Visionaries
Mystics
and
Stigmatists
down through the Ages

Bob and Penny Lord

Journeys of Faith®
1-800-633-2484

Other Books by Bob and Penny Lord

THIS IS MY BODY, THIS IS MY BLOOD
Miracles of the Eucharist Book I
THIS IS MY BODY, THIS IS MY BLOOD
Miracles of the Eucharist Book II
THE MANY FACES OF MARY, A LOVE STORY
WE CAME BACK TO JESUS
SAINTS AND OTHER POWERFUL WOMEN
IN THE CHURCH
SAINTS AND OTHER POWERFUL MEN
IN THE CHURCH
HEAVENLY ARMY OF ANGELS
SCANDAL OF THE CROSS AND ITS TRIUMPH
MARTYRS - THEY DIED FOR CHRIST
THE ROSARY - THE LIFE OF JESUS AND MARY
VISIONARIES, MYSTICS AND STIGMATISTS
VISIONS OF HEAVEN, HELL AND PURGATORY
TRILOGY BOOK I - TREASURES OF THE CHURCH
TRILOGY BOOK II - TRAGEDY OF THE REFORMATION
TRILOGY BOOK III - CULTS, BATTLE OF THE ANGELS
SUPER SAINTS BOOK I - JOURNEY TO SAINTHOOD
SUPER SAINTS BOOK II - HOLY INNOCENCE
SUPER SAINTS BOOK III - DEFENDERS OF THE FAITH
BEYOND SODOM AND GOMORRAH

ISBN 0-926143-57-3

Table of Contents

Dedication

We want to thank *Mother Angelica and the Poor Clare Nuns of Perpetual Adoration* for their prayers and support.

This is one of the most important books we have ever written. We needed a great deal of help in researching it. Most of our information was given to us overseas at the shrines. We want to give special thanks to those people who went out of their way to make this book a reality.

Shrine of St. Catherine of Bologna, Bologna, Italy
Fr. Angel Rodriguez Guerro, Custodian of the Shrine
Shrine of St. Catherine of Genoa, Genoa, Italy
Fr. Cassiano, OFM Capuchin - Custodian of Shrine
Shrine of St. Joseph of Cupertino, Osimo, Italy
Fr. Silvano, OFM Conv. - Custodian of Shrine
Shrine of Blessed Kateri Tekakwitha, Fonda, NY
Fr. Jim Plavcan, OFM Conv. - Custodian of Shrine
Shrine of Blessed Kateri Tekakwitha, Kahnawake, Canada
*Fr. Jacques Bruyère, S.J. Postulator for Cause of Kateri
Shrine of St. Margaret Mary Alacoque, Paray le Monial France
Sisters of the Visitation Chapel
Shrine of St. Louis Marie de Montfort, St. Laurent-sur-Sevres, and Pontchâteau France - Daughters of Wisdom and Custodian
Shrine of St. Veronica Giuliani, Cittá di Castello, Italy
Mother Abbess Maria Caterina and Sr. Serafina
Shrine of Bl. Anna Maria Taigi, St. Crisogono Church, Rome
Trinitarian Fathers - Bishop Francesco Vollaro, Madagascar
Shrine of St. Gemma Galgani, Passionist Church Lucca Italy
Mother Vittoria, custodian of Giannini House
Shrine of Bl. Brother André, St. Joseph's Oratory, Montreal
Custodian of the Shrine
Shrine of Bl. Sister Faustina - Warsaw & Cracow, Poland
Sr. Siepak and Sr. Gratia, Cracow - Mother Paola, Warsaw
We want to thank, in addition, our own *Luz Elena Sandoval, Brother Joseph* and *Lura Daws*

iv

Introduction

My brothers and sisters in Christ, we are at a pivotal point in our Church and our world. We are approaching the third millennium, the twenty-first century, and we need help. The world has gotten away from us; we don't know how to handle it. In every country we visit, we see a resurgence of tradition and values. We've been on a roller-coaster plummeting downward, completely out of control. We have called a halt! People want to go back to all they cherished and somehow lost through the deadly influence of the secular Media. In our country in particular, we see a return to this healthy traditional trend strongly in books, films and merchandise. We want our country back, the land founded under God. We want our freedoms, guaranteed under our Constitution and Bill of Rights, back. We are sending out a message, loud and strong! We are no longer the silent minority; we are the vocal majority.

We need our Holy Family; we need Mama Mary. The family of God is fragmented, divided by the *enemy*. *Mama!* Whenever we have been in trouble we have called on our earthly mothers or our Heavenly Mother. It's time for Mother Mary. We have a great urgency to know our Heavenly Family hears us; we want to hear them. *We need Signs and Wonders.* We are rushing from one reported visionary or mystic or inner Locutionary to the next, trying desperately to grab onto Our Lord Jesus, Our Lady, the Angels and Saints. We want to see them, even if in a haze, a translucent presence, something. We want a whisper, a breeze, a word, anything. And in the midst of all this, Bob and Penny bring you a book on *Visionaries, Mystics, and Stigmatists.*

Why do we need another book on *Visionaries, Mystics, and Stigmatists?* One very important reason is, we feel an urgency to share with you some of the Blesseds and Saints whose messages have been affirmed by Mother Church as *coming to the Faithful through Divine intervention.* The Visionaries, Mystics and Stigmatists we will be presenting to you have passed the test of time; much of what they have prophesied has been fulfilled or is coming to pass.

A more important reason for this book is a danger to which we the people of God have been exposed. We are in the days of many *alleged* Visionaries, Mystics and Stigmatists. We cannot go to a church, a village, or a city that we are not asked to visit *this* local Mystic, or someone does not have a message for us from *that* Visionary. We are not saying that Our Lord and Our Lady are not appearing and speaking to Their children; the dire condition of our Church and of the world would most certainly prompt Them to do so. But holy prudence would dictate we carefully wait upon the word of the Church.

What are we to do? What and whom are we to believe? In many instances there are *Signs and Wonders, even Miracles* that are hard to ignore. This gives us even more reason to be prudent in whom and what we believe. We are in serious times, very serious times! Our Lord, in His Word warns us:

> *"...there will be great tribulation, such as has not been from the beginning of the world until now, no and never will be. And if those days had not been shortened, no human being would be saved; but for the sake of the elect those days will be shortened. Then if anyone says to you 'Lo here is the Christ!' or 'There He is!' do not believe it. For* **false Christs and false prophets will arise and show great**

*signs and wonders, so as to lead astray, if possible, even
the elect."* (Matt 24:24, Mark 13:22)

Our Church is being torn asunder by two forces: *One is
obvious in that it is spawning a heresy* encompassing many
seriously destructive heresies from the past, which Mother Church
dispelled through her Popes and Bishops calling Councils down
through the centuries. But *sadly* they're back, and they are *now
collectively* attacking all we hold dear. This force is dangerous
because often what is being taught is so *close* to what we have
learned in the past, almost a mirror image. This has always been
the work of the enemy, taking the Truth and distorting it for the
demise of the Church he so fiercely hates. Down through the
centuries, we have not realized these are errors and we have been
led astray. *Another* subtle but no less deadly action of this force *is
the intentional manipulation and elimination of parts of the Bible,*
thereby changing its meaning. The most apparent of this trend is
the attempt by an influential minority to rewrite the Bible, using
inclusive language. One of the reasons there are so many splinters
of the True Cross is due to the first changing and elimination of
parts of the Bible by Martin Luther, a former priest.

Another focus of this destructive movement, sometimes
composed of forces within our Church, is the blatant fostering of
disobedience to the Pope by word and example *a*nd the ridiculing
of the Magisterium (the teaching authority of the Church - *See
Catholic Catechism # 889-892*). This force, by its dissent and
disobedience to the Pope, whose authority was given to him and
all our Popes by Jesus Himself, leads to confusion and division.
"A house divided against itself will fall and crumble." In every
house there is a father, a head, an authority whom the other
members of the family obey. Even Martin Luther wrote of the
wisdom of Jesus to leave us a father in our Pope whom the members
of The Mystical Body of Christ obey and follow, to whom all
obedience and allegiance we must render. Was the Lord speaking
of this time?

"There were also false prophets among the people, just as there will be false teachers among you, who will introduce destructive heresies and even deny the Master Who ransomed them, bringing swift destruction on themselves." (2 Peter 2)

Some know the enemy on the far left side of our path to the Kingdom. But there can be an even more perilous force attacking the Church by those who *appear* to love Mother Church. Now we're not saying that they are necessarily, knowingly, deceiving the Faithful. Possibly, some of these alleged Mystics, Seers and Visionaries really believe they are seeing the Mother of God or are receiving inner locutions. Have they, perhaps, been tempted by the enemy? Did he promise them fame if they would use this sure-fire attention-getter which would draw tens of thousands of innocent people, seeking Our Lord and Our Mother in this troubled world, to come to them, and use them erroneously as spiritual fortune-tellers? Another great fear is that this can lead to confusion among the Faithful and an eventual attack on Mother Mary and apparitions *accepted* by the Church.

Mother Mary came and brought warnings to her children. Some alleged visionaries are claiming they are receiving messages that closely resemble those of accepted visionaries of the past. We have to beware; remember Satan is the great copycat with not an original idea. Will important messages left by Mother Mary become a mockery, if and when the revelations of these self-proclaimed present day prophets are judged human and not Divine? Our Lord is speaking to us through His Word, as we read:

"Beware of false prophets, who come to you in sheep's clothing, but underneath are ravenous wolves" (Matt. 7:15)

The saddest problem we have is, if someone today was really receiving messages from Mother Mary and Jesus, would we believe them? We must depend on the wisdom and timetable of Mother Church. With this book, we will try to help you discern, through the words, lives and examples of the Visionaries, Mystics and Stigmatists, *w*ho have been accepted by Mother Church, *who* to believe and *what* to believe, that you will not fall victim to the...

   "Many false prophets (who) *will arise and deceive many;"* (Matt 24:11)

   How will we know *who* are authentic and *who* have agendas of their own? With these prophets we write about, you will hear *faithfulness* to the Word of God and to the Magisterium. You will see them point to Our Lord and His Mother, not to themselves, often reluctantly writing of their revelations only out of obedience to their Spiritual Directors, always seeking *anonymity.* As an example, Saint Mary Alacoque and Saint Catherine Labouré were Visionaries whose holy experiences were *virtually unknown* to those around them, with the exception of their Spiritual Directors or Superiors who ordered them to write them down. You will see *obedience* to their immediate Superiors, Spiritual Directors, Bishops, and to Mother Church.

   What are we trying to do with this book? We want to give you a definition of a Mystic, a Visionary, a Stigmatist, a Locutionary, anyone who has had a very special relationship with Jesus and Mary, not from Webster's dictionary, or from the Catholic Encyclopedia, but from how they lived their lives. You will never hear them promoting themselves. You will never hear them using the *"I"* word. If anything, they will always take the attention away from themselves and focus it in on Jesus. This may be the whole reason why the Lord wanted us to write this book, so that *you,* the people of God, will be able to discern what is a true *Mystic*, what is a true *Visionary*, what is a true *Stigmatist*, from those who are claiming to be. We hope to give you a basis for comparison. When Padre Pio[1] was given the gift of the Stigmata, he begged Our Lord Jesus to take it away, and the Lord gave him an Invisible Stigmata, in which Padre Pio suffered all the pains of the wounds of Christ, without actually showing the outward signs. This went on for ten years, until the *Lord* decided

---

[1] Read about Padre Pio in Bob and Penny Lord's book: *"Saints and other Powerful Men in the Church."*

it was time for Padre Pio to be a visible sign. What is the point here? What are we trying to tell you?

These are important times in the battle for our Church. The Lord *is sending powerful messages* to us through His people. But the messages can be blocked and discredited by false prophets, and possibly even good people who have too much of a need to be known, recognized and adulated, who are willing to sell their souls for the attention that is given to Visionaries, Mystics and Stigmatists. In order for you to be able to hear and act on the word of the Lord, the din, the great roar of noise emanating from the world and from all those who would give you misinformation, has to be recognized and muffled. We pray that by sharing with you *these* brothers and sisters who have passed the test of time and been given the approval of the Church, you will be able to discern the real from the false. Finally and most importantly, pray to our Heavenly Family for guidance. *We love you!*

St. Catherine of Bologna

Visionary, Mystic, Role Model for Abbesses, Incorrupt Body

St. Catherine of Bologna

St. Catherine was born Catherine de Virgi in Bologna, Italy on Our Lady's Birthday, September the 8th, 1413. Her father, Giovanni de Virgi, was a member of the nobility of Ferrara,[1] as well as a highly-respected lawyer and lecturer at the famous University of Bologna.[2] He married Benvenuta Mammolini who was also of a noble family of Bologna.

Catherine was blessed to come from a very pious mother who devoted herself to her precious child from the moment she was born. Catherine was always obedient and very sweet-natured, unlike many of her class who had a tendency to be proud and haughty. She possessed wisdom beyond her years, and maybe

---

[1]Ferrara is well-known by the Church as containing a Miracle of the Eucharist and a well-known Shrine to Our Lady. You can read more about this in Bob and Penny Lord's book *This is My Body, This is My Blood, Miracle of the Eucharist*, Book II

[2]Some of the first Universities were started in Bologna. Bologna is also the city that has the body of Blessed Imelda, who went into ecstasy and died the first time she received Holy Communion. Bob and Penny Lord write about her in their book *This is My Body, This is My Blood, Miracle of the Eucharist*, Book I

because of her mother's influence, applied it to the enrichment of her spiritual life, spending as much time as she possibly could praying and distributing alms to the poor. When they tried to thank her, she insisted, it was a gift from Jesus and they should praise Him, not her.

As her father Giovanni was in the service of Niccolo III of Este, Marquis of Ferrara, the little family soon joined him there, moving from Benvenuta's beloved Bologna. A very famous jurist, his duties as a diplomat brought her father very often to Venice on important missions. Imagine when he returned home, the stories he told his little girl who had such a thirst for learning.

Catherine's piety came to the attention of the Marquis who chose her to be a lady-in-waiting[3] to his daughter Margaret. Writers of her day say that although she was not very pretty, being short and thin with a pale complexion, she held everyone who met her, spellbound; her gentleness, her charm, her gracious ways captivating all who knew her.

She was a bright girl. What with her eagerness to learn, coupled with her outstanding, keenly perceptive intellect, she mastered all her studies, excelling in grammar, literature, poetry and arithmetic, as well as in painting and music, so much so, had the Lord not chosen her for His own, she would have most probably been lauded as an accomplished musician or highly acclaimed painter.

As we have seen with Mother Angelica and her Poor Clare Nuns of Perpetual Adoration, God wastes nothing, using the gifts, He has bestowed on His precious brides for His plan for the salvation of His Church and for His glory; as we will see later, as we continue our story of this great Saint.

An education which included Latin would enable her to write the most profound poetry, rivaling that of any of the great poets of her day. But God did not give her this talent for the world.

---

[3]This is decidedly an honor, when a family of the nobility choose a young lady to be a companion to their daughter.

Above: ***The Miracle of the bread of St. Catherine of Bologna***

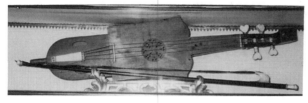

Left:
***The violin
played by St.
Catherine of
Bologna***

Below:
***Bob and Penny Lord with Father Angel
Rodriguez Guerro, the Custodian of
the Shrine of St. Catherine of Bologna in
the Monastery of Corpus Domini in
Bologna, Italy***

Above:
***A Baby Jesus doll
that was hand made
by St. Catherine of
Bologna***

Instead, her mastery in Latin would help her to print her breviary in her own hand; her talent as a painter would be used to beautifully illustrate it. Had she not been specially courted by the Lord, she might have pursued a career in classical writing.

But the Hounds of Heaven pursued her from an early age, leading her to Holy Scripture and the works of the Early Church Fathers. We are what we read; we believe that strongly. And in Catherine's case, the path to sanctity was paved with the spirituality derived from the Holy Spirit Who spoke to her through the Word and the authentic glorious teachings of those great men of God who went before us.

Once her mind and heart belonged to the Lord, she was free to totally abandon herself to Him and His Plan for her. This was essential for Catherine, because she would soon be stripped from all earthly consolation and support, as her father went to the Father in Heaven, her mother remarried, and finally her dear and closest friend Margaret left for Rimini. Although she had pleaded with Catherine to join her and her future spouse, the Lord of Rimini, Catherine chose instead to remain in Ferrara. In the eyes of the world, Catherine had nothing left in Ferrara; but with the Eyes of God, there was nothing else she could do. He had plans for her!

With her father's passing, Catherine became a wealthy heiress. She definitely became the target of friends and family who either wanted to marry her or knew some fine young man who did. What they did not know is, she had already been chosen to be espoused to the King of Heaven and Earth. She had said yes to placing her life in His loving Hands. She completely turned herself over to Jesus. She had chosen the best way and there was no turning back. There is no one who can equal Jesus as Suitor and Spouse.

At age fourteen, she made the commitment to love Him faithfully to the exclusion of all others, forever. Saying good by to the world, and excitedly looking forward to their new life together, she entered a Religious house which had been founded by an Augustinian tertiary, Bernardina Sedazzari, in Ferrara in 1419, six years after Catherine was born. It was a fairly new

Community, made up of pious women who followed the Augustinian Rule. Years later, it would become a Franciscan Community under the double title of Corpus Domini[4] and Visitation Monastery. It still stands today in Ferrara.

Catherine described so beautifully her feelings in this holy place, living her new life:

"During my tender years, enlightened by Divine Grace, I entered God's service in this Monastery with good intentions and much fervor. My life was filled with prayer, day and night. Any virtue I admired or heard of in others, I tried to imitate in my own life. I did so not out of envy, but to please God in Whom I had put all my love."

Catherine battles with the devil

Whenever we are under attack from the *slimy one*, it is difficult to remember that God is in charge, and He is allowing this to strengthen us for even greater battles. The honeymoon over, God stood by and permitted Satan to tempt our little Catherine. But Sister Catherine was not so little that she could not tell the devil off when he tried to tempt her. When he really got under her skin and wouldn't let up, she rebuked him, saying: *"Be sure, evil spirit, you will not tempt me so openly nor so stealthily without my knowing it."* Or to quote one of our young members of the Junior Legion of Mary, "I recognize you sucker, scram!" The enemy was determined, she would fall; but God was more determined. She learned a very essential lesson from this which was: human nature is fragile; never underestimate the devil and his cunning. He is the one who makes jokes that he doesn't exist, that concern over the devil is all nonsense. The Lord wanted to make sure that she would never pridefully believe she was a match for the devil and his cohorts.

For what seemed an endless *five* years, from ages fifteen to twenty, the *prince of darkness* relentlessly attacked the one whom he knew was his mortal enemy. In her book, *The Seven Spiritual*

---

[4]Body of Christ

Arms, our future Saint would not only write to warn future novices, but all Christians for generations to come. Catherine recounted battles waged and won. She dug into the horror of those years and wrote with pain remembered, so that the novices under her care would be forewarned and not fall prey to the father of lies.

She shared her tears. Sometimes they were tears of blood like her Savior before her. Do you ever wonder what Jesus suffered in the Garden that He shed tears of Blood, and now, what Catherine experienced that she did as well? In the end, she vanquished the enemy. God was the victor! The Cross triumphed! She had glorious wounds, sustained in battle to remind her always and to pass on that truth that Satan is alive and he never sleeps. But she also learned, God is always nearby; we are not alone.

As we read and write, we discover and rediscover that attacks by the enemy are always on *obedience*! God has always acted on *obedience*, as far back as Genesis, counteracting disobedience with obedience. Satan attacked Adam and Eve by tempting them to disobey! God raised up a faithful son who would obey; *Abraham* obeyed the Father, but that was not enough. Then, God asked a little virgin and Mary obeyed the Father. Finally, God asked His only begotten Son and Jesus obeyed the Father; and because of *His* obedience, the Father on Calvary forgave the sins of the world. But that is not the end of the story. God has been asking for obedience of His Saints and acting through that obedience down through the centuries. Catherine was one of those Saints.

Because of the power of *obedience* and the destruction caused by one act of disobedience, Satan attacked Catherine mercilessly. First, he tempted her to disobey her Superior. Then, Satan appeared as Jesus Crucified, and using the holy form of Our Savior, attempted to devastate her by berating her for feigning remorse over her rebellious disobedience of her Superior. Although Catherine was confused and trying to recall when she had done so, she knew that Jesus would not lie, and so she was mortified. She cried, judging herself the worst sinner. Satan hates contrition for our sins. He knew he had failed and so he attacked her with vile thoughts, uttering blasphemies against the Lord that ripped away at her very soul! Another attack did not go as he expected. Satan came disguised as the Blessed Virgin, accusing Catherine of desiring sinful love, telling her, the Lord would withhold His precious Love from her.

She came through those attacks weary but not beaten. Knowing her devotion to the Blessed Sacrament, how she spent hours, day and night, consoling Our Lord in the Tabernacle, Satan pulled out all stops, and went after her belief in the Real Presence of Jesus in the Eucharist. He put doubts into her mind, torturing her because suddenly she did not feel anything towards the Eucharist. She agonized over the dryness she felt during the elevation of the Host at Mass. Satan so tormented her, she collapsed on the ground before the other nuns, almost out of her mind with grief.

At last! One morning during Mass Our Lord revealed to Catherine that He was truly Present in the Eucharist. When she received Holy Communion, *"she felt and tasted the sweetest, purest Flesh of the Immaculate Lamb, Christ Jesus."*[5] Then her beloved Seraphic father St. Francis appeared to her and encouraged her to be faithful and to stand firm, assuring her that God was always with her, even when she did not understand. In thanksgiving for the Lord manifesting this *Miracle of the Eucharist* to confound the enemy, Catherine became an advocate of frequent Communion at a time when this was not an accepted practice of the Church.

"....Whom the Lord loves He reproves, and He chastises the son He favors."[6] Our Lord never left Catherine alone. Lest she forget, God gave her a glimpse of the Final Judgment, during one of her ecstasies. It was so horrible, so terrifying, so revolting, she never forgot it. This burned such an image on her mind, she developed an intense repulsion for even her smallest transgressions,

---

[5]*Treatise of the Seven Arms* by St. Catherine of Bologna
[6]Prov 3:12

seeing each and every imperfection, as an ugly scar on her soul. [We received a book on Purgatory at EWTN. After reading it, we began to look at each action with how much time in Purgatory it would cost. And so, the luxuries, we sometimes take, committing what we judge, minor infractions (as they are called today) or more aptly venial sins, takes on different dimensions. Suddenly venial sins do not look so venial.]

The Monastery faces great trials

After the death of their foundress, the nuns faced hard times. Mother Bernardina had heavily financed the Community and now with her gone, they found themselves about to be closed down. Thanks be to God, because of the generosity of the Marquis Niccolo III's assistance, they were able to buy some time. But sadly, the financial crisis seemed critical and it looked as if their worse nightmare had become a reality. At the same time, the Community was facing this dilemma, poor Catherine was being barraged by well-meaning friends to ask the Pope to release her from her Religious vows. She prayed and prayed, lifting her cries up to Heaven, against these temptations that were flooding her soul. The Lord answered His sweet, suffering bride. He told her it was His wish that she remain in the Monastery and not to be afraid; things would get better.

We have contended and we can see it here, once more: *There are Saints and Saint-makers.* Catherine would grow spiritually through Sister Taddeo Pio, the first Abbess elected. She, like Catherine, was from a noble family. Here were two former women of gentility, and the road they walked to perfection was through performing the most *humble, menial* tasks. The Community was having problems because of the way that the Monastery was built; it did not afford the nuns the necessary privacy for enclosure; a new building was necessary. Catherine, with her delicate, slim fingers, carried the heavy materials needed to do the job.

Catherine was assigned to be the doorkeeper. She took this position very seriously and would interrupt her work and even her prayer time to answer the many visitors who rang the bell. There was a pilgrim who came frequently to the door, begging for alms. [In those days, pilgrims traveled with one tunic, a pair of sandals, a walking staff, a piece of bread and a jug of water. Their provisions soon ran out and they had to depend on the generosity of the villagers on the way to the holy Shrines.] To repay her generosity, he left her a small bowl that he said the Blessed Mother had used to satisfy her Son's thirst. Catherine treasured this relic with great devotion. She thought he was just leaving it with her for safekeeping, and that he would most certainly would return to retrieve it. But he never came back! Later in her life, Saint Joseph appeared to our Saint and informed her it was he to whom she had been so generous. [This relic can still be seen in the Monastery of Ferrara.] Although her daily tasks took much out of her *physically*, as she was always very frail, Catherine never complained and tried bravely to hide her exhaustion.

God showers great graces on Catherine

Our Lord was tremendously pleased with the way Catherine handled all the trials, He allowed to come her way, with such genuine humility. He began to bestow upon her many gifts. We will site just a few of them, here.

Conversions come about! On May 19, 1451, the day that St. Bernardine of Siena[7] was being canonized in Rome, Catherine was praying that all who attended the glorious occasion of one of her Seraphic father Francis' sons would receive special blessings. All of a sudden, she went into ecstasy and before her was her Guardian Angel; he swooped her up and transported her *mystically* to the Canonization. In the midst of the excitement of this great moment, Catherine did not think of herself; instead her mind and heart became filled with her brother who had allowed Satan to take over in his life. She begged the newly acclaimed Saint for her

---

[7]Saint Bernardine was a great reformer of the Franciscans. He was also known for his great devotion to the Blessed Sacrament. You can read more about him in Bob and Penny Lord's Book *This is My Body, This is My Blood, Miracle of the Eucharist*, Book I.

brother's conversion. Her petition was answered; he abandoned his sinful ways, turned to God, and lived a holy, virtuous life until his last days. The power of prayer! We can be sure that this was not the first time Catherine prayed for her brother, and we're sure she must have thought that he would never turn around, but she never gave up on him or the Lord's generous Love.

The miracle of the bread! Catherine loved to take on the lowliest chores of the Community. One that she was particularly fond of was kneading and making bread. One day she had just finished placing the bread in the oven when the bell sounded for prayers. Always obedient, Catherine made the Sign of the Cross over each of the loaves and rushed to the Church, leaving the bread baking. When she was able to return to the kitchen hours later, she was sure the bread had burned. To the contrary, the room was filled with the most delightful aroma of bread baking. When she opened the oven to take out the loaves, she discovered they had not only *not burned*, but had a lovely honey color. The nuns commented on how delicious the bread tasted, the best she had ever baked. This became known as the *bread of obedience.* [We love the sound of that. We recall that because Mary obeyed in Bethlehem (House of Bread) the Bread of Life was born.]

Like Saint Teresa of Avila, Catherine found Jesus everywhere, even among the pots and the pans. She never lost an opportunity to pray, meditate and contemplate the Lord and His Goodness. Even in her varied duties she found God, making every task a prayer.

Although Catherine was totally happy with her humble assignments, God had different plans for her. She was elected Mistress of Novices. She protested that she was not capable or worthy of such an awesome responsibility, but she obeyed! However, Catherine insisted that the novices *not* call her Mother Mistress, but instead continue addressing her as *Sister Catherine.* Catherine taught the novices not only by word but by example, how to live a life of Christian meekness like the Savior, through *humility, charity and obedience.* One of the acts of *humility* which greatly touched them was her insistence, they correct any fault they might perceive in *her*.

God is the God of order and balance. As Catherine was being besieged by attacks from the prince of darkness, God was balancing the scales, granting her heavenly visions, ecstasies and special favors such as the gift of Prophecy. There are two visions that we would like to share with you.

(1) *Jesus speaks to Catherine from the Cross!* There was a huge, breathtakingly beautiful Crucifix in Catherine's cell. One Friday, she was kneeling before it weeping, recalling Our Lord's Passion on Golgotha, when Jesus spoke to her. He revealed His pain on the Cross, the bitter and heart-rending affliction He suffered. Was He talking of the bitter taste of His children's unfaithfulness and rejection, more bitter than the gall that was offered Him to drink? Was He speaking of His Heart being *spiritually* pierced before it was struck by the centurion's sword, by those who just stood by apathetically and did nothing? But, He said mournfully, there were no blows no Wounds so painful as those He endured, watching His Mother suffer at the foot of the Cross. He thanked Catherine for sharing His Cross by meditating on His Passion, and said He would reward her for all her efforts to spread this devotion to others.

(2) *Mother Mary places the Infant Jesus in Catherine's arms.* It was Christmas Eve, and instead of joyous anticipation, Catherine was suffering the worst trials. It seemed to Catherine that Jesus was withholding His Divine Love and consolation from her. She had been weeping day and night for days, as if her heart would break. Her Savior's birth was approaching and Catherine asked her Abbess permission to keep vigil before the Blessed Sacrament. She wished to contemplate the wondrous, glorious moment when the *Word* came into the world. She said, she wished to recite one thousand *"Hail Mary's"*[8] in honor of the Mother of God, Mary most holy.

---

[8]This practice has been perpetuated in the Corpus Domini Monastery till today, as well as the faithful around Bologna.

Catherine had said a great many *"Hail Mary's"* when the Blessed Virgin appeared to her with the Infant Jesus in her arms. She lovingly entrusted the precious Babe to Catherine, gently placing Him in her arms. Catherine drew Jesus close to her heart, and tenderly rested her cheek on His adorable Face. Oh, our hearts feel as if they will burst just thinking of it, to be so close to the Lord! But then, at the moment we receive Jesus in the Eucharist, inside us, are we not touching, feeling Him close to us? The Saint wrote in her Treatise, she felt as if she were melting, like she was in a fire. She further wrote:

"The perfume that emanated from His Pure Flesh was so sweet that there is neither tongue that can express, nor such a keen mind imagine, the very beautiful and delicate Face of the Son of God, when one could say all that was to be said, it would be nothing."

The other nuns soon realized something had happened. A heavenly fragrance filled the room! Catherine was beaming, her face flushed, a joy radiating from her face. They turned to her and inquired what had transpired. Out of obedience Catherine shared what, out of humility, she had wished to keep secret. She wanted to savor it between herself, the Lord and His Mother Mary. What Catherine most feared came to pass - the Miracle of Christmas Eve spread throughout the region making Catherine's sanctity known.

The move to Bologna

The Monastery in Ferrara became famous for its holiness, and vocations came from all parts of Italy to join the Community. Now, since Catherine was born in Bologna of a mother who stemmed from the nobility of Bologna, the citizens thought it only right to have a House of these pious cloistered nuns there among them with Catherine as Abbess. Before long, the nuns from the Monastery in Ferrara and their newly elected Abbess Catherine sadly left the village they loved. They departed in the dead of night; it was too painful to say good-by to the villagers. As they traveled, the sides of the road became lined with people lighting their way with torches. The heartbroken citizens of Ferrara had discovered their Religious were leaving, and they would not let them leave without them seeing them off. They tearfully waved good-by. But down the road, there were the faithful from Bologna, excitedly *awaiting* the entrance of the nuns who would bless their city. A cortege of the most important citizens of Bologna, representatives of the different Religious Orders and members of the nobility of Bologna accompanied the little company of nuns. They entered Bologna on July 22, 1456. The streets were alive with the townsfolk rejoicing, singing *"Blessed is she who comes in the name of the Lord."*

As the new Monastery was not ready for them, the nuns were temporarily housed in the small hospice of St. Anthony of Padua. Because so many of the faithful, especially the women and their daughters, had longed to have them in their midst, the restricted enclosure of the Cloistered Community was lifted for three days. This proved to be very fruitful, as six of the young local women entered the Convent shortly after.

Vocations grew! Of the eighteen nuns who started the new Monastery, fifteen were fully professed (nine of them from Bologna), two were Converse Sisters and one a Tertiary, third order,. Third order nuns, like St. Catherine of Siena, took the vows of the religious, but were not required to live a cloistered life. Many third order lived at home. In this instance, the third order candidate was Catherine's mother who asked to join the nuns, after she was widowed a second time. Four of these holy nuns would be raised to the glory of the Altar: Saint Catherine of Bologna, Blessed Giovanna Lambertini, Blessed Illuminata Bembo (the nun who wrote Saint Catherine's biography), and Blessed Paola Mezzavacchi. *Saints and Saint-makers*; here is another instance in this Saint's life where this great truth comes to life.

Catherine as Mother Abbess

The spirit of humility, obedience and poverty soon filled the new Monastery. The nuns were so happy! Catherine had been Abbess for three years when one day they were visited by the

Father Provincial of the Friars Minor who announced that the Abbess and all her nuns were being summoned to Chapter. He showed Catherine and the nuns the Apostolic Brief restricting the length of office of an Abbess of the Poor Clare Monasteries to only three years. Blessed Marco was trying to correct certain problems arising from Monasteries where the Superior was elected for life. He felt secure in beginning with Catherine, knowing her humility and her desire to obey. He had not placed his hopes in the wrong quarter; Saint Catherine was pleased to retire from being Abbess so that she could go back to her joy, serving the other nuns. One of the nuns who had come from Ferrara was elected the new Abbess, but she developed serious eye problems and had to step down after only one year. So poor Saint Catherine was back as Abbess, until she was retired by the angel of death.

As the holiness of Saint Catherine and her nuns became known throughout Italy, it became necessary to enlarge the Monastery to accommodate all the new entries. As some of the women were from wealthy noble homes, Catherine had the necessary funds to bring this all about. But more importantly, Catherine worked to make the enclosure a *sacred one* filled with nuns who would live a life of true holiness. She was a living, walking example for them to follow. At times, she would become so deeply enraptured in the vision before her of God, the nuns had a difficult time bringing her back to reality.

Catherine and the nuns prayed not only for their salvation, but did penance and mortification for the atonement of sins and crimes committed against the Lord. Through prayer comes holiness and through holiness comes miracles. The people of Bologna had been right - with the nuns they would be blessed!

Miracles start to happen in the Monastery of Bologna

Now one of the nuns, Sister Lucia Cadagnelli was a strong girl of sturdy peasant stock. One day she was working in the orchard, hoeing the soil and clearing the weeds. Chopping away at the high grass a little distractedly, the sickle that she had been swinging back and forth struck her right foot and severed it from the leg with one blow. Hearing her screaming in agony, the nuns ran to see what was wrong. When Saint Catherine arrived she immediately began to pray to Our Lord to have mercy on this, her daughter. And with that, she made the Sign of the Cross on the severed foot and attached it to the rest of her leg. There was not the smallest sign, an accident had happened; the leg was as good as before the accident. Sister Lucia was able to use her foot and walk about normally. The crisis over, like a true mother, Catherine told the young Sister to care for the foot from that day on as if it were Catherine's property, and to be watchful that no harm came to it.

Miracles and mothering, the two go together. We have seen, over the years, how a mother's prayers have brought about miraculous healings of mind, body, and spirit. Conversions have come about, even impossible reconciliation after years, all through a mother's prayers. And, Catherine was a mother to all her nuns at the Monastery!

Saint Catherine, Author, Poet, Painter and Musician

Saint Catherine was gifted by the Lord with a multitude of gifts: *human* talents - painting, music, poetry and a mastery in Latin; *spiritual* favors - mystical experiences, visions and ecstasies granted by God. These would first and foremost be used by God to touch and form the nuns of her Monastery; but the light that emanated from this great woman, Saint, Mystic and Spiritual mother has and will continue to enlighten and instruct the faithful in all walks of life. A cloistered nun, Catherine's writings and her life have succeeded in her being raised up by Church historians, to the great hall of contemplatives, alongside Saints like Clare of Assisi and Teresa of Avila.

As author, Catherine did not take quality time from her daily commitments to write her Treatise *The Seven Spiritual Arms;* she performed all her duties faithfully and then snatched time in the daytime, amid many interruptions and countless distractions; and in the evening, after prayers had been faithfully said. As a Mistress of Novices and then as Abbess, her daughters came first. We sometimes think we can do no more, but this frail woman, delicate in health and strength, did the work of an army. What can God do with our Yes?

Catherine wrote the Treatise out of strict obedience to her confessor and hid it from the other Sisters. Her wish was that it be read after her death, and then, only for the express purpose of aiding the novices in their spiritual formation. While still in the Monastery of Ferrara, she stitched the book between the leather covers of her chair,[9] trusting it would be safely hidden there. But one of the nuns found it one day and showed it to the other Sisters. Now, as she did not want to take the chance that her mystical experiences would become known while she was still alive, Catherine burned the book. But God had set a different course. *He* ordered her to write it, again. And, dear family, this was all *handwritten!*[10] Man has an agenda; God has a plan! Humans with their limited vision see the tiny present, but God in His Wisdom sees the grand picture. His design was that this book be a guide, not only for her sisters but for all Christians from all walks of life.

Catherine however, stubborn Italian and soldier of Christ, was determined to keep this Treatise hidden during her lifetime; therefore, when she moved to the Monastery in Bologna, she hid it in her mattress where it would be safely concealed from inquisitive eyes. As she was dying, again out of obedience, she handed it over to her confessor with the wish, upon her death, a copy be sent to the Monastery in Ferrara and the original left in Bologna (It is still there, along with other Relics of Saint Catherine).

As Poet, her knowledge of Latin shines in her lengthy poem *"Rosarium"*. Those who have written of Catherine say that this is the finest source of insights into her personality and spirituality. You get to know her more deeply as you read her meditations on the fifteen mysteries of the Rosary. She ends with these very tender,

---

[9]This chair and other relics are still in the *Monastery of Corpus Domini in Bologna* in the Relic Room in back of the Chapel where Saint Catherine is seated till today, ready to hear your petitions.

[10]We have filmed for our Series on the Mystics this handwritten document and other Relics of St. Catherine that provide insights into this great Mystic.

very loving, stirring words to the One she loves and Who loves her: *"I wear myself out in tears, when I think of the day when I will meet You."*

As Painter, our Saint not only wrote her Breviary, she beautifully illustrated it. It also contained prayers she had composed. Catherine painted poignant miniatures of our Lord, portraying Him as the Savior and as the Infant Jesus, wrapped in elegant swaddling clothes befitting a King. What Jesus did not have, at the time of His Birth choosing to be born of humble estate, His little Spouse clothed Him with almost fifteen hundred years, later. [When you travel in Italy, you will see many Images of the Infant Jesus majestically robed.] Catherine also lovingly portrayed Mother Mary with the Baby Jesus nestled in her arms. Was she remembering that time when the Blessed Mother placed the Infant Jesus in her arms?

As Musician, Catherine's education included playing an instrument. Among her Relics we saw the *"violeta"*[11] that the Saint played often and requested when she believed she was dying.

Catherine begins the final Way of the Cross

A fragile constitution to begin with, compounded by fasting and penance for the atonement of the sins of the world, Catherine prepared the Sisters for her final journey. Burning up with a *raging* high fever, she called all her Sisters to her. She asked that her bed be moved to the middle of the nun's dormitory. She would give them her last Spiritual Direction. She thought she was going Home, and she was joyfully looking forward to seeing the Beatific Vision of her Spouse in Paradise. Her long wait was about to be over, but she did not count on the prayers of her Sisters.

One of them, fifteen year old Sister Mary Magdalene Rose, was assigned to help Catherine who was now bedridden. One day, after the young sister had washed Mother Catherine's feet, she was so overcome with love and devotion toward her Abbess she bent down and kissed them. You see, she and the other Sisters already looked upon Catherine as a Saint. Considering the youthful

---

[11]small violin

innocence of the young sister, Catherine *gently* scolded her and
forbade her under the vow of obedience to ever do that again.
Inspired by the Holy Spirit, the little novice said,

*"My dearest Mother, such is the celestial scene that
radiates from those feet that I felt compelled to kiss them.
However, if at the present you forbid me to do so, you will
never prevent people after your death, from all over the
world, reverently kneeling and kissing your feet."*

This foretelling of the veneration of the Saint would be
fulfilled and continue for the next *five centuries.* "Out of the
mouths of babes!" The Lord had chosen this young girl to speak
these prophetic words.

Catherine was getting weaker and weaker. Believing this
was the end, the nuns called a priest who brought the compassionate
Last Sacraments of the Church. The nuns were all around her
bed, crying and praying, when Catherine had a vision. When she
came to, she told the nuns that she had been in a garden filled with
rows and rows of the most fragrant flowers of different colors and
shapes, breathtakingly beautiful, each in its own uniqueness.

She related that in the middle of the garden, Our Lord was
seated on a golden throne, surrounded by a dazzling light.
Standing to His right and to His left were St. Lawrence and St.
Vincent with myriads of Angels glorifying the Lord. A majestic
Angel (most likely the Archangel Gabriel) stood in front of the
Savior. He was singing to the accompaniment of a violeta: *"Et
gloria eius in the videbitur"* (His Glory will radiate on you).
Catherine said that the music was so sweet she felt as if her soul
would soar out of her body. Then from His throne Jesus stretched
out His Arm and drew her close to Him; with that He explained
the full meaning of the Angel's message. He told her, she was
supposed to have died as a result of this last illness, but because of
the prayers of the nuns, especially one of them, she had been spared
for a little while longer.

Her community had witnessed her many times, when she was

consumed by an ecstasy, but this time, she was so deeply under, the nuns thought she was close to death. Instead, when she awakened, she asked for her violeta. Raising herself, she began to play the little violin and sing, *"Et gloria eius in the videbitur."* When she stopped, she told the nuns what the Lord had told her, that it was the prayers of one nun in particular that persuaded the Lord to have her stay a little while longer. She said to the rejoicing nuns: *"May the Lord forgive her who through her prayers has still kept me in this world."*

Catherine improved so rapidly and thoroughly, the nuns thought she would be with them for a long time. But Catherine knew she had a short time to prepare her daughters for her going Home to her Spouse, and always the Mother Abbess, she began renovating the Monastery. She went about all her responsibilities with new energy, laboring tirelessly with even more of an urgency than before (if that is possible). But with all that, her focus never changed; the sanctification of her nuns and that of herself was uppermost in her heart and mind.

It is time for Catherine to go to her Spouse

It was February 25th, the first Friday in Lent. Catherine called her nuns to Chapter, and gently told them she was about to leave them for her much-awaited journey to her Lord and Spouse. She talked to them for three hours, going on about Heaven and how the heavenly Family was making a place for her. No one could have imagined the excruciating pains, she was experiencing, her head pounding with one of the worst headaches she ever had. She had lost a lot of blood and extremely high fevers racked her poor body; yet she was leaving them with a mission: to carry on faithfully the Rule of their Mother Clare,[12] to love one another as sisters, and to do God's Will. She assured them, if they and those who followed were faithful to this promise, she would protect them, now and forever. She reminded them to revere their Mother Vicar (Blessed

---

[12]For more on St. Clare, foundress of the Poor Clare's, read Bob and Penny Lord's book: *Saints and other Powerful Women in the Church.*

Giovanna Lambertini), and to care for her mother who was still alive. (She died shortly after her daughter.) Catherine was gently but firmly speaking to them, preparing them for *her* ascent to Calvary and then to Heaven, just as her Savior before her, had prepared His disciples at the Last Supper.

During her last week she confessed often; each time this Sacrament of Mercy filled her face with more and more joy and peace. She handed her Treatise of *The Seven Spiritual Arms* over to her confessor, begging him to fulfill her wishes that a copy be sent to the Monastery in Ferrara and the original remain in Bologna. Then turning toward the Sisters, she asked forgiveness for the times she had failed them and pardon for any hurts, she might have caused them. She lapsed into agony, sharing her Savior's last hours.

Rather than her looks diminishing as happens most often to those dying, instead her face took on a beauty she had never possessed before. She turned toward the weeping Sisters, her eyes sparkling because she was going to her Spouse, yet sad because she was leaving them, her beloved family of nuns. She whispered the Holy name of Jesus three times for each Person of the Blessed Trinity and said no more. Our precious Saint Catherine passed away gently, with her Savior, her Mother Mary, and the whole Heavenly Army of Angels there to escort her *Home*. Catherine was not yet fifty years old. Her family which had begun with *eighteen* nuns when the Monastery of Corpus Domini of Bologna was founded, had grown to *sixty* nuns; and they were all around their Mother, as she breathed her last. The ecstasy she fell into now was for all eternity.

Miracles kept happening, after Catherine was dead

The sisters prepared their Mother for her burial. Not only was she more beautiful in death than in life, her body emitted a heavenly fragrance! Miracles began to happen! When the nuns placed her body before the Blessed Sacrament, *she bowed her head*; she was worshiping even in death that Lord Who had been her total life. The Eucharist had always been her Lord truly present, and not even the angel of death could keep her from adoring Him.

The day had arrived. While she was with them in the convent in repose, she looked so beautiful, it was hard to believe that she was dead. But now, the funeral was in progress and the nuns were sobbing, inconsolably. They processed with the body to the Monastery's graveyard and watched their mother truly leaving them, or so they thought! The Sisters took turns kneeling at the tomb, guarding it and praying. A sweet perfume kept rising from the grave, filling the air with a haunting, delightful fragrance, more beautiful than any they had ever known.

Their Mother Abbess was not dead! They prayed and through her intercession, now in Heaven, they were answered. One Sister who was badly crippled was completely healed. The number of miracles that immediately took place could fill this book, and them some.

In obedience to the Franciscan Rule, Catherine was buried in the ground without a coffin. But the Sisters could not bear that their beloved Mother had been placed in the ground without special honors; and so, they asked for (and received) permission to exhume her body and place her in a coffin befitting their Abbess, and then to bury her again. They opened the grave. To their sorrow, they discovered that the wooden plank that had been placed over the body to protect it, had broken under the weight of the earth, soaked by days of pouring rain. The plank had smashed Catherine's face and had caused other wounds that were now bleeding!

They lifted the body, tenderly, from the grave and carried her to the Cloister. They prayed beside the Saint for days. Her face resumed its former loveliness, the wounds on her body healed and returned to normal. And if that was not enough, *rigor mortis* had not set in; she was as supple as the day she had breathed her last. Now, the fastest way for a body to decompose is in water. Catherine had been soaked in water and yet her body was incorrupt! In addition, that same sweet fragrance of fresh Heavenly flowers filled the Monastery.

Try as they may, the nuns could not bury the body. Every

time, they attempted to carry her to the grave, a mysterious force shoved them back, propelling them to the Choir. They took this as a sign that Catherine was to be placed in a coffin close to the Altar of the Blessed Sacrament, her Lord Whom she adored.

She looked so alive, the nuns would not elect an Abbess for a year! Finally, when the decision was made that it was time for a new Superior, a Chapter was called. As none of them felt worthy to follow the Saint, they turned to the Monastery in Ferrara for an Abbess.

Signs, Miracle and Wonders

The Church does not determine the Sainthood of one for whom the Cause for Beatification or Canonization is open, based on the gifts they received during their lifetime, but rather the virtuous life they lived according to their vocation. However, there is the requirement of two Miracles which comes about through the sole intervention of the one whose Cause is open, after he or she is dead. Miracles occurring during one's lifetime do not count.

In Catherine's case, Miracles started to happen at once; the nuns at the Monastery were the first to receive God's mercy through Catherine's intercession. Just as *"A city set on a mountain cannot be hidden,"*[13] news of God's special grace and miracles cannot be hidden. And so it was with our Saint. Word got out, and soon religious and laity from all walks of life and stations, rich and poor, prince and peasant, came first from all parts of Italy, and then from abroad, to obtain special favors and graces from God and miraculous healings of mind, soul and body through the intercession of Catherine..

One of the many Miracles was that of a fifteen-month old baby who was dying. He was the son of a knight from Imola, Italy. The child was so far gone, the doctors had given up any hope of his recovering! But then, there was the child's aunt. Kneeling beside the child's bed, she prayed to Saint Catherine to intercede with the Lord. The child was immediately restored to good health.

---

[13]Matt 5:14

In 1589, a nobleman from Milan was burning up with fever. He was near death. His aunt prayed to Saint Catherine, and he was immediately healed. Years later, he became seriously sick once again, and was declining fast. This time, *he* petitioned our Saint, and he was healed again.

A noblewoman from Parma, Italy, after fifty days of doctors unable to break a dangerously high fever, appealed to Saint Catherine and her fever broke and she was perfectly well!

At the beginning of the twentieth century, Anna Codice became critically ill in December of 1908. She was declared incurable and the doctors had her on an artificial respirator. The girl's parents turned to Saint Catherine, believing in faith that God can do all things. Then after having been blessed with one of the Saint's Relics, the young woman began to breathe on her own and was restored to perfect health.

Perhaps, one of the greatest Miracles is the incorrupt body of our Saint, seated on a regal throne in a Chapel to the left of the main altar in the Church of Corpus Domini in Bologna. It remains intact, never having decomposed for *over five hundred years!* In the beginning, after they realized they could not place her body in the grave, four nuns would carry Saint Catherine's body to the parlor on a wooden stretcher, every time visitors came to view the body, or the faithful wanted to venerate the Saint. *This went on for twelve years!* Then the nuns decided that the faithful could view her better if she were seated on a chair. To their amazement, her body which had lost none of its suppleness, rigor mortis never having set in, became stiff, and the nuns could not place her in the chair. It was only when the Abbess ordered her, did Catherine, out of obedience, sit unaided in the chair and in the same position she can be found to this day.

Our Saint wanted to be where all the people of God could venerate her easily, and so she appeared to one of the nuns of the Monastery of Corpus Domini and told her she wanted a Chapel built close to the outer church. Previously, she had been in a Chapel inside the Monastery.

From the very beginning, Saint Catherine's Miracles and fame have brought people from all parts of the world, not only the simple faith-filled believers who fill and enrich our beautiful Church, but also future Saints, Kings and Queens and scholars. Among the first to come was Queen Isabel of Naples, Italy, who arriving in her regal finery, venerated our Saint and then left her ring as a token of her affection. She was followed by Popes (one of whom was Pope

Incorrupt body of St. Catherine of Bologna

Clement VII), Cardinals (including St. Charles Borromeo who gifted her with a precious vestment), Emperors, Princes and all kinds of personages.

Pope Clement VII granted the nuns permission to say the Office and celebrate Holy Mass in honor of Saint Catherine on March 9th which became her Feast Day. He inscribed her name in the Martyrology of Saints of the Roman Catholic Church. He was followed by other Popes who have granted indulgences and privileges to pilgrims coming to the Sacred place to venerate the saint. The process for her Canonization was started in 1669 and was solemnly concluded on Trinity Sunday, the 22nd of May, 1712 when Pope Clement IX proclaimed to the whole world, to the whole Roman Catholic Church that we had a Saint!

The first time we went to visit Saint Catherine, it was out of holy curiosity; *her body was incorrupt!* But when we got there, we discovered a very powerful Saint who became very personal to us. We have loved her since 1977, the first time we brought our grandson, all of ten years old, to Europe with us. We hope reading about her that you will turn to her and get to know her with your head and heart, as we have. We love you!

Saint Catherine of Genoa
Wife, Humanitarian, Christian Model, Mystic

St. Catherine of Genoa

Catherine was born into the Fieschi family, at that time, the most influential of the Guelf families of Genoa in the Province of Liguori in the Northern part of Italy. This famous family produced the powerful, very dynamic Pope Innocent IV in 1234 and then his nephew Adrian V as Pontiff (for only a few weeks). The Fieschi family reached the pinnacle of fame and fortune in the *fifteenth century*, raising up a Cardinal, and a Viceroy James Fieschi.[1] James would marry Francesca di Negro of Genoa, of an ancient noble family, linking two strong aristocratic families of Genoa. But the Lord had a greater plan; He was to send Catherine, fifth and last of their children, who would some day become a Saint.

It was 1447. Just as Jesus brought His favored three to Mount Tabor to strengthen them for the next high place, Calvary, so would the Lord raise up a Saint to balance in holiness the devastating blow that another, born in that century, would inflict upon His Church. Catherine Fieschi, later known to the world as *Saint Catherine of Genoa*, would become a *Role Model*, not only to the Catholic Church but also a much admired inspiration and unifying force to the entire Christian world, bringing back home those whom Martin Luther, the other child of the fifteenth century, separated from Mother Church.

---

[1] descendant of Robert Fieschi who was a brother of Innocent IV

She was destined to be wholly dedicated to the Lord, as His faithful bride, from her youngest years. At eight years old Catherine began to do penance, exchanging her soft luxurious bed for a bit of straw on the hard floor, and her fluffy pillow for a tree stump. She was an obedient child and showed signs of holiness even at that early age.

When she was twelve years old, Catherine had her first glimpse of God's love; He shared with her some of the pain He had suffered during His Holy Passion. At thirteen, she disclosed to her confessor her desire to become a nun. As he was also the confessor of the Nuns of Our Lady of Grace Convent where her sister Limbania was already a canoness regular, Catherine pleaded with him to intercede on her behalf. The Superiors rejected Catherine, because it was not their custom to accept girls of such a young age. This greatly hurt Catherine, but she never lost faith in her Lord and His love for her. Then, a year later in 1461, her father died.

A marriage of convenience is arranged for Catherine

With the death of Robert Fieschi, political maneuvering was necessary. How does a family keep its position? They marry off their children, uniting two strong families. And so, although Catherine must have thought sixteen years of age *finally* would be a suitable age to enter the convent, she became a political pawn, and a marriage of convenience was arranged for her. Her heart was again broken, but she obeyed and was married to a young noble of the prominent, well-to-do Adorno Family, also of Genoa.

The marriage was certainly not made in Heaven; the young husband Giuliano was the direct opposite from Catherine. Whereas she was holy and religious, he was wild and self-indulgent to the sacrifice of everything and everyone. The first ten years of married life were stark, unadulterated hell! He squandered all their wealth on good times and wild women. Catherine, after suffering five years of loneliness, unable to endure her husband's infidelity and lifestyle, feeling deserted from everyone, even God, turned to the

Above: ***Stained-glass windows in Genoa of scenes
from the life of St. Catherine of Genoa***

Left:
***Bob and Penny
Lord with Father
Cassiano,
Capuchin who is
the Custodian of
the Shrine of St.
Catherine of
Genoa in Genoa,
Italy***

frivolous life of her class, going to parties and becoming more and more involved with the next party and new dress she would wear. Although her attempts at finding some meaning in life were innocent, they did not bring her the joy and peace she sought so desperately; and so the depression she had attempted to overcome grew worse.

God takes over in Catherine's life, and she is never the same

But God never leaves us alone. It was the Feast of St. Benedict, March 21, 1473. Catherine's sister Limbania suggested Catherine go to *her* confessor. The moment she knelt in front of this holy priest, Our Lord overshadowed her and wounded her so powerfully with His unsparingly unconditional Love, she was lost in ecstasy, and was unable to confess her sins. Catherine was suddenly filled with remorse for the life she had been leading. God appeared to be unfurling her life before her, like a film, showing her the many times she had betrayed the love He had for her. But, at the same time, through this *Divine Wound* as she called it, God revealed the sweet Love that never ended, the Love He had for her and all His children. With this striking contrast of God's Love and the world's false gods of empty promises, she became repulsed by all that her society had to offer and cried out: *"No more world, no more sin!"*

When we are faced with the absolute, unreserved Love, Our Lord has for us, it is as if a giant, brilliant light enters our soul, and even the smallest transgression, compared to God's generous Love becomes to us, a monumental sin. And who is to contradict the great Saints on this point? Are we not taught: *To those who much has been given, much is required?*

Catherine went home and wept through the night. When the Lord saw how very remorseful she was, He appeared to her, covered with blood, carrying the Cross. As He shared that part of His life and pain, she became deeply filled with His Love and, through that knowledge, a heavy sadness for the last ten wasted years, years she could have spent loving Him. For the next fourteen months, the more the Lord revealed His Love and her sins, the more she desired to be cleansed and lead a new life in Him. As one by one her sins were revealed to her, she repented, and they disappeared, consumed by the flames of His Love, never to reappear.

One day, while praying before the Crucifix, Catherine was lifted up to Our Lord's wounded Heart on the Cross. This Heart, Which had been pierced out of love for all mankind, was on fire, glowing with the same flames that burned inside her own heart; it was the same fire that He had enkindled in her, the same blaze which had consumed her sins, never to resurface. This so affected Catherine she relived it for years, crying out: "(I) *Have no longer either soul or heart; but my soul and my heart are those of my Beloved.*"

Catherine was changed! She became totally absorbed in Her Savior. No longer did she need or desire the world and its trappings. After Our Lord appeared to her on the Cross and drew her up to Him, after she felt herself like John the Beloved resting her head on His precious Chest, she saw everything through His Eyes. She no longer had to decide what was right or wrong; rather how it was revealed in the Light of God. *How would Jesus feel? What would Jesus do?*

She made a general confession on March 24th (three days after her prior confession) and her new life began! We always say, God has a sense of humor. Of course, as calamity strikes, it is difficult to see beyond the darkness to the Light which is about to shine through. Catherine's husband Giuliano's life caught up with him and they were reduced to almost total poverty. We do not know if the new-found strength, displayed by Catherine, brought about the change, along with her unrelenting prayers for his salvation, or the frailty of the world's possessions and glory; but you guessed it, Catherine's husband was converted!

Catherine's journey from riches to rags and eternal joy

Giuliano agreed to live a celibate life with Catherine, a life of perpetual abstinence. He became a Franciscan Tertiary. They moved out of their palace to a small house which was conveniently close to the hospital, where the two would serve the sick and helpless. Giuliano tended to the poor and the infirm, selflessly and tirelessly, until his death on January 10, 1497.

In 1479, six years after their first move from the luxurious to the austere, they went from their modest home to two small rooms in the hospital. They supported themselves, with a small pension Catherine received from her parent's estate. They served without pay, the poorest of the poor and the most destitute. For eleven years, Catherine served as a nurse, taking on any and all tasks, small and great. In 1490 she was asked to take over the administration of the hospital. Although she would have preferred caring full time for the ill, she took on her new task with the same kind of dedication and zeal. She handled financial matters efficiently, scrupulously accounting for every penny, never taking any recompense for her services. But she did not do this at the expense of her prayer life or her service to the poor and the sick.

In 1493, a deadly epidemic spread throughout the province, claiming 80% of the population. Those who contracted the disease died, after suffering excruciating pain accompanied by high fevers. There was a very pious woman in the hospital dying from this highly contagious disease. She underwent the greatest trials, enduring unbearable agony for eight days. Catherine visited and tended to her often. Try as she may, the woman was unable to call on Jesus, the Shepherd for help. Catherine repeated, over and over again, *"Call on Jesus."* No matter how she tried, the woman could not reach out to her Savior for consolation. She tried mouthing the words, her lips forming the Name of Jesus, but no sound came forth! One day, seeing the noble effort put forward by her holy patient, Catherine kissed her lips. Hours later, dizziness, flushed cheeks, accompanied by a raging high fever confirmed Catherine's suspicions, she had contracted the deadly disease. Catherine narrowly escaped death. This close call with the angel of death, however, did not deter her from performing all her hospital duties. She returned to her patients, including the highly contagious, before she herself was completely recuperated.

We see in Catherine, the powerful balance of the Love she had for God, (the First Commandment) and through that Love, the love she had for neighbor (the Second Commandment), the same quality of Love shown by the Savior when He walked the earth - love for His Father, giving all credit to Him, and love for those He came to save, saying: *"I am the good Shepherd; I know My own and My own know Me, just as the Father knows Me and I know the Father; and I lay down My life for My sheep."*[2]

Those who would stress *social justice* to the sacrifice and omission of *Divine Love*, should remember that Judas was reminded by Jesus of the importance of putting God first when Judas criticized Mary for wasting precious ointment anointing Jesus' Feet. He said, *"You have the poor with you, always; you will not always have Me."*[3] If we put God first, *He* will, through our hands and hearts, do *good* for our neighbors.

"Whatsoever you do for the least of My children..."[4]

When Catherine learned of her husband's former mistress and the illegitimate child he had sired during his sinful days, she treated them with utmost kindness and concern, caring for them as if they were her very own. She went further, leaving the child an inheritance from her estate. The child's mother eventually entered a convent and led a pious life until her death.

Now, thinking of the family and the traditions of the Italian people of that time and times past, this is a complete mystery, if you see with the eyes of the world and not those of the Lord. Catherine became, through *the overpowering outpouring of Love* from her Savior, what we are all called to be, and find so very difficult - a contradiction in the world. Her forgiveness of her husband and his years of infidelity, which had been compounded by his irresponsible lifestyle impoverishing them, could not be construed as anything but conversion through *Divine intervention*. Only the Heart of the Savior could have melted her heart, forgiving

[2]John 10:14
[3]John 12:8
[4]Matt 25:40

Giuliano for all the years of aloneness and pain he had caused her, the wounds she carried as he was holding back his love from her, robbing her of all those years of innocence. But when the Lord with His open Heart melts our hearts of stone, placing our wounded hearts into His, we begin to love again, only now with the Heart of the Savior, Whose last words on the Cross were pleading with the Father to forgive His persecutors. But it is so hard, Lord!

Catherine and the Eucharist

On the Feast of the Annunciation, following Catherine's conversion, Our Lord gave her a burning desire for Himself in the *Eucharist*, a love she never lost. Contrary to the rule of that time, Catherine was given special permission to receive Holy Communion every day. She became a daily communicant, which was most unusual for those days. Only Priests were permitted to receive Communion daily. Others risked being accused of repenting for some scandal, if they were observed receiving every day. What we take for granted, and often do not take advantage of, being able to receive Our Lord *daily* in Holy Communion, was first instituted by the holy Saint Pope Pius X at the beginning of the Twentieth Century.

Once Catherine was able to receive her Lord, daily, she never stopped, except for one time. One day, a holy religious asked her, *"Did you ever think there might be something wrong with your receiving Communion every day?"* Although it caused her much anguish and sorrow, fearing she might be doing something wrong, she abstained from receiving daily. The religious, seeing how she preferred to suffer, rather than offend God, directed her to return to receiving Holy Communion daily.

After her conversion, Jesus invited Catherine to be with Him in the desert for forty days, in remembrance of that time He fasted without food or water, suffering temptation from the devil. Catherine ate nothing during that Lent until Easter Sunday, *subsisting solely* on the Eucharist. Her love for Jesus became so great, and her desire for the Eucharist grew to such proportions, all other food became distasteful during the forty days of Lent as well as the forty days of Advent, each year. At that time Catherine supplemented the Sacred Host with only a small bit of salted water or bitter tasting water and vinegar.

The fasting did not diminish her physical capabilities and endeavors, nor lessen her mental proficiency. She was sharper than ever; she looked better than she had in her entire life and was able to do *more* in *less* time. Try as she may, even under obedience, she could not withhold the feeling of nausea that swept over her, when she ate during those periods. But, when the days of Lent and Advent were over, she was able to eat heartily, enjoying all that was placed before her.

Catherine maintained this practice of fasting from 1473, when she began at 26 years of age, until 1507, when at age 60, she became ill and was ordered to curtail all her fasting, including fast days set down by Mother Church. During two of the most holy periods of our Church - *Advent*, when we are awaiting the Birth of the Baby Jesus, and *Lent*, when we prepare for His death on the Cross and Resurrection, she fasted. Although, for 34 years, her only sustenance had been the reception of Holy Communion and a bit of water mixed with a bit of salt, she was active until she died at age 63.

Once, she was so ill, the doctors told everyone, she was dying. She could take no food or water, no nourishment of any kind. Catherine requested the Holy Eucharist, saying if she could receive her Lord just three times, she would be cured. She received Communion and was immediately healed, returning to her activities, once more, as if she had never been ill.

As we know, the Eucharist is the Source of life![5] When Catherine was deprived of Holy Communion for any reason, she suffered such unbearable, excruciating physical pain, all who attended her knew it was the Will of God that she be united with her Spouse in His Body Blood, soul and Divinity through His Eucharist. They say Catherine rarely cried, but one night she awakened, drenched with tears she had shed. She had dreamt,

---

[5]Catechism of the Catholic Church

she would not receive Holy Communion, the next day!

She would have travelled many miles, enduring all kinds of pain and fatigue, struggling through and overturning all obstacles, to be able to receive her Lord in Holy Communion. The day that Our Lord had appeared to Catherine, covered with Blood, carrying His Cross, and she was converted, she was chosen to be one with her *Savior Crucified*! Is it any surprise, she would adore Him in Holy Communion? Do we not believe that the Same One Who came to her on His Way to Calvary is the Same One Who came to her, and comes to us, in the Form of a Consecrated Host during the Sacrifice of the Mass![6]

At times, she would not hear or see any part of the Mass, until the very moment she was about to receive Communion, her spirit was so engrossed with anticipation of encountering Our Lord in Holy Communion. She would awaken, as if from a trance, and beg the Lord for His forgiveness, crying:

"O! my Lord, it seems to me that if I were dead, I should come to life in order to receive Thee and if an unconsecrated host were given me, that I should know it by the taste, as one knows wine from water."

She shared that when she received Holy Communion, she felt a ray of love deeply pierce her heart. We wonder, if it was like the red hot arrow that pierced the hearts of such Mystics as Saint Teresa of Avila, Gemma Galgani, Veronica Giuliani, John of the Cross, and Padre Pio, when they received transverberation of their hearts, from the hands of an Angel.[7]

So great was Catherine's love for her Lord in the Eucharist, she told Him she desired nothing but Him and Him *wholly*. *She asked Him not to grant her visions*, nor any earthly consolations;

---

[6]Read more about Miracles of the Eucharist and Jesus' Real Presence in the Host after Consecration during the Sacrifice of the Mass, in Bob and Penny Lord's book: *"This is My Body, This is My Blood, Miracles of the Eucharist, Book II."*

[7]You can read more about St. Teresa in *"Saints and other Powerful Women in the Church"* and John of the Cross and Padre Pio in *"Saints and other Powerful Men in the Church"* both by Bob and Penny Lord.

she rather would *"walk by faith."* The great Love that she embraced, through her partaking of the Eucharist, was enough for her.

The Agony and the Ecstasy

For four years following her conversion, Catherine had practiced mortification and penance, disciplining her senses. She wore hair shirts that itched, irritated, scratched and cut into her delicate flesh. She abstained from meat and fruit of all kinds. She slept on sharp, pointed objects, their blade-like edges cutting into her body, causing it to bleed. But while practicing great austerity, *she was careful to not neglect her everyday duties.*

She allowed little or no temptations to lure her from her God, spurning all human respect in favor of that of the Divine. Temptations, like insects attracted to a burning candle, would be consumed by the flames within her heart, which burned with the Love of her Lord. She spent six hours in prayer each day, and yet was able to fulfill all her commitments.

She lived, subject to others, serving others to the neglect of herself, her desires and needs. And when she had the slightest tendency to fall prey to her natural inclinations, the Lord revealed them to her, giving her the opportunity to identify and rebuke them.

When the four years ended, Catherine was no longer allowed to practice these acts of penance and mortification. Although she desired to do so, the Lord said that it had been *His* Will, she do so for four years, not her will. Now it was His Will she cease. And she obeyed!

Though her inner spirituality was drawing her into ecstasy, she remained a faithful servant of the needy. She always showed concern for others, but did not allow her desire to serve the poor and helpless to take away from her family. She used just enough from her modest inheritance to barely sustain herself (that she might not take from the much needed assets of the hospital). This was so she could leave some form of security to her family, especially to her unwed nieces and the widows.

A very healthy characteristic which we see running through most all the Visionaries, Mystics and Stigmatists is the desire for *anonymity* and their seeking discernment as to the authenticity of the supernatural source of their gifts. Catherine consistently turned to the Lord, begging Him to reveal if it was He, herself or the evil one. She healthily questioned miraculous occurrences such as: her fasting for 40 days in a row, twice a year, during Lent and Advent; and although she had just been at the point of death, being restored to perfect health and new strength. Her inner spirit would soar when someone was in need, overturning her outer weakness.

But Catherine never took her gifts for granted. As she grew closer to God, *she* disappeared and all that was left was her God fully in charge. At one point, the Lord told her, *"Never say `I will'* or `I will not'. Never say `mine' but always say `ours.'"* And this is a rough one, but again consistent with the other true Mystics, the Lord told her, *"Never excuse yourself, but always be ready to accuse yourself."* Can you imagine being able to live this kind of life without the Lord fully in charge? Can you try to fathom the dying to self, this required of Catherine?

Catherine's battle between Divine Love and self-love

Catherine said that she saw a vision of *self-love* whose lord and master revealed himself as the devil himself. She shared that a better, more descriptive title would be *self-hate*. The Lord told her that because of the evil that a human brings about, when he seizes the bait of *self-love* on the devil's fishing pole, his soul is on its way to eternal damnation. Once a soul gives consent to this sometimes subtle scourge that permeates the world, it spreads like a rampant, highly infectious epidemic. Have we not seen, in this, the end of the 20th Century, the results of the cancerous philosophy of self-love that has been covering the earth like a giant plague, robbing our Church of vocations, destroying families, pitting brother against brother, children killing without remorse, and mothers killing their own unborn babies?

Once someone shared that his confessor said it was all right to think impure thoughts, as long as you did not act on your fantasies. We said that he probably misunderstood the priest. We shared that Jesus and the Church He founded teaches that evil begins in the mind and *then* travels to the flesh.

The *spirit* displayed in self-love has, first and foremost, little or no concern as to whether it attacks its own body and soul or that of its neighbor. The soul, so absorbed with self-love, will go to any lengths to accomplish its end. When it has set its sites on a certain diabolical course, neither promises nor threats can dissuade it from wielding its lethal blows; causing enslavement and impoverishment, death of reputation through scandal, it cares not if the results are damaging to itself or others. Then finally, when there is not a glimpse of the goodness of the precious soul that God created, it cares not the cost and sounds the death knell, but not for its adversary but for itself, condemning itself to Purgatory or even Hell.

Catherine further said that once a soul has allowed self-love to take over, not even the promises of wealth, position, and fulfillment of every earthly desire, can persuade it to turn around, not even the knowledge, it will lose eternal happiness and peace in Heaven. And so, deafened and blinded to the Truth, the soul condemns itself willingly and openly to Purgatory or the never-ending agony of Hell.

A priest once said that if someone were to open the gates of Hell, no one would leave. How devastating! It causes your heart to break, when you think that possibly someone you love has taken that road. But, fear not, the Lord is not finished with any of our souls on earth and He will reach out, through our prayers and sacrifice to bring those we love home to Him; because He never stops loving!

She further shared that *self-love* is a subtle thief who steals even from God Himself; claiming souls as his own, he uses God's gifts against God and His loved ones. The evil of self-will is insidiously deluding the soul that is so inundated by its lies that it really believes *the end justifies the means*. It thinks nothing of robbing from others, in the name of doing good. The soul which is permeated with *self-love* is often difficult and may appear impossible to detect. Saint Catherine warned that *spiritual* self-love is far more deadly than that which is bodily, in that it is often disguised as sanctity and cannot be easily detected; it can appear as charity; it can arouse our pity, calling us to defend it against those who try to expose it. It uses so many deceitful masks, it makes one shudder, fearing for the innocent lambs of the world. But, we have seen it come to pass; the Lord in His Light, in His Love, will not allow His loved ones to be deceived for long. God, in His Truth, will set us free!

Jesus reveals Purgatory and Hell to Catherine

Through the Divine fire Which burned inside Catherine, while she was still on earth, she was able to understand the state of souls in **Purgatory**. The Lord had purified her soul, in the furnace of His Love, as gold is refined of all its impurities, by *fire*! Cleansing her of every stain of sin while she was still in the flesh, he was perfecting her on earth, so that when Catherine passed to the next world, she would be ready to appear before Him. God told her that the soul is like gold; once all the impurities are burned away, no matter how great the fire is, it can do it no harm to the soul. God said He keeps the soul in the flames of His Divine Love until every stain of sin is burned away and the soul reaches the highest perfection it is capable of (each according to its own vocation and capacity), and once this is accomplished, the soul rests completely in Him.

He further told her that, as the sun cannot penetrate a covered surface (like a dark shade) so as to allow light to flow into a room, not through any defect in the sun but simply from the blockage of the covering, so it is with the rust of sin which darkens the soul; it blocks the *Son's* Love from coming through. In **Purgatory**, the compassionate flames burn away all the rust of sin, layer by layer, allowing the Divine rays of God's Love to come through, the rust of sin decreasing as God's Love increases. This does not take away the torment which no one can ever truly describe, nor anyone truly understand. The vision of Purgatory that the Lord revealed to Catherine so impressed her, she could not wipe it from her mind and heart. God revealed to her:

On Sin: *"The source of all suffering is either original or actual sin. God created the soul pure, simple, free from every stain, and with a certain beatific instinct toward Himself. It is drawn away from Him by Original Sin, and when actual sin is added afterwards, this (actual sin) draws the soul still farther away from God; and as the soul removes itself more and more from Him, its sinfulness increases and its communing (or communication) with God decreases, till there is less and less of Him and more and more of the dark shade of sin blocking the soul from Him."*[8]

Have you ever noticed that when someone is living in sin, the first thing they do is stop going to Mass? Rather than going to confession, unburdening themselves of all that has separated them from God and living a new life in Him, they remain in the Hell that they have created on earth for themselves, walking farther and farther from God.

On Hell and the Soul: *"As the purified spirit finds no repose but in God for Whom it was created, so the soul in sin can rest nowhere but in Hell, which by reason of its sin has become its end."*

On Purgatory: *"The same thing is true of Purgatory: the soul leaving the body, and not finding in itself that purity in which it is created, and seeing also the hindrances which prevent her union with God, conscious also that Purgatory only can remove from them, casts herself quickly and willingly therein. And if she did not find the means ordained for her purification, she would instantly create for herself a hell worse than Purgatory, seeing that by reason of this impediment she is hindered from approaching her end, which is God; and this is so great an ill that in comparison with it the soul esteems Purgatory as nothing. True it is (as*

---

[8]We have paraphrased Catherine's words, to a degree, to make it more understandable to today's reader.

I have said), like Hell; and yet in comparison with the loss of God it is as nothing.

"I will say furthermore: I see that as far as God is concerned, Paradise has no gates, but he who will may enter. For God is all mercy, and His open Arms are ever extended to receive us into His glory. But I see that the Divine Essence is so pure-purer than the imagination can conceive-that the soul, finding in itself the slightest imperfection, would rather cast itself into a thousand hells than appear, so stained, in the presence of the Divine Majesty. Knowing, then, that Purgatory was intended for her cleansing, she throws herself therein, and finds there that great mercy, the removal of her stains.

"The great importance of Purgatory, neither mind can conceive or tongue describe. I see only that its pains are as great as those of Hell; and yet I see that a soul, stained with the slightest fault, receiving this mercy, counts its pain as naught in comparison with this hindrance to her love. And I know that the greatest misery of the souls in Purgatory is to behold in themselves anything that displeases God, and to discover that, in spite of His goodness, they had consented to it."

God entrusts His sole direction of Catherine, to another

Catherine's walk was spiritually guided by God himself for twenty-five years. Every time she believed that she was to have an earthly spiritual director, the Lord spoke to her inner spirit: *"Trust Me and doubt not."* Only when she approached her last years, suffering from physical exhaustion, her body giving out from years of service and physical deprivation, did the Lord choose a director to care for the needs of her body and soul. He heard her confession, said Mass for her, and brought her Holy Communion whenever he could. This priest would be the instrument to share with the world, the mysticism of this great and holy lay woman, truly a contradiction in this world.

The Lord continued speaking to Catherine; only now He

determined, she share it with her confessor. The Lord, in His Divine Wisdom, willed she be dependent on her confessor in her last years, as a means to get His message out to generations upon generations of Christians who would be touched and enlightened by all that He had revealed to Catherine.

As with other Mystics, her inner spiritual experiences so weakened her *physically*, she had to divert her mind from the spiritual to something external. This caused Catherine to suffer intense pain and burning in her heart. One day, having languished in this state for days, unable to stand the agony any longer, she took her Spiritual Director's hand and placed it on her feverish face. Suddenly, a sweet aroma gently spread over her flushed face, flowing downward like a cool breeze, cooling her fever-wracked body. At last, her suffering was relieved!

She shared with her confessor that God had sent the *Odor of Heaven*, as a means to alleviate the pain in her body and soul. Its fragrance heavenly, its aroma sweet and rich, this gift from the Divine struck her with such an impact, it pierced her heart deeply. Although with Catherine the feeling and fragrance lingered for days, when her confessor raised his hand to smell what Catherine had experienced, there was no scent of any kind on his hand.

This priest, who had been wisely directing her, found himself being powerfully directed. Catherine explained, the Lord does not grant such gifts to those who *desire* them. As we research miracles that the Lord manifests, we discover over and over again that signs such as these have been brought about in cases of profound need, most often to bring about the salvation and glory of His Church. *"Remember always that I will not leave you orphans."*[9] *"I will be with you till the end of time."*[10]

The Lord revealed to Catherine that this was a tiny foretaste of what the body's senses will experience in Heaven. She was able to smell the aroma of celestial flowers for days. This was to remind her of the Lord's ongoing power which would continue to

---

[9]John 14:18
[10]Matt 28:20

strengthen and refresh her, until that day when she would go to Him and His whole Heavenly Family.

Catherine and her Director are victims of gossip

As the world with its sinfulness, deprived of the Light Who is Jesus, is blind and sees everyone in its darkness, tongues began to wag. *Why was the confessor always at Catherine's side? Was it proper for a priest to be in the company of someone of the opposite sex?* This not only wounded her director, he scrupulously stayed away from Catherine for three days, questioning his motives. When he discovered the pain the holy victim had suffered because of his absence, he repented his doubts and continued directing her, confidant that this alliance was formed by Divine Will and not by human origin and design. You can believe that the Lord chastised him for doubting, after all the signs he had witnessed attesting to the holiness and virtue of the saintly Catherine.

That battle fought and won, the two remained friends, she confiding in him as her confessor and director; and he growing more and more sensitive to when she was sharing *all* the Lord was telling her, as opposed to when she was withholding something. It has always been difficult for the true and tested Mystics to reveal their experiences, whether they were with Our Heavenly family or the devil himself. First, they always questioned the origin of the apparition or locution. Secondly, they did not desire to bring attention to themselves. Some, like St. Thérèse the Little Flower,[11] were afraid they might lose the gifts from the Lord and Our Lady if the Lord felt they were using them in a form of boasting. It happened with Saint Clare of Montefalco who bore the crucified Lord in her heart as well as the tools of crucifixion.[12]

"St. Clare of Montefalco was constantly striving for a more ascetic type of prayer, that is the type of union with

---

[11]read more about St. Therese in Bob and Penny Lord's book: *"Saints and other Powerful Women in the Church"*

[12]from the chapter on St. Clare of Montefalco in Bob and Penny Lord's book: *"Saints and other Powerful Women in the Church"*

Christ that calls for self-denial and deep contemplation. It seems she was just beginning to reach that Union of 'Complete Oneness' when God put an end to it.

"Clare was having a highly Spirit-filled, engaging conversation with Marina (another contemplative) when the enemy of pride surfaced and she gave into it."[13]

We are not sure why Catherine chose to withhold some of her experiences from her Spiritual Director, but it would appear she did; because one day, he confronted her, advising her of *all* she had failed to share with him. She knew that what she was hearing could only have been revealed to her Director by the Lord. She not only divulged all that she had omitted, she never kept back any part of her spiritual journey from him again. Because of and this relationship, the Lord would use this holy priest and His little vessel Catherine to reveal to His children His involvement in mankind! The tools, methods and vessels He chooses need only to be available to do His Will, so that the world will know *He* is the Power and to *Him* goes all glory!

Catherine - instrument of Healing

Marco de Sale had cancer of the nose. He had tried every means that medical science of his day knew, to no avail, and he was dying. His anger became uncontrollable; he would fly into wild rages of frustration. Once a holy man, he now behaved as one possessed. His wife Argentina went to the hospital and pleaded with Saint Catherine to come to her home and pray for her husband that he might have a peaceful death. Saint Catherine prayed with the sick man, compassionately, imparting words of hope and encouragement and then left for the hospital, accompanied by Argentina. On the way they stopped at St. Mary of Grace Roman Catholic Church. Upon entering the church, Catherine felt herself being brought down on her knees, the Lord commissioning her to pray for the stricken man. She obeyed and Argentina joined her.

---

[13]quote from the chapter on St. Clare of Montefalco in Bob and Penny Lord's book: *"Saints and other Powerful Women in the Church"*

Argentina accompanied Catherine to the hospital and then left for home to attend to her husband. When she entered her home, Marco was a different man. He was no longer a man driven, as if by demons, but one with the angelic peace that could only come from the Lord and His Mother, and their Heavenly Army of Angels. He asked his wife to bring Catherine back, the next day; which she did. Now Catherine knew the condition of the sick man, as the Lord had interiorly enlightened her, and had inspired her to pray before visiting him.

When she arrived at his bedside, Marco said to Catherine:

"The reasons I have asked you to come here again are, first, to thank you for your charity towards me, and then to ask you one more favor, which I pray you will not deny me. After you left me, Our Lord Jesus Christ Himself appeared visibly to me, under the form He appeared to Mary Magdalene in the garden, gave me His most holy blessing, pardoned my sins and said that He appeared to me because on Ascension Day I was to go to Him; therefore I pray you, most kind mother, that you may be pleased to accept Argentina as your spiritual daughter, keeping her always close to you; and I pray that you Argentina consent to this."[14]

Having received their mutual agreement, Marco asked for a priest that he might hear his confession and give him Holy Communion. Then he followed with a request that a notary public be summoned in order to put his house in order. Although they tried to dissuade him, because he looked in the best of health, the husband acted in faith on what the Lord had told him. That accomplished, when the vigil of the Ascension arrived, Marco sent again for a confessor. He made his last confession, received

---

[14]excerpt from *"The Spiritual Doctrine of Saint Catherine of Genoa"* by Tan Publications

his Viaticum[15] and Extreme Unction,[16] in preparation for the journey *Home*.

Night approached, and Marco sent the Priest back to the monastery. When he and his wife were alone, Marco handed her a crucifix, saying, *"Argentina, I leave you this for your Spouse; prepare to suffer, for I assure you will have to do so."* Argentina indeed would suffer mentally and physically, as she shared the heavy cross, her spiritual mother was to always carry.

With the early rising of the sun, Marco turned to his wife and said, *"Argentina, God be with you, for the hour has come."* With that he closed his eyes and passed away on to his new *Home*! The confessor shared that the man's spirit, having left his body, knocked on his window and cried out: *"Ecce Homo."* With this, the priest said he knew that Marco had entered the Kingdom of Heaven to be with His Lord. Catherine took Argentina into her home and heart, Catherine bringing her wherever she went. One day when they were passing by Our Lady of Grace, the church where they had prayed for Marco, Catherine said to Argentina: *"This is the place where grace was obtained for your husband."* The Lord placed these words in Catherine's mouth that all who read her life would know, not only of the miracle that had come to pass when Catherine listened to the Lord's prompting and prayed, but, more importantly, what can happen when we just trust in the Lord and His Mercy and Power!

Catherine prepares to go Home

For *nine years* preceding her death, Catherine suffered from a disease that did not have signs of earthly or Divine origin. There was nothing that could be done to relieve her most excruciating pain. Her condition continued to deteriorate. Many times, during those nine years of endless suffering, she appeared so feeble, everyone thought: *This is it; she is dying.* The last year of her

---

[15]"...name given to Holy Communion when it is given to someone in...danger of health, during an illness...When Anointing of the Sick is given at the same time, Viaticum precedes." Catholic Encyclopedia - Broderick

[16]now called the Sacrament of the Anointing of the Sick

life, she lived on relatively nothing, eating in a week's time less than one would consume in a day. The last six months, she sipped a bit of broth and nothing but the Eucharist.

Towards the end, Catherine could keep nothing down, with the exception of Holy Communion. Her body became truly united with her Savior, as she physically and spiritually shared in His Passion. She had said *Yes!* when she was commissioned by her Savior to be spouse of the *Crucified Lord*, and He was taking her up on it, trusting her with the agony and desolation He underwent in the Garden of Gethsemane. Like her Spouse, every inch of her body cried out in pain. Because it was such a heartache to watch her writhing in pain, she was not even to know the comfort, the companionship and the uplifting support of dear friends.

Even sleep was denied Catherine, her anguish and torment was so unbearable. Screams involuntarily escaped from her cracked, parched lips, giving painful testimony of her final walk with Jesus to the Cross. When You were scourged at the pillar and then nailed to the Cross, Lord, did You *want* to cry out in pain, but did not? Now, was your spouse Catherine crying out Your pain? Were Your silent screams given a voice, through Catherine?

At the very end, she had so surrendered her will that she became one with her Savior, no longer she but He, arms outstretched on the Cross, near death, dying of thirst, totally and completely vulnerable to the Will of the Father in Heaven. She was sharing Our Lord's final moments on the Cross! But the pain had left her face. She resembled the Resurrected Christ, the signs of His Wounds still visible for the eyes of the world to see; her interior spirit reflecting the joy of one who had already seen Heaven from afar, saluted it, and now was on the threshold of entering into her long awaited eternal life with Her Spouse Jesus. When her director inquired about the happiness reflected in her face, she shared she had seen a vision so beautiful of what was ahead, her spirit was already soaring heavenward.

When word got out that their Saint was dying, the faithful came to see her for the last time. As her Savior before her, although racked in pain, she was radiating such a blinding love, her light filled what could have been a gloomy room. As she spoke with such joy, of the Lord and His Love for them, they felt they were at a celebration. And indeed, although they were sad they would not have her *physically* present, they knew she would be interceding more powerfully before Jesus in Heaven.

A Saint is dead; long live the Saint!

September 13th, Catherine began to bleed so profusely, the little blood left in her body was consumed finally by the raging fire that had been burning inside her for so long. She received Holy Communion and continued talking, her pulse very weak but her mind alert and very much alive. The next evening, she was once again asked if she wanted Holy Communion. She replied, *"Not yet,"* and pointed towards Heaven, advising them her next Communion would be with her Lord in Heaven. Knowing that her Spouse was waiting to escort her to the Kingdom, she closed her eyes for the last time, uttering the words of her Savior, *"Into Thy Hands, O Lord, I commend my spirit."*[17]

On September the 14th,[18] Love triumphed over death; a little Saint, with a *great* mission, gave up her spirit to the Lord, and once again we have the *Triumph of the Cross*.

Catherine is welcomed into the Company of Saints

Catherine's body was at first interred in the hospital where she had so faithfully and tirelessly served for so many years. They discovered a year later that water was streaming through the wooden coffin in which the holy body had been placed. When they opened it, there were all sorts of worms and creatures surrounding it, but not one touched the body. It was not only dry but had not suffered the slightest decomposition.

Others hearing about the Saint's miraculously incorrupt body, word got out, and the faithful flocked to the hospital to view this miracle, and to pray to the intercession of the Saint, to kneel before

---

[17]Luke 23:46
[18]Feast of the Triumph of the Cross

St. Catherine of Genoa in Glory

her body present, so m i r a c u l o u s l y preserved. Her clothing was covered with mildew and showed signs of deterioration, as did the wooden coffin; therefore, how much more extraordinary was the sign of our Saint's body, untouched by the ravages of death, there before them, just as she appeared the day she was buried.

Miracle after miracle began to happen, through prayers to the Lord, through His servant Catherine. A dear friend of Catherine was critically ill and confined to her bed. She had a vision of Catherine in Paradise, rejoicing in the Light of her Spouse. She asked to be carried to the hospital that she might be placed next to the body of the Saint. They placed pieces of cloth that had touched Catherine's incorrupt body, on the parts of her friend's body where she was suffering the greatest pain. The friend asked for the Saint's intercession and was *cured, immediately* !

Others hearing about the Saint's miraculously incorrupt body, and the miracles coming about through her intercession, came, prayed, and touched the body to such an extreme, the body was placed in a glass sarcophagus that all who came could view this miracle and pray, but not touch. We have visited the church in Genoa where her body is still incorrupt and on view for all to see that we might know and believe that the Lord can and will do all things to let His children know He is the Power and can do all things, even preserve the body of a holy child of His; that they might have faith and know they have nothing to fear!

Saint Catherine died in 1507. Even before her death, while she was still alive and active, the townspeople called her a Saint. The faithful began to flock to her immediately after her death. She was proclaimed *Blessed* by popular acclaim! [This was before Urban VIII issued a Bull restricting this title, and that of *Saint*, to only those formally declared so by the Holy See. On May 18, 1737, Catherine's Spouse Jesus crowned His little bride, welcoming her to the Heavenly Company of Saints, through Pope Benedict XIV, adding her to the Roman Martyrology with the title of Saint Catherine.

You have asked us to write about powerful lay faithful who have been made Saints. This is only one of them. Has she challenged you to be more? Has she spoken to your heart? Does your heart burn with the fire that finally consumed her? Then, read again this chapter that you know and realize, the way is not easy; it is the Way of the Cross. *Do you still say Yes?*

St. Rose of Lima

Saint Rose of Lima

Patroness of the Americas

This is a very difficult chapter, in that there is so much to tell you about this most powerful Saint, and this time in the history of the Church, and of the world, we don't know where to start. These Visionaries, Mystics and Stigmatists have such powerful teachings. We have tried to focus on the gifts the Saints had been given: their visions, their mystical experiences, and their sufferings. But what the Lord has to teach us through their lives is so broad, so all-encompassing, we can't leave much of anything out. So bear with us. We have so much to tell you. Rose of Lima is a very important Saint; you've got to know all there is to know about her. You will learn from her life, from her experiences, and from the gifts the Lord gave her.

Rose Flores, raised to the level of Sainthood, for all the world to know, and renamed for posterity, St. Rose of Lima, is the first canonized Saint in the Americas, thus her title, *Patroness of the Americas.* She was born the product of two great cultures - the Spanish, who conquered and ruled the New World and the Inca Indians, a brilliant, comely race of people. Her great-grandmother was reported to have been of the Inca culture.

The Incas were not dark-skinned like the Aztec or the American Indian. They were white-skinned. The children born of Spanish and Inca unions were usually breathtakingly beautiful.

Rose was a stunning, very fair child with light brown hair. She was part of a trio of powerful men and women in the Church of the early days of Peru. St. Martin de Porres, and St. Toribio de Mongrevo, Archbishop of Lima, were both from the same time period, and from the same city, Lima, Peru. Martin was a very close friend to Rose and Archbishop Toribio baptized and confirmed her.

Rose could very easily have come by her strong faith belief as a result of a Caucasian evangelist who came to the land of the Incas centuries before the Spanish arrived. Legend says that it could have been St. Thomas the Apostle. It could also have been St. Brendan of Ireland, who voyaged up and down the western hemisphere in the Sixth Century. St. Brendan is credited with having brought the Faith to the Mexican Indians. Whatever the case, and whoever the Lord sent to touch the hearts of His children in this, His New World, the evangelist taught the people a set of values very similar to those of the Catholic Church. He taught them about the Cross. He even put a Cross on top of the hill of Cuzco, one of the main cities of Peru.

Down through the centuries a strain of Catholicism ran all through the Indian religious beliefs. For example, the Incas believed in Heaven, Hell and Purgatory. They had what they called Huacas, Holy Things. They believed in the Resurrection; they fasted; there was a sense of sin; they believed in confession and penance. But after the great evangelist left, they lost the values of the teachings. The Cross on the hill remained, but nobody knew why it was there or what the Cross meant. They lost the sense of what suffering and adversity meant. They believed, much like the Biblical Job, that suffering and adversity, misfortune of any kind, were punishments from the good God for sins committed.

This was the spiritual society into which Rose Flores was born on her mother's side. Her father was a Spanish soldier. Gaspar Flores was born in 1531, (the year that Our Lady came to Tepeyac Hill in Mexico) while his parents were en-route to Puerto Rico from Spain. It is believed Gaspar was possibly born on a

St. Rose of Lima

ship, or right after the family arrived in Puerto Rico. From his earliest days, his life was filled with stories of conquistadors and battles between the Spaniards and the Incas. He grew up with a thirst for combat. At fifteen, he left Puerto Rico and went to Panama to take part in the battle on the side of the Spanish conquistadors. He had been very involved in most of the wars in Central and South America for Spain, either against the natives, or the British, or the French. From as far back as he could remember, there was always a war or the intrigue of a war, or the spoils of a war going on somewhere in his world. Gaspar spent his life in the military until there were no more battles to be fought, or until he was judged too old to take part in them.

He finally settled in Peru after having traveled and lived in most of the New World of the time. He met a beautiful girl, Oliva, who was sixteen when he was forty five. She was completely feminine, with none of what we would consider the special spiritual qualities necessary to be the mother of a Saint, much less a mystic like St. Rose of Lima. She was completely wrapped up in the social life of Lima of the Sixteenth century. She also possessed the exact qualities Gaspar Flores wanted. He fell in love with her and asked for her hand in marriage. He was considered a great catch to Oliva's family, despite the age difference.

Planning their married life became Oliva's *entire life*. She fantasized how it would be. While Gaspar, her betrothed, was not rich, he held a noble position. Oliva envisioned them as becoming a part of the social gentility of Lima. That called for a special house in a great neighborhood with all the trappings of middle-class Lima. One day, while they were house-hunting, they came across a little parcel of land owned by the Church of St.

Dominic. Oliva fell in love with some rose bushes in the back of the property. Gaspar told her that if they bought this land for their home, the rose bushes would be part of their property. She became ecstatic. He further told her that the roses were from the first seeds planted in Peru. She went out of control, as any sixteen year old girl would. The decision was made on the spot; they had to have that property for their house.

But Whose decision was it really? We don't believe in coincidence, unless it's Holy Coincidence. Who chose Dominican property, with roses playing a dominant part in the landscape, which would be the home of a powerful Third Order Dominican whose name would be Rose? The Lord had a plan for Rose of Lima from before she was born. He knew what part she would play in the lives of the people of Lima, but especially the poor slaves who came to Lima from Africa. Everything was planned in advance. We're reminded of the inspired words of St. Paul the Apostle as he wrote in his letter to the Romans,

"We know that in everything God works for good, with
those who love Him, who are called according to His
purpose.
For those whom He foreknew He also predestined
to be conformed to the image of His Son, in order
that he might be the first-born among many brethren.
And those whom He predestined, He also called;
and those whom He called, He also justified,
and those whom He justified, He also glorified."

Romans 8:28-30

After the death and canonization of St. Rose of Lima the question that everybody asked was whether it was coincidental that her parents bought the property on the location where the first rose was planted, or was it by Divine design? Those who believed in the power of God were sure it was His intent that the child be born in this place.

A Miraculous Name

Even the name she was given came directly from Heaven. Originally she was named Isabel after her maternal grandmother. But a miraculous occurrence took place while the child was an infant, before her Baptism. She was in her stroller with the Indian servant Mariana. All of a sudden the maid began to cry out to Rose's mother and the children assembled in the room. *She saw the child's face turn into a beautiful rose!* The children ran over to the stroller. They saw something different. They cried out that they saw a rose above her head, suspended in mid-air. Her mother, Oliva, took this as a sign from Heaven that the child was to be named Rose. We believe it was a sign from Heaven also, even though it caused a lifetime of bad feelings between Oliva and her mother, Isabel, for reasons which are pretty obvious. This was just the beginning of the mystical experiences attributed to St. Rose of Lima.

When it was time for the Baptism, Rose's grandmother, Isabel was still determined to have the Archbishop, Toribio de Mongrevo, baptize the child with her given name, Isabel. But the Archbishop, who heard about this miracle from his sister, being justifiably fascinated by the possibility that this might truly be a miracle from Heaven, baptized her with the name Rose, ignoring the name Isabel altogether. Whether he did it intentionally, or was inspired by the Holy Spirit, is not certain. Do you think there may have been a little intercession from on high? We do.

We believe that God had a very special plan for this child in the religious development of the people of this New World. If we just look at the parallel world, Europe, in this same time frame, we may be given some indicator as to why God was working so hard to make the Church strong in Peru. The year of Rose's birth was 1586. What was happening in Europe in 1586?

The heresies of Martin Luther had wreaked havoc on the Church of Europe from the beginning of the century. But the movement faltered, even under the rule of Calvin, who was much more violent than Martin Luther. It was in great danger of collapsing, until Henry VIII of England started his own church in an effort to legitimize his lustful and adulterous behavior. He wanted to marry many women and couldn't get the Pope to annul his previous marriages. Henry decided to throw out the Catholic Church and start a new church, with him as the head. This from a man who had been given the title of *Defender of the Faith* by the Pope for his defense of the Faith against Martin Luther.

Henry VIII's daughters played a game of one upmanship on him, treating those who would not come over to the Church of England worse than Henry did. By 1570, Elizabeth I, his daughter from Ann Boleyn, declared her Act of Supremacy,[1] and in 1585, it became illegal to be a priest in England under pain of treason. Priests and religious became non-persons. This was Elizabeth's way of getting back at Pope Pius V, who excommunicated her as a heretic in 1570.

In 1588, a rumor was started that the Pope and the King of Spain were planning an invasion on England and Ireland. All priests who were in captivity or who were able to be rounded up, were taken to Canterbury and executed. Most were hanged, then drawn and quartered.[2] They were called the Martyrs of Canterbury.

During the time Elizabeth and her cronies were enjoying killing their own countrymen, she decided it was time to subject the Irish to her particular type of terror. Thus began the Penal times for the Irish, the age of the persecution. Thousands of Irish people, faithful to the Church, were slaughtered or starved to death in an effort to bring Ireland under English Rule and the Church of

---

[1]The Act of Supremacy basically stated that the throne of England was head of the Church in England or its possessions, under penalty of treason. At first, it wasn't enforced very strongly. But it became a tool to persecute the enemies of the throne.

[2]Drawn and Quartered was a cruel and brutal way of slaughtering people. The prisoner was tied to four horses, one extremity to each horse, i.e., the two legs to two horses, and the two arms tied to two other horses. At a given command, the four horses were hit with a stick, and forced to gallop at high speed in four different directions. The body was ripped to pieces.

England. It never happened. This was followed by Oliver Cromwell, who subjected the Irish to inhuman terror.

In France, the Huguenots[3] began Wars of Religion, in which they looted and destroyed churches, kidnapped and murdered priests and nuns, dug up bodies of Saints and profaned them, all to put down Catholicism in France.

So if you wonder why Our Lady came to Guadalupe in 1531, and Our Lord Jesus gave us Martin de Porres, Rose of Lima, and Toribio de Mongrevo in Lima Peru at the end of the Sixteenth century, the answer may be all too clear.

Saint Rose of Lima

A Rose from Heaven

In the midst of so much political activity in Lima, little Rose was born on April 20, 1586 to Oliva and Gaspar Flores. From the very beginning of her life she exhibited a great deal of mysticism. She was the only child of Gaspar and Oliva's eleven children who did not cause her mother any labor pains. All the children before, and those subsequent to Rose, caused her a great deal of pain in child-bearing. Rose, on the other hand, caused her mother a great deal of pain after she was born.

She was the recipient of God's graces from an early age. Barely able to walk, she would be found lost in contemplation before the big crucifix in her mother's room. At three years old, she endured surgery from an accident without crying at all. A heavy lid from a flour jar fell on her finger, causing a blood clot and great pain. The surgeon had to cut back her fingernail, and apply acid to the finger. All of this was done without anesthetic. The acid had to stay on the finger for several days. When she was complimented on her behavior, Rose commented on how much

[3]Huguenots - French followers of Calvin

more Jesus had suffered.

Later, she was stricken with an excruciating earache. When asked if it hurt badly she stated, *"Yes, but Our Lord's Crown of Thorns must have hurt much more."*

During Rose's recuperation period from the blood clot, her mother tried teaching her how to read, using secular material. It was impossible. The girl could not read anything. Oliva gave up in despair. She threw the book across the room and told little Rose to get out of her sight. Then her grandmother began to teach Rose from her prayer book. Sometime later, little Rose came out of her room with the prayer book, having read several pages from it. When Oliva asked her daughter who taught her to read and write, she replied, *"I asked the Baby Jesus to teach me, Mama, to save you the work and He did."* Rather than being elated that her daughter could read and write, Oliva punished Rose for what she considered defiance. Rose took her punishment without a word of complaint.

In an effort to establish a truce with her own mother, Oliva allowed Rose's grandmother, Isabel, to bring Rose to confession to whatever church she desired. When Rose became five years old, Isabel brought her to the Jesuit church. Rose immediately asked her new confessor if she could make a vow of Chastity. The priest was somewhat surprised, especially in view of the fact that she was only five years old, but after prayer and counsel with superiors, he allowed her to make the vow. It would be a problem for Rose in later years, when her mother wanted her to marry, but at this time, it seemed harmless to the priest, and to our little Saint, it was an important gift to give Our Lord Jesus.

Through a controversy which took place between the government and the Archbishop of Lima, the Lord moved Rose and her family from the Jesuit church to the church of St. Dominic, to which Rose became extremely attached. There was a special statue in this chapel of Our Lady of the Rosary. Many of the faithful of Lima flocked in time of need to petition favors of Our Lady. In this chapel, Rose had many encounters with the Mother of God, some of them actual apparitions, others inner locutions, and still others just down-home conversations with Our Lady.

At this particular time Rose was only six years old, but a thought pattern was established which would stay with the Saint all her life. Peru was in danger of revolution and civil war. All the people were praying for peace and an end to the crisis. Rose began, at this very early age, to pray for the people of the city, the people of the country, and for the officials of the government and the Church. Rose would offer this form of prayer for the rest of her life.

Lima boasted many miracles, and miraculous images which attracted many to chapels of pilgrimage. Rose grew up in an atmosphere of miracles. They were taken pretty much for granted in Lima at that time. We have to keep this in mind when we learn how naturally St. Rose and her family, indeed, most of the people of Lima, took miraculous occurrences. When Rose began to work miracles, she paid little or no attention to them. They had virtually nothing to do with her. They were the works of the good Lord and our Mother Mary.

The Lord worked very powerfully in the life of Rose of Lima, especially when it came to helping His people. Nothing was impossible when it came to doing the Lord's work. The time would come when the very flowers and trees would dance at her bidding, and bees and birds would join her in psalmody. Yet she saw in this a fact no more extraordinary than their creation. To her, life was all faith; she never descended from the supernatural, and what might amaze others was of little account to her. In many ways, she reminds us of Padre Pio of Pietrelcina in Italy.[4] Padre Pio began having apparitions of Our Lord Jesus, our Mother Mary, the Angels and Saints as early as five years old, as did Rose. These apparitions became such natural occurrences that both these holy people believed that *everyone* had visits from our

---

[4]Read about Padre Pio in Bob and Penny Lord's book, *Saints and Other Powerful Men in the Church*

Holy Family.

Rose and Obedience

We would be hard-pressed to give just one outstanding characteristic of St. Rose of Lima. There are no end of special virtues with which she was blessed. But high on the list, perhaps at the top, would have to be *Obedience*. She practiced what had to be perfect obedience, even at the risk of suffering physical and spiritual pain. There were times when her mother claimed she was *too obedient!* We would like to share just a few examples.

Food was an expensive commodity for the Flores family. There were the mother and father, the grandmother, and three children. So there were certain rules which had to be obeyed. A definite one was nothing to eat in between meals. But a special rule which Rose's mother liked to impose on Rose was not drinking any water unless she asked permission. Rose, who looked for any excuse to practice self-denial, would go for *two to three days straight* without asking for a drink of water. The mother, not realizing it had been days since the daughter had asked for water, would sometimes refuse permission for Rose to drink water. Rose never complained, which would extend the fast to four or five days without drinking water.

Another much more serious incident took place when the family had to move to Quive, some distance from Lima. Rose's sister Mercedes, died there. Soon after, Rose began feeling a coldness in her extremities, i.e., fingers, toes, which was then followed by numbness and eventually paralysis. The doctors were stymied as to the cause. However, they pronounced her incurable. The situation became graver with each passing day. Rose's mother had heard of a cure for paralysis which had to do with covering the patient's body with the uncured hide of a recently killed animal. Rose's brother, Fernando, had just been given the gift of a pet llama which he loved dearly. But he loved his sister even more than his pet. So when Oliva asked Fernando to sacrifice the llama so that it could be killed and used for a cure for his sister, he gladly turned his favorite pet over to be slaughtered.

The animal was killed and skinned. The hide was taken immediately to the mother, who in turn brought it to her daughter. She said to Rose, "Here is the skin of a freshly killed llama....I am going to bind it on you tightly. When the proper time has passed, I shall come and take it off. *Now, do not loosen these strings no matter how it feels.*"

Oliva had a tendency to forget things. One of the things she should not have forgotten was to take the hide off Rose's body. After being distracted by many things, she finally came into the child's room and began to take off the wrappings. She apologized to Rose, and asked how she felt. Rose looked pale, but avoided the question. All she said was, *"The hide has not cured me, Mama. But I have not unbound it or loosened the strings since you put it on."*

Oliva said, "That is good; you are obedient." With that, she took the strings off and began to unravel the hide. She was shocked by what she saw. Rose's skin came off with the hide. A huge ugly rash covered her body. Her back was ulcerated. She was in excruciating pain. The mother was in shock. "Why didn't you loosen the strings? You must have suffered terribly." Rose answered, *"But you told me not to loosen the strings or unbind the hide! What could I do but to obey you?"*

If this story were about anyone else, we would have to say the child was being precocious, trying to show the mother how stupid or incompetent she was in jeopardizing her daughter's health in that way. But knowing Rose, and how committed she was to obedience, we have to hold fast to the fact that she was doing as she had been ordered. She was being obedient at all costs, even at the cost of her health.

In this particular account, there's a happy ending, and what might be considered a double miracle. The following Sunday, it was announced at Mass that all candidates for Confirmation should be prepared shortly, as the Archbishop, Toribio de Mongrevo would be arriving in a few short weeks to administer the Sacrament. Rose was a candidate for Confirmation. But she had lost all desire to live after the incident with the llama hide. She was still in bed, paralyzed. When her mother told her when Confirmation was going to be, she came to life again. She wanted to receive Confirmation. She began to pray hard for a healing. At the other end of the spectrum, Archbishop Toribio also prayed, not for Rose in particular, but for all the children who were to be confirmed. We believe the power of prayer of these two Saints brought about the complete healing of Rose just in time for her confirmation.

Rose and St. Catherine of Siena

The parallels between the lives of St. Rose of Lima and her mentor, St. Catherine of Siena are remarkable. Both girls had a strong vocation early in life. Both took a vow of chastity, and claimed Jesus as their bridegroom. Both were mystically married to Jesus. Both lived at home and worked as Third Order Dominicans. Both treated the sick, although Catherine's greatest accomplishments were the writing of her book, *Dialogs*, for which she was given the title of Doctor of the Church, and bringing the Popes back to Rome from Avignon. Both had to go through tremendous struggle with their families when it came to marriage.

For Rose, the conflict arose when she was twelve years old. The question of marriage surfaced as was natural for that time. As we said, Rose had already taken a lifetime vow of virginity. But her mother was not having any of that. To give Oliva credit, Rose was exceedingly beautiful. Remember what we told you about the combination of Spanish and Inca. The children were most beautiful. Rose was possibly the most beautiful of the Flores children. She was so beautiful that biographers have detailed every fine turn of her face, the curve of her cheeks, the soft texture of her skin, the color of her lips and eyes. To research Rose of Lima is to fall in love with her.

Considering all of that, we can understand why Oliva was looking forward to her most beautiful daughter marrying *well*. A suitable marriage could mean comfortable living for the child and her new family for life, and could also be helpful to Oliva and

Gaspar, whose financial condition had always been on the verge of bankruptcy. Plus, to be sure, Oliva had fantasized for years how it would be for her child to be married to someone from a good family, raising grandchildren as beautiful as Rose and the continuation of the lineage. She would be the grand-dame of the family, taking the place of her mother Isabel, who had always been the head of *her* family.

It's also not hard to understand how devastated Oliva was when Rose told her she would never marry. She had consecrated herself to God at an early age, but this was the first time she had to confront her mother with it. It took a lot for Oliva to come to terms with her announcement, but once she did, she insisted the girl enter a convent. When Rose asserted, she desired to become a third order Dominican, Oliva was beside herself. Rose had become very close to St. Catherine of Siena over the years, and she wanted to follow in her footsteps. Finally, her mother accepted this; but neither she nor the rest of the family could empathize with her decision.

Rose and her brother made a little retreat out in the back of their parents' property. It was a very small room, but it became Rose's living quarters for her life. She lived an austere but extremely happy life with her Lord Jesus and the Saints. She did all she could, however, to help her family, whose financial situation never got better. She grew beautiful flowers in her little yard and sold them. The Lord blessed this venture, and gave the family much-needed money through her efforts. The family knew the child was extremely loved by her Heavenly Family, but didn't know how far the Lord would go out of His way to please her.

Once, Gaspar had over-extended himself financially for two of his sons. They were given the honor of joining a royal galleon to fight the British. The cost of outfitting them for this position went far beyond the normal expenses of the family. Add to that the expense of a wedding of another daughter. The normal income from Oliva's needlework was not forthcoming because she had concentrated on making a trousseau for her sister. Gaspar was informed by creditors that he must come up with the money by ten o'clock the following morning, or pay the consequences which could include prison. They tried never to bother Rose with their problems, but the whole family was so depressed that she could not help but be aware of it.

At her mother's urging, Rose asked her father what the problem was. He shared their financial situation, ending with *"all is lost. It is the end."* Rose went to church with her brother. She kept telling him to have faith. He too, was very depressed about what was happening to the father. Rose prayed as hard as she had ever prayed. As she and her brother walked out of church, a man came up to Rose and handed her a packet of money. He said to her: *"I have this package of money for the señorita. Give this to your father for his present needs."* Needless to say, it was the exact amount that Gaspar owed. Also needless to say, from that time forward, no one ever questioned Rose's special relationship with Jesus.

Rose and Mortification

From her earliest days, she asked her confessors' permission to perform various forms of mortification, from fasting and abstinence from water or food, to physical mortifications which were common at that time, and which had been practiced by Saints before her. She was always trying to do more than she had done previously. There were times when she would become accustomed to the disciplines she inflicted upon herself. This happens when the body builds a tolerance for pain or deprivation, whether it be self-inflicted or not.

We have a tendency today to criticize our brothers and sisters of long ago for practicing such penances as mortifications, disciplines, fasting and abstinence. But it's really important to understand the moral fiber of the people of the Church of that time. We of today's society find that hard to understand or accept. Our problem is that we've never tried to control our senses. A common philosophy today is *"If it feels good, do it."* This is the culture we were born into; this is how we were raised, not necessarily by our families, but by the world around us, the influences of television, movies, magazines and materialism.

As an example, there is a movement to close the various military academies in the United States, West Point and Annapolis, because of the furious scandals coming out of them, and because of the low moral character of their students and graduates. A Senator, who was a graduate of either West Point or Annapolis, was questioned about whether the academies should be closed. To paraphrase his reply, he said, *"Don't blame the institutions for the behavior of the students. Blame the society that sends that type of student to the military academy. We can't change in four years, a lifetime of immoral or amoral behavior."*

Based on that philosophy, perhaps we should not pass judgment on those who came before us, but on the moral character, or lack of it, of this generation of ours. So when we share about someone who did a great deal of fasting, rather than attribute it to a weakness based on the latest psychological theories, give them credit for wanting to control their appetite for food for the sake of the Kingdom.

There were also other reasons for these forms of discipline, positive motivations. The most apparent is that our Saints were attempting to share in the Passion of Our Lord Jesus. Remember, this overpowering love for Jesus was their *raison d'etre*, their reason for being. They wanted so much to emulate the Savior. Add to that the state of their particular world, be it the religious or secular world.

The world has always had need for souls who would participate in Redemptive suffering. It's been lost on the last few generations, but for those of us who date back to the Great Depression, we understand the value of this gift. Simply stated, it's offering up our sufferings for the redemption of sins, of our families, our Church, our world, conversion of sinners, and reducing the time souls spend in Purgatory. This is one of the reasons we have such a problem with the Suicide doctor, Jack Kervorkian. His philosophy cheats people of being able to offer their pain to the Lord, for many possible intentions. Their illness, which could have been a shared experience of the Passion for the Glory of God, becomes and ends as an egocentric, lonely finish, taking away much of the meaning of life. Could you picture a Rose of Lima, or Francis of Assisi, or Thérèse of Lisieux, or the many thousands of brothers and sisters before us, giving up the privilege of being able to suffer for the Lord? I don't think so.

Rose would not give that up. Having received permission from her confessor to practice fasting, abstinence and mortification, she asked her parents, because the priests's permission was contingent on obedience to her parents. We talked about that before. Obedience was the most important gift Rose or any of the Saints could give to the Lord. One time she asked permission to give up red meat for life and to fast on bread and water. Her parents didn't really go for this too much. Her mother said Rose could fast and abstain from meat until she felt Rose needed that nourishment, and then she would be required to eat meat.

Penance became a normal part of Rose's life. A small example would be her wearing of a crown of sharp, pointed metal thorns inside her veil, and then covering them with a garland of roses. She was able to persuade her mother to allow her to wear a penitential band, but she didn't tell Oliva it would be around her head. Rose had an adjustable band made to which she attached steel points. She could adjust them so that she could share in the pains of Jesus crowned with Thorns for the conversion of sinners.

St. Rose wore the headband in this manner, covered on the outside by the garland of roses, until a situation arose where her father grabbed his stick to hit his son, who had made a disrespectful remark. Rose got in the way and the cane hit her on the head. The pointed steel pressed against her head, causing her to bleed. Her mother saw this, and took the headband away, showing it to Rose's confessor, who had not given her permission to use the pointed steel. He filed them down, so that they became nubs, rather than points. Out of obedience Rose wore the head band this way for the rest of her life.

Rose and St. Toribio de Mongrevo

Visions, mysticism and miracles had become a normal part of Rose's life but not for those around her. For years little miracles would occur to help the family in time of need. Rose's mother always knew about these, but did not say anything to her children. However, one time when Gaspar was ill, and no money was coming into the house, the family had come to the end of their resources. They didn't even have honey for bread. Everyone in the family, Oliva, Mariana the maid, each of the sons individually, went down into the basement to look for honey in the barrel, but each one saw it was empty. They were filled with despair. Then Rose went down and came back with a jar full of honey stating that there was a big barrel down there.

Her brothers, instead of thanking God for a miracle through the hands of Rose, went down together, saw the honey and came up angry because Rose had somehow contradicted them. Could it be the devil? She had better be careful or the Inquisition would call her in. Doubts began to arise in the family as to where these gifts were coming from. Were they from God or the evil one? That poison soon invaded the heart of Oliva, and before long, the entire neighborhood murmured gossip that Rose could be possessed by evil spirits.

Word came from Archbishop Toribio de Mongrevo that the Inquisition was looking into the mystical character of Rose's life, and that unless these supernatural occurrences stopped, they might call her in. Actually, the Archbishop was trying to protect her from a very unpleasant possibility. He even came to the house to try to talk the family into sending Rose into the convent. Oliva's hair stood on end. She had *plans* for Rose *to marry*. She was not happy with the Archbishop recommending the convent. Archbishop Toribio's niece had entered the Poor Clares. He suggested that to Rose.

The mother countered with the fact that Rose already had a vocation, helping all the sick who came to the infirmary at the house. The Archbishop did not consider that a vocation. Oliva said Rose would most likely marry. The Archbishop turned to Rose and asked her how she felt about entering the Religious life. She replied,

> *"It is true that I have often longed for the retirement and consecration of the religious life. Still, as my mother says, I have much to do here at home caring for the poor who come for medical help, as well as for the members of our family."*

As she spoke about the poor, everyone in the room could see her eyes gleaming, her face flush; the poor were her great love. She continued,

> *"I would miss this work exceedingly; but if I am called to the cloister, God's will is all. I would willingly forfeit everything for this treasure."*

A subtle battle ensued between Oliva and the Archbishop. The family was too poor; they couldn't possibly come up with a proper dowry. The Archbishop offered a dispensation from the dowry. Oliva came back with the fact that Rose's embroidery was a major factor in the financial life of the family; without the income from her work, they would be reduced to total poverty. The Archbishop pointed out that Oliva had another grown daughter as well as sons who could provide income for the household. Finally, Oliva put her foot down, stating that her daughter was not entering any convent, much less the Poor Clares, and that she would marry.

The Archbishop took this as her final word and accepted it. However, the seed that had been planted about going into a cloistered atmosphere began to grow. It haunted Rose. She went to her confessor, a Jesuit priest, and asked him his opinion. When he heard that the Archbishop, whom everyone agreed was a holy man, had recommended the Poor Clares, he urged her to join immediately. Then she went to the Convent of the Holy Rosary, Martin de Porres' Dominican Community, where she had gone to Mass and Communion for years. They agreed, she should go into the convent, but recommended the Dominicans. She went back to her Spiritual Director, the Jesuit priest, to ask if he concurred with the Dominicans. He was furious that she asked the opinion of someone else after he had told her what to do. She told him it was because her mother would never take the suggestion of her Spiritual Director alone. He told Rose not to tell her mother and father until after she had entered the Community. He also suggested she go to the Augustinians with whom he was friendly. He went to arrange everything with them, and told Rose to go there the following Sunday morning after Mass.

Rose recruited her brother Fernando to help her in the clandestine plot. He would take her to the Augustinian convent. She was not really happy with the turn of events. In addition, she did not like the idea of deceiving her mother and father. She would rather have gone to the Poor Clares, because it had been the recommendation of Archbishop Toribio. But she felt this must be what the Lord wanted. She prayed as we often do, and as we have heard Mother Angelica say so often, for the Lord to open the right doors and to close the wrong doors. And that's exactly what He did.

Rose and the Miracle of the Dominicans
The following Sunday morning, Rose and Fernando left as if they were going to the eight o'clock Mass at the Convent of the Holy Rosary. The only difference between this and other Sundays was that Rose had a little suitcase which contained all her worldly possessions, not very much. As they passed the Convent of the Holy Rosary, Rose asked Fernando if she might not go into the chapel and say a prayer. Fernando advised her to hurry. She went in and knelt down. Fernando stayed outside in the doorway of the church, but felt uncomfortable because his family's front door was right across the street from this entrance. If they should come out and see him standing there, all would be lost.

After what he felt was a reasonable length of time, he called to Rose, to get a move on. Rose seemed not to pay attention to him. Finally, he went inside and snapped at her, *"You will have plenty of time to pray after you have entered the convent."* She looked up at him, perplexed. *"I would certainly like to leave, Fernando, but I cannot move."*

Exasperated, he grabbed her arm and tried to pull her up. He couldn't move her. He exerted all his strength; she didn't budge. Finally Rose turned to the statue of Our Lady, to whom she had been praying. She seemed to realize why she couldn't get up. She spoke to Our Lady, *"Good Mother, if you deliver me, I promise you to go back to my mother and live at home with my parents as long as you order me to do so, instead of in the convent."* She rose from the kneeler as if she were being lifted by Angels. She turned to Fernando who appeared aggravated on the surface but was secretly thrilled that his sister had such a close personal relationship with Our Lord Jesus, our Mother Mary and all the Angels and Saints.

Rose said to him,

"I am sorry to have caused you so much trouble, but evidently it is not the will of God and our Lady that I should enter the cloister. I must stay at home, at least for the time being."

Fernando could only reply, "You and your miracles!" and with that, the cloister was forgotten forever but not the vocation.

Shortly after this incident, the saintly Archbishop Toribio died. Rose felt a great loss as did all the people of Lima. There would never be so special an Archbishop as Toribio. They were correct, although they didn't know for sure at that time, why they felt that way. Toribio was one of the three who lived in Lima at the same time, who became Saints. He was canonized in 1726, St. Martin De Porres in 1962, and St. Rose of Lima in 1671.

After the Archbishop's death, Rose knew she had a Saint in Heaven, interceding for her to know God's Will in her life. Within a few short months after his death, God's Will was made known to her most clearly. She was in the garden working on her embroidery with her mother and sister. A beautiful black and white butterfly flew into their presence. Oliva cried out, "Be still, Rose; I believe that it is going to light on you!" Sure enough, the butterfly rested on Rose's heart. The butterfly stayed there, but its wings fluttered back and forth. When it flew away, the black markings stayed on Rose's breast.

Rose spoke very gently,

"It means that God wished me to be a Dominican Tertiary. I was just praying that he would make His divine Will known to me, when the butterfly came. As it rested on me, I had an interior light explaining what it meant."

And although her mother tried to pawn it off as the work of the devil, the die was cast. Rose knew what her vocation was to be, and she went forward with full steam. After a few weeks of resistance, Oliva finally gave in and accepted her daughter's decision, even though she felt that being a third order Dominican meant that she could still marry. Rose was probably too exhausted by this time to bother telling her *again* that she would never marry.

St. Martin de Porres, who was a member of the Holy Rosary Convent, was completely elated when he heard of Rose's decision to enter the Community. Although they had always been close, a strong spiritual bond was formed between the two that was obvious to all who saw them together. They worked closely in ministering to the sick and the poor. Rose's infirmary, located in her home, was only a block away from the Holy Rosary Convent. It was easy for the two to bring patients back and forth and meet at the chapel to share gifts from the Lord.

Even though Rose's mother had agreed to allow her daughter to become a Dominican Tertiary, she was still fighting the program. When they came back from the clothing ceremony, Oliva felt exceedingly tired. Rose told her to go into her bedroom and rest. Rose went to show her grandmother her habit and scapular. Oliva fell off into a semi-sleep until she was awakened from her reverie by Angels all around her. She found herself in the clouds, and right in front of her was the Blessed Mother, in her title of Queen of the Most Holy Rosary. She was dressed in the white habit of St. Dominic. On her knee was the Infant Jesus, dressed in a Tertiary habit. Our Lady spoke to Oliva,

"This rose represents your daughter, my Son's cherished flower. I plucked her for Him from your garden and He will not let her go. Only see how grateful He is to you for having tended her for Him and for having given her to me!"

Our Lady held out the Baby Jesus to Oliva so that she could feel His hand touch her cheek. She said to Oliva, *"Now, see the reward that my Son has prepared for those who love Him. This reward will be yours if you are faithful in His service."* At this point, Oliva saw a young woman in the Dominican habit kneel at the feet of Our Lady and Our Lord Jesus. It was Rose. She kissed the Baby Jesus. Oliva heard the words spoken, *"Come, spouse of Christ, accept the crown the Lord has prepared for thee from eternity."*

The rose in the hand of the Baby Jesus transformed into a crown of roses, glowing with the brilliance and the fragrance of Heaven. Rose bent her head and received the crown of roses. She took the Baby Jesus into her arms, pressing Him to her heart. Oliva swooned. She was finally convinced that her daughter had chosen the right path. When Rose came into the room an hour later to see how she was, Oliva opened her eyes, smiled and said, *"You are not the only one who has visions, Rose. I have just had one myself, and I must say that it was consoling."*

St. Rose was a third order Dominican. She was in charge of the infirmary, which was in her home. She welcomed people of all classes and colors. There was at that time in Peru a great influx of black slaves from Africa. She and St. Martin de Porres ministered to them. Her work was so important that you know she had to be under constant attack. In the writing of this book, our Ministry, and we personally, have been bombarded by the *enemy*. Whenever that happens, we know it's because we're doing something important. And so it was with Rose. She was centuries before her time. She was the Saint of Social Justice, along with St. Martin de Porres, who was a peer of St. Rose. They worked exclusively with the poor. Wherever possible, they worked together. But each had their own individual ministry to the poor. Because of the success Rose was experiencing, she was open to ferocious attacks.

No sooner had Rose taken the habit of the Dominicans than she became very popular with her religious brothers and sisters. They flocked to hear her. They adored her. They heaped praises on her. Now this was a new form of temptation for her. She had always been on her guard against praises from the secular world on her beauty or her skills in flowers or embroidery. She did not have this guard up with her brothers and sisters in religious life. She could not equate this kind of praise with that which she was so wary against from the world. She enjoyed this attention from her peers. She couldn't see the harm in it, but she attempted to offset the satisfaction she received from this flattery, by practicing the disciplines more harshly, too harshly. Eventually, when she tried to inflict the same tortures on herself that the men were imposing on themselves, she had to be stopped.

The Dark Night of the Soul

This title has been used in the life of every great Saint. For most of the Saints, the *dark night* is one of desolation, complete desertion from God. For Rose, her dark night began with Aridity, a dryness in which she could not feel the presence of God. She prayed constantly but felt nothing. Teresa of Avila suffered Aridity for twenty years, during which time much of the fruitful work of her Ministry was done. Under normal conditions, when the Saints were subjected to Aridity, they tried harder. Rose was just like the rest. She prayed more, disciplined herself more, fasted often, and pleaded with her spiritual directors to explain what was happening to her. Nobody knew what to tell her. Their explanations ranged from epilepsy to insanity.

We have always had a question as to why the Lord allows this dryness, and these violent attacks from the *evil one* to plague our Saints, like Thérèse of Lisieux, Teresa la Grande of Avila, John of the Cross, Francis of Assisi, and on and on. We believe the Lord has finally given us and St. Rose of Lima, the answer through St. Martin de Porres, her brother-in-Christ.

Visions began

From the time she was a child, she had always had visions. But they were beautiful visions of Our Lord Jesus, His Mother Mary, all the Angels and Saints, especially her mentor, St. Catherine of Siena. They had always given her great comfort. She received teachings from her visions. But these new visions were ugly, foul-smelling, filthy, sensual, sexual visions, conjured up from the bowels of hell. She fought them fiercely with prayer and with all the penances she could come up with. She concocted a bed of nails and broken glass and pottery which she laid on to take her mind off these visions. One night, deep in prayer in her garden, a handsome young man, dressed in white, accosted her and tried to have his way with her, She broke away from him, and managed to get inside her home. She shook with fear, not so much of the man, but of the possibility that she might give in to the temptation.

Her family became aware of the toll this was taking on Rose. They suggested she sleep during the day if the visions were going to attack her at night. She tried that, but found that she was under constant assault at all times, day or night. In her visions, Rose saw the Angels, the Saints, her family, everyone she believed to be good and holy, reject her, and thrust her into the fires of hell. She couldn't cope with it.

Finally in desperation, she appealed to her brother-in-Christ, Martin de Porres. Through his God-given wisdom he granted her the peace she needed. He explained what had happened and why. First he asked her why she had the feeling of Aridity. Then he answered the question for her, *"I have heard you say you suffered from Aridity before; would you say that it made you love God more?"*

Rose answered, *"Yes. I kept seeking Him, and striving to be better to please Him."*

"And that, my dear sister," Martin replied, *"is why the Lord sent you that Aridity. Now, why do you think He is permitting these visions of the judgment in which you feel that you are*

damned?"

Rose could see the simple logic before she answered the question. She smiled in her agony.

"To make me love Him more and seek for ways of pleasing Him better, so that I may escape hell and enjoy His presence?"

Martin smiled. *"I am not at all surprised at this purification the Lord allows you to bear. I should be more surprised if you had not begun to suffer some such trial. It is the lot of those whom God wishes to raise to the highest sanctity to pass this way. You should find in the very violence of your trial a source of encouragement, since He purifies most, those for whom He has destined the most perfect union with Himself."*

It was so simple! It was so logical! Rose could not help but be in total awe of this humble but brilliant servant of God. She knew the Lord could heal her completely through the intercession of this brother. She continued, and was given the most powerful answer she had ever heard. She asked him, *"Then why have the priests whom I consulted not understood, Brother?"*

He looked at her with so much love in his eyes, tears welled up in them. ***"God Wills it; that is all."***

This was not the end of the Dark Night of the Soul for St. Rose of Lima. The battles with the visions continued until the end of her life. But there was a great difference. While she was having visions of the great judgment upon her, she knew who was attacking her. She knew God loved her, and was protecting her. So in the midst of Hell, she could see Heaven through the smoke and stench. Satan could not have his way with her. God was victorious. We hate to tell you this, but the lesson behind this story is that the closer you are to the Lord, the more merciless the attacks will be. But to quote St. Paul, *"My grace is enough for you, for power is made perfect in weakness."*[5] Thank You Jesus; thank you St. Paul; thank you, little Rose of Lima.

---

[5]2 Corinthians 12:9

The Inquisition

From the time Rose became a Dominican Tertiary she had to give up her Jesuit Spiritual Director. It was difficult for her to find a strong priest to take the place of her Director. She had a need for two great strengths she would receive from a Spiritual Director, **obedience**, which she loved dearly, and a **guarantee of safety**. She knew that the right Director would not let her go astray and would advise her against anyone who would be harmful to her immortal soul. The right Spiritual Director was hard to come by. However, a Dominican priest, Fr. Juan de Lorenzana, was drawn to Rose from the beginning of her ministry with the Dominicans. He found her piety and reverence profound. That, coupled with the stories which constantly circulated around the church and convent about miracles attributed to her, the ongoing presence of out-of-season flowers on the altar, her raptures and ecstasies, made him want to be more involved in her vocation.

There was a slight problem, however. He was the provincial of the Dominicans as well as the Head Inquisitor. This created a twofold difficulty: his time was extremely limited, and more importantly, being the Inquisitor he was constantly investigating people like Rose who claimed apparitions, mysticism, and special relations with the Supernatural. When Rose announced that he had agreed to be her Spiritual Director her mother saw the potential dilemma immediately. She panicked. She moaned out loud, *"Oh my God! What will become of us! You have taken the Inquisitor as your Director! You are going to open your soul to him! Daughter, you are mad!"* The problems she predicted were not long in coming.

It was really a comedy of errors. It began because everyone was concerned about Rose's health. She had fasted and abstained from nourishing food for so long, and had practiced physical penances and mortifications for so long, that signs of physical as well as emotional breakdown were surfacing. A new benefactor, Don Gonzalo de la Maza, who loved her very much, had granted a long time wish of Rose's to build a hermitage outside her house.

She didn't live in it very long before she became seriously ill. Her mother blamed the dampness of the hermitage, which, coupled with her Asthma and Arthritis, had forced Rose to bed. When at last she was able to beat her illness, she was left very weak.

Her Spiritual Director, Fr. Lorenzana, became very forceful in his orders that she not overdo her penances while she was still in a weakened state. Whereas previously he had allowed her to whip herself one hundred strokes each time she disciplined herself, which could have been two or three times a day, now he ordered her not to whip herself more than a hundred times in an entire week. Rose, being always obedient, gave her word. However, when she did her discipline the next time, while she only gave herself the proportion of a hundred strokes, she hit herself with all her strength each time.

A good friend, Isabel de Mejía, who also loved Rose very much, saw her in her hermitage beating herself. She knew that Rose would not last long if she kept up this abuse of her body. Isabel went to Fr. Lorenzana and begged him to make Rose curtail her disciplines. Fr. Lorenzana assured her he had already taken care of this. Isabel went back to the hermitage to find Rose whipping herself to the cadence of the psalms. Now her love turned to hate. She believed that Rose had disobeyed her Spiritual Director, in which case she was not a Saint but a pretender. Furious, she returned to Fr. Lorenzana to make a formal complaint against Rose.

Fr. Lorenzana had just finished listening to a complaint against Rose accusing her of witchcraft. In addition, the priest was experiencing a great deal of difficulties administering to his Community, which had problems, and taking care of his job as Grand Inquisitor, which was a full time job in itself. When Isabel came in with this new charge against Rose that she had disobeyed Fr. Lorenzana, he just blew. It did not occur to him at that time to address the real reason for his anger, his difficulty in handling his too many jobs. He never bothered to get the particulars on the complaint, or to give Rose the courtesy of questioning her about this. When next he saw her, he told Rose he would no longer be her Spiritual Director, and accused her of being a hoax. She had no idea what was going on, and protested her innocence, but the priest would have none of it.

In addition, his outlook on Rose took on the same complexion as Isabel's. If she had disobeyed him in this one thing, and then lied about it, what about all the other claims about her, the miracles, the bilocation, the super-piety. Add to that the charge he had received of her practicing witchcraft. Were all her supposed gifts from the evil one? He didn't act immediately, but held all these things in his heart. He would wait and see.

Now, at the beginning of this story, we told you how Rose's vow of Virginity, taken when she was about five years old, would come back to haunt her, when her mother wanted her to marry. Well, the time had come. A very handsome suitor came calling on Rose at the house. Remember, though she was a Tertiary, she had not taken the vow of chastity, because she had already done so secretly at age five. Her mother thought Rose was available to marry because she had not taken the vow of chastity when she entered the Dominican order. So each time this young man came calling, Oliva became more and more optimistic that this might be the one. Rose developed a very good, spiritual relationship with the young man, and so she told him that she had given herself over to Jesus at age five and would never marry. The young man loved her so much, he was willing to live in this celibate relationship with her.

The problem arose when Rose's mother and father were becoming impatient that the young suitor had not asked for their permission to marry Rose. Finally, Gaspar asked the young man what his intentions were. The reply was that he would marry her in a minute if she hadn't taken this vow of virginity. Gaspar tried to correct him. Rose had not taken the vow of Chastity when she entered the Dominicans. Then the young man told him about the vow she had taken when she was five. Gaspar maintained his calm, but when the young man left, he became ballistic. He blew like an atom bomb.

He ran into the room where Rose was working on embroidery with her mother and sister. He began yelling at her, accusing her of being disobedient to her parents all these years. As soon as Oliva caught wind of what was taking place, *she* became furious. She was followed by Rose's sister Juana who was followed by the brothers. Before the end of the day, everyone in the family had vent their anger against Rose.

But the real problem came about the following morning, when Rose prepared to go to morning Mass. Her mother gave a strict edict that from this time forward, they would only go to *Sunday* Mass and Communion; Daily Mass would be eliminated. Visits to the Blessed Sacrament chapel were out also. Rose was obedient to her mother. It didn't create a real difficulty for Rose. She bilocated to the different churches in Lima for Mass and devotions. The difficulty arose because no one could see her in these churches.

Her superiors in the Dominican Community across the street knew nothing about Oliva's ban on morning Mass. They only knew that Rose was not attending Mass or services at the church or chapel any more. This, coupled with what was perceived as very strange behavior on the part of Rose and the accusation of her practicing witchcraft, was justification enough for the Grand Inquisitor, her former Spiritual Director, Fr. Lorenzana, to call for an investigation of Rose. Three priests and one doctor showed up at Rose's doorstep one day, and the heat was on.

However, God is in charge. He is always in charge. Perhaps it was necessary for this to happen so that the Lord could let these people know how they were pulling this child apart, who had no desire other than to love Him, and serve Him. During the course of the questioning, it became obvious to Fr. Lorenzana and Oliva and the wife of Don Gonzalo de Maza who was allowed to stay, just how Rose had been unwittingly and unintentionally manipulated and victimized by those who loved her. Fr. Lorenzana repented of his judgments on her. He had always loved her. He just felt that she had disobeyed him and that was as much as saying she didn't trust him.

Rose was vindicated by her beautiful testimony. She never accused anyone of misjudging or mistreating her, although everyone knew the part they had played in this terrible indictment against her character and her spirituality. Actually, *because* she refused to put the blame on anyone, she was exonerated completely and brought back into the good graces of church and family.

Rose's Last days

The scandal to which the Flores family was subjected lived with Oliva for the rest of her life. She and Rose never had the same relationship. Actually, Rose and her whole family experienced a death to their relationship. Things became so bad, the tension so great, that the friends of the family, Gonzalo de Maza and his wife, asked Rose to come to live at their house. There were token objections by Oliva and Gaspar and none at all from the brothers and sisters. The objections were overcome easily and Rose was on her way. She was never consulted as to whether she wanted to live at the de Maza's' home. Once the families had agreed on it, it was decided.

Rose was not happy at the beautiful home of the de Maza's. There were too many things which had been a part of her life which were taken away from her. She could not work with the sick at the infirmary anymore. She could not go to her hermitage. Her beloved church of Santo Domingo was too far distant for daily visits. In addition, she couldn't have her own room. She had to live with the daughters because Gonzalo and his wife wanted her holiness to rub off on their children. But Rose did not object. She knew she was being made ready to go Home to her Heavenly Lover, her Jesus.

As Rose drew nearer to earthly perfection, to union with God, she experienced the worst physical sufferings imaginable. She knew these would happen in advance; and she said yes to them. With each of the sufferings, she was given a splendid grace, to console her and bring her to the next level. As part of her acceptance of these sufferings, she proclaimed *"Lord, increase my sufferings and with them increase Thy love in my heart."*

It was Palm Sunday of the year she was to die, 1617. That Lent had brought her so close to perfection. Every one of her God-given gifts were sensitized to near perfection. She looked forward, with great anticipation, to a long-standing tradition whereby the Tertiaries are given a blessed palm to carry in procession during the Mass. She looked forward to this special gift she knew she would be given. She spoke to Jesus,

"Jesus of my soul, how happy I am to carry this palm in Thy honor! This palm will be the symbol of my soul, which with the help of grace, will always praise Thee and move in harmony with the slightest breeze of the Divine Spirit."

She waited with eager anticipation for the sacristan to bring the palms to the Tertiaries. Her heart beat wildly as he approached her and the other Tertiaries. She watched as he handed out the palms to each of her sisters-in-Christ. When it came to her turn, somehow, he just passed her by. She couldn't believe it. She watched as he passed her, sure that he would return to her. He continued to give out palms to the people in back of the Tertiaries, and then returned to the altar. She was completely crushed. Why hadn't she gotten a palm?

After Mass, she went into the Chapel of the Rosary to be alone with the Lord. She cried her heart out. But as the time passed a calm came over her. She looked at the statue of Our Lady and the Baby Jesus. She smiled, somewhat embarrassed that she had made such a fuss about the palm. She spoke to Our Lady, *"Please God, O my Mother, may I no more regret a palm given by mortal hands."*

Our Lady looked at the Baby Jesus who then looked at Rose. Rays of light cascaded from His eyes. They enveloped Rose with such a warmth and compassion. She knew she was in the presence of her Savior. The lips of the Baby Jesus began to move. He spoke to her. He said one short sentence, the most important words she would ever hear, ***"Rose of My heart, be thou My Spouse."***

Rose thought her heart would burst. She couldn't believe she was hearing correctly. This was what she had yearned for all her life. Jesus took her as His bride in Mystical Marriage. It was more than she had ever dreamed could happen! She looked at Jesus. He was waiting for a response. Her mind raced. What can I say that will have any meaning? The perfect response was given to her by her Angel, *"I am Your Servant, Lord. I am the docile slave of Your ageless Majesty. Yes, if You wish what I should not dare, I shall be Yours and ever be true to You."*

Our Lady looked at Rose. She said, *"See, daughter, the rare honor Jesus deigns to pay you in taking you as spouse in so wondrous a way. Can He better prove the greatness of His Love?"*

This was the culmination of the life of St. Rose of Lima, the beginning of her most rewarding spiritual relationship with her Lover, her Jesus. It was also the beginning of the most intense period of pain she would ever endure, consummating with her total surrender to the Lord, her death. Rose was given the knowledge of how she would suffer, and when she would die.

She had a vision. She saw herself in the middle of a great light which extended from the Source, God, in every direction to Infinity. In the middle of the light, she saw a large rainbow covering a smaller rainbow, in the middle of which was a Cross covered with blood. The sign *"Jesus of Nazareth, King of the Jews"* could be easily seen, as well as the nail holes in the Cross. In this same image, she could see Our Lord Jesus in His Glorified State. He was brilliant; she had never seen Him in this way, nor could she ever have envisioned such a sight. Radiant beams shot out from His Heart in the form of tongues of fire. They permeated her soul. She could feel herself leaving her body.

Next to Our Lord Jesus stood a set of scales. Myriads upon myriads of Angels came and worshiped and adored Our Lord, as well as souls who had not yet entered into the Kingdom. Then the Angels began to bring weights, which they placed on one set of scales. On one side of the scale were placed numerous weights which seemed so heavy that nothing would get them off the ground.

But then the Angels placed on the other side of the scale trials and tribulations enough to balance both sides of the scales. Jesus began to lift the scales. When they were at a certain level He distributed all the sufferings, trials and tribulations to the souls who were standing there waiting upon Jesus. The weight of the sufferings He gave to Rose was enormous. When all the sufferings were given to the Faithful, and the one plate was empty, the Angels piled it high again, only this time with graces. The graces were disbursed in the same proportion as the sufferings.

Our Lord Jesus spoke, *"Affliction is always accompanied by Grace; Grace is proportionate to Suffering. The measure of My gifts is increased with the measure of trials. The Cross is the true and only road that leads souls to Heaven."*

Rose felt the surge of graces and sufferings enter her body. She knew she was on her final road Home to the Kingdom. She began to put her house in order. She went back to her home, to her natural parents, her grandmother Isabel, her faithful Indian maid Mariana, and her brother and sister. She wanted to be sure she could spend this last time with them because she didn't know exactly how intense the suffering which the Lord had given to her would be.

After that she went to the Monastery of the Dominicans. She spoke briefly to Fr. Lorenzana, and shared all that she had received from the Lord, including the day of her death, the type of sufferings she would endure, and asked for his prayers. She wanted to see Martin, and so she asked if he were home. The priest told her that no matter where he might be, even if it be in Quito, Ecuador, which was over 800 miles away, he would be with her immediately. As the priest predicted, Martin was next to her in an instant.[6]

Martin greeted Rose with that beautiful smile of his, which would take away depression or melancholy from anyone. She explained what had happened to her:

"I am in dire need of prayer, Brother Martin. I have before me a trial such as I have never experienced, and

---

[6]St. Martin had the gift of Bilocation

shall never experience. To pass through it according to God's Will, I must have extraordinary help. It is for you and my other friends to obtain this grace for me. Without it I shall fail."

Martin knew what she was to endure, but he wanted her to tell him.

"Since you so often honor me with your confidence, may I ask what this great trial will be? You have suffered so much, surely there can be nothing you have not borne."

Rose looked at him firmly, but with great love.

"There is no comparison between this trial and what I have suffered in the past. In it there will be nothing natural. All will be far beyond the strength of any mortal to bear. But blessed be God who gives me this share in His Cross. It is my death of which I speak; it will come on the vigil of St. Bartholomew (August 23)."

Martin spoke to her very tenderly.

"You will not fail, Sister, even if this mulatto fails to pray for you. But wretched as I am, and the least of all, I shall promise you in God's name all the help you will need."

That was the last meeting that Rose and Martin had in this life.

Rose suffered brutally, physically, spiritually, emotionally and mentally until that final day. First, she suffered paralysis on one side, followed by the feelings of hot irons going through her entire body. Her joints were on fire; her head felt like it would explode. She coughed up blood, each cough ripping through her chest, projecting more and more blood to her mouth. She experienced a maddening, unquenchable thirst, which tortured her and stayed with her to the very end of her life. She begged for water. The doctors had refused it to her. She prayed for her Guardian Angel to bring her water. It was refused her. Her comments to Martin had been, *"These pains exceed the bounds of nature."*

Her suffering lasted until midnight. She blessed her whole

family. She gave instruction to her brother and sister. She asked once again for water. It was denied her. She asked to be put on the floor. They couldn't do it. She asked for the pillow to be taken away, which they did, and she asked for the candle to be brought close to her. Her mother brought it over, her eyes filled with tears. Rose called out, *"Jesus! Jesus! Jesus!"* Then she paused, and spoke her last words, *"Jesus be with me!"*

She went into an ecstasy, from which she never returned. Immediately, testimonies were taken by people from all over Lima. One woman, Luisa, some miles away, was awakened by the image of Rose rising to Heaven surrounded by Angels and Saints enveloped by brilliant colored lights. Two people in the room where Rose died, saw her crowned in glory. When they laid her out, the room was aglow with the aura of the Saint.

Rigor Mortis did not set in. Her body remained soft and supple, her cheeks flushed. Her eyes stayed open, her lips parted, and she smiled.

There are reports that when her body was brought into the chapel of Our Lady of the Rosary, the statue of Our Lady with the child Jesus came alive and smiled at the Saint.

During the time the body of St. Rose was laid out, the faithful followers kept cutting pieces of her habit, so that her vestments had to be changed many times.

The throngs of friends that came for the viewing of the body were so great, guards had to be posted to keep order. But the people would not allow the priests at the church to bury the Saint. They feared a riot would break out if the body of Rose was taken away to be buried.

The friars decided to play a trick on the people. They left the chapel at noon, making enough commotion to be sure everyone knew they were leaving. One thing about Latins, they don't let anything interfere with their meals. When the friars left for lunch, they were quickly followed by all the people, who also went to lunch. But the friars sneaked back into the church, and took the body away clandestinely. Rose was buried in the cloister in an

St. Rose of Lima

unmarked grave.

There was a tremendous outbreak of violent protests. Where had St. Rose been taken? Where were her relics for the faithful to keep in their homes in places of honor?

Three years later, Pope Urban VIII gave permission to open the cause for the beatification and canonization of St. Rose. Within a short period of time, it was concluded. In 1671, St. Rose was canonized. She was given the title of St. Rose of Lima, Patroness of the Americas by the Pope, being the first canonized Saint of the New World. She was also given the title of Patroness of Peru, the Indies and the Philippines. Her Feast Day is August 23.

We said at the beginning of this chapter that the Lord had blessed the New World, and especially Lima, Peru, with the presence of three powerful Saints, of which Rose was the first to be canonized. In life, but especially in death, she brought together the people of Lima. The blacks and Indians, who were considered low class in the social structure of Lima, were honored and glorified by the life of St. Rose of Lima. Perhaps the greatest gift she was given came after her death. Her mother joined the convent which Rose had always wanted to build, and died as a Dominican Tertiary. God evens out all things, and makes them right. Praise be the name of God.

St. Martin de Porres

Apostle of Charity, Saint of the Slaves

St. Martin de Porres

The Holy Spirit is so powerful; He works in marvelous ways. We began the chapters on St. Martin de Porres and St. Rose of Lima on the Feast Day of St. Toribio de Mongrevo, who baptized St. Rose. He was the Archbishop of Lima, Peru and had a tremendous effect on the spirituality of St. Rose of Lima and St. Martin. The lives of these three Saints of Lima, Peru are strongly interwoven.

Although this is not an account of the life of St. Dominic, the father-in-faith of Saints Rose and Martin, a special tribute has to be paid to this great *"Watchdog of God."*[1] St. Dominic was a powerhouse during his lifetime, a true defender of the Church, a watchdog of God. His followers have been commissioned and mandated to be an order of Preachers, to bring the word of God to the whole world and as part of that commitment, to defend the Church in the name of God against her enemies. The two Dominicans we have written about in this book (as well

---

[1]translation of *Domino cane* in Italian or Latin which means watchdog of God, the true charism of the Order he founded.

as St. Catherine of Siena, the role model of St. Rose of Lima), truly followed in the footsteps and charism of their founder, St. Dominic.

This is how the Lord works. He never leaves us alone. He doesn't just give us one Saint, one powerful man and woman in a period of crisis, but we find ourselves leaning on *many* of the brothers and sisters who came before us. The whole foundation of our Church lifts us up. We feel their strength behind us, as we encounter attacks from the enemy, experiencing uncertainty about whether we're doing what the Lord wants, or what we want, in our everyday struggles, and what path we are to take to the Kingdom. Martin de Porres was to lean on *his* brothers and sisters in Christ, especially those children of St. Dominic.

Martin has been given many titles over the years including Apostle of Charity, Saint of the Slaves, Patron of the Negroes, Patron of Social Justice, and others, all true, all describing one or more of his attributes, but none actually goes to the heart of who this Saint was. He was love; he was Christian; he was truly son of the Father, brother of the Son, and vessel of the Holy Spirit.

It's hard to describe all the charisms of St. Martin de Porres, or cover all the gifts he received from the Lord. The more we read about him, the more we realize what a powerful instrument of God he was. He had the gifts of *bilocation, healing, multiplication of food, reading men's minds, raising the dead, levitation, ecstasy, visions, inner locution;* it goes on and on. Martin de Porres was one of the most powerful and yet one of the gentlest Saints in the history of our Church, and without doubt, a true disciple of the Lord in the New World. We will try to give you just a taste of how the Lord worked in this hemisphere through this Saint.

Martin was born in 1579, in Lima, Peru. It was only 83 years after Columbus placed a small Spanish flag on the island of San Salvador, claiming it and the entire new world for the Catholic Queen, Isabella, as it was she who had financed this expedition in thanksgiving to God for deliverance of Spain from

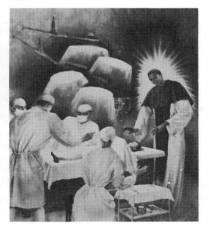

Above:
*Saint Martin de Porres
serving the sick*

Above:
*Painting depicting one of the
Miracles which were verified to
support his Canonization. A twelve
year old boy was miraculously
healed by the Saint's intercession.*

Above: *St. Martin de Porres
Lover of the Cross*

Above:
*Painting of St. Martin de Porres
used at his Canonization*

the Moors. In 1535, the city of Lima was founded, and in 1551, the Dominicans began a university there. [An aside, the Dominicans were the first order of religious to preach the gospel in Peru.]

Martin was born of John de Porres, a Spanish nobleman and Knight of the Order of Alcantara, and a black free woman, Anna Velazquez. Martin's father was not very happy to find his child was black. He did not want to be connected with the child in any way. As a matter of fact, on the baptismal record there was no mention of the father at all. The Baptismal certificates read only "Martin, son of an unknown father." But some years later, he officially acknowledged Martin as being his son. We're not sure if John ever married Anna Velazquez. If he did, he didn't treat her very well. He spent most of his time in other countries, leaving Anna and the children, Martin and his sister Joan to fend for themselves. Though Martin was not from a poor background, you would not have known it by the way he and his family lived. They were always at least borderline poverty, and sometimes full-blown poverty.

But none of this had any detrimental effect on Martin. If anything, it gave him an understanding and empathy for his poor brothers and sisters. From his earliest days, he focused completely on his Lord present in the tabernacle of all the churches of Lima and in helping out the poor. His mother became furious with him in the early days. She would send Martin shopping for food, entrusting to him the meager pennies the family had, just enough to get some bread and a few necessities to see them through their meals. Martin inevitably took the money and gave it to the poor. When he returned home with nothing in his basket, his mother would let him have it. "How can you give to the poor? *We are the poor!* It's bad enough that you will not eat today, but what of your sister and me? We didn't volunteer to starve!"

He got lost in the churches. This was his most favorite time. When he entered the dark, cool church, the entire world was left outside. He was in a haven. He spent hours before the Blessed

Sacrament, before the Crucifix looming high on the altar or a statue or painting of Our Lady. This was truly his home. He was an orphan on pilgrimage, journeying through this time on earth in preparation for his trip to his heavenly *Home* in Paradise.

Although John de Porres only came to Lima on very rare occasions, he must have been shamed by his relatives or neighbors who could see the way Anna and the two children were living. They needed some kind of home, education, food and clothes. Anna also had need, but John had never cared much about her well-being, so it was not thought that he would now spend any amount of time and money, taking care of her or her children. Never mind that he was the father. Although he had *finally* recognized them as his own, his behavior towards them was the same as towards a slave. However, when Martin was about eight years old, the father came and took him and his sister back to Ecuador with him, which was where he was living at that time. The children went to school; they were fed and clothed properly. The father actually admitted to being the parent of both children to his various relatives whom they met in the few years they lived in Ecuador.

But when John de Porres left Ecuador to govern Panama, he *again* dropped the two children off in Lima, at the home of their mother. This time, he left her enough money to get them out of poverty and put Martin through school where he would learn a trade. This was a very important move, and we're sure it was orchestrated by the Holy Spirit. Martin chose to learn the trade of a barber. Now you may say to yourself, "*What's the big deal about being a barber?*" Well, in Europe, as well as in Central and South America, a barber was an honorable profession, like a doctor or a lawyer. It carried with it the same prestige. As a matter of fact, as part of learning to be a barber, Martin also learned surgery, or the surgery of the day, which was letting blood with leeches, healing wounds, broken legs and arms, fractures, and giving out medicine for illness. So the barber was also a surgeon, doctor and pharmacist. [When Penny was a child in Brooklyn, her grandfather's profession was a barber. He brought that profession over from Sicily. As barber-surgeon-doctor, he was very well respected by the people of Brooklyn.]

For Martin, this was a God-given gift. He was remarkably good at this profession. Remember, we're talking about a twelve year old boy, beginning his apprenticeship as a barber. He learned quickly and well, and before very long, he was outdoing the teacher. The instructor was able to leave him in charge of the shop, knowing full well that whatever happened during his absence, the young barber could manage it as well or better than he. The instructor was very astute in this assumption, because being left on his own was the opportunity Martin wanted and needed. He handled himself brilliantly in many situations where the patients who were brought in, were in very bad condition. He cured them and had them back to work in a short time. His clinic was like an emergency room. Soon, people came into the shop, not looking for the owner, but for Martin. And he never disappointed any of them.

At the beginning, this was a good way for Martin to continue the works of mercy he had begun as a young boy, when he used to go to the market and wound up giving the family's money to the poor. Now, he *treated* the poor and would charge them nothing. This was his way of serving the Lord and putting back in the pot, so to speak, paying the Lord back for the gift of healing which had been given to him through his profession. His fame spread throughout the entire city of Lima. People came for any and every ailment imaginable, and the professional young mulatto[2] barber was able to heal them, through the gifts of the Holy Spirit. Martin never forgot where his gifts were coming from. He never for a moment thought there was anything about him that caused these healings to come about. They were from the Lord, and he knew it.

St. Martin's Miraculous Lemon Trees

It was also at this time that the beginning of his special gifts became apparent. One of the first and most lasting was a fruit

---

[2]Mulatto - Anyone with mixed Negro and Caucasian ancestry

tree, a lemon tree which Martin planted in the courtyard of his house. No sooner was it planted than it bloomed immediately, and its blossoms gave forth fruit abundantly. The tree continued to yield fruit so bountifully, the branches, weighed down by its yield, often appeared as if they would break. This tree would provide lush lemons until well after Martin had died. It came to be called *Martin's Miraculous Lemon Tree.*

Martin loved Jesus so much, he could not spend enough time with his Lord. He went to the church as often as he could. He would just stay by Our Lord Jesus, adoring Him in the Tabernacle. He spent all his evenings alone in his room, arms outstretched in the form of a cross *"en croce "*[3] praying, concentrating, in ecstasy. He focused his attention on the Crucifix in front of him. He blocked out every other image in the world but Our Lord Jesus on the Cross. There was a fervent expression of love on his face. This was witnessed by a close associate of his, who peeked in on him through the keyhole of his room as he prayed there on many occasions. Martin and Jesus were becoming so close that anyone or anything else was a distraction. The few hours, he was able to spend before the Blessed Sacrament, were not enough. Martin wanted to spend *all* his time with Jesus, adoring Him as he did in his cherished hours away from the barber shop.

During the four-year period of his apprenticeship as a barber/surgeon, he became so proficient in his healing profession, his name became very famous; most especially among the Indians and blacks in the town, both slave and free. He was their symbol of respectability. *He gave them self-worth!* In an era when the question, often asked among Catholics, was whether blacks had souls and could warrant being baptized, this beautiful young black child of Jesus was proof positive that Jesus was the God of all creatures, large and small, and the blacks in Lima were no exception. This is one of the reasons that his decision to leave his profession and turn his entire life over to God as a Dominican

---

[3]the Italian expression

brother threw them into a panic. His people needed him to be highly visible. They needed him as a representative of the poor and often unwanted people in the city. They needed him to remain an important figure in the town.

Martin had his own needs, however, and he believed his greatest need was for total consecration to the Lord. He had always felt that he served the Lord best through his work with the poor of Lima. He found himself being pulled apart. [We're reminded of one of his role models, St. Catherine of Siena. She wanted more than anything to lock herself up in her small cell, and spend the rest of eternity with Jesus. But she also knew, He wanted her to be for the people. If she would have become a nun,[4] she would have disappeared behind the cloister, and never would have been able to touch the people in the way that she did.] St. Martin de Porres had the same dilemma. We believe the reason, he chose to be the lowest of the low in the Dominican order, a donado,[5] was so that he could have the best of both worlds. He could serve his Lord, concentrate His life on Jesus, and still serve the poor, the brothers and sisters who looked to him to give them respect in the Community. He was sixteen when he joined the Dominican order as a donado.

Most likely Martin had made his decision without asking the advice of his father, and definitely not his consent. Although John de Porres had never been a real part of his son's life, he felt that Martin was his son, a possession, and was dragging the good name of the family down. He had no problem with Martin entering the Order of Preachers, the Dominicans. His problem was where Martin was entering the order. John felt he should at least be a lay

---

[4]In those days, all nuns were enclosed in Cloister.

[5]Donados were members of the Third Order, who gave their services freely to the Monastery, and lived there, receiving food and lodging as compensation for their work. Theirs was the most menial, the most difficult, the heaviest manual labor. They were considered the lowest of the low, below the lay brothers in rank. They wore a white tunic and black cape. This was the only indicator that they were members of the Dominican order. They didn't wear the scapular, which the first order Dominicans wore.

brother of the First Order (the priests), but definitely not a lay brother of the Third Order. This was the lowest of the low. He appealed to the Father Provincial, Fr. Lorenzana, who was more than willing to allow Martin to enter on the higher level. But Martin refused. He insisted on being the lowest of the low. Perhaps Martin wanted the world to know that he was nothing; Jesus was everything. To quote St. Paul,

"Yet I live, no longer I, but Christ lives in me; insofar as I now live in the flesh, I live by faith in the Son of God who has loved me and given Himself up for me."[6]

We know that John de Porres was not very happy with the type of work for which his son had volunteered. But Martin dove into his new career of sweeping the cloisters, scrubbing the corridors, and cleaning the toilets, with the same enthusiasm and dedication he had shown for barbering and tending the sick. He never stopped doing these loving tasks. No matter how important he became in the eyes of the world, and a time was to come when he would be sought out by the most important people in the known world, he never forgot who he was, and Who It was Who was working through him. And lest he ever get a swelled head, the filth of the mud and dust being trampled in from the outside, the foul stench of the toilets would bring him out of his reverie very quickly.

There's a really important point, to *stress* here. Don't for a moment believe that Martin de Porres enjoyed cleaning toilets or sweeping floors. This was a reality check. This was his way of disciplining himself to understand and accept his role in this life, the role the Lord asked him to take on, and to which he said *Yes*. At one point in the life of St. Bernadette, the little visionary of Lourdes, a famous photographer came down from Paris. At the time, Bernadette was one of the most famous women in France, though she was only fourteen years old. He said to her, "Bernadette,

---

[6]Gal 2:20

come with me to Paris. I will make you rich and famous." to which she replied, *"But no Monsieur, I would much rather stay here in Lourdes and be with the poor people. This is my place in life."* At another time, when she was deathly ill in the Convent of Gildard in Nevers France, she was asked why she would not return to the Grotto at Lourdes for a healing, and she replied, *"The Blessed Mother used me like a broom. What do you do with a broom when you are finished with it? You put it behind the closet door."*[7]

So Martin brandished his broom as a knight would wield his sword. To this day, when you see paintings of St. Martin de Porres, or statues of him, you will always see his weapon of Sainthood-his broom. He was Don Quixote, the Man from La Mancha, the dreamer of impossible dreams. In Lima, when pilgrims go to venerate the great Saint, they are often given a broom as a sign of the humility which Martin embraced so happily.

Martin had a tendency to reward those who treated him badly. As a matter of fact, he showered them with gratitude. An example of this was when he continued his profession of barber-surgeon after joining the Dominicans. Now, instead of the clients he was used to serving in the clinic, his clientele was mostly brothers and priests of the Dominican Order. Martin tried his best to remain a humble servant; he desired neither praise nor recognition for doing what he believed was his duty. He would never take credit for being a good servant.

At the cause for Martin's beatification, a priest gave testimony of Martin's great humility. When the priest, Fr. Francis Velasco Carabantes was a novice, he wanted to talk to Martin, who was busy at his duties as barber. The novice did not want his hair cut; he felt great disdain for the way the Dominicans shaved their heads in the tonsure style (The entire crown was shaved bald, while the smallest section of hair was left around the head). Perhaps our novice, Brother Francis at the time, had a little vanity left over from his secular days. At any rate, he just wanted to talk to Martin.

---

[7]Read about St. Bernadette in Bob and Penny Lord's book: *"Saints and other Powerful Women in the Church."*

But while he was deeply engrossed in thought, trying to determine how he would approach his mentor, Martin grabbed him, put him in the barber's chair, and began working on his head. By the time Brother Francis became aware of what was happening to him, his head had been shampooed, shaved, and was being dried. He went into orbit.

He jumped out of the chair and berated Martin with every expletive he was supposed to have forgotten when he entered religious life. He called him a mulatto dog, a hypocrite, a cheat. At that point, Martin was still lost in his job of tonsuring the novice's hair, during which he always prayed deeply. It was, as though the Angels were doing the work, while Martin was conversing with Our Lord Jesus and His Mother Mary in ecstasy. So he was going through the motions of drying the novice's hair, when he came out of his ecstasy and realized he was being scolded.

By this time, one of the rectors, Fr. Gamarra, had witnessed the entire outburst. He grabbed Brother Francis and began to criticize him severely for his attack on Martin. Meanwhile Martin wanted the novice to look at his head in the mirror, so that he would realize he didn't look bad with the tonsure. Brother Francis backed off on his attack. But the rector inflicted a severe punishment on Brother Francis and sent him away. This was when Martin went into action. He went to the Superior and begged forgiveness for Brother Francis. He tried providing the brother with every excuse he could. He even tried to justify *how* Brother Francis might have called him a mulatto dog and a hypocrite. His mother was Negro, while his father was white. That took care of the mulatto part. He was a Dominican, which meant *"Watchdog of God!"* That could loosely have taken care of the dog slur. In an effort to close the case in favor of the brother, his final argument was, *"Everyone knows what a sinner I am."*

The rector, who was also the disciplinarian, knew too well what a Saint Martin was, and how he berated himself. He could not refuse Martin, so he forgave the novice and relented of the punishment. As if that was not enough of a reward for Brother

Francis, Martin sent him fresh fruit, a rare delicacy in the monastery.

In a very short period of time Martin was asked to take care of the sick, for which he was well-trained as part of his profession as barber, and so the cycle was complete. He was now doing everything he had done in secular life, only he was doing it for the Lord as a *religious*. Most of the sick who came to him were the black slaves who had been brought over from Africa. This became a major part of his healing ministry. Oftentimes, he would miraculously increase the food portions which he gave to the people. He would go out of his way to do anything he could, to make their sufferings lighter. This done, his greatest gift was to be able to spend time in the chapel with the Lord. Martin could not have been happier.

He was treated badly very often by those to whom he ministered. But he never let that bother him. He offered up everything for the glory of God. More often than not, people he accused him of false modesty and humility. He agreed with them when they reviled him, criticizing the work he did. They really hated when he agreed with their insults. His Superiors, after much investigation, ascertained that he really did believe himself the lowest of the low, the worst sinner; whereas they all recognized the true Saintliness of the little brother.

One aspect of Martin's life which all his biographers found most exceptional, including *Butler's Lives of the Saints* and the *Acta Sanctorum* was that he handled three major jobs: barber-surgeon, wardrobe keeper, and infirmarian. Each of these loving tasks was a full-time job, requiring a tremendous amount of work and concentration. However Martin managed all three of these jobs with ease, with joy, and with a great deal of competency. Now remember, he did these in addition to all his other non-assigned tasks and spent hours each day in the chapel, adoring Our Lord Jesus in the Blessed Sacrament. One way he was able to accomplish these goals was by not sleeping.

The Gift of Bilocation

Martin was in an excellent position to evangelize in his ministry as barber-surgeon. He was an ardent follower of St. Dominic, his father in faith. He believed firmly in Dominic's commitment to teach the people of God. St. Dominic maintained that the cause of a great deal of the heresy which was rampant throughout the world was ignorance and neglect. Wherever he went, he found these two evils. He was convinced that the only way to stop heresy was to preach and teach. In this way, freeing it from the basic causes of evil, Christian society would be restored to the Church that Jesus founded. St. Dominic named his order, "The Order of Preachers" for that reason-that they would go out and teach the faithful.

The enemy finds his richest soil in the ignorant. Martin had an open invitation to preach to the unlearned. They came to him every day, not looking for spiritual aid, but physical and material aid. What better opportunity to share the word of God? He had a captive audience. As he filled their stomachs and healed their bodies, he fed their souls with stories of this great Church and its Saints.

In many ways, he reminds us of Blessed Juan Diego, the visionary of Guadalupe. He became the sacristan in the little chapel built after the apparitions of Our Lady. When people came into the little chapel, Juan Diego told them the story of the Indian and the Lady from Heaven. Pretty soon, they would find themselves seeking out the priests, and they were on their way to conversion.

Most of the poor, uneducated people who came to Martin were slaves, or former slaves from Africa, who had come to Peru on the slave ships. But as part of his outreach ministry, Martin had what he termed the *"Pain of Desire."* He reached out to Dominican missions in Japan and China. There were Spanish prisoners in infidel countries, such as Turkey. Martin ministered to those brothers also, not in Peru, but in whichever country they were located. How did he do this? He was given the gift of bilocation. Witnesses testified having seen Martin in *China* and

Japan, sitting with little street people all around him, teaching them about the love of Jesus, erasing the ignorance to which they were the victims.

Another example of bilocation occurred one day when Martin instituted a new medical treatment in the infirmary, relatively new in Lima and not really tested. The brothers questioned him on it. They asked him how he was sure it was safe to use this procedure. To which, Martin very matter-of-factly replied, *"Oh, I saw it done this way in France, in the hospitals of Bayonne."* The brothers looked strangely at Martin. They knew he was not making up a story, and yet, they knew he had never been out of Lima, Peru from the day he entered the Dominican order. It was, in effect, an admission of the powers the Lord had given him to bi-locate.

One day, a Spaniard came to the Dominican Monastery of the Holy Rosary. He passed Martin, and stopped in his tracks. He was awestruck. He called out to Martin, *"Father! Liberator!"* Martin brushed him off with a smile, and a quick assurance he would speak to him later. The Spaniard rushed to the other brothers to tell them how he had been a prisoner in Turkey, when Martin visited him and his fellow prisoners. He brought them whatever he could to make their condition more livable. He brought food for the body and food for their souls. He left them a little money. This was not once or twice, but often during long years of imprisonment, the Spaniard further testified. He said, it was the little money that Martin brought over the years that finally gave the Spaniard what he needed to pay a ransom to the guards to get out of prison. While the brothers were astonished at the tale, they were not really surprised. They knew there were many times when Martin was off by himself in deep meditation. Who knows where the Lord brought him during these times?

Martin and the locked doors

The brothers knew firsthand, some of the things he did in the Monastery. It was a known fact that the doors to the infirmary and the doors to the novitiate, where Martin had his quarters, were locked with heavy locks, and the keys were in the possession of the Superior. On more than one occasion, when a sick or dying brother in the infirmary would ask for Martin to come to aid or console him, the infirmary personnel would run to the Superior to get the keys to open the doors so that Martin could enter. Then, as they were running towards the locked door, to let Martin come in the infirmary, they would find him already in the patient's room, ministering to the sick person, without interference from locks and benefit of keys.

Another instance of Martin and locked doors occurred when two novices ran away from the Monastery. The Master of Novices, in a panic, asked Martin to lift them up in prayer, as Martin's prayers always got the desired results. Martin began to pray and immediately knew where to look for the two runaway brothers. He went to the place where they were, two miles from the Monastery. The door was locked; that meant nothing at all to Martin. He went through the door, and awakened the brothers, who had been fast asleep on cots. Rather than berate them for fleeing the Monastery, he spoke to them in the gentlest tone he could muster. Within minutes, they were eager to go back to the Monastery. But now a new problem arose. How would they get back into the Monastery? We know it was no problem for Martin, but what about the brothers? How would they get in? No problem. They just huddled next to Martin, and as he went through the locked doors, they just went in with him.

Sometimes when Martin would pass through locked doors, he would be carrying heavy things with him. Nothing seemed to get in his way. He had a lot to do, and a limited amount of time, so he couldn't be bothered with things like locked doors or cumbersome objects.

He would always comfort the sick. It could be any hour of day or night. If Martin felt it necessary to be with a sick brother, he would just appear out of nowhere with sheets, or linens, or a brazier.[8] When the patient awakened, he would find Martin sitting

---

[8] A metal pot filled with coals to warm up the room.

there, with whatever it was that the sick one had been craving, whether it was water to cool a fever, or something to eat. He would mop the brow of those who were perspiring heavily. He was just there. Another gift was that after Martin left the ill person, they usually improved greatly and very often experienced a total healing.

Martin and the Dying

One of Martin's special gifts was a little scary. *He knew when someone was going to die.* The brothers would watch him when he paid a lot of attention to a particular patient in the infirmary. They knew that person was going to die. There was even a saying among the brothers, "That brother will soon die, because Martin goes to see him often."

A dear friend of Martin's, Fr. Cyprian de Medina, became very ill. He was admitted to the infirmary, but according to the doctors, he was a hopeless case. Five of them had given up on him, advising everyone in the Community, it was time to administer the Last Rights of the Church. But Martin had not come to his room to console him. Now, Fr. Cyprian knew well that Martin always consoled and prepared those who were ready to enter the Kingdom. He also knew the prognosis of the doctors. The question that kept going through his mind was, *"Where's Martin? Has he abandoned me?"*

It was late in the evening. The brothers began a death watch over Fr. Cyprian, not believing he would last until the morning. Fr. Cyprian asked for Brother Martin. No one could find him. The hours flew by. Fr. Cyprian became very nervous. He prayed for Brother Martin to come. It was now about three in the morning. The priest and the brothers had given up hope of Martin arriving in time to see Fr. Cyprian before he died. All of a sudden, very quietly, Martin entered the room. The priest thought he was seeing a vision. He was so happy to see Martin, he had new energy and used it to really let Brother Martin have it for not being at his bedside at this, his hour of death. Martin just sat there, head bowed, while his friend went through their entire life together, all the time complaining, he could not believe that Martin could have abandoned him at this time; and then adding, he had been sure he would die without Martin praying over him.

Finally, after Martin felt that Fr. Cyprian had gotten all his hurts out of his system, he raised his head and said very quietly, *"Father, you should have realized that you were not in danger. Everyone knows that when I make frequent visits to the cells of the sick, it is a bad sign. Do not be upset if you have grown worse. This crisis will only serve to end your illness more swiftly. But you will not die now. God wills that you should live and give Him more glory by continuing to serve Him in Religion."*

Naturally, Martin's prognosis was correct. Fr. Cyprian recovered; he and Martin remained the best of friends; and he continued in his ministry for many years. As a matter of fact, Fr. Cyprian ministered to Martin at his death.

Martin, Wardrobe Keeper and Beggar

Many of the jobs, Martin took on himself, were out of Holy Coincidence. He would do any task, others did not care to do. The job of wardrobe-keeper was thrust upon him because he was in charge of the infirmary. Actually, he was responsible for two areas of the Community: he had to be sure they had enough habits for the brothers that they were in good shape, and clean, and he had to be responsible for the infirmary, and all the supplies necessary, such as bed linens, blankets, pajamas, and the like. One reason, he was assigned the job, could have been that the cupboard was virtually bare. There were no supplies, and the powers that be knew that it would take a miracle to restock the bare shelves, and the only one who was good at asking God for miracles was Martin.

We don't know if he did or didn't want this job. Martin knew that it was a necessary task which needed organization, and he was great at organization. When he saw the condition of the supply department, he immediately put his logical mind to work. They needed supplies, but didn't have any money with which to buy them. They needed money, but where would they get it? From those who *had* money. Martin began to build a list of benefactors, who would be most happy to cooperate with Martin and the Community. He was very well known in Lima. Even if it had not been that his father was a political figure of the town, Martin, by his years of service in the Community, and the word of his closeness to God, had developed quite a name for himself.

When he went looking for help, it came fairly easily. Martin was able to purchase a complete new set of everything the Community needed. But while he was a good fund-raiser, he was also frugal. Once he had all this equipment, he made sure that it was well taken care of. He gave all the brothers a number. He attached the number to their clothing. He also set up a cubbyhole system in the supply room. Each week, he would distribute clean clothing and pick up the dirty clothing. He organized a similar setup in the infirmary. Things were a little more difficult to handle there. The items-like sheets, pillow cases, blankets, mattresses, beds, were all items in demand by the local people. And they had no qualms about stealing *whatever* they could, when they could.

The problem was that Martin was no fun. He knew where everything was. One day, when Martin left a patient alone in the supply room, the man shoved a few sets of sheets in his trousers, which were very blowzy. When Martin returned to the room, the man casually headed for the door. Martin, very lovingly but firmly, ordered him to return the sheets, saying *"The sick have so little linen, they can't get along without even this pair of sheets."*

Then there were the mattresses and the beds. Once, he had left a mattress on the line to air out. When he went to retrieve it some time later, it had disappeared. He immediately went with another brother to a dark storeroom, directly to the spot where it had been hidden. Another time, a whole bed was stolen. The black worker, who had been using it, complained to Martin that it was missing. Martin told the man to wait for him in the infirmary. He then went to one of the priests, whose servant had stolen it. He told the priest *"Father, if that servant has no bed, please see to it that he gets one, but he should not take the bed of the Negro who works in the infirmary."*

Martin and the Mice

St. Martin de Porres and the mice remind us of St. Francis of Assisi[9] and Lupo, the Wolf. The farmers in the town of Gubbio were going to kill a wolf who was attacking their chickens and cows, and eating all their crops. Francis asked to speak to the wolf. He met him in the forest and pleaded with him to stop his vandalism immediately. Francis said he realized that the wolf, whom we now call Lupo, was hungry. He said he would make a deal with Lupo. If he would stop vandalizing the farmers' crops and animals, Francis would guarantee that the farmers would feed him. Lupo stopped vandalizing the farms; the farmers took turns feeding him, and Lupo not only became their friend, he also became their greatest defender against invaders. To this day, there is a statue of Lupo in the center of the town of Gubbio.

When you look at a prayer card, or the canonization painting of St. Martin, you see him wielding the broom, as we said before. Then you see the dog. But to his right, on the floor, there is a dish, with a cat and a mouse and a dove all eating from it at the same time. The mouse is a very important symbol of the ministry of St. Martin de Porres. It began with a problem.-St. Martin's wardrobe room. After all his work, getting new clothing, shirts, sheets and such, one day he found that there were mice in the room. They were nibbling on the shirts and sheets, making holes, and doing their business there, making a terrible smell. Martin didn't know what to do. His Superior suggested spreading poison to kill the mice. *That would do it.* But Martin wasn't having any of that. He waited and watched until, one day he was able to catch one of the little enemies. He held him in his hands. The mouse was sure this was his end. His little heart was beating so fast.

But then Martin spoke to the mouse, softly and gently. In a short period of time, the mouse relaxed. He had no fear of Martin.

---

[9]Read about St. Francis in Bob and Penny Lord's book: *"Saints and other Powerful Men in the Church."*

Martin explained the problem. They couldn't have the mouse and his friends chewing up all the supplies needed for the Monastery and the infirmary. He realized it was because they were hungry and were not getting enough food. Martin worked out a deal with the mouse. If he led his friends to the far end of the garden, where they would find a new place to live (which Martin would show them), Martin promised that he would be sure they received more than adequate food *every* day.

We're not going to say the mouse actually answered *"Okay"* but in effect it seemed like he agreed with his eyes. When Martin put his little newfound friend down, the mouse scurried away. Within minutes, from all over the wardrobe room, the heads of hundreds of little mice appeared from every nook and cranny. Martin led them out of the wardrobe room, out to the garden where there was a whole area which would be suitable for them. They immediately began nuzzling into the dirt, making holes where they could set up their living quarters.

Martin was good to his word, as the mice knew he would be. Every day, after he finished feeding everyone else-the shut-ins, the workers in the Monastery and the street people, he would go out to the garden with food for the mice. For their part, they never came back to the wardrobe room or disturbed the Monastery in any way.

The Mystical Gifts of St. Martin

St. Martin de Porres was a very specially blessed child of God. The Hand of the Father was on everything he did. Mystical gifts abounded in Martin, to such a degree that they were accepted as daily occurrences. The Lord had blessed him with seemingly all the gifts from Heaven. But they were all for the benefit of the children of the Kingdom.

A perfect illustration would be what we would call a repeat of the biblical *Multiplication of the Loaves and Fishes*; only in this instance, it was not loaves and fishes, but soup and bread. One of Martin's tasks, which we did not classify up above, with that of "Barber-surgeon," "Wardrobe-keeper," and "Infirmarian," but which in itself could have been a full time job, was that of *feeding the poor*. At the beginning of every day, there was never enough food. By the end of each day, there was not only enough food, there were baskets filled with food, left over, for the little animals that waited hopefully at the kitchen doors to be fed.

Martin would come every day to the refectory where he would feed the poor. He would look at the meager provisions available for that particular meal, then look at the swarm of hungry mouths waiting to be fed. One of the brothers who helped out in the kitchen, Brother Aragonés, testified that he watched as Brother Martin began to serve them. He prayed, first for the Salvation promised by Jesus, and then he prayed, *"May God increase it through His infinite Mercy."* What was in the pots was enough to feed four to six people, meagerly. What was waiting to be fed was anywhere up to two hundred and fifty. Martin began to pour and serve, as more and more poor people came to be fed. Every one of them was given huge helpings, yet there was enough for all, and then for the little dogs and cats. Remember, Martin had a great love for the animals.

Martin was also known to *levitate*. There were many eyewitnesses to this miracle. It had a blessed effect on the people who witnessed it. They were strengthened greatly in their vocations. One priest, Fr. Ignatius of Dominic, proclaimed this throughout his priesthood. "I've said it and I've repeated it millions of times, that I decided to become a Dominican because I saw Brother Martin de Porres in prayer, *lifted high above the earth, almost embracing the crucified Christ in the chapter room.*"

Unfortunately, this great espouser of the mystical gifts of Martin was not alive when it came time to give this testimony at the Beatification process. The Superior whaled, "If only Fr. Ignatius were alive to give his testimony." A surgeon, Marcel de Rivero asked, "Isn't my testimony enough? I saw him, just as Father Ignatius did, high above the ground, in the chapter room, and my word is just as good as his!" We get the impression that Marcel de Rivero was a little miffed that his word might not be as good as the deceased priest.

The Saint of Social Justice

The term Social Justice has been bandied around a great deal in this 20th century. Martin has been called the *Patron Saint of Social Justice*. But we must clarify what is meant here by Social Justice. On the surface, Social Justice would seem to mean feed and clothe the poor. And that is so. It does mean that, but not just that. Feeding the body is not the entire extent of it. That's only part of it. We have heard that in some dioceses in the United States, those reaching out to the poor are not even to *mention* the name of Jesus. They are to find out what the physical needs are, and take care of them. That's not Social Justice, at least not *Catholic* Social Justice. Without Jesus in the center of it, it becomes Socialism. With Jesus in the center of any program, be it feeding the poor, visiting the sick or clothing the naked, it will be abundantly blessed and prosper. Without Jesus in the center, these programs are Socialism at best, and Communism at worst, and they will fail.

Martin spent a great deal of his life taking care of the poor. He did all of the things above, and more. But he had *one* focus. *"Martin's whole apostolate of charity had only one purpose; to awaken the love of God in souls; in all souls, without exception, in the souls of the rich as well as the poor."*[10] There's the difference. His charity was God-centered. Many of our brothers and sisters of today could take a lesson from our little Saint of Lima.

St. Martin and the devil

It would make a great deal of sense for Satan to hate St. Martin.   Martin was one of his worst enemies. Martin did everything he could to keep souls out of hell and on the road to Heaven. The Lord gave him the power to take away all the excuses people have to sin. They looked at this simple man and saw Jesus. He took away prejudice and bigotry. He was a black, the lowest of the low in Lima of that time. Yet, he was the special one of

---

[10]St. Martin de Porres, Apostle of Charity

God. He took away starvation. People came to Martin, and they were given Manna from Heaven. It went on and on. Whatever Satan could come up with to drag people down to the depths of hell, Martin could counter with Jesus and His promise of everlasting life in Paradise.

It only stands to reason that Satan would have his demons attacking Martin at every opportunity. One evening, Martin was rushing from his room to the infirmary, loaded down with supplies. He used a rickety stairway which had been closed down because it was too frail and dangerous. He wasn't supposed to use that stairway, but it was the most direct route between his room and the infirmary, and he felt he was under the protection of the Angels anyway, so it should be okay. Right? Wrong!

As he was moving along at breakneck speed, he was stopped in his tracks by this monstrous, unbelievably hideous demon from hell. It's impossible to describe accurately, except that it was revolting. A very ugly face emanated from the body. Martin addressed the thing with great anger: *"What are you doing here, accursed one?"*

The creature replied, "I am here because it pleases me to be here, and because I expect to profit by being here."

Martin replied, *"Away with you to the cursed depths where you dwell!"*

The demon held his ground. Martin dropped his supplies, took off his belt, and began whipping the creature, who disappeared immediately. Martin took a coal from the brazier, which he always carried with him, and made the Sign of the Cross on the wall, and prayed in thanksgiving to the Lord for taking care of him.

Another instance of demonic attack was witnessed by Francis de la Torre, an officer of the guard, who was sharing Martin's cell, the night of the battle. Martin's cot was in the back part of the cell, and the captain's was in the front. Francis was preparing to go to sleep when he heard a door open and close, and Martin spoke. Francis could tell something was wrong by the tone of Martin's voice. Now you have to understand that Martin was a man who never raised his voice, who always spoke gently and with a great deal of love. To hear anything other than that emanate from Martin's mouth was to know that there was a serious problem afoot. Martin's tone was angry. He said, *"What have you come here for, you troublemaker? What are you looking for? This is not your room. Get out!"*

By what Francis could make out from the sounds that he heard, there had to be more than one demon. It could have been as many as a legion of devils. At any rate, they attacked Martin with a vengeance, knocking him about the room. Francis went to the alcove separating the room. He wanted to come to Martin's aid. He looked at the scene. He could see Martin being thrown from one side of the room to the other; he would flinch, move his head from one side to the other, back and forth, and then again, back and forth as if he were being struck. He doubled up with pains in the stomach and he went flying to another part of the room. But Francis could not make out even a hint of anyone beating up Martin.

Suddenly, the entire room was in flames. Francis ran to help Martin. He couldn't let Martin burn to death. He burst into the room and, with Martin's aid, put out the flames. The fire extinguished, the noises stopped. The room abruptly returned to a harsh silence. The two men went back to their beds, and as soon as their hearts stopped pounding, they fell into the sleep of the innocent.

A few hours later, Martin rose to ring the dawn bell. He lit a candle for Francis and left the room. Francis jumped out of his bed to assess the damages from the fire and the brawl which had taken place there a few hours before. As he looked around, he could see no signs of a battle. There were no burn marks; no broken furniture; nothing was in disarray. Francis de la Torre was bewildered.

Martin was a simple man of few words. He showed an inner

control, almost a total peace. He was the epitome of humility. In everything he did or said, he projected the best of his father-in-faith, St. Dominic and all that was espoused in the Dominican family of brothers and priests.

But when he did speak, you could count on whatever he said. In addition to his gentle, lilting voice, the content of his speech was so solid, so filled with the Spirit, his listeners were enraptured by him. Martin was so concise, his words so well-chosen (although not deliberately so), he brought his points home so effectively, it was obvious these gifts were coming from above, as he was just a lay-helper, the lowest of the Dominican Order. He didn't waste his time talking about sundry things; he concentrated his efforts on things above, rather than of things of the earth. He took to heart the Scripture passage, *"Do not seek what you are to eat and what you are to drink, and do not worry anymore.... Instead, seek His Kingdom, and these other things will be given you besides.... For where your treasure is, there also will your heart be."* (Luke 12:29-31,34)

Martin embraced the vows of Poverty, Chastity and Obedience as an alcoholic would embrace a drink, or a man stranded in the desert for 30 days and nights would embrace food and water. There are those who *take* the vows of Poverty, Chastity and Obedience. There are those who actually *embrace* these vows. But Martin *ate, breathed and lived* these vows. *They became part of who he was,* the fiber of his very existence. He woke up in the morning, for his vows; his last thought of the day were these vows; they brought him closer to Jesus.

Martin goes *Home!*

We believe that Martin spent his whole life as a pilgrim on his Journey of Faith to the Kingdom. Everything he did, everything he said, was in preparation for that time when he would shed his earthly body and be with his beloved Jesus in Paradise.

The Lord made him work for sixty years before allowing him to leave the earth. Martin went to his Heavenly on November

3, 1639, but he could not leave his beloved Dominican Community without preparing them for his absence Towards the end of the preceding summer, his body just fell apart on him. He had abused it for decades, in an attempt to break the chains that shackle us to our flesh. Physical mortification was a nightly practice, all the years he was a member of the Dominican Community. Because of his special relationship with the Lord, his Superiors gave him more leeway with this than they might have given an ordinary brother. Apparently they felt Our Lord Jesus or Our Lady or St. Dominic would have stopped him if he were embarking on areas which would prove dangerous to his health.

Martin knew when he would die. There were indicators which the brothers shared in the beatification process. The first indicator that death was in the offing came when one day, out of the blue, Martin wore a new habit. That may not seem unusual, but when you consider that he wore the same old beat-up habit for *twenty five years*, without ever changing it, the sight of a new habit would draw stares from everyone in the Community. When Fr. John Barbazán said in surprise "What happened," Martin smiled his gentle smile and responded, *"This is the habit I am to be buried in."* Martin had never spoken about his own death before.

This statement put a chill in Fr. Barzabán's heart. He loved Martin very much. Martin was his mentor; he considered himself one of Martin's spiritual sons. Fr. Barzabán was leaving the Holy Rosary Monastery shortly to take a teaching position in Cuzco. He feared, if Martin's demise was as imminent as he made it appear, he would never see Martin again. He knew he could not return to Lima before the end of the year. But when he was to depart Lima, Martin said to him, *"We will see each other very soon, because you will not be absent from Lima very long."*

Fr. Barzabán replied, "I cannot possibly return before the end of the year, because the Superiors are sending me to teach theology." So the priest left with a heavy heart, fearing he would never see his friend Martin again. However, Martin was correct again. Shortly after Fr. Barzabán left Lima, he returned. His trip was postponed indefinitely. He was there to say good-bye to Martin when he left for Heaven.

Another man, John Figueroa, came to Martin, asking for him to pray for his soul at his hour of death. Martin told him, *"I shall die first."* Then, a few days after he put on his new habit, he became violently ill. Now we come to a very unusual part of the story. For most of his life, the Lord had given Martin the power to heal people. He raised people from the dead! All he would have to do is touch a person and they would experience a healing. And yet, when he became ill to the point of death, he had no power to heal himself. It may be ironic, but it is not unusual. Many Saints experienced the same thing. When it came to their own illness, they were not able to help themselves at all.

What does this prove to us? We believe Jesus is trying to tell us very clearly in these instances, that He is the Healer, and no one else. If Martin were truly healing the people, he would have no problem healing himself. However, possibly to prove to the people that he was not the healer, he couldn't heal himself.

He suffered excruciatingly during the months of September and October. His Superiors insisted he not sleep on the hard board he had used for a mattress for so long, and to exchange his old sackcloth habit for a good, lighter habit. Martin was always obedient to his Superiors. But the new habit caused him so much more pain than the old one had, he asked permission to take off the new habit and replace it with his old sackcloth habit. Permission was granted. Martin de Porres, out of obedience, did sleep on a proper bed for a change.

One of the greatest struggles for the bedridden Martin was his inability to go about his daily duties. In addition to not being able to minister to the sick and poor, healing and feeding them, he just couldn't do anything. He couldn't run all over the place, handling his chores as barber-surgeon, wardrobe master and infirmarian. He was not able to serve his brothers and sisters, and that saddened and frustrated him.

But through all of it, the Lord was still showering Martin

with many blessings. Towards the end, a high official came to Martin to say good-bye-to a friend and a counselor. The brothers led him to Martin's cell and knocked on the door. There was no answer. They looked in; Martin was in ecstasy. The viceroy insisted, he would wait until Martin came out of it. He went outside and talked to the brothers about Martin. It was about fifteen or twenty minutes before Martin came out of his ecstasy. At that time, he saw his friend, bid him farewell, and asked for his prayers.

The Superior was upset with Martin for having made this important man wait for him outside. Martin said nothing in his own defense. Finally, the Superior, who really just wanted to know what was going on in Martin's ecstasy, ordered him to explain why he made the viceroy wait so long. Martin pointed to a small altar on which the Blessed Sacrament was in reserve, waiting to be given to Martin at the moment of his death. Martin told the Superior that the Blessed Virgin was over there by the altar, and St. Dominic, his father-in-faith and St. Vincent Ferrer, along with many other Saints and Angels were there as well.

Martin said to the Superior, *"I was so occupied with those holy visitors that I couldn't receive any other at that moment."*

Martin suffered greatly, physically as well as spiritually. Satan felt that this was a perfect opportunity to snatch the holy Brother of God and cast him into the bowels of hell. He took advantage of Martin's weakness to try to weaken him spiritually. However the Angels and Saints came to his aid, and he defeated the power of Satan. On November 3, 1639, after receiving the Blessed Sacrament for the last time, Martin surrendered his body and soul into the Hands of His Heavenly Father. He let go of the Crucifix which he had held onto so tightly. It was finished.

However, that was not the end, but the *beginning* of the miracles. As they were preparing to bring his body downstairs to be venerated by the faithful, bloodcurdling screams were heard from one of the priests. He was in agonizing pain. One of the brothers shouted out to him, *"Invoke Martin de Porres, whose loss we all feel so keenly."* No sooner had the words been spoken than the priest's pain disappeared, and he was completely cured.

Martin was dressed in the new habit, he prophesied would be the one in which he would be buried. He was brought into the church for the people of Lima, his brothers and sisters, those for whom he labored all his life, to say good-bye. As the brothers were keeping watch with him the night before the crowd was to come in, Father Cyprian de Medina, whom Martin had brought back to life from the brink of death, touched his body. It was stiff. Fr. Cyprian had the kind of relationship with Martin where he could joke with him, in life and in death.

He said to him, *"But what's this? So stiff and rigid? Brother, don't you know that as soon as day breaks the whole city will come to see you and praise God in you? Ask God to make your body flexible, for you know we would render Him infinite thanks for that!"* Within a matter of minutes, the body was loose and flexible. The face lost that hard look of death. Fr. Cyprian and the brothers lifted Martin's body to a sitting position, so that he looked alive and ready for a visit with his people.

Miracles after his death, began almost immediately. As a matter of fact, they began at the veneration of his body. Sick people were carried to the church and up to the body of Martin. When they left, they were able to walk home, cured from their illnesses.

Two days after Martin's death, a brother was on the throes of death, in agonizing pain. Then the next morning, he awoke completely healed. He said Martin had come during the night with Our Lady, St. Dominic and St. Catherine of Siena. Martin said, *"This visit will cure you."*

The miracles went on and on, and continue to go on and on. Devotion to this powerful man of God has never ended, never slacked off. The miracles through the intercession of St. Martin de Porres have never let up. In 1837, he was beatified, and on May 6, 1962, Pope John XXIII proclaimed him a member of the Church Triumphant, a Saint of our Church. Praise Jesus for St. Martin de Porres and his powerful sign in the Church, in the world.

Above: *The Madonna and Child given to St. Joseph of Cupertino by his Superiors*

Above: *Basilica of St. Joseph of Cupertino in Osimo, Italy*

Above: *Sacramentary used by St. Joseph of Cupertino*

Above: *The triumph of St. Joseph of Cupertino*

St. Joseph of Cupertino

The Flying Saint and Patron Saint of Students and Aviators

Saint Joseph of Cupertino

Save My Church Which is in ruin

The Church in the 16th century received a devastating blow, unlike any attack the *enemy* could level. Oh, he had been working hard at destroying the Church, what with all the heresies[1] which kept cropping up. But Mother Church, perfect mother that she is, always set her children straight through her sons, the princes of the Church on earth - the Popes, down through the centuries, writing Bulls, convening Councils, condemning and dispelling these errors, once and for all, only to have them resurface, again, with a different face but the same disobedient heart (sadly, often using our priests, the Church's own ambassadors of Christ as instruments). Not even the devil's fondest dream of fracturing the Church through the Schism in the East in the Eleventh Century could deal the death blow.

But, the day came when the bells tolled mournfully, Mother

---

[1]Read Bob and Penny Lord's book on Heresies that attacked the Church: *"Scandal of the Cross and Its Triumph."*

Mary crying, as her dear children in Europe left the Church founded by her Son. What one priest (Luther) began, one former Defender of the Faith (King Henry VIII) would complete, the procession of 6,000,000 unsuspecting Faithful from the Church that flowed from the Heart of her Son on the Cross, robbing them of the Sacraments.

Through the betrayal of King Henry VIII, the attack on the Church, which had failed under Martin Luther, began to spread throughout Europe. Would Hell prevail against His Church? *No!* Jesus had made a promise and He would keep it to the end of the world; He would return and head the Church Himself. Whenever our Church has been in danger, the Lord has raised up powerful men and women. In the 16th century, he raised Saint Teresa of Avila and Saint John of Cross (to mention a few), to save His Church.

And now, in the 17th century the battle not yet won, Our Lord chooses another precious soul from a humble family and a little-known village, Joseph of Cupertino.

To us, a Saint is born

Our story takes us to Cupertino, a tiny farming village near Lecce, at the heel of the boot of Italy. Farming has always been a hard life, but in the south of Italy you can keenly see the ravages of weather and disappointment on the farmers' leathery faces, furrowed and cracked by the merciless, unrelenting beating of the sun's rays.

Conditions were no better in the year 1603 when Our Lord sent a son to Felix Desa and Frances Penara.[2] Felix was a carpenter, a very good one. His only problem was his heart was bigger than his pocketbook. He guaranteed loans for friends. When they could not pay, creditors demanded restitution from Felix. Since he could not satisfy the debts, the creditors seized his home as part payment and then threatened poor Felix with imprisonment,

---

[2]In Italy, as in many European countries (as well as in Mexico), the woman is always known by her maiden name, even when her name is listed in the Obituary notices.

Above: ***Bob & Penny with Fr. Silvano, Rector of Osimo Shrine***

Above: ***St. Joseph of Cupertino rises above the Altar during the Consecration of the Mass***

Below: ***Shrine of St. Joseph of Cupertino at Osimo***

Above:
St. Joseph levitating up to a statue of the Blessed Mother

Right:
The habit of St. Joseph of Cupertino

to satisfy the rest. Without the possibility of help forthcoming, Felix fled to a holy place and asked for asylum. In those days soldiers could not enter any Church property, as it belonged to the Vatican which was considered another State (equivalent to a separate country with the Pope as head or prince).

Frances, in the last days of her pregnancy, heavy with child, without the aid of her husband, had to flee as well. But do not let me paint a false picture of Frances, mother of a future saint. She was no delicate flower that the slightest wind would blow away. The women of Italy, especially peasant stock of Southern Italy, are strong, the real power and force behind their husbands; they are the heart and strength of the family which keeps it together. Running from the authorities, unable to reach a friend's home before Baby Joseph made known his urgency to be born, Frances found shelter in a stable. Here, as with Jesus before him, Joseph would be born June 17th, 1603, with only farm animals as witnesses. He was later baptized in *Our Lady of Snow* Church. Although not present, you can be sure his father was close by, looking on.

With no father to discipline the growing Joseph, the task fell to his mother who, fearing he might get into trouble, wielded a heavy hand. As many of that generation, Frances rarely showed the boy affection while he was awake, afraid he might take advantage of her love and judge her weak and incapable of controlling him. Years later Joseph would jokingly say, he had no need of a novitiate as a religious; he had gone through *his*, under his mother.

Joseph experiences his first ecstasies

To his delight, Joseph's mother often took him to church. When he was eight, he made a little Altar at home, where he would recite the Rosary and Litanies to Blessed Mother and the Saints, day and night. His ecstasies began at that time. Experiencing them even at school, oftentimes the book Joseph was reading dropped to the floor; his eyes traveled heavenward, his lips parted, his mouth opened and he was in another world. Imagine the fun the other children had, calling him name, one of the kindest being, *"bocca aperta."* [The English translation *"open mouth"* loses some of its sting.] Because of this, many mistakenly took him for *being retarded.*

Joseph developed ulcers on his legs. His only comfort was attending Holy Mass. Unable to walk, his mother carried him to church each morning. Hearing a hermit had the gift of healing, Frances brought Joseph to him. The hermit prayed and then resorted to excruciating surgical means to remove the diseased flesh with forceps heated in fire; still no reprieve from pain, no cure in sight. Throughout all this useless torture Joseph never complained, always seeking his relief in the Blessed Sacrament. When all looked hopeless, as a last resort, the hermit took some hot oil from the lamps burning before the image of Our Lady of Grace and placed it on the sores. Joseph, suddenly free from all pain, walked to a church *nine miles* from his home, aided only by a cane.

His life *more and more* became God and His Church. He visited different churches, assisting at Mass, as often as they would allow him. He ceased eating meat, subsisting solely on vegetables he had seasoned with a bitter herb. He fasted sometimes two or three days in a row, abstaining from food of any kind. As he practiced *more and more* austere forms of penance and mortification, he desired *more and more* to leave the world and unite himself with things above.

Joseph, a prophet unknown in his own land

The Lord said, *"A prophet is unknown in his own land."* So it was with Joseph. When he asked his uncle, Father Francis Desa to help him join his Order, the Conventuals, he ridiculed Joseph for *dreaming* he could ever become a priest with his lack of education. Well, as with his Seraphic father Francis, if Joseph could not enter through the front door, he would come through the back door. Joseph went to the Provincial of the *Capuchins*, Father Antony of Francavilla, and begged him to accept him as a lay-brother. Joseph received the habit in August, 1620.

Joseph's thoughts were first and foremost *on above*; he could never have been accused of focusing on things below. This would cost him dearly, as he served white bread when asked for wheat, as he broke dishes when they fell out of his hands, and as he upset pots of food cooking on the open fire when he attempted to add firewood.

God's ways are not our ways. A sad and wounded Joseph was relieved of his beloved habit and dismissed, actually thrown out of the Order eight months after his joyful entry. His agony was so great that years later he would say, *"It seemed to me as if my skin was torn off with the habit and my flesh rent from my bones."*

As he believed he was entering the Order for *life*, he and the brothers had taken little notice where his secular clothes were placed on the day of his entry. And so, eight short months later, our little rejected soul walked away from his dreams, his head bare, his hat gone, no shoes or stockings to cover his feet. He thought he would by-pass Cupertino and all the snide and painful remarks he would encounter there. He bleakly walked toward Vetrara and his uncle, Father Francis Desa who was preaching the Lenten services.

When Joseph arrived, his uncle, true to form, received him by lashing out at him, calling him demeaning, derogatory names. Joseph fell prostrate at his feet, humbly responding when asked why he had come, because *"I am good for nothing."* Fr. Desea, softening at his nephew's apparent sincere humility, allowed him to remain with him until after Easter when he accompanied him to Cupertino to act as a moral support for the moment Joseph dreaded, facing his mother. She did not disappoint him; she greeted him with blows to the head and cuts to the heart. Now do not think for a minute she did not love him. She was afraid for him. Joseph had been safe in the Monastery. Now, he was home; what would happen to him? Her husband dead, Frances pleaded with the authorities not to imprison her son to satisfy his father's debt.

Next, Frances took on the Order of Conventuals. If you have ever known an Italian mother, she is the persistent woman, Jesus spoke of in Holy Scripture. You can just imagine what the Conventuals were subjected to until they grudgingly accepted Joseph as a *tertiary.* He was ecstatic over his new apostolate, tending the mules and his other barnyard friends. He whistled happily as he performed all sorts of menial tasks for the brothers and went into town to gather alms for the monastery. He served the brothers humbly and joyfully.

Although Joseph never felt worthy, evidently God did, as He went executing His plan to make Joseph a priest. On June 19th, 1625, Joseph entered the novitiate in the Monastery in Grotella. The other brothers testified that the qualities Joseph most exemplified as he walked closer to God and farther from man and his approval, were *"humility, patience and obedience."* Although their respect for him grew, he insisted he was the most to be despised of all sinners, and he most assuredly received his habit out of pity. As with Jesus before him, he never defended himself, when accused falsely, accepting punishment although innocent. He willingly submitted to every trial imposed on him to test his virtue. The brothers of his Order ultimately came to recognize Joseph as a true man of holiness in their midst. Because of his obvious virtue, although not having the required education, he took his solemn vows and made his profession as a Franciscan, his heart bursting, his eyes shedding rivers of joy. *He was home!*

Joseph received *minor orders* without the necessary preliminary evaluation on January 30, 1627, was admitted to the subdeaconate February 27th, barely a month later, and became a deacon on March 20th of that same year. God was with him all the way. When interviewed for the diaconate, he was questioned[3] on the *only* Gospel passage he could remember and explain. It began, *"Blessed is the womb that bore thee."*[4] On the day of his examination for the priesthood, the Prelate, who was impressed with the answers given by the first friars he cross-examined, passed

---

[3]This is one of the reasons St. Joseph of Cupertino has been designated "Patron Saint of Students."

[4]Luke 11:27

the rest of the candidates, assuming they had the same grasp of Theology. *And so, Joseph was ordained March 18, 1628.*

Joseph begins to Levitate

Joseph returned to the Monastery at Grotella after his ordination. As soon as he entered, he ran to the Image of Our Lady to thank her for intervening for him, worthless and least of all her sons. During his first Mass, at the moment of consecration, when he touched Our Lord in the Holy Eucharist, he was so overcome with his unworthiness that he begged the Lord to purify his heart and cleanse his hands of all impurity. Each day, after his work was done, Joseph would steal away to a tiny room or remote hideaway. As he meditated on the Lord and the real world *above*, he would become engulfed in ecstasy and find himself levitating in mid-air. The brothers later testified at his Beatification, his ecstasies and levitations recurred so frequently, Father Joseph was not allowed to take part in spiritual exercises with the other brothers or walk in processions, lest he disturb the proceedings.

Father Joseph's life, through his own design, became more and more austere, as he deprived himself of all eating utensils and all but one poor garment. Throwing himself before the Crucifix, he cried, *"Look upon me, Lord; I am divested of all things; Thou art my only good; I regard all else as a danger and ruin to my soul."* The Lord's response was to take away all *His* consolation from Father Joseph, plunging him into the *Dark Night of the Soul.*[5] His agony became so unbearable one day, he cried out in anguish, the cry of his Savior before him, *"My Lord, why hast Thou forsaken me?"* A religious appeared to Joseph, someone he had never seen before. He handed him a new habit. Upon donning it, suddenly Joseph was no longer alone; he could feel the presence of his heavenly companions. Who was this stranger? Was he an Angel? Father Joseph believed so.

Father Joseph chastised his body through means of

---

[5]Read more about the Dark night of the Soul in the chapter on St. John of the Cross in Bob and Penny Lord's book, *Saints and other Powerful Men in the Church.*

mortification to tame and empty it of all earthly consolation, so he could be free to accept the graces poured down upon him by the Holy Spirit. During his priesthood, he felt so keenly the responsibility and the privilege of his vocation that he ate no bread for five years, drank no wine for ten years, and subsisted on herbs, dried fruits and beans flavored with the most bitter powder. One of the brothers tasting it, later testified that he got so sick to his stomach, for days all food made him nauseous. Joseph fasted almost unceasingly, observing 7 fasts of 40 days each (280 days), the same fast observed by his founder Saint Francis before him, eating no food on Thursdays and Sundays. Living solely on the Eucharist, after receiving his Lord, color would return to his face and renewed strength to his weakened body.

Saint Joseph of Cupertino is called before the Inquisition

He became famous, people of all stations in life flocking to him for spiritual direction. A Vicar-General, unaware of his holiness, brought Joseph before the Inquisition, charging he performed miracles, attracting the faithful to *himself* as a Messiah and Healer rather than to Jesus. Nothing could have been farther from the truth. There was suspicion about anyone having visions and what appeared to be phenomena, the Church always prudently investigating: *Were they of man, of the devil, or truly Divine?* Father Joseph willingly agreed to appear before the Inquisition. Always obedient, always humble, he was looking forward (as with all the visionaries and mystics, accepted by Mother Church) to the findings and proclamation of the Church in the matter of his gifts.

His call to the Inquisition in Naples came as no surprise to Father Joseph. Three years before he had told a brother he would be called to Naples. Shortly before Joseph was to leave, Jesus came to him as a Child, His clothes shabby and ripped, His little Body weighed down by an enormous Cross, forewarning His little priest of the Way of the Cross he was about to walk. Was the Lord strengthening him for the forthcoming trials and attacks, he would suffer? Father Joseph had a choice! He could join his pain and rejection to the agony, His Savior encountered as *He* walked to His final act of love which would bring about the salvation of the world; or like the Disciples, he could run away from the persecution.

When he arrived, Joseph set out for the Palace of the Inquisition. A young, very handsome *religious* caught up with him. Walking beside Joseph, he spoke gently, instilling confidence in him, bolstering his courage, fortifying him for the trial ahead. As he was about to enter the Palace, Joseph looked back to his companion who had begun to pull back; he was gone! Father believed, to the end of his life, that *Saint Anthony was the religious who walked beside him.*

Armed with the two edged sword, "*the armor of God*," a peace-filled joyous Friar appeared before the Sacred Commission. The members of the Inquisition questioned him for weeks. But at the end of intense inquiries, they found him without any stain of self-interest or guile. Although Joseph did not agree, always judging himself a worthless sinner and scoundrel, the Inquisitors all concurred, he was leading a virtuous life of piety. As if their findings were not enough, the Lord manifested His Majesty once again through Father Joseph. He was asked to offer Mass in their church. Upon raising the Host in consecration, Father Joseph levitated, oblivious of everyone around him, completely enraptured in ecstasy.

News of his vindication spread, just as that of his questioning and possible condemnation by the Inquisition had. To his pain and utter anguish, his fame grew more widespread than before. Princes, royalty from far and wide came to him, often satisfied just to see him. [We have always hungered for the Supernatural, the evidence of God working in our lives. We believe that because some of the members of our Church are disputing and casting doubts on the Supernatural, the Faithful are seeking signs and wonders, running to this alleged visionary and that supposed apparition, sadly no longer waiting upon the test of time and the wisdom of Mother Church.]

Father Joseph goes to Rome and then on to Assisi

The Inquisition over, Father Joseph was directed to bring the message to the Father General in Rome that he was to be sent to a secluded monastery. When he entered Vatican City, the magnitude of the ongoing succession of generations of Disciples faithfully following Jesus Christ through obedience to His Church, so touched his heart that he, in imitation of *his* founder St. Francis, desired to enter as a *poor one*. Joseph left even the last small coin he had on the city wall, entering the Vatican as he would leave the world, without anything but his love for the Lord and His Mother.

Now the news of his holiness and flights of ecstasy reached many countries and members of the Body of Christ and came to rest on not only Cardinals but on the Pope himself. His Father General brought Father Joseph to an audience with Pope Urban VIII. Upon kissing the feet of his Holiness, Joseph became so in awe of this sweet Christ on earth,[6] he went into ecstasy and levitated, remaining mid-air until his Father General ordered him to awaken. The Pope said that if Father Joseph were to die while he was still alive, he would give personal testimony as to this miraculous occurrence, and to the holiness of this priest. Because of Father Joseph's piety and holy virtues, the Pope commanded the Father General to send Joseph to a monastery best known for its strict observance of the Rule of St. Francis. And so, Father Joseph was sent to the Monastery in Assisi!

On April 30, 1639, it was a truly jubilant son of Francis who entered the ancient city of his Seraphic father. But like father Francis before him, he would know "*perfect joy.*"[7] His old friend Father Antony, Superior of the Monastery in Assisi, did a complete reversal, ignoring Joseph as if he didn't know him, avoiding him, at times almost looking through him, pretending not to see or hear

---

[6]St. Catherine called the Pope her "Sweet Christ on earth."

[7]Read more about St. Francis' definition of Perfect Joy in Bob and Penny Lord's book *Saints and other Powerful Men in the Church.. "Above all the graces and gifts of the Holy Spirit which Christ gives to His friends is that of Perfect Joy...willingly enduring sufferings, insults, humiliations, and hardships for the love of Christ."*

him, and upon acknowledging his presence, humiliating him in the company of the other friars, treating him with the greatest suspicion and disdain. Rather than being hurt and resentful of these unwarranted attacks, Father Joseph, believing he deserved this and more, became even more obedient to his superior.

Now, without the love and support of his old friend and superior, his brother friars looked upon him as a hypocrite and charlatan. But none of this was to compare with the *Dark Night of the Soul*, he would once again suffer as Jesus withdrew *His Love and comfort* from Father Joseph. No more ecstasies; no more encounters with his heavenly family. When he read the Word of God, he felt nothing! Praying the Divine Office had always enriched him and instilled courage in him; now he experienced nothing! But most painful of all, during the celebration of the Holy Mass, he felt dead! He felt alone! Father Joseph cried out to the Lord, but it seemed God was deaf to his pleas and blind to his sorrow.

Without the consolation of God, the devil thought he would have a field day. Oh, how he delighted in attacking Father Joseph! The devil likes to get us off, alone, to himself. He taunted Father Joseph with temptations, followed by impure thoughts, besieged by horrible nightmares. This went on for two years. Father Joseph, receiving no consolation from the Lord, alone and under relentless attack by the devil, weakened by the lack of peaceful sleep, rather than succumbing and falling victim to the *evil one*, became stronger and more resolute in his convictions and love for the Lord. God's Grace was enough for him. He didn't need to feel. He knew God loved him, and that's all he had to know to get through the dark nights of assaults and grieving.

Father Joseph desired to return to his Lady of Grotella in Cupertino. Instead, his superior sent him to Rome. It was there, after two years of silence, the Lord spoke to him and told him he would return to Assisi. His heavenly gifts returned; he was once again experiencing heavenly ecstasies.

Our future Saint's return to Assisi was met with joy and

celebration not only by the friars but by everyone in the village. They led him into the church. Upon raising his eyes to the fresco of Mother Mary[8] on the ceiling, Father Joseph cried, *"Ah, my dear Lady, you have followed me!"* and flew approximately 40 feet upward, toward his Mother, his arms outstretched to embrace her. It had been so long! With tears flowing he pledged his undying love to her and her Son.

⁊ Father Joseph's ecstasies increase

The trial over, Father Joseph was now in the bosom of his Heavenly Mother and his soul seemed to soar to Heaven more than ever, almost detached from his earthly body. When he heard the Names of Jesus and Mary, when organ music filled the church, when he heard a homily on God, he would become enraptured, sighing aloud, *"O Love, O Love!"* He desired the whole world to know and love Jesus and Mary. Upon meeting others who proclaimed love for God, Joseph's heart would begin to swell with joy, and he was lost in ecstasy to the world. He would go up to *religious* pleading, *"Would you die for Christ?"* One of his greatest desires was to be a martyr for Christ, never realizing he was already a *"Dry Martyr."* When sharing God's grief, over the sins that offend Him, Joseph's sorrow would be so great that blood would gush from his mouth.

His ecstasies became more frequent after he was ordained a priest. They were manifested with such close intervals, they were almost *uninterrupted* constant rapture. At the mention of God, Joseph would become impervious to pain. When he was subjected to needles piercing his flesh, repeatedly struck by blows from heavy iron rods, his body burnt by the flames of a torch, there was no reaction whatsoever. He would remain transfixed, his eyes heavenward, his body poised mid-air. During St. Joseph's ecstasies, when the pupils of his eyes were pressed by an index finger, he never even blinked. Only when God released him, or under obedience to a Superior, was he able to come out of his

---

[8]similar to the one of Our Lady of Grotella.

heavenly encounters and feel pain or experience any effect upon his senses. In the history of the Church, rarely has it been documented in the life of another Saint or Mystic, the phenomenal amount of divine ecstasies, miracles of healing and supernatural occurrences that have been attributed to Saint Joseph of Cupertino, a humble, holy friar who only felt worthy to serve his friends of the barnyard world.

In the 17 years he spent at the Monastery of Grotella,[9] Father Joseph levitated over 70 times. The most spectacular occurred when the friars of the Monastery were erecting a Calvary. The middle Cross that was to hold the *Corpus*, was over 36 feet high, and by far the heaviest of the three. Try as they may, 10 men could not lift the Cross. Upon seeing their plight, Joseph flew 70 yards, scooped up the cross, as if lifting a feather, and planted it in its appointed spot.

It was Christmas Eve. As Father Joseph was processing up to the Altar, strains of bagpipes and flutes serenading the Baby Jesus about to be born, filled his heart with so much hope for the world, he began to dance and weep tears of joy. And then, with a loud cry, he flew through the air like a graceful bird to the main Altar, almost 8 feet away. He remained there for 15 minutes in a state of ecstasy, disturbing nothing, the candles never burning his vestments.

Another time, on the Feast of St. Francis, our flying priest, vested for Mass, levitated up to the pulpit, close to 6 feet from the ground and remained there suspended, in an attitude of prayer, his knees bent, his arms outstretched like his Savior before him on the Cross.

On Holy Thursday evening, Father Joseph was praying with the other friars of his Order before Our Lord Jesus Who was reposing in the Tabernacle, His Holy Sepulchre, high above the main Altar. Overcome with the sad reality that His Lord would suffer the ongoing agony of Gethsemane that evening and that of

---

[9]where his favorite statue of Our Lady of Grotella was.

His Passion on the Cross the next day, and feeling the terrible emptiness in the church without His Presence until Easter Sunday, Joseph could no longer contain his grief and levitated, soaring high up to the ciborium which contained His Lord.

Joseph and the Lord in the Blessed Sacrament

Joseph had a strong sense of the Real Presence of Jesus in the Eucharist. To test him, someone knowing he was entering a particular church for the first time, asked if he knew if the Blessed Sacrament was present. As the Sacristy Lamp was not burning, Joseph replied he did not know. But all of a sudden he levitated toward the Tabernacle, embraced it and through it his Lord, the willing Prisoner within.

The Eucharist was very *personal* to Father Joseph. He did not see a piece of unleavened bread, but with the eyes of faith, he saw His Lord in His Body, Blood, Soul and Divinity. There were also times that the Lord favored this loyal son with a miraculous sign showing that He was truly present, which Joseph would see with the eyes of the flesh. One day when he was celebrating Mass, Joseph came to the moment of consecration. As he held His Lord between his fingers and raised Him high in adoration, what Joseph beheld was Jesus the little Boy Who played beside his foster father Joseph as he worked in his carpenter shop; the Virgin Mary's Son Who was lost and found, after she and Saint Joseph searched for three days.

Father Joseph always pointed to, and focused everyone who came to him for help, on the Lord and His Presence in the Sacraments. When someone came to him, tempted by the fallen angels who roam the earth seeking the ruin of souls, he would advise them to receive the Sacraments often.

Joseph exorcised demons

His Father Superior ordered him to exorcise demons. But Father Joseph, feeling unworthy, would address the demons in these words: *"Out of obedience, I ask you to depart from this person, but if you do not wish to, do not. All that is necessary is that I obey my Superior.* " This humble act of obedience would so baffle the fallen angel, he would leave the tortured soul.

One day, a seriously disturbed nobleman was brought to Father Joseph, bound tightly in a chair. He was asked to exorcise a demon from the poor soul. Before he began to pray, Father directed them to untie the man, then to hold him down, in a kneeling position. This accomplished, Father implored the nobleman to believe that the Lord can do all things, including heal him. He then instructed the nobleman to consecrate himself through the Mother of God to her Son Jesus. Then, letting out a sigh, Father Joseph lifted him by the hair and sailed through the air with the jubilant nobleman, completely cured. He joined with Father Joseph rendering praise and thanksgiving to the Lord for performing His wondrous Miracles through His servant Father Joseph.

Another time, while exorcising a demon from a possessed woman, Father Joseph was savagely struck on the face by the evil spirit. Appearing unaware and untouched by the furor of his attack, he calmly handed the demon his Superior's written orders to exorcise demons, exclaiming, *"Here, take it. It is enough I obey."* Then Joseph knelt and began to pray the Litany of Loreto to Our Lady. Powerless before such child-like obedience, and impotent before the priest's devotion to the devil's arch-enemy, Mother Mary, the demon fled, leaving the tortured soul at peace and free at last.

Joseph had the gift of converting men's hearts

Father Joseph was responsible for the conversion and return to the Catholic Faith of Lutheran Prince John Frederick. The Prince, then 25 years old, came to Assisi expressly to see Father Joseph, accompanied by two companions (a Catholic and a Protestant). He entered the chapel where Father Joseph was offering Mass. During the consecration of the Host, Father Joseph found himself unable to break the Host; It was so hard, he had to return It to the paten. Father cried out in pain, and levitated to almost 3 feet above the ground. Uttering another anguished cry, he returned to the altar and again tried to break the Sacred Host. This time, although it took great effort, the Lord in His Eucharist allowed the Host to be split in two.

Later, when his Superior asked him why he had wept so bitterly that morning at Mass, Father Joseph replied, *"My dear brother, the people whom you sent to Mass this morning, have hard hearts, for they do not believe all that Mother Church teaches, and therefore the Lamb of God was hardened in my hands so that I could not break the Sacred Host."*

Upon hearing of this, the Prince asked to attend Mass the next day. As Father Joseph elevated the Host, the cross on the Sacred Host turned black. Father let out a pitiful cry and was once again raised from the ground and remained in this position for 15 minutes with the Host held aloft for all to worship. Was it the miracle of Father Joseph levitating before him, or was it Father elevating the Sacred Host so reverently that melted the prince's heart? All we know is that he returned to Assisi and made his Profession of Faith before Father Joseph and remained a faithful son of the Church, with a special devotion to Saint Joseph of Cupertino. And the Protestant who had accompanied him? He said, "Cursed be the hour in which I came to this country; for at home I was much more at peace and now my conscience is tormented by the furies of doubt."

Miracles happened through Saint Joseph of Cupertino's intercession, as stated at his Beatification: *"His prayer was never in vain, but always obtained what he implored for the welfare of the soul and body; even those who merely commended themselves to him, received the desired favor at the moment he prayed for them."*

Father Joseph and his relationship with Mother Mary

Father Joseph never accepted credit for any miracles, pointing always to Mother Mary. He had a deep and abiding love for Mary, his earthly mother having always spoken to him of this Mother who would never let him down, who would love him forever. He called Mother Mary *his* Mother, he, the loving son, bringing her flowers with which he would bedeck her statues, and she, the loving understanding Mother who enjoyed her little son, who would playfully say:

"My Mother is very strange; if I bring her flowers, she says she does not want them," ... *"and if then I ask her what she desires, she replies, 'I desire thy heart; for I live in hearts.'"*

This Mother had this son's heart. Whenever he spoke of her, or sang sweet songs to her, he endearingly referred to her as his *Lady*, his *Patroness*, his *Protectress*, his *Queen*, his *Mother* and *helper*. All it took for him to go into ecstasy, was for someone to mention her name. When he stood before the Image of Mother Mary, he would involuntarily rise up to meet her, so great was his love for His Lady.

Father Joseph would pay honor to Our Lady of Loreto[10] by reciting repeatedly the Litany of Loreto. One day, when the shepherds who usually stopped in the middle of the day to recite the Litany with Father Joseph, were unable to come to the chapel near his monastery, he began to call out to the sheep which he could see in the far distant fields: *"Come here to revere the Mother of your God and my God."*

With this, the sheep began to run toward the chapel, the shepherd boys trying unsuccessfully to catch up with them. This priest, truly *"in persona Cristi,"*[11] had the Supreme authority of the sheep's true Shepherd Whose Voice they knew, and they followed that Voice. When they arrived, Father Joseph began the Litany of Loreto. Every time he said *"Holy Mary,"* the sheep would bleat *"Baa."* When the Litany was over, the sheep frolicked back to the pastures and continued grazing.

When we are under attack and feel helpless, when the enemy has even the holiest fooled, what do we do? We cry out against the injustice and angrily strive to defend ourselves, trying to expose the enemy, all to no avail. Why do we not do what Father Joseph did when people came to him? He would direct them to

---

[10]Read more about Our Lady of Loreto and the Holy House of Loreto (Nazareth) in Bob and Penny Lord's book, *Heavenly Army of Angels*.

[11]in persona Cristi - the priest stands before us in the Person of Christ.

Mother Mary saying, *"Go to Mother; Go to Mother."* When they pleaded with him to exorcise demons, he told them to kneel and pray the Litany of Our Lady of Loreto with him. Through this and our Saint's invocation to Mother Mary to intercede with her Son Jesus, he was able to help the broken in mind and body, exorcising demons and freeing the possessed.

Father Joseph always asked people to turn to Mother Mary. To a priest who had lost his way, he advised, *"Take refuge in Mary; she will hear you!"* Blessed Mother heard and answered his prayer; the priest remained faithful to his vocation and to the Church.

Another time while ministering to a dying man, Father Joseph pried open his lips and gently poured some liquid into his mouth. When he asked the man if he felt better, and the man replied he did, Father Joseph said, *"Then say nothing about me to anyone, but rather say the Mother of God, who is your mother and mine, has made you well."*

In life, St. Joseph went to Jesus through his Mother Mary; and in death he went to the Lord, calling out her name, a faithful son to the end. Why do we tell you of his love for the Mother of God, how he always gave her all credit, humbly accepting none for himself? Read and learn. As with Father Joseph who would become Saint Joseph, are those who are claiming to be special messengers of Our Lady and Our Lord humble, remaining in the background - the focus being on the Lord in the Eucharist and the Church? If it is Mother Mary speaking or her Son, you will hear a call to you to grow closer to the Church and to the Sacraments, not to a particular person.

Father Joseph had the fragrance of Heaven

When Father Joseph encountered a person in sin, he would detect an odor so repugnant, he could barely stand it. It lingered for a long time afterward; no amount of washing with hot water and soap was able to drown out the stench. On the other hand, coming from Father Joseph one could detect the sweet fragrance of flowers, *"the odor of sanctity,"* lingering, not only on those whom he touched but on objects he handled, for weeks. He had only to walk through a room to fill it with a haunting, lingering, heavenly bouquet, a touch of Paradise in their midst, for days.

Father Joseph would say that the soul was like a glass pitcher filled with clear water. It was a treasure, especially to those dying of thirst, a means of life, without which the body was not able to live. But when the smallest bead of oil is dropped into that water, it becomes spoiled and repugnant. So it is with the soul; when the smallest sin enters, it too becomes tainted.

Father Joseph embraced Lady Poverty

Like his founder St. Francis, our future Saint not only embraced Poverty, he adored her. He sought the most tattered, patched habit for his own, went without sandals, walking barefoot even in the coldest weather, donning foot covering only in public. He would not allow anyone to rob him of his Lady Fair, Lady Poverty. Even when he was close to death, he refused the two handkerchiefs offered him because they were of fine linen, insisting the friars exchange them for cloths of coarse material.

To control the demands of the flesh, Joseph used all forms of mortification on his body. He fasted! Those few times, he did eat, his meal would consist of a few herbs and vegetables, *rarely* any fish, *never* meat, except out of obedience. And then, when he did eat meat or fish, it caused him so much grief, he had to make a concerted effort, to eat at all.

His ecstasies came frequently, without warning. Fearing, they would disturb the other friars as they dined in the refectory, Joseph ate alone in his room. His cell was austere, with furniture consisting of a kneeler, two wobbly chairs, a tiny rough table and some modest paper pictures of Saints. His bed consisted of several boards haphazardly put together with some straw for a mattress.

Money was oppressive to him; when someone offered him a donation or stipend, he would ask them to hand it to his Superior. One time, without his knowledge, someone dropped some coins in his habit. He began to breath heavily, as if a huge weight was on his chest. He moaned, *"I cannot bear it! I cannot bear it!"*

Only when the friars discovered and removed the money, did his breathing return to normal.

Our Saint exercised total abandonment and obedience

"My God and my all!" God was everything to Father Joseph. He renounced even his very self so that he could be free to depend on nothing and no one but Our Lord. *"How do you know if it is God speaking to you?"* Father Joseph lived for God, as Saints before and after him, through *obedience* to his Superior. When his Superior spoke, Joseph heard his Seraphic father Francis speaking and joyfully obeyed, even to the point of altering his prayer life; it was as if God was talking. *Do we place the Face of Jesus on someone in authority over us, Our Pope, our bishop, our priest, our Superior, our mother and father, our husband?* We are so inundated with the culture of *personal freedom*, we fail to hear Jesus saying, *"I have placed this person in charge of you, on earth. Obey and I will work through that obedience."* There is such freedom in the total abandonment that Saints like Saint Joseph of Cupertino had.

He had a great repugnance toward any admiration or attention being shown him. One time a friar brought him a new habit, saying the Princess of Savoy wanted to exchange it for his old habit. Unaware *who* had sent the friar, the Saint refused. But upon learning it was his *Superior's* orders, he immediately removed his tattered habit and replaced it with the Princess' gift, exclaiming, *"Out of obedience, I will give not only my habit but also my skin and flesh."*

Obedience! *Over and over again, we hear obedience!* When Jesus said to Peter, *"If I do not wash you, you have no part in my inheritance."* our first Pope's response was one of obedience: *"Well then, Lord, not only my feet, but my hands and my head as well."* Are some of those who claim to be visionaries and mystics today obedient to Mother Church and her God-given authority? Are their messages in agreement with the teachings of the Church? All Visionaries and Mystics who have been accepted by the Church were; and when their message was not in accord with Mother

Church, they willingly submitted to her findings. Do not make Visionaries, Mystics and Stigmatists, real or imagined, into God. Even those accepted by the Church were *human*, open to human frailties. Their lives of virtue and piety made them Saints! Father Joseph said of obedience: *"It is like a knife that kills the will of man and sacrifices it to God, a carriage that conveys a man comfortably to Heaven, a little dog that leads the blind."*

Gift of Inner Locution - Saint of students

Saint Joseph is Patron Saint of Students. He was never able to master Latin, except in the reading of the Breviary and the Roman Missal. But he imparted such wisdom, responding to theological questions directed at him by theologians, more learned than he; they all agreed his wisdom could only have come from Heaven. One theologian said that he learned more, through the modest Father Joseph, than he had in all the years he had spent studying, receiving a purer, more clearly understandable, *authentic* theology, a theology very much like that of Jesus. Jesus spoke simply, using objects and circumstances everyone could relate to. The Pharisees and Saducees spoke pridefully, *above* the believers' heads. Joseph, using the wisdom of God, reached the minds and hearts of all who came to him. A noted theologian, Father Angeli, said of him, *"In every conversation I had with him, he used to talk always about the Mysteries of the Faith with such ease and clarity that his thoughts far exceeded the little study he had."*

A professor of theology and well-respected author, Father Lawrence Brancati said, *"Being ignorant and having neither studied nor understood much Latin, at every question put before him, about some difficulty which we ourselves have studied, he gave a clear and profoundly doctrinal answer, solving every difficulty."*[12] Father Brancati became a Cardinal and gave full credit to Father Joseph for all he had written about Mystics in *De Oratione,* his book on prayer.

---

[12]from *"Ecstasy, Jail and Sanctity"* by Gustavo Parisciani, O.F.M. Conv.

Joseph read men's hearts - the Perfect Confessor

When someone came to Father Joseph with sin on his soul, Father would tell him to go and wash. On one occasion, a young noble came, seeking help. Father told him to go and wash (make a contrite confession) that his face was black with sin and abhorrent to look upon; then to come back and see him. When the young man returned, after having received absolution Father said *"Now, my son, you are beautiful; wash yourself frequently; yesterday you were ugly."*

If someone said he did not recall having sinned, Father would tell him *the sin*, the *time* of the sin, the *place* where it occurred, and the *situation* which precipitated the sin.

He could read men's hearts. He always knew when someone was falling into temptation and would reach out to save him from sin. One day Father Joseph approached a fellow priest who was about to commit a grievous sin.

"My son, resist this temptation with courage; for it is God's will that you not offend him; this I say to you in all honesty."

Father Joseph always pointed to, and focused everyone on, the Lord and His Presence in the Sacraments. When someone came to him, tempted by the fallen angels who roam the earth seeking the ruin of souls, he would advise them to receive the Sacraments often, especially *The Sacrament of Penance* which cleanses us of serious sin and *The Sacrament of the Eucharist* which strengthens us for the battle.

When Jesus walked the earth, He *first* forgave the sins of the afflicted; He *then* healed them physically. This Sacrament was of such importance, one of His last acts was to leave His priests this Sacrament to be administered, in His Name. Jesus showed He had power over *all* on earth as He commanded evil spirits to leave those possessed. He passed on this Grace to His priests to do likewise, through these Sacraments. Father Joseph stressed Penance and the Eucharist, saying,

"Where God dwells, the enemy of God cannot easily approach; and in the long run God always conquers because by

His Grace He can do more than the devil by temptations."

Joseph had the gift of Prophecy

Reliable witnesses testified that Father Joseph foretold events before they came to pass. He not only foresaw the deaths of Pope Urban VIII and Pope Innocent X, but predicted the time and the day when they did die.

He prophesied not only deaths but also the recovery of people critically ill in *Rome*, which was a great distance from the monastery in Grotella where he was staying. He predicted incidents in his own life, long before they happened. A doctor came to Father Joseph and asked him to pray that he have a son. When his wife was about to give birth, it looked as if she would die before delivering. The husband now asked Father Joseph to pray for her! He assured the man that his wife was in no danger. After the doctor rushed off, Father Joseph said to a fellow-religious, *"Tonight, a son will be born to the doctor. I didn't want to tell him, lest it be said I pose as a prophet."* A son was born that night!

Father Joseph foretold the ascension of King John Casimir to the throne of Poland. While still a Prince, John Casimir asked Father Joseph which religious Order he should join. Father cautioned him not to take *any* Sacred Vows, as God would reveal His Will for him. Prince John, upon the death of his brother, was elected King of Poland! He never belonged to a religious Order, but King John Casimir was an instrument of the Lord, turning always to the Mother of God, Our Lady of Czestochowa for help and guidance. Later when Father Joseph saw the Prince travelling through Assisi on his way to be crowned King, he said, *"Did I not tell you? You will do more to advance God's interests in this state of life than in the religious state."*

Saint Joseph soared with the Angels

One time the Lord would come and rest in Fr. Joseph's arms. Another time the Saints would come and share the awe and wonder of Paradise. Angels would appear to him, and bring him comfort and consolation from Heaven.

But wherever the Heavenly Army of Angels is, the fallen angels are close by, ready to do mischief. One day when a religious was placing a girdle, blessed by Fr. Joseph, around a possessed man in an attempt to exorcise Satan from him, he heard the evil one say, "If you knew the virtue of this friar (Father Joseph) and how pleasing his soul is to God, you would be astonished. I must acknowledge this because God forces me to speak. Friar Joseph is the worst foe we have."

The enemy attacked Fr. Joseph relentlessly. He was praying before the Tomb of Saint Francis in the crypt of the Basilica of Saint Francis in Assisi, when the devil blew out all the candles in the church and proceeded to beat Joseph. All of a sudden, the demon saw Saint Francis emerging from his tomb carrying a candle, and needless to say, he fled!

The devil never stopped trying to do Father Joseph in. He tried everything; he tried to drown him; he tried to kill him by running him through with a sword; he tried to destroy him by gossip. But the Lord Who is Almighty is far mightier than that sucker.

Saint Joseph the Miracle Worker

Whenever there was a need for food, the cupboard quite bare, Fr. Joseph would pray, place his hands upon what little there was to eat, and what came about was the *multiplication* of honey, bread, wine and whatever food there was before him. At other times he simply called upon his Lady to intercede and *behold*, food miraculously increased.

He would place his cap on a blind man's head and his sight was restored. The lame and the crippled walked after they kissed the Crucifix Joseph held out to them. During the plague which claimed many lives, he blessed a poor soul burning up with fever, making the sign of the Cross on his forehead; the fever immediately dropped, and his temperature returned to normal. With the sign of the Cross, St. Joseph brought the dead back to life.

An arrogant nobleman contemptuously challenged Fr. Joseph: *"Impious hypocrite, it is not you, but the religious habit you wear that I respect and because of it, I trust that if you make the sign of the Cross on my wound, it will heal."* Cheerfully, Joseph humbly agreed with the nobleman that what he said was absolutely true and wise. Then he blessed the nobleman's wound, whereupon it was completely healed.

Saint Joseph and the gift of Bilocation

An old man in Cupertino asked Father Joseph to be with him at the hour of his death. Father Joseph unknowingly prophesied when he said that he would be with him even if he were in Rome. When the time came, Father *was* in Rome! One day, he knew it was time to go to his friend's side and give him the Last Rites of the Church. Many witnesses in Cupertino saw and heard Father Joseph prepare this precious soul to enter the Kingdom. One of them, Sister Teresa Fatali, testified that when she had questioned Father Joseph's presence there, he said, he had come to help his friend *Home*, and when he had done so, he vanished before their eyes.

As Father Joseph's mother was approaching death in Cupertino, he was in Assisi. She was weeping because she would not see her son before she died. Suddenly a bright light filled the room. When she saw her son standing before her, she cried out, *"Oh Father Joseph! Oh my son,"* closed her eyes and expired. At that very moment in Assisi, Father Superior was asking the weeping Joseph why he was grieving, to which he replied, his mother had just died. Many witnesses swore, they had seen and heard Father Joseph assist his mother on her deathbed, in Cupertino!

St. Joseph goes before the Second Inquisition

Fearing for his sanctity in the light of his fame, people from all walks of life flocking to him, Pope Innocent X directed the Father Inquisitor at Perugia to have Joseph moved to a remote place where he would be able to continue leading a virtuous life. An order came through that Joseph was to be taken from Assisi to the secluded Monastery of the Capuchins in Pietrarubbia. He cried as he kissed the tomb of his beloved Francis. Although unsure of his next home, he submitted, and kissed the feet of the Father Inquisitor.

Upon arriving at the Monastery in Pietrarubbia, he was isolated from all but his fellow Capuchins. He never questioned why he was sent there or why such restrictions were placed on him. His tears were never for himself but for his Savior's suffering. He continued to have ecstasies, especially during Holy Mass. He could see future events; miracles came about through him, even in this obscurity.

Although the Inquisition's purpose was to hide Father Joseph away in this remote hideaway, God would not permit this light to be hidden *under a bushel basket*. People came from far and wide and the church became too small to hold all the worshipers at his Masses. They pulled off the roof to get in, and knocked holes in the walls. They built humble huts near the monastery, even some inns for the many to stay. He remained three months, after which the Saint was called to another remote Monastery. Again, the light could not be hidden. Although he was ordered to celebrate Mass alone, people soon discovered he was there. So after three years, Father was once again called away. He was always a consolation to his fellow friars, no matter where he was sent to live. The more he was isolated from man, the more God drew him to a closer communion with Him, favoring Joseph with more and more ecstasies and countless gifts.

Father Joseph goes to Osimo

Although the Conventuals pleaded with Pope Alexander VII to have Father Joseph returned to Assisi, he ruled in favor of Osimo. All this Father Joseph foreknew and foretold.

Father Joseph had to wait till evening to enter the town so as not to be recognized. Standing on the porch of the Monastery, he inquired of the cupola in the distance. His heart leapt with joy when he discovered he was so close to the Holy House of Nazareth and his Lady of Loreto. [On Pilgrimage, each year, when we first spot that cupola, our hearts, too, leap.] He entered the Monastery on July 10, 1657. He was not to communicate with anyone except the bishop, his Vicar-General, the other friars of the Monastery, and when necessary, a doctor or surgeon. He lived a solitary life which to many would have appeared hell but to him was Paradise.

His ecstasies continued, lasting as long as seven hours. The religious finding him enraptured, would carry his stiff body (as if dead) to bed. He ate little and never complained when his brother religious forgot to bring him food for a couple of days. God was his strength and only consolation, as the devil took every occasion to attack him, mercilessly.

Father Joseph foretells his death

He foretold the day of his death, prophesying to his fellow religious, he would die when he could not receive Holy Communion. On August 10, 1663, he developed a high fever. When his brother friars pleaded with him to ask God to heal him, he replied, *"No, God forbid!"* For five days his fever rose dangerously and then dropped hopefully, our Saint only retreating from his bed to celebrate Mass in his private chapel. At his last Mass, on the Feast of the Assumption, the ecstasies and levitations were greater and more powerful than ever. When he was so debilitated by high fevers, he was no longer able to celebrate Mass, he pleaded to *assist* at Mass. Whenever he beheld the Eucharist, the Lord in His glory, his face would begin to glow! And then, upon receiving his Lord, he swooned, his face losing all color. His passion for his Savior grew, as the days moved closer and closer to the end of his life. He said,

"I desire to be dissolved and to be with Christ."

After he received his last Kiss from his Savior, Holy Communion, and then Extreme Unction,[13] he sighed: *"Oh what sweetness of paradise."* He asked that the Profession of Faith be recited; and then asked pardon of his brother friars. He implored them to bury his body in a secluded spot.

Our little friar was notified that he was to receive the Papal

---

[13]Today it is called The Sacrament of the Anointing of the sick.

blessing by special decree of His Holiness the Pope! After he collected himself, he asked to be helped to his chapel where he knelt as he tearfully received the sacred gift.

Before he drew his last breath, he cried out, *"Take this heart, burn and rend this heart, my Jesus."* Our Saint died at midnight, September 18, 1663, at the age of sixty. When they opened the Saint's body to embalm, they found the pericardium[14] of the heart had shriveled up and the ventricles of the heart were without blood; the heart itself withered and dry. Remembering how at times, they would see Joseph clutching his chest, trying to rip it open, to cool the fire raging within that was consuming him, the friars agreed this was another *physical* sign of his burning love for His Lord and Lady. As Padre Pio would in later years, Saint Joseph gave his all, to the last drop of his blood.

The body was prepared and placed on a sheet. For some unexplainable reason the sheet caught on fire and flames swept over him. Their worst fears, that his body would be burned beyond recognition, were not to be realized. When they put out the fire, they discovered to their amazement and relief, the body had no signs of the fire that had attacked it; even his beard, and the hair on his head escaped without a single hair being singed.

They laid Joseph out in state, so that all those who had not been able to see him the six years he was in Osimo could come, at last, to love their Saint in death.

Miracles began to happen immediately after his death

Two years after his death, Pope Innocent X commissioned the Bishops of Nardo, Assisi and Osimo to investigate the life of the future Saint Joseph of Cupertino.

The inquiry continued under Pope Clement XII who, in 1735, on the Feast of the Assumption of our Lady, declared *publicly* that Father Joseph had led a virtuous life. Now, the next step, *Miracles!*[15]

---

[14]pericardium - the thin, closed membranous sac surrounding the heart and the roots of the great blood vessels, containing a clear serious liquid. (Webster's dictionary)

[15]Miracles manifested during a candidate's life do not count toward his or her Beatification or Canonization.

The Cause for Beatification was soon opened as documentation of Miracles continued to pour in. On the Feast of St. Francis, October 4, 1752, Pope Benedict XIV proclaimed two miracles had been accepted as having been manifested through the sole intercession of the *Servant of God, Joseph of Cupertino.* On the Feast of St. Matthias,

Tomb of St. Joseph of Cupertino in Osimo

February 24, 1753, Joseph of Cupertino was solemnly Beatified by his Holiness Pope Benedict XIV.

Miracles kept happening through the intercession of Blessed Joseph of Cupertino, so much so that the Conventuals were joined by bishops and members of royalty entreating the Pope to open the Cause for Canonization.

The Pope accepted the Sacred Congregation's findings and approved the three Miracles credited to him, and Blessed Joseph of Cupertino went from the ranks of the Church Militant,[16] to the Church Suffering,[17] to the Church Triumphant,[18] as Saint Joseph of Cupertino was entered into the Company of Saints in Heaven, on July 16, 1767.

---

[16]The Church Militant is made up of living members of the Body of Christ (you and us) who are actively working out their salvation within faith, love, and hope - Virtues given by the Sacraments and the teachings of the Church. (Catholic Encyclopedia - Broderick)

[17]The Church Suffering is that group who have died in grace and whose souls are being purged in Purgatory. (Catholic Encyclopedia - Broderick)

[18]The Church Triumphant consists of known souls in Heaven, the Blessed Virgin Mary, the Saints and all who are united with Christ and enjoy the Beatific Vision. (Catholic Encyclopedia - Broderick)

Blessed Kateri Tekakwitha

Lily of the Mohawks
Mystic of the
New World
Fruit of the Martyrs

Blessed Kateri Tekakwitha

The Lord takes us into the wilderness of a new, uncharted, untouched world, to share with us the beauty of His creation and the power of His works through the first beatified native person born in this country. In our book, *Martyrs, They Died for Christ*, we wrote about a new breed of Evangelists who came upon the horizon, whose images cast a broad shadow on a new world. These were brave, totally committed men of France, the Jesuit Blackrobes, who came to our continent in the early Seventeenth Century with only one goal - to bring Jesus to the pagans who inhabited the land.

The move by these French priests was spearheaded by an observation made by Samuel Champlain as he traveled the breadth of the St. Lawrence River, which then broadened out to Lake Ontario. He noticed as he sailed past all the Indian villages, there were so many children of God who knew nothing about Our Lord Jesus, our Savior. He wrote, in his journal, how sad it was that most of these people would live their entire lives never having heard the name of Jesus and would die without the grace of having known Him or being a part of His Church through Baptism.

When this word came back to the Church of France, an

avalanche of fervor swept across the country. But it was the newly-formed army of Ignatius Loyola, the Company of Jesus, the Jesuits,[1] who took it as a call to spiritual arms. The French contingency of that order accepted the challenge put to them. They embraced St. Paul's plea to the Christians of another time, the early days of the Church, as a call to arms. They used his words as their battle cry.

"For everyone who calls on the name of the Lord will be saved.

But how can they call on Him in whom they have not believed?

And how can they believe in Him whom they have not heard?

And how can they hear without someone to preach?

And how can people preach unless they are sent?"[2]

They came over to New France, as Canada was called at that time. They came with hearts burning to spread the word of God to the Indians and to die as Martyrs for Evangelization to the New World. By the thousands they came. They set up missions, worked in the wilderness, learned the language and customs of the Indians and gently, very gently taught them about Jesus. Their progress ranged from slow to full stop. But they persevered! They had many obstacles to overcome, many of which were caused by their own people. Before the Blackrobes ever got to Canada and upper New York State, they were preceded by trappers and fur traders who cared little or nothing for the people who lived on the lands, the natives of our country. They represented nothing but a way to satisfy their greed.

These were followed by the Military, whose only purpose was to obtain and maintain control and keep the Indians in their grip. Neither group would have won any popularity contests among the Indians. What they did manage to accomplish was to create an atmosphere of suspicion and distrust for any white men. The Blackrobes became victims because of the iniquities their

---

[1]Founded by St. Ignatius Loyola in Spain in 1534, barely a hundred years before the Jesuits began coming to the New World.
[2]Romans 10:13-17

Above: *The Mission of Saint Francis Xavier at Kahnawake, Québec founded in 1667*

Above: *Statue of Bl. Kateri Tekakwitha at her Shrine in Fonda, New York*

Left: *Books printed in Iroquois for Mission at Kahnawake Québec*

Above: *Bob & Penny with Fr. Jacques Bruyère, S.J., Postulator for Cause of Bl. Kateri*

Above: *Oldest known painting of Bl. Kateri*

countrymen and others[3] had inflicted upon the natives of America.

Add to that the Indians' own culture, which was so completely different from the French settlers. Both the French and the Indians focused on the things which separated them, rather than try to find a common denominator- those qualities which could unite them. The Iroquois, who were the strongest of the Indian tribes, hated the Hurons, who traded with the French; therefore, the Iroquois hated the French. They were friendly with the Dutch and the British who were at odds and sometimes at war with the French. That could account for a great deal of the hostility between the Iroquois and the French.

But the real victims had to be the Blackrobes, the Jesuit Evangelists. They were blamed for everything. If the Iroquois attacked the Hurons, it was the fault of the Blackrobes. If the Hurons suffered drought, it was the fault of the Blackrobes. If the crops failed, it was because of the black magic of the Blackrobes. If illness were to take its toll on the Indian population, because of strains of bacteria, brought into the continent by the French, Dutch and British, it became strangely enough the fault of the Blackrobes. To this day, there are those in Canada who blame the Jesuits for the rampant disease to which the Indian population was subjected, and because of which they died in great numbers.

But what was the justification to blame the Jesuits? They were no more responsible for spreading the viruses than any other foreigner who emigrated to the country. However, they were the most vulnerable. They were the easiest to attack and the least able to defend themselves. There came a time in 1649, after the torturous execution of John de Brebuf, Gabriel Lalemant, and others in Huronia, when the wholesale slaughter of the Blackrobes became too much for the Superiors in Quebec to accept, and so they closed down the missions, burned to the ground Saint Marie of the Hurons, the settlement which they had built as a headquarters for the missionaries, and left to go back to Quebec. The mission

---

[3]British and Dutch settlers, both of whom did their share of abusing the natives

venture to Huronia was a failure. The wilderness reclaimed the lands in which the Blackrobes had labored and died, their blood left as fertilizer for the growth of the new missions, the fruit of the Martyrs.

In Ossernenon, which is modern-day Auriesville, New York, the first of the North American Martyrs *René Goupil* was martyred in 1642, tomahawked for making the Sign of the Cross on a young Indian's forehead. At that same place, St. Isaac Jogues and St. Jean Lalande, a lay *Donné*,[4] were martyred also. The Missionaries left and the cause seemed lost. But on that soil, in that place, the Lord was to plant the seeds of Evangelization into the blood-soaked earth, which would grow into what would be the first Native American Blessed *Kateri Tekakwitha*, the Lily of the Mohawks, the Mystic of the Wilderness. And when she is canonized, finally brought into the Communion of Saints, she will be the first Native American, first fruit of the North American Martyrs.

Kateri is born - the Seed Bears Fruit

The Lord moves in great sweeping motions when He wants to accomplish something. The fruit of the Martyrs had to be a strong focus of the Lord from before the death of the Martyrs. In Trois-Rivieres, today a part of French Canada, in the province of Quebec, a young Indian Maiden of the Algonquin tribe was raised under the mantle of the French Jesuits. She was baptized in Trois-Rivieres and lived with French settlers for a time. When the Jesuits pulled their missions back to Quebec in 1649, as a result of violent raids by the Iroquois and the outrageous executions of the Blackrobe missionaries, the Algonquins were left on their own and came under the domination of the Iroquois. Kateri's mother was taken prisoner and brought down the Mohawk river with the rest of the Indian captives. She landed in Ossernenon, a beautiful Mohawk village in what is today, Auriesville, in upstate New York.

It was in Ossernenon that she met her husband, a chief of one

---

[4]Donné - French for a lay volunteer to the Jesuits. Most were people who wanted a religious life and wanted to work in the missions but didn't feel the calling to the priesthood.

of the villages. They married, and settled down there. Now, we have to remember that Kateri's mother was as much a captive as she was the wife of the chief. Nothing is known about her relationship with her husband or the people of the village. She was a foreigner, who spoke a different language, and had different customs. We're sure that she was not able to practice her Christian religion, because the Blackrobes had not yet returned to this area. How she must have grieved, especially over the loss of her Lord Jesus in the Eucharist.

She and her husband had two children, Kateri, born in 1656, and her younger brother. They lived a comparatively peaceful life in Ossernenon. Her mother tried to impart in the children at least the virtues of Christianity, if not the actual beliefs of the Faith, to the best of her understanding. She also tried to incorporate the teachings of the Church with the positive values of her Indian background, even though her Algonquin beliefs varied somewhat from the Iroquois or Mohawk.

Kateri was a beautiful child, possessing the best features of both mother and father. She was very loved by her parents, and respected as the daughter of a chief of the village. But all that was to come to an end swiftly when she was about four years old. A deadly epidemic of Smallpox erupted, and swept through the village like wildfire. It had no respect for age, sex or position. Kateri's mother died first, then her brother and her father. Kateri's mother had always prayed for the baptism of her children, and possibly they were baptized with the Baptism of Desire. But in her lifetime, Kateri's mother did not see her children officially baptized. Kateri's brother was never baptized. It would be 16 years after her mother's death that her prayer for Kateri would be finally answered.

After the death of her family, the most difficult period of Kateri's life began. She was taken in by her uncle, her father's brother, who was made head chief of the village. However, as much as he loved Kateri, the uncle's personality was different from Kateri's father, from what she could *remember* of her father. Her actual upbringing was put in the hands of various aunts who loved her as a relative, but they were definitely not her mother.

The Smallpox epidemic had devastated the village and Kateri personally. In addition to losing her family, she was permanently scarred from the disease. Her face, beautiful before the Smallpox hit her, became extremely pockmarked. Her eyesight was severely affected to the point of being almost blind for the rest of her life. She walked with her head down, mostly to protect her eyes from the sunlight, but also because she couldn't see clearly in front of her. It worked out to her favor after her baptism as she then walked in this manner, as an expression of humility. It was because of this condition that she was called Tekakwitha. Her uncle looked at her as she struggled to walk around, in the early days after her eyesight was affected. He called her Tekakwitha, which means literally *"She pushed with her hands."* But Tekakwitha has a very special meaning among the Mohawks. It means the *ideal woman, one who works hard and keeps everything in good order: a prudent, industrious, provident, loving wife and mother.* The chief didn't know it, but he was prophesying about the qualities Kateri would possess when the Lord put her to work for the Kingdom.

Ossernenon was considered an evil omen to the villagers. It had been the scene of almost total destruction to the people there. Everywhere they looked, they could see in their minds' eyes the bodies of loved ones who had died from the epidemic. In addition, Smallpox was still ravaging the tribe. The chiefs determined it was best to leave Ossernenon, because evil spirits were there.

Her uncle, as main chief of the village, supervised the building of the new village, with the *palisades*[5] for protection and the *longhouses*[6] for living. They chose a spot on a hill facing the river, about a mile to the west of Ossernenon. It was called

---

[5]spiked logs, forming a high fence around the entire complex

[6]Indian form of communal living. A longhouse was a dwelling for anywhere from thirty to forty people, all from one family, sort of an extended family living set-up.

Caughnawaga,[7] which meant "by the rapids." In addition to being very beautiful, it was a very strategic location. From this vantage point, they could see their enemies approaching. This is where Kateri spent her childhood.

When she was seven or eight, our little Saint was taught the basic duties of an Indian woman. She was required to go out and pick up dry wood for firewood, which was stacked outside the longhouse in anticipation of the cold weather and snow. She drew water from the stream and ground the corn for the favorite meal of the people, *Sagamite*.[8]

She was taught all the Indian crafts: how to make beads, how to make leather shoes and clothes from hides. She did all the tasks an Indian child would have done in those days. But perhaps the most important job she was trained for was *marriage*. The women who were involved in her upbringing most likely had her wear beautiful buckskin clothes with beaded ornaments, to let any prospective suitor know she was the daughter of a chief of the clan. Getting a girl married was of the utmost importance, not only so that she would not become an old maid, but also for the well-being and survival of the Community.

Kateri knew this, but she did not feel the same way her relatives did about marriage. She didn't know why at the time; she only knew she didn't see herself as being married. The Lord had planted a seed in her heart from her mother, and it would bloom at the proper time.

The Word of God is taught to the Indians

The Indians and the French went through a series of battles against each other, one time the Indians winning, next time the French winning. Peace Pacts were signed, only to be broken by Mohawk raiding parties. The Indian Community, i.e, the council of Indians, did not really want war. They didn't want the French because most of them hated the French. But they didn't want the

---

[7]Today the village is called Fonda, New York, site of the National Shrine to Blessed Kateri Tekakwitha.

[8]Ground corn, seasoned with dried fish, meat, oil and other seasonings

constant threat of invasion hovering over them, either.
Nevertheless, individual chiefs, like Kateri's uncle, loved to go
out and raid French camps. It was fine when they were victorious,
but when the French finally had had enough of it, they brought
together all their heavy artillery and attacked the Indians with all
their force. Kateri's beautiful little village of Caughnawaga was
devastated by one of those attacks.

There were so many French soldiers, and they marched with
such strength and confidence that the Mohawk chiefs fled at the
sight of them, running for their lives. Kateri and the other women
of the village fled in another direction to avoid being captured, and
God knows what else at the hands of the enemy. The magnificent
village was burned to the ground, after all the food stores had
been used by the French. The chiefs of the village were petrified.
They immediately asked for peace. They sent gifts to the French
leaders and asked for terms of peace - including Jesuit Blackrobes
to be sent into various villages. When the French heard this, they
knew the Indians meant business; they acted immediately.

Three Jesuits were sent on this mission, Frs. Jacques Frémin,
Jean Pieron, and Jacques Bruyas. They were accompanied by
Donnés - Charles Boquet, and Francois Poisson. They were
supposed to go to the village of *Tionnontoguen*,[9] which was the
most important village in the Mohawk Community. But they
were detoured to the village of Caughnawaga, where they met
Kateri Tekakwitha. The Indian reasoning behind the detour was
that there had been a big drinking party going on in Tionnontoguen,
and the chiefs were not in any condition to receive the Jesuits.
They felt that by sending them first to Caughnawaga, they would
have some extra time to prepare for a *well-planned* ceremonious
welcome. The chiefs were so frightened of another war, they
wanted nothing to spoil this peace gesture.

That was their thinking and their reasoning, but it was not

---

[9]Modern-day Albany, in upstate New York

God's plan. He wanted Kateri to meet these Jesuits, especially Fr. Frémin who would have a lasting effect on her spiritual life. When the Blackrobes came into the village, little Kateri, who was eleven years old at the time, was given charge of taking care of their needs. She was able to observe them at close range for the entire length of their visit. She made their meals. She observed them as they went around the village, ministering to the Christian Huron prisoners who were there. She watched as they set up a longhouse as a chapel and prayed there. They spent much time in prayer. She commented later in life how this influenced her, how gentle they were, how sensitive and kind.

She was also able to perceive the workings of the Blackrobes in another woman of the village, who had a great desire to be baptized. When the priests came to the village, she asked to be brought into the Church. Fr. Frémin said he would give her instructions and baptize her at a later date. She asked if at least her son, who had never sinned, could be baptized. They agreed and the child was baptized. The woman went through great struggles learning enough about the Faith to be baptized. But finally she was ready, and Fr. Frémin baptized her.

No sooner did Fr. Frémin baptize her than the woman's *real* struggles began. Her husband died. His family blamed it on the new religion she had embraced. They began to mistreat her terribly. Then her son took ill. The family harangued her even more. Then she contracted a disease where her body and eyes swelled so badly that she couldn't see and she could hardly walk. Yet through all of this, she maintained her faith. Her husband's family now accused her of trying to kill herself. They taunted her with: It was not bad enough she killed her husband by embracing the new Faith; now she was going to kill herself, and who would take care of her child?

This dear lady suffered this persecution until she could escape from the grip of her husband's family. Then she went to a Huron convert who knew a remedy for her swelling. In a few months, her body and eyes were well. Through all of this she never stopped believing in her Lord Jesus, nor did she stop teaching her four-year old son his prayers and the teachings of the Church.

Kateri made the acquaintance of this lady and marveled at her faith in the face of so much conflict. She never believed that her Faith or her God had anything to do with her problems. She always believed that He would take care of her and deliver her from her affliction. What is amazing is that although the faith of this woman and her love for Jesus and the Church impressed Kateri so much, it did not give her the desire to go to the priests and ask to be taught about the Faith. It was not time yet. When it would happen, Kateri would be ready.

Kateri was in a difficult position. She was the *daughter* of a chief and the *niece* of a chief. Her uncle hated the Christians and the Jesuits. Because of the political situation, he had to be courteous and tolerant of the Blackrobes, but it was a cold, hateful tolerance. He had to allow them to build their chapel in one of the longhouses; he had to stand by and allow his people to be evangelized by these men. But he was not happy about it. He would just as soon have taken them captive, tortured them the way he and his tribe tortured their enemies, and kill them. He couldn't, because the Mohawks had to maintain peace with the French.

But one thing Kateri's uncle could do was to make sure the Christian message, the acceptance of *"Iesos Christos"* (Jesus Christ) as Savior and God, did not invade his household. No one from his longhouse was allowed to take part in any of the Christian activities that went on with the Blackrobes. Kateri had such a longing to learn about the Catholic Faith! All she knew about it was what her aunt Anastasia, who was Christian, shared with her about her mother, how she had been baptized into the Faith, and had always wanted Kateri and her brother to be baptized.

Kateri recalled the time she had been given the privilege to be with the Blackrobes the first time they came to the village. She listened to them pray. She recalled the words of Fr. Bruyas as he responded to her uncle's welcome speech, when they first came:
"The true God is the Father of all men, the red as
well as the white. He loves all human beings; and everyone

- man, women and child - may speak to Him, for He hears
every whisper and sees what is in every heart."

These words never left Kateri. She prayed, possibly for the
first time to the Great Spirit, *"O God, help me to know You and*
to love You." The seed had been planted; it would have to be
nurtured and grow.

Young people would go to the Chapel longhouse for
teachings about Jesus, the Saints, and the truths of our Church.
She couldn't wait to eavesdrop when they returned. What had
the Lord taught them through the Blackrobes? Kateri circulated
among the groups of young natives, listening to their excited
sharing, but she was not able to be part of it. She yearned to learn
about the Faith, but she knew her uncle would be really upset if
she had anything to do with the Blackrobes. Kateri's aunts knew
his will, and watched her carefully, to be sure she didn't get involved
in what was going on with those studying with the Jesuits.

Kateri retreated into herself. She became quieter than she
had been; she became more removed from everyone in the village.
All she wanted was to learn about the Lord, and she wasn't
allowed to, so she stayed by herself. Her aunts thought she was
lonely, and needed to find a spouse, so she could get married.
She wasn't getting any younger. She was fourteen or fifteen at
this time. They couldn't take the chance of waiting until she was
in her twenties. She would then be considered an old maid and
would have become a source of shame and embarrassment to the
family. So the aunts started a campaign to get Kateri married.
This was definitely not what she wanted.

Marriage was a casual thing with the Indians. There were
many ways in which a boy and girl would be married. Sometimes,
they were given to each other as children. Then as they grew up,
they lived together. Then there were those married couples who
lived separately for long periods of time, or even permanently.
One form of making a marriage arrangement was when a brave
would be chosen by the girl. Then he and his family would be
advised that she wanted to marry him. If they accepted, a date

was made. Prior to their marriage, the boy and girl would not communicate with each other. On the day of the wedding, the boy and his family would come to the girl's longhouse. He would be seated, and the girl would serve him sagamite, the favorite food of the Mohawks. If she served it and he accepted and ate it, they were married.

On this one particular occasion, Kateri came in from the fields, and was told to dress in her finest clothing *immediately*. She assumed her aunts had invited someone important for dinner. After all, her uncle was the chief. She did as she was told. She also made the sagamite. In time, a handsome young brave walked into the longhouse. He was introduced to Kateri. She was very polite. She thought something was peculiar when he sat next to her rather than in one of the other places. Her aunts told her to feed the brave. This was a natural thing for her to do. She always took care of serving guests at the house. So she got up to prepare and serve the brave his dinner.

She had the food in her hand and was walking over towards the brave when something hit her. We know it was the Holy Spirit or her Guardian Angel. Kateri realized what was happening, what she was doing. If she had given the food to the brave and he ate it, she would be married. She immediately ran out of the longhouse, threw the food on the ground, and ran into the woods. Her aunts were furious! They ran after her but to no avail. Kateri was nowhere to be seen. The brave did not get married that night.

Kateri answers the Call to Jesus

Kateri felt the call of Jesus more and more compellingly. But she couldn't say anything to the priests, or to anyone for that matter, because of her uncle's animosity towards the Blackrobes and Christians. To make matters more serious, *many* of the members of the tribe were turning their lives over to Jesus. They were completely enraptured by the new way, *"the Prayer"*[10] the peace

---

[10]The Natives called the new Religion, anything that had to do with the Christian Faith, "The Prayer."

and love of Christianity. The chief became more and more concerned. In the Spring of the year, fifteen of the best braves of the village converted to Christianity and left the village to go to the Huron mission in Quebec, Notre Dame de Foy. There they could practice their Faith freely, without persecution from their fellow tribesmen.

Her uncle, and the other chiefs of the tribe now had *real* concerns. They were afraid they were losing their best men, and the tribe would dwindle down to nothing. There were only 450 braves to defend the whole nation. How much would it take to be conquered by one of the stronger tribes? Another fifty braves and their families planned to follow the other braves who had departed for Quebec. They had their canoes packed with supplies, and they were ready to go. However, the fear that they may be leaving their tribe vulnerable, unprotected in the event of an attack, made these families wait for a more expedient time. This growing momentum now made Kateri's uncle opposed to any of his people further joining the Christian movement! Naturally, he wouldn't hear anything of it in his own home.

Kateri longed to take part in the beautiful ceremonies of the Christian Community. At Christmastide the Blackrobes made a Nativity Scene, the first they had ever made in the Missions. The Indians loved the tradition and the hymns which were sung, French hymns which the Indians intoned in their own language. It was beautiful. But Kateri could not be part of it. She didn't have the confidence to go to Fr. Boniface, or Fr. Bruyas, who were there during her teenage years. She had no relationship with them and feared to speak to them, because of her uncle. But in midsummer of 1675, Kateri's nineteenth year, a new Blackrobe came upon the scene, Fr. Jacques de Lamberville. When Kateri saw him, she knew that she could talk to this priest. He had a great deal of sensitivity and was very gentle with the Indians.

But still she hesitated. The Lord knew that if this was ever going to happen, if Kateri were to become the sign and symbol of the Church among the Indians, He was going to have to make it happen. So one day, while Fr. de Lamberville was making his rounds of the longhouses, he passed by Kateri's. He knew the women of the longhouse would be out in the field working; they were so industrious. So he first passed by the longhouse without entering. But then, a few yards away, he thought to himself that there might be a sick person in the longhouse who would need his attention. So he picked up the flap and entered.

There, to his surprise, he saw Kateri lying on her mat. She had injured her foot and wasn't able to go out into the fields with the other women. She wasn't able to walk very well at this time. As soon as she saw Fr. de Lamberville, she got up. She had never dared to go to any of the priests before; but now, since the priest had come to her, and no one else was in the longhouse, she opened herself to him. She poured out her entire heart, sharing how she longed to learn about the Catholic Faith, and how she wanted to be a Catholic. The priest could see from their very first interview how powerfully the Holy Spirit would work through this girl. But he brought her along very gently, very slowly, so that she could absorb all that was to be learned about the Faith.

As soon as her foot healed, Kateri began going to the Chapel to receive instructions from the priest. Strangely, or according to the Will of God, her aunts did not stop her from going to the chapel to learn about the Faith. Actually, the aunts were believers; but they were so very afraid of the uncle, they had to be extremely cautious about mentioning Catholicism.

This was the beginning of the most beautiful part of Kateri's life. Everything she had ever experienced was in anticipation of this time. She loved the teachings of the Church, about the Saints and the Angels, about the Eucharist, and our Lady. Kateri found a mother in our Lady. She immediately fell in love with her. She couldn't hear enough about Mother Mary. Remember, she had lost her natural mother at an early age. She had not known the warmth and tenderness of a mother's love for fifteen years. Now, she was given the Mother of God as her mother! Kateri derived great strength in and through Mary. It was important for her, and actually for the rest of the women of the tribe, that there be a woman who was a powerful sign in the Church. For Kateri, Mary was that sign.

In December, 1675, a Miraculous statue of Our Lady was brought from Dinant, Belgium, to Canada. She was called Notre Dame de Foy. The statue was found carved in the middle of a giant oak tree. It was given to the Blackrobes in Canada. When Fr. Bruyas received it in an other mission, *Tionnontoguen*, he installed it with great pomp and ceremony. He began the unveiling ceremony on the Feast of the Immaculate Conception. Then, for the next few Saturdays, he unveiled the statue again and again.

The people of the village testified that a strong surge of spirituality went through the Community as soon as the statue of Our Lady was brought to them. Prior to this time, while there had been a great deal of success in the evangelization of Tionnontoguen, there remained many who were violently against the Faith. Once the statue of Our Lady showed her strength in the parish, a great deal of piety blanketed the village. Those who had criticized the new Belief found themselves as converts, asking to be accepted into the Church. People from all over the area came to Tionnontoguen to pray the Rosary in front of the statue of Notre Dame de Foy. They had to walk ten to fifteen miles each way to take part in this rosary, and during cold weather! Nevertheless, they came. New converts blossomed, as well as an infusion of renewed, more powerful spirituality among the older converts. Kateri was among those who made this pilgrimage to the shrine of Our Lady. For her, it was an extra special sacrifice, in that she was walking in the cold, with poor eyesight which was extremely sensitive to sunlight and snow. She couldn't look up, and she couldn't look down. But she persevered; she would not have missed it for anything.

Kateri was a vibrant example of how a convert should be. She embraced everything she could regarding the Faith. At Christmastide, she stayed by the Nativity scene as long as she could. She absorbed everything the Church had to give her. She was so eager to be baptized, she looked as if she would burst with joy. Father de Lamberville was as excited as she; he couldn't help it. Her piety and reverence were infectious. However, although anxious to bring this special child of God into the Church, Father waited and went through many formal procedures. But he couldn't see Kateri waiting the two years, normally required for Catechumens to be baptized. He decided that Easter Sunday, April 5, 1676, would be the perfect day for her Baptism, as it was the most important day in the Church calendar.

The ceremony was glorious! Father baptized Kateri and two other converts at the same time. Almost the entire village turned out for the ceremony. Kateri waited with baited breath while the priest asked the questions just prior to her baptism. As is traditional, the catechumens waited outside the church. The priest came to the door, and asked Kateri,

"Catherine,[11] *what do you ask of the Church of God?"*

"Faith," she answered with a firm voice.

"What will Faith give you?"

"Eternal life."

"If you wish to enter eternal life, observe the commandments, love the Lord God with all your heart, with all your soul and with all your mind and your neighbor as yourself."

Fr. de Lamberville then took his stole, placed half of it on Kateri's shoulder and the other half remained on his. The two of them walked into the Church together, the stole on each of their shoulders.

Kateri knelt. She was overcome with emotion. She prayed the Creed, and the Our Father. The priest then went into the sacristy and changed from his purple vestments for Lent to white for purity, with a cope[12] for adult baptism. He stood over Kateri. Her eyes

---

[11]She took the name Catherine, after St. Catherine of Siena, which translates to Kateri. So the name Kateri was only given to her at her baptism into the Faith.

[12]A vestment used for other ceremonies than the Mass itself, made in a semicircular shape, worn draped around the shoulders full length, and fastened in front across the upper chest by a clasp called the morse.

were filled with tears. He spoke gently but firmly to her.

"Catherine, do you renounce Satan?"

"I do," she said.

"And all his works?"

"I do."

At this, the priest took water, placed Kateri's head over the Baptismal font, poured the water on her and said the words, *"Catherine, I baptize you in the name of the Father, and of the Son, and of the Holy Spirit."* She stood up. A white veil was placed on her head. She was given a lighted candle. She stood there in the middle of the church, while a children's choir sang hymns in honor of the occasion.

But Kateri couldn't hear any of it. Her heart was about to burst. It was as if Heaven opened up before her, and she could see, in her mind's eye, a Heavenly Army of Angels gently swooping down towards her, with Our Lord Jesus, our Mother Mary, and all the Saints, especially her namesake Catherine of Siena, surrounding her, embracing her, welcoming her into the Body of Christ. She was home. She would never leave.

As if the gift of Baptism was not enough, Kateri was now going to be allowed for the first time to take part in the celebration of the Mass. As the priest came out on the altar, the voices of the choir burst into the opening hymn, *"I have risen, and I am with You, alleluia. You have laid Your hand upon me, alleluia. How wonderful it is to know You, O God, alleluia."*

Tears of joy cascaded freely down Kateri's face. She was being given the privilege of being in the presence of Our Lord Jesus, as He came down on the altar during the Consecration of the Mass. She watched as her fellow Catholics went up to the altar to receive the Body and Blood of the Savior. She longed for the day when she would too be able to receive Him in her body, though she knew it would be another four or five years, according to the Jesuit tradition.

Kateri lives the life of a Catholic

Life was so exciting for Kateri. Each day she learned something new about the Church. If it wasn't about our Lady, it was about the Saints, or the Angels, or the Eucharist. She became completely absorbed in her new Faith. Her life was one of great peace and involvement in the Christian activities of the village. Prior to her Baptism, she had been a rose in the shadows, hidden in her longhouse, never being able to show her great love for Jesus. Now, she bloomed into a model convert for the Community.

The Blackrobes were able to use this outstanding example of Christianity to show those in the village who had converted in name only, taking on the mantle of Christianity but practicing their pagan ways the same as they had before their conversion. Fr. de Lamberville pointed to Kateri, and those who had gone back to their old ways were reconverted, back to the promises they had made to Jesus and the Church.

Kateri was radiant. With all her pock marks and her difficulty in seeing, she was so filled with the love of Jesus that she beamed. People couldn't get close enough to her. Everyone jockeyed for position to be closer to her during church services, just to feel the warmth of her aura. She exemplified the living Christian, as she participated faithfully in the Mass, prayer, instructions, fasting and abstinence. These were mandatory. She embraced them with such joy that her brothers and sisters in Christ didn't consider them obligations when they were in her presence. They were more like gifts, given them by the Lord.

At the beginning, she lived in comparative peace. Even her family allowed her to take part in her newfound Faith. They would never call her Kateri however, which was her Christian name. They only referred to her as Tekakwitha, her Indian name. They probably were not aware what an effect she was having on the whole Community. But little by little, word got back, especially to her uncle, how she was turning those who had left back to the Faith. Braves who had converted to the Faith were leaving the village and moving to the Mission of Francis Xavier where they could practice their religion in peace. So the flames of anger built up in Kateri's uncle and were aimed at her.

She became the model of purity and modesty, which was a cause of conflict between her and the Community. Fr. Pierre Cholenec, who later became her spiritual director, wrote about her. He praised Kateri's firm commitment to purity and virtue. He said,

> *"I have found more than thirty people whom she helped to get back on the right road; among others, she delivered several from violent temptations of the flesh and obtained for them the gift of chastity. It is mostly in this area that she has worked wonders for souls."*

Kateri had always been a hard worker, as was everyone in her longhouse. Now, however, she would not work on Sunday or Holy Days. She went to the chapel where she attended Mass as often as possible, prayed the Rosary, and took part in any devotional practices available. Her aunts, who had never been strong Christians, began to become annoyed with this behavior. They berated her, calling her lazy. They criticized her newfound Christianity as having been the reason she no longer did her duties in the longhouse. They tried to change her by not leaving any food for her on the days when she went to the chapel. This had become a standard practice among Indians with those who had converted, and went to chapel instead of work. They tried to starve them out if they wouldn't change their ways.

Kateri put up with all the insults and degradations, her family had to give her. That only made it worse. The more she accepted the denunciations, the more they piled them on. Within a short period of time, the persecution which had originally been imposed on her only by her family spread throughout the entire village. *Everybody* began taunting her. Little children pointed fingers at her; the local medicine men, called jugglers,[13] as well as the women and drunks made fun of her. They called her "Christian" in the

---

[13]They performed ritual dances.

tone they would use to call her "bitch," according to Fr. Chauchetière, another of her biographers. She felt a great joy at being singled out to suffer for the Name of Jesus.

But the situation became out of control. Her uncle once sent a warrior into her longhouse with a tomahawk. No one knew for sure if he wanted her killed or just frightened. But when the warrior stormed into the longhouse, with tomahawk poised to come down on her head, Kateri just bowed her head in acceptance of the Will of God. This shook her attacker so, he stopped in his tracks and ran out of the longhouse, never to return.

Kateri had been spared this time, but Fr. de Lamberville feared for her life and for her spiritual well-being. The situation was getting worse and worse in the village. She was too much of a sign of the Lord Jesus in their presence. Either the Indians loved her with a passion or hated her with a vengeance. So Father suggested she leave Caughnawaga and go to the Mission of St. Francis Xavier, the *"Village of Prayer"* in Montreal. Although she was initially stunned by the idea of leaving her home and her family, she soon came to realize that she was no longer part of this family. She had already given them up when she became a member of the family of Christ.

Once she got used to the idea, Kateri really began to look forward to her move. She came to desire it with all her heart. A plan was conceived by her adopted sister and her husband, who had left Caughnawaga some time ago to live in the Village of Prayer, which had by this time moved to a section of Montreal called Kahnawake. Her sister's husband enlisted the help of a powerful Indian convert, called *"Hot Ashes"* and another volunteer, a Huron convert. Together, the three men set out for Caughnawaga to rescue Kateri.

When they arrived at Caughnawaga, the men went to the longhouse of Fr. de Lamberville. Immediately, they were surrounded by Christians who wanted to hear about the Village of Prayer. Hot Ashes shared the beauty and tranquility, they had known there. He talked to Fr. de Lamberville about how to get Kateri out of the village. The priest was happy that they had come to take her away. They worked together on a plan. Once they had determined the plan, Kateri's brother-in-law went to visit her secretly. He told her of the plan to get her out of the village, to go and live with them in Canada. Hot Ashes was going on to preach to his people in Oneida, so his place on the canoe was reserved for Kateri. All the men had to do was steal her away from the village.

Now you may be wondering why all the secrecy in getting Kateri out of the village. Remember, for whatever it was worth, she *was* the niece of the chief. He was vehement about losing any of his people to the prayer village in Canada. But the idea of his *niece* leaving would be more than he could have taken. The disgrace would have been too much. So the rescuers knew they had to do it in a clandestine manner. They waited until the middle of the night. Then they came for Kateri. They made an animal sound which had been predetermined. Although she was very tired, she jolted out of her sleep, put a blanket over her shoulders, and quietly left the longhouse.

The three of them traveled through the night, until they came to a place where they had to *portage*[14] through the woods. The brother-in-law had to go to Schenectady to buy provisions for the trip. Kateri and the Huron waited at a prearranged place for him. What no one knew was that the feared uncle was also in Schenectady selling skins to the Dutch. When news of Kateri's disappearance became known in Caughnawaga, the fastest-running brave was sent to Schenectady to tell the uncle that she had been kidnapped. The brave arrived shortly after the brother-in-law, whom the uncle had never met. The brother-in-law got his provisions and left immediately to warn Kateri and the Huron convert that the uncle had found out what had happened.

The uncle loaded his musket with three shells to kill anyone

---

[14]lift the canoe over their heads, and travel on land for a distance - from the French verb, Porter, which means to carry.

who had kidnapped his niece, and maybe *even* his niece, Kateri. The chief set out to find them. He knew what path they would have taken. He was right. Kateri's brother-in-law was aware, he would be coming after them, and he would be much faster then they. The chief didn't have to carry provisions and was not slowed down by Kateri, who could not walk as fast as her uncle. So the brother-in-law made a plan. Kateri and the Huron convert were to walk half a mile ahead of him. When the uncle finally caught up with him, he would pretend to be a Mohawk hunter in the woods. He would fire a shot which would warn them that the uncle was coming. They were then to hide out in the stumps of trees off the road, until the uncle passed them. Then the brother-in-law would catch up with them, and they would continue on until they approached the river where they would canoe up to Canada.

Everything worked exactly as planned. The uncle walked quickly and caught up to the brother-in-law who shot into the trees, as if he were trying to kill a squirrel. The uncle asked if he had seen two men and a woman walking this way. The brother-in-law pretended he didn't understand what the uncle was talking about. He was dismissed by the uncle as an idiot, and the uncle continued onward. Kateri and the Huron had hidden in the brush as per their agreement. They saw the uncle pass them by. Shortly after, the brother-in-law joined them. They all continued on their journey to the Village of Prayer in Kahnawake, Canada.

Everything went smoothly, according to plan - except for one thing, the internal turmoil going on inside Kateri. No one considered that Kateri was leaving her homeland, a place where she had lived all her twenty years. She loved this Mohawk valley, so breathtakingly beautiful. She would miss the river and the streams. She would even miss her family, although they had been extremely cruel to her. She thought about what she was giving up; then she thought about what she was getting in return. She turned herself over to Our Lord Jesus completely. Kateri was truly a pilgrim. She had no place to call her own, no place to lay her head. She was a pilgrim journeying through this life, on her way to Heaven.

Kateri's new life among the Christians

The trip to the new world, Kateri's new Jerusalem, was breathtaking. Even with her limited vision, she saw rolling green hills and clear blue water, with majestic mountains in the background. She was in constant joy, in constant prayer. They headed north, from modern day Albany, up Lake Champlain, to an area across the St. Laurence River south of Montreal. About seven days after they had left Caughnawaga, they arrived at the Village of Prayer of the Mission of St. Francis Xavier.

The welcome received by Kateri at the Mission of St. Francis Xavier was not to be believed. First she had a reunion with her sister whom she had not seen for years. Then an old friend, Anastasia, who had been very close to her mother in Ossernenon, renewed her relationship with Kateri. On that day, Kateri also met many of her former villagers who had left Caughnawaga for this better life. They were so happy to see her. They knew she belonged there, that it was just a matter of time until the Lord would bring her to this place. Kateri couldn't help but notice that there was no cursing at her, no insults, no badgering, no drunkenness, none of the things she abhorred about her former home. There was one thing which was missing, for which she thanked the Great Spirit of God, and that was craven fear. She no longer felt jeopardized every time she left her longhouse. When she went to sleep at night, she did not fear that she would not be alive the next morning. She felt a great...*peace!*

When Kateri brought letters from Fr. de Lamberville to the priests at the mission, she remembered that she had met two of them when she was eleven years old, the first time they came to her village. She handed Fr. Cholenec a letter addressed to him. It read

"Catherine Tekakwitha will live at the Sault. I ask you to please take charge of directing her; it is a treasure which we are giving you, as you will soon realize. Guard it well and make it bear fruit for the glory of God and the salvation

of a soul which is certainly very dear to Him."

Fr. Cholenec commented that he had to go no further than look at the face of the child before him to know what Fr. de Lamberville was talking about. Kateri arrived at the mission in October, 1677. Some months later, during the winter of 1677, Fr. Cholenec was to write his own observations:

"There is one who walks with a limp; she is the most fervent of the whole village, I believe, and though she is cripple and always sick, she does some amazing things."

Kateri threw herself into her new life with great joy. She went to the first Mass every morning at five o'clock. In the afternoon she attended instructions for the newly converted Catholics. During the day, she worked at a job, just like all the other members of the Community. She collected firewood and hauled water from the stream to the longhouse. She crushed the corn, cooked meals and served the dinner. Kateri also made moccasins, and decorated clothing with multicolored wampum. She did all of this with great delight.

But her happiest time was in the chapel, in front of the Blessed Sacrament. She *longed* to receive the Body and Blood of Our Lord Jesus in the Eucharist. She prayed to Our Lady to make the time go faster, so that she could have her Son inside her heart. The Jesuits gave a solid, well-organized program of religious instruction before a newly baptized Christian could receive Our Lord Jesus in the Eucharist. It usually took five years. Kateri had been baptized just over a year and a half. She went to all the instructions. In addition, she had her mother's old friend Anastasia, who had been a Christian for over thirty years, to instruct her in areas she didn't understand and was too shy to ask the priests. Anastasia proved to be an exceptional teacher for Kateri.

Kateri gathered enough courage to go to her priest Fr. Cholenec and meekly whisper that she longed to receive Our Lord Jesus in Communion. He looked at her with such love. He knew how special she was and what a strong personal relationship she had with Jesus. This gift of receiving Him inside her body should not be held back from her any longer. He smiled, and told her she would receive First Holy Communion on Christmas Day. It was the beginning of Advent, just a few short weeks away.

Kateri prepared for this first physical encounter with her Lover and Savior more than she had ever prepared for anything in her life. She fasted from any food or drink all day until evening on every Wednesday and Friday during Advent. She brought her meals to the sick people in the village. She went to Mass every day, received instruction, stayed for the Rosary at night, and then after the others had left, she stayed for personal prayer with her Lord. Because of her poor eyesight, Kateri pulled the blanket over her head, so that the brightness of the lights would not disturb or distract her.

On Christmas Eve, Kateri received the Sacrament of Reconciliation. What a great gift this was for her. She had never experienced the release afforded her after she told her sins to her priest. She admitted her unworthiness, everything she thought she might have done wrong at any time in her life. She could feel the burden of sin lifting off her shoulders. She felt lighter; she was new; she was in love with her God. She thanked Him for allowing her to receive this special gift in preparation of receiving her Lord in Holy Communion.

Then the time came. Midnight Mass and Christmas Eve was a special time for Kateri, as it was for the entire Community. She always looked forward to celebrating the Birth of her Jesus. But today, *this day*, Christmas Day, 1678, had to be the most important day of her life. She waited as the hours ticked by. She spent most of her time in prayer. Her mentor Anastasia recommended she wear fancy wampum jewelry for the occasion. But Kateri wanted nothing to disturb or interfere with this first meeting with the Lord. She wore a plain garment, without any ornamentation. It was just her and Jesus.

We believe that this time, when she first received Our Lord Jesus in the Eucharist on her tongue, Kateri experienced her first ecstasy. It actually lasted in some form the entire length of

Christmas Day. She was in union with her God, *in Communion with her God* through the consecrated hands of her priest. She stayed in the church those first few hours of Christmas with her Jesus. She was in a dreamlike state, filled with the joy of Jesus. She spent the rest of the day as one floating on a cloud. She radiated as she went through the village, bringing food to the sick, and special Christmas presents to those she loved so dearly. Towards the end of the day, Kateri returned to the church to be with her Lord again in quiet time. As she spent the last hour of the day with Him, Kateri could feel herself being lifted up to the heights of Heaven. She could feel the strong, gentle Arms of our Lord Jesus embrace her mystically. She did not want to come back to earth. She held onto Him in the Eucharist. She would not be allowed to receive Him again until Easter Sunday, which was four long months away.

There is a tradition in the Indian culture which coincides with the end of the Liturgical year. After Christmas, the tribe would go out to the wilderness for a three month winter hunt. At this time, they would live out of tents and bring enough provisions into the Community to last them through the Spring. The whole family went on these hunts - husbands, wives and children. It was the same with the Christian Community. Kateri was hesitant about going because she wanted to be near the Chapel for Daily Mass. However, her spiritual director advised her to go, and so she went. She kept the discipline which she always followed in the village. Since there was no Mass celebrated on the hunt, Kateri went off by herself to pray during the time when Mass would be celebrated at the camp. She practiced forms of discipline, such as flagellation, and spent much time during the night in prayer.

An unfortunate incident occurred during this, her last hunting trip. One of the men had been hunting all day. He came back late at night. The fire had gone out and vision was at best difficult. When he came in, he didn't bother to eat anything. He just dropped where he was, out of exhaustion, and went to sleep. The next morning, his wife was looking for him, because he hadn't been with her all night. She saw her husband sleeping next to Kateri's mat. She had never had any trouble with him. He was a good husband, very faithful. But perhaps, she thought, he might have sinned with Kateri. She was not a pretty girl, because of her pockmarked face, but she was so sweet and innocent. Perhaps her husband had taken a shine to her.

The woman didn't say anything, but waited until the hunting trip was over, and they had returned to the village. She went to the priest, Fr. Cholenec, and accused Kateri of committing adultery with her husband. She had seen Kateri leave the camp quietly every day for an hour. She thought she was having a rendezvous with her husband.

In addition to speaking to the priest, the woman also told Kateri's spiritual mother Anastasia, who then had a talk with Kateri. She vaguely made references to familiarity with a married man. Kateri had no idea what she was talking about, but just sat and listened. At the end of the conversation, Kateri just walked away confused.

The major problem in this whole incident was that the woman who had made the complaint was a holy and pious woman, and everyone knew that, so the priest could not take her grievance lightly. He called in Kateri and asked her in veiled terms, if she had done what the woman charged. Kateri didn't understand fully what he was intimating, but she knew she had not even talked to a man, so she just denied the charges. What the priest was asking her was the same as Anastasia had! The priest, not satisfied with the sincerity of her answers, asked her to think about it and come back in three days.

During that time, other women in the village heard the story, and all were against Kateri. Even Anastasia asked her to repent what she had done. Kateri became very distressed, which only provided added further credence, to the gossips of the village, that she had admitted her guilt and had been admonished by the priest. Kateri spent a very sad three days. At the end of that time, she went back to the priest. She said she had done nothing wrong.

He asked her if she had stolen away every afternoon, so that the women would not see her. Kateri responded that she had. The priest was taken back by her answer.

"Did you meet someone out in the woods?"

"Yes, Father, I spoke to someone in the forest, but not a human. I prayed to God out there." With this, she broke down in tears. Then she shared about how she had done her hour of devotions in the forest.

As far as the priest was concerned, she had exonerated herself. But Kateri continued,

"I beg you, Father, not to tell anyone what I did when I stole away from the women. I would rather be suspected than have my sweet secret revealed and talked about in the whole village."

She composed herself and added, *"If you wish to check on the truth of the story, you will find a cross I cut into the bark of that tree."*

Fr. Cholenec respected her wishes and told the outraged wife that he had investigated the complaint, and that she had nothing to be concerned about. But he didn't tell her why. She held onto her suspicion, as did other women in the village, because the priest didn't tell any of them either. But as time went on, and Kateri continued to be Kateri, the women rejected any possibility she could have done anything wrong. As a matter of fact, after Kateri's death, and the barrage of miracles which immediately followed, the woman who had accused Kateri pleaded with God *openly* to forgive her for ever having doubted Kateri.

For Kateri, this was just one more skin to shed. At first she was very hurt, mostly by the priest, thinking he didn't believe her. When wounded, she shared with the Lord that she had given up everything - home and country, marriage, everything for Him, did the Lord say, *"Will you give this up to Me, also, your reputation and your honor? Will you give up all for Me?"*

Kateri was achieving unity with the Lord through *Infused*

Knowledge.[15] She was not a learned girl. What instructions she received from the Blackrobes were not of an advanced spiritual nature, such as she was experiencing. She had to get it directly from God, as did her namesake Catherine of Siena received it, by infused knowledge. Kateri moved through levels of the mystical life. She had gone through the first, *personal* special relationship; then the level of purging herself, *shedding* everything that was not of God, or which would not lead her to God; and finally the level of union, *unity with God*, a Mystical Marriage with Jesus. From that level, there is only one place to go, to Paradise.

Kateri's commitment to the Lord

Kateri had an ongoing battle with almost everyone in the village about Marriage, including her sister, her adopted aunt Anastasia, and even the priest Fr. Cholenec. They all insisted she get married. It came to a head when her sister became very upset with Kateri and called the priest to talk sense into Kateri. The logic was that Kateri was a drain on the sister and her husband, because she was an extra mouth to feed and clothe and shelter. She should have set up her own family by this time. Kateri insisted she would eat very little, and she had plenty of clothes. She went to the priest and proclaimed her desire to keep herself for Jesus only.

To this end, she asked to be able to take a formal vow of virginity, to which the priest agreed. However, Father said it would have to take place on the Feast of the Annunciation, March 25, 1679, and she would have to prepare herself for this. Because of her bad experiences on the winter hunt, Kateri was given permission by the priest to remain behind in the camp. In this way, she was allowed to go to Mass daily, and receive Communion often. She spent hours on her knees in church in meditation, after having received Communion. She practiced many forms of mortification and penance, in order to purify her body and soul for the great event of March 25th. When the long-awaited moment

---

[15]Knowledge given her directly from the Holy Spirit

came, she was in ecstasy. She was the first Native American to take the vow of Virginity. From that time on, Kateri lived the life of a nun, even though she never entered a religious Community. Kateri advanced far beyond any of her peers in spirituality. She spent all her time in communion with the Lord. But her union with the Lord, the highest form of relationship with our God possible, inflicted a heavy toll on her body. Forms of penance and mortification that she and another pious woman in the camp practiced, were impossible for the average person in their existing circumstances to pursue and survive. The toll very quickly showed itself on Kateri's face and body. Remember, she was only twenty-three years old; but her body betrayed her, reacting against the harsh punishment she had inflicted upon it. She joyfully endured her penances for the conversion of her people, the Iroquois, and in reparation for the terrible sins they had committed in the previous forty years against the Blackrobes.

From the middle of the summer of 1679, when she fought a furious fever, until Holy Week of 1680, Kateri suffered terribly. She continued with her mortifications and penance, giving herself over as victim-soul for the conversion of her people. She had taken on her shoulders, the sins of her people. A little less than three hundred years later, a Jewish sister, Blessed Edith Stein, would take the burden of the sins of her enemies, the Nazis on her shoulders. She said, *"If I don't pray and sacrifice for them, who will?"*

It was almost as if Kateri suffered the Passion of Our Lord Jesus. From Palm Sunday to Spy Wednesday, she suffered so brutally. She tried to maintain a smile for everyone who came to visit her. She gave last words of thanksgiving and encouragement to all, especially the woman who had done so much penance with her. Her last day on earth coming to an end, she summoned all the strength she had left to pray with the priest and her Community as they renewed her baptismal vows and commended her body and soul to Our Lord Jesus in Heaven. She waited until her *sisters*, other women who had taken the vows she had taken, were all in the room. Her last words, *"Jesus, Mary, I love you."* she went into her final agony. Slightly after three in the afternoon, everyone noticed a slight twitch on her mouth. Then, her entire being relaxed. She had passed over. It was Wednesday, April 17, 1680. She was twenty-four years old.

The Miracles of Kateri begin

The first miracle of Kateri Tekakwitha occurred within *fifteen minutes* after her death. Her face, which had been scarred from Smallpox from the time she was four years old, all of a sudden lost all the scars. She was transformed into the beautiful girl she had been as a child. The witness, Fr. Cholenec, who had stayed at her side to pray her into Heaven, let out a shout. He, who was not by any means one given to sensationalism, drew everyone's attention to Kateri's face, which was now magnificent and radiant.

After that, people flocked to her grave, people with all infirmities - the blind, the lame and the sick. Healings took place in mammoth proportions. After a while small packets of dirt from her grave were handed out and given credit for healings and conversions. Some testified that merely thinking of Kateri, asking for her intercession, brought about miracles.

Her first apparition came on Easter Monday, *six days* after her death. Fr. Chauchetière was praying in his room at four in the morning. Kateri appeared in front of him, surrounded by dazzling light. She didn't say anything, but he heard a voice (not hers), say in Latin, *"I appear every day."*

Fr. Chauchetière explained what happened. "The vision remained for two hours, with prophetic signs appearing on either side of Kateri. On her left, he saw a church toppled over, and on her right, an Indian tied to a post amid flames."[16]

Both of these prophesies were *fulfilled* within seven years. The first, in which the church toppled over, occurred on August 19, 1683. The second, in which he saw the Indian tied to a post

---

[16]Taken from "Kaia'tano:ron Kateri Tekahkwitha" by Fr. Henri Béchard, S.J., Page 158

Right: ***Original burial location of Bl. Kateri near Kahnawake***

Below: ***The present tomb of Bl. Kateri at her Shrine in Kahnawake near Montreal***

amid flames, referred to an Indian who was burned alive seven years later, whose name was *Stephen Tegananokoa*, the first Indian Martyr. He was followed by two heroic women, *Frances Gannonhatenha* and *Marguerite Garongouas*, also martyred.

Two days later, Kateri appeared to her instructor, Anastasia in the longhouse. In her own words,

> *"...I had barely gone to sleep when I was awakened by a voice calling me and saying, `My mother, get up and look.' I recognized Kateri's voice; I sat up at once, and turning to the direction from which the voice came, I saw her standing beside me. Her body was surrounded by such a bright light that I could only see her face, which was of extraordinary beauty. `My mother,' she added, `look*

carefully at this Cross which I am wearing. See how beautiful it is; Oh! how I loved it on earth, Oh! how I still love it in Paradise! How I wish that all those of our longhouse loved it and valued it as I did.'"

With that, Kateri disappeared.

Many apparitions and healings have taken place through the intercession of our little saint. The greatest miracle was the conversion of her people, the rush of Iroquois men and women to follow in the footsteps of this Lily of the Mohawks, our Mystic of the Wilderness, Kateri Tekakwitha. Pope John Paul II beatified Kateri on June 22, 1980. She is the first fruit nourished by the blood of the North American Martyrs. *Praise Jesus!*

St. Margaret Mary Alacoque

Mystic and Visionary of the Sacred Heart

St. Margaret Mary holding Image of Sacred Heart of Jesus

Specially chosen by the Lord to bring the Message of His Sacred Heart to His children.

"What hast thou, dust and ashes that thou canst glory!"

With these words, Our Lord called Sister Margaret Mary to humility, reminding her that she was *His*, and that renewed, more powerful devotion to His Sacred Heart was *His* will and *His* design, not hers; cautioning her, she was nothing; He is all! She was simply to say *Yes!* to Him and not become puffed up that He chose her for His will on earth. Are not His words to St. Margaret Mary, to us the Faithful as well, lest we think otherwise and fall? Did not St. Paul tell us that no one may boast; for we have faith, and are part of the Mystical Body of Christ by the Grace of God and His merciful Love.

Our Lord, the Potter, has molded us from clay, from the very beginning. No one has ever been exempt from the need of His Grace and Love. Was this not Our Lord's way of telling her and us that only two were born holy, without the stain of original sin, Our Lord Jesus and His Mother Mary? Is He not reminding us that even the Saints, Visionaries, Mystics and Stigmatists were sinners, subject to Him and His laws? Is He not trying to teach us that they were just souls who fell in love with the Lord, simply brothers and sisters like us, only specially chosen by the Lord for a mission on earth? Are they not to be an example to us of what God can do with our Yes? The choice was theirs; they could have said Yes or No. Here is the story of a sinner who said *Yes* and became a Saint.

From her earliest years as a child, the Lord prepared this Mystic and future Saint for her mission, by molding her into the vessel necessary to carry out His commands. She wrote in obedience to her spiritual director the following words to her Savior:

"O my only love! How indebted I am to You for having predisposed[1] me from my earliest childhood, by becoming the Master and Possessor of my heart, although You well knew how it (my heart) would resist You! As soon as I could know myself, You made my soul see the ugliness of sin, and impressed such horror of sin upon my heart, that the slightest stain caused me unbearable torment; and to put a stop to my childish impetuousness one needed only to tell me it was offending God. This stopped me short, and kept me from doing whatever I was eager to do."

The Molding of a Saint

Step into the Lord's special helicopter and fly with us to Paray-le-Monial, a quiet little town with a great message. As we walk through the narrow streets of this quaint village nestled unobtrusively in the center of France, if we are still, we can hear Our Savior's most passionate cries. Here Our Lord will speak to our hearts just as He did to a little nun in the 17th century, over a period of 17 years. Here, in a small Chapel, Our Lord shared His Sacred Heart, wounded and bleeding, because of His Love, unreturned.

Shhh! Pause a moment! You can still feel the presence of

---

[1]to make receptive beforehand

Monastery of the Visitation Paray-le-Monial, France

Vision of the Sacred Heart of Jesus to St. Margaret Mary

Chapel inside Monastery of the Visitation at Paray-le-Monial

our Lord Jesus, as you climb up the steps to the Chapel. But not so keenly as when you enter the Chapel. He is here, a *faithful* God to an *unfaithful* people. Our Lord Who asked Margaret Mary to share His message of Love with those who had grown cold, who had traded Him in for lesser gods, He is here! You can hear Him with the ears of your heart, as He once again cries out that tremendous love that drew Him to become Man and suffer death on a Cross. He is the same God Who showed His wounded Sacred Heart to Margaret Mary, revealing the pain He feels because of the neglect and apathy of the family, for whom He suffered and died, the same One Who commissioned her to tell us that His Heart, pierced on the Cross, still bleeds out of love for us, His ungrateful children. *"My enemies placed a Crown of Thorns on My Head, My friends on My Heart."*

Be still; close off all the distractions of the world and come with us into the *real* world of Jesus Christ. According to St. Louis Marie de Montfort, it most assuredly appears that we are in the days of great Saints. If your heart's desire is to be a Saint, come with us, as we share with you, the life and visions of St. Margaret Mary Alacoque, the little nun who would suffer greatly and willingly for her Savior.

Margaret Mary consecrated herself to her Lord as His bride

Margaret Mary Alacoque was born in Charolles, a farming village bout twenty miles away from Paray-le-Monial, on July 25, 1647. Little did her family know when she was born, how powerfully the Lord would use her one day; nor did they have any idea that she was to be the instrument, He would use to bring about renewed[2] devotion to His Sacred Heart, and the nine first

---

[2]We say here *renewed devotion* to the Sacred Heart, because this devotion is found in the Gospel itself when Our Lord Jesus says: *"Take My yoke upon you and learn from Me; for I am gentle and humble of Heart and you will find rest for your souls. For My yoke is easy and My burden is light."* On the Cross, we again see Our Lord's *Heart* when It is pierced by the Centurion Longinus' sword; it is that *Sacred Heart* from which the Church sprung. When we think of the *heart*, do we not think of love, the love we have for one another? Our Lord's *Sacred Heart* was pierced on the Cross, out of love for us. Our

Fridays.

Our little future Saint was baptized three days after she was born, in the little parish church of Charolles. Between the ages of four and eight, she spent much time at her godmother's chateau. The saintly woman taught her the Faith, greatly influencing her future walk towards Jesus. At the age of four and a half, Margaret Mary made a vow of *perpetual virginity* in front of the statue of Our Lady in her godmother's garden. She later wrote:

"Without knowing what it was, I continually felt the need to say these words: 'Oh my God, I consecrate my purity to You.' Once, I said these words between the two elevations of the Holy Mass, which I usually attended on my bare knees, however cold it might be. I did not understand what I had done, or what the word 'vow' meant either, any more than what chastity meant. My only desire was to hide in some forest, and the only thing that held me back was the fear of finding people there."

Margaret Mary, first as a child and then as a young adult, spent long hours on her knees, adoring Our Lord Jesus present in the Blessed Sacrament in her far-off parish church. The first nine years of her life were filled with joy and a family steeped in spirituality, praying the Rosary and going to Mass together. But this was to come to a devastating end. When her father died, Margaret's only consolation was the Lord in the Blessed Sacrament. But even that would be denied her. After his death, her whole family was left under the control of her father's brother. As their home was jointly owned by her father and her uncle, Margaret Mary, her mother and two brothers were forced into a life of servitude, their uncle taking over full control of the property and his family treating them worse than servants.

Lord showed His *Sacred Heart* to the doubting Thomas, one of the Apostles He had chosen. Our Lord manifested His *Sacred Heart* in the Miracle of the Eucharist of Lanciano when the consecrated Host turned into a Human Heart.

By the grace of God, Margaret Mary was sent away to the Urbanist Poor Clares of Charolles, where at age nine she received First Holy Communion. She writes:

"I was placed in a house of Religious where I received Communion when I was about nine years old; this Communion made all pleasures and amusements so bitter to me that I could not enjoy any of them, even though I sought them eagerly. But when I wanted to engage in some of them with my companions, I felt something draw me away and call me into some little corner, giving me no rest until I complied. And then, it would make me pray, almost prostrate, or on my bare knees, or making genuflections, providing no one saw me. It caused me strange torment when someone saw me."

Margaret Mary was strongly influenced by the nuns, and the stories they told of the Saints at the convent school she attended. Considering all nuns to be Saints, she watched them closely, believing if she became a nun, she too would become a Saint. This special time was to end for Margaret Mary when, at eleven years of age, she became ill and had to return to her home. She was struck down by a crippling rheumatism that would confine her to the prison of her bed for the next four years. Bedridden and with no sign of relief, recovery seeming hopeless, Margaret Mary prayed to the Virgin Mary. She made a vow, if Mother Mary would intercede for her to her Son, she would someday become one of her nuns. Margaret was immediately cured! Now under our Lady's Mantle, Mary would be there for her in the difficult days ahead. She instructed Margaret in the ways and Will of her Son:

"The most Blessed Virgin Mary has always taken the greatest care of me, who turned to her in all my needs; she saved me from very great dangers. I didn't dare address myself to her Divine Son at all, but always to her, to whom I offered the little crown of the Rosary (five decades of the Rosary) kneeling on my bare knees, or genuflecting and

kissing the ground each time I said a `Hail Mary.'"

To Margaret Mary, her vow to the Blessed Mother to be one of her daughters as a nun, meant becoming a nun of the *Order of the Visitation*, because these nuns were called *"Daughters of Mary."* But nine years elapsed before she asked for admittance to the Order. What happened to the child who had made a vow to the Lord at four and a half years old, and the girl who had made a promise to Mother Mary to be one of her daughters?

As with so many of us, she was healed through the intercession of Mother Mary, and then she went about her life enjoying her great health, not paying much attention to, if even remembering, the vows she had made. But God had a plan for her and He executed it, taking away all earthly pleasures from Margaret Mary from age fifteen until she reached eighteen.

The persecution suffered by her mother at the hands of her father's family was now to be shared by Margaret Mary, with even the family's servant inflicting insults on them and taking delight in their acts of tyranny. Mother and daughter could do nothing or go nowhere without prior permission of at least three persons. Everything was under lock and key, often depriving them of something presentable to wear to go to Mass. Without any earthly consolation, Margaret Mary again turned to Jesus in the Blessed Sacrament. At that time she had no knowledge of devotion to the Sacred Heart. But even the Lord in His Real Presence was to be denied her. When one of her familial jailers agreed she could go to church and spend time with the Blessed Sacrament, the other two refused. When Margaret Mary begged to be allowed to go to Mass, she was accused of wanting to sneak off and meet young boys.

Unable to be with her Lord present on the Altar during Mass, or afterward when He awaited her in the Tabernacle, Margaret Mary went off to a secret place and stayed days on her knees, pouring out her heart to her Lord Jesus through the intercession of Mother Mary. Margaret Mary neither ate nor drank; she was so engulfed in their love and consolation, it was enough for her. But when she returned home, the recriminations began, again. The family took turns berating her, inflicting abuse upon abuse, never giving her an opportunity to say a word in her defense. They accused her of misconduct and selfishness, leaving the house, neglecting the children (the uncle's children) in her care and not doing her household duties. Crying, her heart breaking, Margaret Mary turned to her Lord on the Crucifix.

The Crucifix speaks to Margaret Mary

Our Lord told Margaret Mary He wanted to be Master of her heart; that it was only through sharing His life of suffering, she could ever be one with Him; it was only from unity with the *Cross* that she could understand the love that He had for His children which strengthened Him to endure the pain and the rejection, He suffered at their hands and from their hearts. As she came to understand the Cross, she was not only able to forgive her tormentors, she began to look forward to the pain they inflicted on her. But Our Lord was careful to remind her always that it was only through His grace that she could love them, desire to do for them and to speak kindly of them.

Margaret was to carry ongoing, *excruciating* crosses in her walk with Jesus. One of the most painful was the one ladened down by the suffering of her mother, at the hands of the family who never let up, in their pursuit of cruelty toward mother and daughter. Although Margaret Mary had through Jesus been able to grow in sanctity, achieving peace as she accepted and even welcomed the abuse *she* received at the hands of her persecutors, her mother's suffering was a pain that ripped away at her whole being. It would cause her great anguish when she would be called to choose between the Lord and His will and her mother's Purgatory on earth. Just when she thought her world could not get any more traumatic, that nothing could happen to equal the agony she endured, as she watched her mother dying inch by inch from abuse, her two brothers died.

Margaret Mary turned more and more to the Lord in His Eucharist, desiring frequent Holy Communions and time before the Blessed Sacrament. Our Lord Jesus taught her how to talk to Him and *listen* to Him, preparing her to receive the message He would entrust to her.

"His goodness kept me so completely engrossed in the pursuit of 'mental prayer [3] *that it gave me a distaste for vocal prayers which I could never say before the Blessed Sacrament, where I felt so completely engrossed, I was never bored."*

Very often, we are so busy talking to the Lord, we do not hear the Lord speaking to us. We need to spend *quiet* time with Him, to just *be* with Him, to spend *one hour* with Him, as He asked of the Apostles, consoling Him with our presence for all those who do not believe and hurt Him with their disbelief. Margaret Mary was so completely consumed by the Lord and His Presence, she could spend hours before Him, not eating or drinking. Although it caused her embarrassment, she would go up to the Altar, kneeling as close as she could to the Blessed Sacrament. She considered herself specially blessed by the Lord to be able to do so.

Margaret Mary - new temptations and crosses

Our Lord Jesus required much discipline of Margaret Mary. To those whom much is given, much is required. Margaret Mary's vow of chastity, given when she was four and a half years old, never died or even waned. But her mother, who depended on Margaret Mary marrying to get her out of this life of servitude and cruelty, tried to dissuade her daughter from a vocation as a religious. Although Margaret Mary had this gnawing desire to be a Bride of Christ, she felt herself being pulled in two directions - the Lord on one side, her mother and her needs on the other.

She tried to drown out the sound of the Lord knocking at the door of her heart. When she decided to accept her father's family's decision to marry, her persecution ceased. They began not only

---

[3]St. Teresa of Avila described "mental prayer" as merely having a conversation with Someone Who loves you.

to give permission for her to go out, they encouraged her, dressing her in the finest clothes. Margaret Mary writes that at this time, she committed a crime she would grieve over the rest of her life. When she was a teenager, trying to please the family, she went to a carnival. She took part in the masquerade and dressed in an ornate costume. Right in the midst of the festivities, Jesus appeared to her, scourged from head to toe, His precious skin hanging helplessly, almost falling away from His Body scarred and bruised, ropes painfully rubbing against His hands. His Eyes were hurt as they pierced her heart. He told her that He suffered those wounds and hurts because she had dressed in that fashion, not only because of the worldliness of her attire, but because she had chosen human respect over His Divine Love. Margaret Mary, to the end of her days, considered this one of her greatest sins.

The devil busy at work, never let up; he persisted sending the most eligible suitors to pursue Margaret Mary, the most handsome young men with good and honorable intentions asking for her hand in marriage. This caused her great turmoil. She knew she was consecrated to the Lord and could never be happy separated from Him, but then the devil used as a tool her mother crying constantly, telling Margaret Mary her marriage was her mother's only hope of escaping this life of misery. A terrible battle raged with God on one side, the devil on the other, and poor Margaret Mary in the middle.

Margaret had many temptations. *"Were the vows she took at age four binding? Would it be selfish for her to enter the convent when it meant leaving her mother to suffer never-ending humiliation, abuse and servitude?"* A genuine problem was the love that Margaret Mary had for her mother. The devil plagued her with his "How will you be able to be separated from your mother whom you love so tenderly?" So, Margaret Mary went out socially in obedience to the family and loyalty to her mother. She tried to enjoy herself at the parties she attended. But try as she may, she could not, for that Voice within her heart spoke clearly and sternly to His future Bride.

"At night, when I took off those cursed gifts of Satan, those vain adornments, the instruments of his malice, my Sovereign Master would appear to me, as He was in His scourging, all disfigured, reprimanding me in a strange way; that my vanity had reduced Him to this state - and that I was losing such precious time for which He would require a strict accounting at the hour of death; that I was betraying Him, after which He gave me so many proofs of His love and His desire that I conform to Him!"

Margaret sets out to be a Saint

Margaret Mary wanted to be a Saint. She had read the *Lives of the Saints* and thought *they* had never sinned. Believing herself the greatest sinner, she used many harsh forms of mortification, to make up for the sins that she felt she had committed when she had put human cares, and acceptance, before her Lord's Will. Our Lord Jesus came and chastised her, scolding her that she was doing *her* will and not His, for it was not His desire, she practice these extreme atonements for her sins. He told her she was to remember always that He was the Master of her soul, not she.

He began to infuse her with love and compassion for the poor. She gave what little money she had to poor children. They came back to her and through this, she was able to teach them Catechism, about a God Who cared. As this was not in keeping with her family's agenda, Margaret Mary lost her freedom, *again*. Therefore, when she requested permission to teach the children, the answer was No! The excuse given was, the children would dirty the house and soil the furnishings.

Margaret Mary tended the sick, ministering especially to those suffering from the most odious, ulcerated sores. Although she was greatly repulsed by the odor and the sight of the open festering lesions, she cared for them with the merciful love she had received from her Lord. At times, when she could barely handle it, when she thought she would be sick, she would kiss their wounds. Our Lord, in turn, protected her from the highly contagious, most transmittable diseases and miraculously healed her patients with no other medication than His Healing Providence.

The battle never ended for Margaret's hand, the Lord pursuing her and the enemy following right behind trying to entice her with his tricks. But the Lord never gave up, no matter how many times He felt her weaken. Margaret Mary loved life! She was very much like us, falling victim to all the lures and attractions of the world and its promises, falling but also getting up. One day, Our Lord said to her:

"I chose you as My spouse and we promised to be faithful to each other when you made your vow of chastity to Me. It was I who pressed you to make it, before the world had any part of your heart (age four and a half years old), for I wanted it to be perfectly pure and unsullied by earthly affections. And to keep it that way, I removed all the malice from your will so it could not be corrupted. Then I placed you in the care of My Holy Mother, so she might fashion you according to My wishes."

Margaret Mary's devotion to Mother Mary continued to grow as she walked the only path to her Lord Jesus through His Mother. In 1667, four years before entering the convent, she vowed to fast every Saturday in honor of Our Blessed Mother, to pray the Office of the Immaculate Conception,[4] and recite the seven decades of the Rosary while genuflecting, meditating on the Seven Sorrows of Mary. Six years before St. Louis Marie de Montfort was born, Margaret Mary practiced the *holy slavery of Mary.* She wrote:

"I made myself her slave forever, asking her not to refuse me this role. I used to talk to her simply, like a child to a good Mother for whom I already had a truly tender love."

---

[4]Although this Dogma had not as yet been proclaimed, it was the belief and teaching of the early Church Fathers from the very beginning of the Church. It was made an Infallible Dogma of the Church in 1854.

Margaret Mary and the Triumph of the Cross

Once Margaret Mary *decided* that she would enter the Convent of the Visitation, attacks began with a fury that made all other bouts with the devil seem like child's play. He taunted her with, "Poor wretch, you will never persevere. You do not have the stuff to be a holy nun. You and your family will be the laughing-stocks of the village when you give up the habit and leave the convent."

Although her mother never cried in front of her, everyone told her that her mother wept, every time she spoke of Margaret Mary entering the convent. Well-meaning friends of her mother scolded, she would be the cause of her mother's death, and that Margaret Mary would have to answer to God for abandoning her.

Just as she was about to succumb to the attacks of the enemy and consider marriage, Mother Mary came to her and scolded her for weakening. Then Our Lord came to her and reminded her of her vow to *Him*. One day, after she received Communion, Our Lord showed Himself to her as the most handsome, the wealthiest, the most powerful, the most perfect of all spouses. He asked her how, since she had been promised to Him since childhood, she could think of going with another. He remonstrated,

"Oh, know that if you scorn Me in this way, I shall abandon you forever. But if you are faithful to Me, I shall not leave you, and I shall be your victory over all My enemies."

Now, as with other Mystics, Margaret Mary had a dilemma discerning whether this was from the Lord and His Mother, or was it the work and words of the devil.

"When Jesus said this to me, He instilled such a great calm within me and my soul felt such great peace, that I determined then and there to die rather than change."

This *peace* was the sign for Margaret Mary, of the Lord's presence. The stronger her resolve to become a nun, the more this *peace* covered her, strengthening and protecting her, breaking the enemy's hold on her.

Home, at last

Margaret Mary would never cease having problems. Even when her family finally accepted her resolve to become a nun, there was strife; they insisted she enter one Religious Community of nuns and she was determined to enter the Convent of the Visitation. She walked through the doors of the Visitation Sisters in Paray-le-Monial on June 20, 1671, to begin her life as a religious and she would never turn back. In the parlor of the convent a warm peace settled over her; she heard inwardly: ***"This is where I want you!"*** She answered, she would *"never be anywhere else."*

Out of obedience, she shared her desire for humiliation and mortification as well as her *"mental prayer"* (with the Lord), with her Superiors. Although a former Mother Superior felt strongly that Margaret Mary's special walk was of the Lord, her taking of vows would be delayed for two and a half months.

During the ten-day retreat in preparation for the ceremony, as Margaret Mary was praying in the garden of the convent, Our Lord Jesus appeared to her. He spoke gently, softly, instructing her in the mystery of His Passion. It was the beginning of a very intimate relationship between Margaret Mary and Our Lord Jesus. He told her,

> ***"Here is the wound in My side, so that you may make of it your present and perpetual dwelling. There you will be able to preserve the robe of innocence in which I have clothed your soul, that you may live henceforth by the life of a God-Man, as though (you are) no longer living, so that I may live perfectly in you."***

Before the day of the ceremony, All Soul's Day, Margaret Mary knelt before the Blessed Sacrament and begged the Lord's forgiveness for all the times she had betrayed Him. She then offered herself as a sacrificial victim to Him, her Divine Master. In reply, Our Lord said:

> ***"Remember that it is a crucified God you intend to wed. That is why you must conform to Him, by bidding farewell***

to all the pleasures of life, for there will be no more pleasures for you except those of the cross."

Do we want to wed the **crucified Lord**? Do we want to conform to the *crucified Lord*? Is this what we mean when we say, we desire to know Our Lord better? Is this the Lord Whom we pray everyone sees, in place of us, when we say *"I must decrease and He increase?"* Or is it the Lord Who walked on water, the One Who healed, Who preached, the popular Lord Whom everyone followed, the Lord they wanted to make King?

"I belong forever to my beloved; I am forever His slave, His servant and His creature, since He is all mine, and I am His unworthy spouse, Sister Margaret Mary, dead to the world. Everything from God and nothing from me; everything God's and nothing for me!"

With these words, on November 6, 1672, having made her vows, Margaret Mary became Sister Margaret Mary, Nun, Bride of Christ and future Saint.

Jesus blesses Margaret with His Presence

One of the greatest blessings Sister Margaret Mary received after her profession was that of now being able to *see* Jesus her Spouse, to *feel* Him close to her, to *hear* Him more clearly than when she had seen and heard Him solely with her *heart*. She could not bear to turn away from Jesus, even for a moment with His Real Presence so visibly before her. Sometimes, I wonder, do we truly believe that Jesus' Real Presence is before us, His Body, Blood, Soul and Divinity in the Blessed Sacrament, after our priest says the words of consecration? He is present in the Tabernacle or exposed in a Monstrance. Do we spend an hour with Him in Eucharistic Adoration? Do we believe? Are we distracted at these times? Do we believe?

"He promised never to leave me, saying: 'Always be ready and eager to receive Me, for I want to make My dwelling in you, to converse and talk with you.'"

Is this not what Our Lord says to us, as He opens His Arms and Heart to us, in His Eucharist, every day?

Margaret Mary embarks on the Way of the Cross

Jesus' gift to Margaret Mary was a mixed blessing, if we look at it with the eyes of the world; it brought her unfathomable joy and peace; it brought her great pain and humiliation from within her Community. They did not embrace this kind of spirituality. They did not understand it or her and so they rejected Margaret, delivering *the persecution* Jesus spoke of when he addressed those who sacrifice for His sake,

> *"Amen I say to you, there is no man who has left house or brethren, or sisters, or father, or mother, or children, or lands, for My sake and for the gospel, who shall not receive a hundred times as much, now in this time; houses and brethren, and sisters, and mothers, and children, and lands, with persecutions; and in the world to come life everlasting."*[5]

But because of her obedience to her Superiors and her Community, as with St. Teresa of Avila, she was protected from the heresy of Illuminism.[6] Our Lord demanded she be faithful and obedient to even the smallest regulation of religious life. Although she did not fully understand what the Lord was telling her, she shared it all with her Superiors.

Our Lord showed Margaret Mary a large cross, covered with flowers, saying this was the bed prepared for His chaste spouses; He told her the flowers would fall and all that would be left were the thorns which would pierce her so deeply, she would need to summon all her strength from His Love to endure the excruciating pain. Rather than running from the prospect of such agony, Margaret Mary wrote, she longed more and more to join Jesus in the agony of *His Passion*, to love Him and receive Him often in

---

[5]Mark 10:29-30

[6]Illuminism - a form of Gnosticism, a heresy which flourished during the early Christian centuries that claimed, salvation comes through enlightened knowledge. Then, in 16th century Spain, there were pseudo-mystic Spaniards who claimed to act always under illumination received directly and immediately from the Holy Spirit, and independently of the means of grace dispensed by the Church.

Holy Communion, and to die so she would be finally united to Him in Paradise. Oftentimes, we are so delighted with God's gift of *roses* to us, we fail to recognize His gift of thorns; we embrace the bouquet and reject the thorns.

The devil never left Sister Margaret Mary. He made her fall, caused her to drop things, then taunted her with: "You clumsy fool you; you never do anything worthwhile." The devil would push her down the stairs, and bruise her seriously; but not one bone would be broken. This was a promise the Lord had made to her and He never goes back on a commitment. The devil would try everything and anything to crush her spirit so totally, she would be too weak to relate everything to Mother Superior. He did this, knowing the only way to block his power over her was by obedience and openness to her Superior.

Margaret Mary receives the First Great Revelation

When Our Lord spoke to Margaret Mary through *"interior locutions,"* He would bid her to ponder (as Mother Mary before her) on the Wound in His Side. Although all His Wounds brought deep sorrow to Margaret Mary, it was *this* Wound, this *wounded Heart*, pierced by Longinus'[7] sword which caused her the greatest pain. I wonder if this was not the greatest Wound, the greatest hurt Our Lord suffered, not so much from the sword (as He was already dead) but the pain to His Heart through the rejection of His children. [It reminds us of the time, Our Lord appeared to *John of the Woods* in Bois Signeur Isaac, His Body covered with welts, bruises, and open bleeding cuts. "(His) Eyes pierced (Lord Isaac's) eyes... Finally He spoke, *"Look how they have mistreated Me."*[8]]

When Our Lord Jesus showed His Precious Heart, pierced out of love for us, was He preparing Margaret Mary for His

---

[7] read about Longinus, the centurion and how he became a Martyr, in Bob and Penny Lord's book: *This is My Body, This is My Blood, Miracles of the Eucharist* Book I

[8] excerpt from Chapter XVIII: Bois Seigneur Isaac in Bob and Penny Lord's first book: *This is My Body, This is My Blood, Miracles of the Eucharist* Book I

mandate: *"Tell My children they can soothe My Wounded Heart, through renewed devotion to My Sacred Heart?"* Although devotion to the Sacred Heart was not new to the Church, existing in some form or another, many Saints meditating on Our Lord's Sacred Heart, the Lord chose Margaret Mary to promote this devotion in a way which would touch the hearts of *all* the faithful. He desired, it become an official devotion throughout His Church, *throughout the world, for all time in memoriam.*

Up until this time Our Lord had made His will and presence known to Margaret Mary *interiorly*, but that was to change December 27, 1673. Margaret Mary was twenty-six years old. She had been professed for almost fourteen months. Her job in the Infirmary brought her nothing but rejection, insults and adversity. Her only solace was on her knees, her body pressed against the grill, as close to the Blessed Sacrament as she could get. She found herself enveloped by Our Lord's heavenly presence. *"He opened His Heart"* to her *"for the first time."* He said,

> *"My Divine Heart so passionately loves all men and you in particular that, no longer able to contain the flame of its burning charity (love), it has to pour forth through you, and it must manifest itself to them, to enrich them with its precious treasures, which I am revealing to you, and which contains the sanctifying and salutary graces necessary to snatch them away from the abyss of perdition (sin). And I have chosen you as an abyss of unworthiness and ignorance for the fulfillment of this great plan, so that everything may be accomplished by Me alone."*

> *"After that, He asked me to give Him my heart, which I begged Him to take, and this He did. He placed it within His own adorable Heart, in which He made me see my heart as a tiny atom being consumed in this flaming furnace, and then, drawing it out like an intense flame in the form of a heart, He put it back where he had taken it, saying to me: 'Beloved, here is a precious pledge of My*

Love, which implants in your side a tiny spark of its most intense flames, so as to serve as your heart and consume you until the last moment;....its intensity will not die out or find refreshment except to a small degree in bloodletting,[9] which I shall mark so completely with the Blood of My Cross,....it will bring you more humiliation and suffering than relief. That is why I want (you) to practice what is commanded of you by the rule, so as to give you the consolation of shedding your blood on the cross of humiliations. Although I have closed the wound in your side, you will feel the pain of it forever, and although you have taken only the name of My slave, I now call you the beloved disciple of My Sacred Heart.'"

With this revelation of her future mission, Jesus made it plain to Margaret Mary that *He* had chosen her, but to save her from any slight possibility of pride in Him having chosen her, He revealed she was totally unworthy and ignorant. We hear again the message of Saint Bernadette when she said if the Blessed Mother could have found someone less worthy and more stupid, she would have chosen her instead of Bernadette.

Margaret Mary receives the Second Great Revelation

Every first Friday Our Lord would reopen the wounds in her heart. It was probably on one of those first Fridays, a couple of months after the first Great Revelation, that Our Lord appeared to her a *second* time. She writes that each revelation was richer than the one before. Our Lord dared not show her *all* that He had in store for her, that she might not die. We often say, if we knew God's total plan for us, we would die of ecstasy, our hearts would burst, unable to contain all His Gifts of Grace.

During this revelation, Our Lord's Sacred Heart appeared *"as a brilliant sun of blinding light, whose rays fell directly on (her) heart."* The red-hot flames were so intense, Margaret Mary

---

[9]bloodletting - This is referring to an old practice of bloodletting prescribed, at one time, for individual religious by a Superior of a convent who deemed it necessary for their spiritual life.

felt they "*would reduce* (her) *to ashes.*" He showed her His Sacred Heart "*on a throne of flames.*" His Heart, pierced by our sins, was surrounded by a crown of thorns. He told Margaret Mary, "*My enemies placed a crown of thorns on My Head, My friends on My Heart.*" A cross rose from the top of His Heart symbolizing the cross that He carried in His Heart from the time of His Incarnation, the cross of humiliation, abandonment, rejection, pain and mockery that He, in His Sacred Humanity, would suffer and endure throughout His Life up to His Death on the Cross.

Jesus told Margaret Mary He wanted to save mankind from eternal damnation, and He would accomplish this through His Sacred Heart with Its Love, Mercy, Grace, Sanctification and Salvation. He requested that she tell His children His Heart was to be honored in the form of *Flesh*[10] and the Image of His Heart, surrounded by a crown with a cross above it, was to be exposed in their homes and on *their* hearts. He promised that wherever His Sacred Heart was displayed and honored, He would pour out His Graces and provide protection from the *enemy*.

This was not to come to pass without much questioning and great opposition from her own Community.

The Third Great Revelation - Jesus makes His Will known

Approximately six months passed before Jesus appeared to Margaret Mary, again. The Blessed Sacrament was exposed. Most likely, it occurred on a Friday, during the Octave of the Feast of Corpus Christi. Our Lord was radiant, brilliantly clothed in glory, "*His five Wounds glowing like five suns,*" flames leaping out from every part of His Sacred Humanity. Most pitiful were those flames from His Sacred Breast which was like a roaring furnace. Jesus bared His Breast, revealing His Sacred Heart which was filled with love for His children, although they wound Him so deeply.

He shared that the rejection and ingratitude of His children

---

[10]Our Lord manifested a Miracle of the Eucharist in Lanciano having the Host turn into Human Flesh, a Human Heart. Read more about this and other Miracles of the Eucharist in Bob and Penny Lord's book: *This is My Body, This is My Blood, Miracles of the Eucharist,* Book I

today pained Him even more than that which He had suffered during His Passion. But if only they would return His love, He said, in even some small way, He would count all the pain He had endured for their sake during His Passion *little*, compared to what He would desire to do for them. But He cried, *"They repay love and mercy with coldness and indifference."*

He asked Margaret Mary to console Him by doing as much as she could to make up for their ingratitude, to be what they refused to be, and to do what they have failed to do. When Margaret Mary pleaded, she was weak and had not the strength to bring about His mission for the Church, He told her *He* would be her strength. She was to receive Communion as often as obedience to her Superiors would permit, but most especially on the first Friday of each month.

Then Jesus asked Margaret Mary to make a Holy Hour every Thursday from eleven to midnight. From that time till her death, she made this Holy Hour, prostrating herself on the floor, sharing Our Lord's Agony in the Garden of Gethsemane with Him. Was Our Lord trusting her with the hour, He had offered to His closest Apostles, that precious hour when He suffered, shedding blood and tears for the sins and agony of the world? Was He asking this from her as reparation for the sins which so excruciatingly wounded Him then and wound Him now? Or was it to strengthen her for her Way of the Cross?

Had the Apostles understood? Did they not realize how very much Our Lord in His Humanity, needed them to share this painful time in His Life? Days before, Peter, James and John had not wanted to leave Mount Tabor. We often thought the Lord brought them to the Mount of the Transfiguration to fortify them for His final Walk - to the Cross. And, we still believe that, but now, we wonder if this *Holy Hour* was not also what the Lord was offering His trusted Apostles to strengthen them for the days and then the years to follow? Would they have slept if they had known that they would no longer have their Lord with them, that He would be taken away from them? Did they take Him and His being with them forever for granted? Do we take Him for granted? If we knew that we would never be able to attend Mass or spend time before the Blessed Sacrament again, that as in some European nations, we would not have Our Lord Jesus in our midst for hundreds of years, would we have to be *asked* to participate in the Mass or spend one hour with the Lord in Eucharistic Adoration? Would we not only *kneel* during the Consecration, would we not desire to prostrate ourselves before Him?

When Margaret Mary had protested she was too weak to carry out her Master's Will, what did He offer her, to strengthen her? *Reception of Holy Communion as often as obedience would allow and a Holy Hour before the Blessed Sacrament.* What is the Lord offering us to strengthen us to do His Will, to save His Church, to console Him in these days of crisis and infamy? *Reception of Holy Communion often and to spend a Holy Hour before the Blessed Sacrament.* It is always the same, my brothers and sisters; Jesus is with us; Jesus is alive; Jesus is our power and strength - always present to us in The Eucharist. The weapons which He gave Margaret Mary in the 17th Century are the same He gives us, today. God is constant, consistently, faithfully all-giving.

In this Great Revelation, Jesus gives us two ways to express our love for Him and to make reparation for those who do not.

First to receive Holy Communion often, especially on the first Friday of the month. To make reparation for those who mocked and taunted Our Lord, those who crucified Our Lord, those who stood by and did nothing that first Good Friday, that Jesus suffered and died for us and our sins.

Second, He asks us to spend a Holy Hour with Him, especially on Thursday evening. This is in memory of Jesus' suffering agony in the Garden of Gethsemane and in thanksgiving for His Great Gift of Life and Love, the Eucharist - at the Last Supper. Can we spend an hour with Him, *the hour we could not spend with Him that first Thursday in Gethsemane?* What will we feel, the next time we attend Holy Mass and receive Our Lord eternally with us in Holy Communion? Will we give love for Love, our poor limited love in exchange for the Heavenly Love he bore us that Last Supper, a Love so great His last thoughts were of *us*, the night before He would face death on the Cross?

The nuns found Margaret Mary unconscious. She had been that way throughout the Third Revelation. Seeing she was so weakened physically, not able to walk or talk, they carried her to the Mother Superior. Imagine the Superior's predicament. On one hand, she knew that Margaret Mary was virtuous, but she had misgivings, having an ongoing problem with all the phenomena that had occurred in Margaret Mary's life. She thought, *"Oh not again!"*

Margaret Mary crumbled on her knees before the Mother Superior. Seeing her on the floor, burning with fever, trembling uncontrollably and having difficulty sharing what the Lord desired of her, Mother Superior refused to grant her any of Our Lord's requests. Instead, she replied, wielding a strong tongue lashing, heaping humiliation upon disbelief, forbidding Margaret Mary to comply with any of her claimed decrees by the Lord. *Margaret Mary obeyed!*

Now this must have been horrendous for Margaret Mary. She knew this was the Lord and His wishes, but as with the Mystics and Saints before her, she obeyed her Superiors. And through this obedience, she was able to scuttle the devil's plan. The devil, beginning with the Old Testament in the Garden of Eden, has always tried to get those specially chosen by God to disobey. When Our Lord walked the earth, He gave us the perfect example if we would be perfect as our Heavenly Father is perfect. Our Lord always obeyed first His Father in *Heaven*, then His *earthly* foster father Joseph and Mother Mary. Over the centuries of our beloved Church's history, whenever Jesus appeared to the Saints and Mystics, like St. Teresa of Avila, He always told them to obey their Superiors and He would work through their obedience.

Margaret Mary became seriously ill, so debilitated, it came to her Superior Mother de Saumaise's attention. She became alarmed. She had an idea; this would solve all her questions. She turned to Margaret Mary: "Why don't you ask God to cure you? In this way, we'll know if this comes from the Holy Spirit. Then I will grant you permission to receive Communion on First Fridays, allow your Thursday evening hour vigils - I'll allow everything."

As she was to obey her Superior in all things, she asked the Lord to heal her. Our Lady, along with her Angels appeared to Margaret Mary; she embraced her and said,

"Take courage, my dear daughter, in the health I give you in the Name of my Divine Son, for you have still a long and painful road to travel, always bearing the Cross, pierced with nails and thorns and lacerated by whips. But have no fear, I shall not abandon you and I promise to protect you."

Margaret Mary was restored to perfect health *immediately*, the sign her Superior accepted as proof her messages were of the Lord. But the battle was not over. Her Mother Superior judged wisely that Margaret Mary needed a strong Spiritual Director to guide her and to discern the messages she was receiving. As with St. Teresa, many potential Spiritual Directors came; they did not understand *mental prayer;* they had never received *interior locutions* or experienced an apparition by the Lord, and so, out of ignorance, they completely rejected the Revelations as coming from a Divine Source.

Saint Claude Colombiere comes into Margaret Mary's life

Our Lord Jesus had promised Margaret Mary that His Work would triumph, in spite of His enemies; He kept His promise by sending a loyal son, a Jesuit priest, highly reputed for his wisdom, to His little servant. He sent *Father Claude Colombiere*, who saw the holiness of Margaret Mary and believed in her Revelations. Now Father Claude was not to have Margaret Mary's complete trust and openness in the beginning, until one day as she was confessing to Father Claude, she heard a Voice inwardly tell her: *"Here is the one I am sending you."*

As Father Claude was hearing Margaret Mary's confession

with a darkened grille covered by a black cloth between them, he could not see who the nun was that was receiving messages from the Lord. After he had heard all the nuns' confessions and the black cloth was drawn aside, he was able to see all of them seated on the other side of the grille. He looked right at Margaret Mary and said to her Superior, Mother de Saumaise, *"That is a soul of Grace!"* With this, her Superior had no more misgivings and ordered Margaret Mary to reveal *everything* to Father Claude.

As she learned to trust her confessor, Father Claude, more and more, she experienced more and more peace and tranquility. The battle was not over, however. There was still much suspicion and mistrust among the other nuns who could not accept that which they did not know. Having a Visionary in their house was tantamount to having the devil himself in their midst. They even resorted to dousing Margaret Mary with holy water. This anger and furor would continue even after her death. Margaret Mary rejoiced as this was simply part of the life she was called to by the Lord. She welcomed it as it was as close as she could be to the Passion of Our Lord Jesus when He, too, was accused of being in league with the devil.

Margaret Mary's only pain was seeing the Community's anger and wrath turn on her confessor, Father Claude. The nuns knew little of what had transpired between Margaret Mary and the Lord. But they did know and never forgot how she had been severely chastised by Mother Superior after having been so terribly weakened from a vision of the Lord. To compound the problem, permission had been granted to her to receive Holy Communion on the first Friday of every month and to spend a holy hour every Thursday evening with the Blessed Sacrament. This was not the mode of religious life known to them, and they looked upon it as very unorthodox.

It took all the faith and strength Father Claude had, not to abandon Margaret Mary as others had when the going got rough. More than belief that she had truly received Divine Revelations was the evidence of her holiness, through her obedience that most heavily persuaded him to persist with the little nun. He later wrote that this spirit of humility and obedience she possessed was the key for him, for as a son of Ignatius Loyola, Fr. Claude had learned that,

> *"The devil is capable of doing many things, but he will never, never inspire humility, obedience, love for the Cross - in a word, love for Our Lord Jesus Christ."*

Although Father Claude was to share in the *agony* with Margaret Mary, he also was to share in the *ecstasy*. When we speak of the Heart of Jesus, His most Sacred Heart, are we not speaking of Our Lord in the Eucharist, the Heart of our Church? Our Lord always came and revealed the great Revelations to St. Margaret Mary during the Sacrifice of the Mass. It was after the Consecration that Jesus united His Heart with her heart and that of Father Claude. It was then He gave her the Image of His Sacred Heart.

> *"One day when he* (Father Claude Colombiere), *came to say Mass in our church, the Lord granted signal graces both to him and to me. As I went up to receive Him in Holy Communion, He showed me His Sacred Heart as a burning furnace, and two other hearts were on the point of uniting themselves to It, and of being absorbed therein. At the same time He said to me:* **'It is thus My pure love unites these three hearts for ever.'** *He afterwards gave me to understand that this union was all for the glory of His Sacred Heart, the treasures of Which He wished me to reveal to him* (Father Claude Colombiere) *that he might spread them abroad, and make known to others their value and utility."*

The Fourth Great Revelation

Father Claude directed Margaret Mary to write down all that Jesus told her. Although she found this greatly distasteful, not wanting to draw attention to herself, she did so out of obedience. Then she burned all she had written as soon as she was finished. In this way, she thought she had fulfilled the requirements of obedience set down by Father Claude. But when she confessed this, he forbade her to burn her writings. Our Lord came shortly after and revealed to Margaret Mary *The Fourth and last Great Revelation.*

June, 1675, again *during the octave of Corpus Christi,* the Lord gave Margaret Mary His Fourth and last Great Mandate. *It was the Eucharist!* Jesus told Margaret Mary that although there are those who love and adore Him, there are those who return His unconditional Love Which vulnerably comes to them in the Eucharist, with coldness and indifference. He went on to say that although there are those who claim they believe He is truly present in the Eucharist, and that His Real Presence comes to us at the time of Consecration during the Mass, they go up to the Altar without having gone to confession, receiving Him while in a state of sin. He cried, there are those who claim that they believe His Body, Blood, Soul and Divinity is truly present in the Host reposing in the Tabernacle, and reserved in the Monstrance during Eucharistic Adoration, yet they have no time to go and visit Him. *This Revelation called for reparation for sins committed against Jesus in His Sacrament of Love.*

Margaret Mary was before the Blessed Sacrament when the Lord appeared to her, uncovered His Divine Heart and gave her His last Great message. He told her that she could do no better than to return His great love by doing what He asked of her:

> *"Behold this Heart Which so much loved men, that it spared nothing, even to exhausting Itself, in order to give them testimony of Its love, and in return I mostly receive ingratitude, through their irreverence and sacrilege, and through the coldness and scorn that they have for Me in this Sacrament of Love. What causes Me most sorrow is that there are hearts consecrated to Me who treat Me thus.*
>
> *"Therefore, I ask of you that the first Friday after the Octave of Corpus Christi be set apart for a special Feast in honor of My Heart, by receiving Communion that day, and*

by making solemn reparation and honorable amends to make good the insults that It receives when It is exposed on the Altars. I promise you that My Heart shall deign to shed abundantly the influence of Its Divine Love upon those who rend It this honor and induce others so to honor It.[11]

Father Claude Colombiere directed Margaret Mary to comply fully with the Lord's Will. In addition, his heart was so touched by this Great Revelation, he desired to be the *first* to do what the Sacred Heart of Jesus mandated.

Ten years passed before the Feast of the Sacred Heart would be instituted in the Monastery of the Visitation where the Revelations took place, and this because Father Claude Colombiere had suggested they do so.

Those next ten years would be hard ones for Margaret Mary. Mother Saumaise, who had come to believe and support her, left the Monastery to become a Superior at another Monastery. But before she left, she insisted Margaret Mary tell the nuns what the Lord had commanded her to relate to them. Margaret Mary, more dead than alive, reluctantly obeyed. In front of her whole Community, she shared the punishments that the Lord said He would release upon them and the Monastery. She remained kneeling, humbly in the midst of very angry, rebellious, belligerent, threatening sisters. She later wrote:

"If I had been able to gather together all the sufferings, I had experienced until then, and all those I have had since, and if all of them had continued until death, this would not seem comparable to me to what I endured that night!"...
"I was dragged from one place to another, with unbelievable humiliations."

Most of the nuns felt they had gone too far, and so the next day there were not enough confessors to hear their confessions. The following day, Margaret Mary heard the Lord say that at last peace had returned to the Monastery, and through her sacrifice

---

[11]Quotation from St. Margaret Mary by Msgr. Demimuid

His Divine Justice had been satisfied.

Mother Greyfié became the new Superior. She did not understand Margaret Mary nor her spirituality, and so now we have the new Mother Superior joining in with some of the nuns who persisted in making life the Way of the Cross for Margaret Mary.

Our Lord had appeared to her; He had issued a mandate. But He didn't make it easy for Margaret Mary to bring about this devotion to the Sacred Heart. She knew great pain as everyone opposed her. It was only when the Monastery of the Visitation had a new Superior, *Mother Melin*, that things would begin to happen. With the advent of a new Superior, devotion to the Sacred Heart started to take Its first steps toward being accepted.

Against her will, Margaret Mary was appointed as assistant to the Superior as well as Mistress of Novices. She reluctantly obeyed, protesting her unworthiness. Little did she know that it would become part of the Lord's plan to bring about devotion to His Sacred Heart.

Her life continued to be a roller-coaster, with the greatest highs and the lowest lows. But Margaret Mary, now Mistress of Novices, was to suddenly see her sorrow turn into joy. One day, to her amazement and her delight, she came upon her novices kneeling before an Image of the Sacred Heart which they had made and placed on the Altar of their little oratory.

As her Feast Day was approaching, her novices planned a celebration in honor of the Sacred Heart of Jesus, knowing nothing could please their Mistress of Novices more. Imagine how surprised and shocked they were when one of the most devout nuns refused to attend, stressing the young novice advise her Mistress of Novices to teach *sound devotion*, according to the Rule and Constitution of their Community. But this attitude was about to change.

Sister Margaret Mary's dear confessor and spiritual brother Father Claude had died in 1682. As God would have it, shortly after his death, his book *Spiritual Retreat* was published. He had been so moved by Jesus' last Great Revelation to Margaret Mary, he took what she had written with him when he left for England, and later included this message from the Lord at the end of his book, *Spiritual Retreat.*

Here it was ten years after Claude Colombiere had shared great spiritual experiences with Margaret Mary and he was still helping her. As Father Claude had always been considered holy, and his teachings reliable, the nun in charge of choosing the readings for the refectory never bothered reading the book of the day ahead of time. Toward the end of the book, Father Claude was sharing his experience before the Blessed Sacrament, how his heart would "*overflow*" on the point of bursting, with an elation and joy from the Lord he did not understand himself:

"I realized that God wanted me to serve Him by carrying out His wishes concerning the devotion He recommended to a person to whom He reveals Himself very freely, and for whose sake He has deigned to make use of my weakness."

His words touched not only the nuns, but Margaret Mary herself as she recalled the experiences she shared with the Lord and her deceased spiritual brother Claude Colombiere. But she was to awaken from her reverie of days long past. The nun continued reading. Near to finishing the book, she came to Margaret Mary's account of the last great Revelation to her from Jesus, written under obedience to Father Claude. The realization that the one whose writings were being read was their own Margaret Mary, excitement spread throughout the refectory. After all, this book was written by the widely respected Jesuit priest, Father Claude Colombiere!

Margaret Mary bowed her head, praying no one would recognize her as the *person* to whom Father Claude Colombiere was referring. She had had no idea he had kept her accounts of the Revelations, no less included them in his book. She was happy that the nuns were listening to the Lord's Revelations through Father Claude; she was just unhappy her sisters might focus on her as the recipient, rather than on the message. But inside, she knew that this was the beginning of the fulfillment of the Lord's mandate to her. Margaret Mary had waited ten years for this moment. At last devotion to the Sacred Heart would spread and spread throughout the Church as her Savior had commanded.

Margaret Mary's other Apparitions

Margaret Mary knew (and had apparitions) of Jesus, not only as the God-Man but He even came to her as a *Baby*. It was the vigil of the Feast of the Visitation. Margaret Mary was in Choir with the rest of the nuns. They were singing *"Te Deum,"* when suddenly Margaret Mary lost her voice. She tried to sing; she opened her mouth, but nothing came out. She couldn't sing! All at once, the Baby Jesus appeared in her arms. Her voice returned, and she sang with the rest, in praise and glory of Our Lord.

On another occasion, as she was praying with the other nuns in the garden, Margaret Mary's mind and heart left her sisters and she had a vision of the Sacred Heart of Jesus surrounded by Seraphic Angels. The Angels made a pact with Margaret Mary at this time: *They would suffer with her. She in turn would rejoice with them.* It is said that once Our Heavenly Family visit a place, their presence never leaves. This garden has become a special shrine where we often bring our pilgrims to pray. It has been renamed fittingly, *"The Garden of the Seraphim."*

The Chapel of the Visitation, Yesterday and Today

We have entered the Chapel of the Visitation and celebrated Mass many times over the last nineteen years of leading pilgrimages to the Shrines. As we kneel at the beginning of the Eucharistic prayer, we find our eyes and hearts drawn to the area above the Altar of Sacrifice where there is a powerful mural depicting that moment when the Heart of Jesus united Itself forever with St. Margaret Mary's heart and that of St. Claude. We see Our Lord Jesus hovering over St. Margaret Mary, His Heart on fire out of love for her and for us.

We cannot fail to ponder: Is Our Lord not offering to unite

His Heart with ours at the moment we receive Him in the Holy Eucharist, that He might envelop our hearts inside His, that we might love and forgive with His Heart, our heart no longer alive but His Heart in us, beating with every thought we have, every act we perform? As we kneel there, the years melt away and we are present at the Mass, that fateful day when St. Claude Colombiere brought Margaret Mary Holy Communion, and Jesus united Himself *forever* with His two faithful servants.

Our eyes travel to the right side of the main Altar where there is a grille till today, where the nuns still hear Mass and receive Holy Communion. It is here, behind this very grille, that Margaret Mary heard Mass and received Holy Communion. This is where she went into ecstasy, where Our Lord Jesus, present in the Blessed Sacrament exposed on the Altar, gave her the message of Love she was to spread to the whole world. It was here that He showed her His wounded Heart and asked her to establish a Feast in honor of His Sacred Heart.

We are kneeling. It is over 300 years later. Our priest has just consecrated the host and the wine into the Body, Blood, Soul and Divinity of Jesus Christ. As we prepare to receive Our Lord in Holy Communion, we must ask ourselves if we adore Our Lord in the Blessed Sacrament, as Margaret Mary Alacoque adored Him? She longed for the Eucharist and knew great suffering because she was not allowed to receive the Eucharist daily or often times *weekly*. It's really ironic that we have been given this gift to receive Our Lord often, daily if we wish, through the compassionate actions of our saintly Pope St. Pius X in the early years of the twentieth century, and we take it for granted. The dear Saints who preceded us, longed for Jesus in the Eucharist, and out of obedience, had to be content with the once a month, or once every few weeks, they were allowed to receive Him. To try to understand, we need to hear with our hearts what Margaret Mary Alacoque was to say:

*"I could have passed whole days and nights there, (*in front of the Blessed Sacrament) *without eating or drinking, or knowing what I was doing, except that I was being*

consumed in His Presence like a burning taper, in order to return to Him love for love....

"...I never failed to go as near as I could to the Blessed Sacrament.

*"I envied and counted those alone happy (*only happy those*) who were able to communicate (*receive Communion*) often and who were at liberty to remain before the Most Holy Sacrament.*

"It happened that once before Christmas, the parish priest gave out (said) *from the pulpit that whoever should not have slept on Christmas Eve could not go to Communion; as in punishment for my sins I was never able to sleep on the vigil of Christmas, I did not dare communicate* (receive Communion). *That day of rejoicing was consequently for me a day of tears which took the place of food and pleasure.*

*"My greatest joy, in the prospect of leaving the world (*in becoming a religious), *was the thought that I should be able to receive Holy Communion frequently, which up to then I had not been permitted to do.*

"I would have thought myself the happiest person on earth, had I been allowed to do so often and pass the nights alone before the Blessed Sacrament...On the eves of Communion, I found myself rapt in so profound a silence, on account of the greatness of the action, I was about to perform, that I could not speak without great effort; and afterwards I would have wished neither to eat nor drink, to see nor speak, owing to the greatness, consolation and peace which I then felt."

Margaret Mary goes Home to her Lord and Savior

Sister Margaret Mary predicted the day of her death. On the evening of October 17, 1690, she commended her soul to her Savior. Above her tomb in the Church of the Visitation there is a sign which reads: *"Thou shalt love the Lord thy God with thy whole heart."* Jesus had loved God the Father with His whole Heart. Margaret Mary had loved Jesus with her whole heart. And so at last, she was able to plunge herself into the heart of her Savior Whom she so dearly loved to the exclusion of all else. Her last words were, *"I need nothing but God, and to lose myself in the Heart of Jesus."*

Sister Margaret Mary was not to see the Lord's wishes and her hopes for Devotion to the Sacred Heart fulfilled before she died. But three short years later, in 1693, Pope Innocent XIII began a momentum which would spread to the four corners of the earth. He issued a papal bull granting indulgences to all Visitation Monasteries, which resulted in the institution of the Feast of the Sacred Heart in most of the convents. The establishment of Confraternities of the Sacred Heart was followed by cities, dioceses, and entire nations clamoring for a Feast of the Sacred Heart. In 1765, Pope Clement XIII introduced the Feast in Rome!

Then, in 1856, Pope Pius IX extended the Feast to the entire Church! And with this, Devotion to the Sacred Heart became a perpetual part of the Liturgy and Devotions of the Catholic Church. So, although our Visionary was never to see the promise, she was to salute it from afar.[12]

Not only were the revelations to Margaret Mary from Our Lord Jesus accepted by the Church, but because of the virtuous, selfless life of this nun, she was raised to the Communion of Saints in 1920 by Pope Benedict XV.

We have discovered, through our journeys of faith into the lives of the Saints, that there are Saints and Saint-makers. Just nine years after the Canonization of Margaret Mary, her confessor Father Claude Colombiere became Blessed Claude Colombiere; Pope Pius XI beatified him in 1929. And then in 1992, Blessed Claude joined his spiritual sister Saint Margaret Mary as he became Saint Claude Colombiere. Mother Church, through one loyal son, Pope John Paul II, honored her other son, by raising him to the Company of Saints. So the two friends, spiritual brother and sister

---

[12]*cf* Heb 11:13

The Tomb of Saint Margaret Mary Alacoque

on earth were reunited, still at work, only now in Heaven, promulgating honor and glory to the Sacred Heart of Jesus

Our Lord Jesus promised that wherever the Image of His Sacred Heart had a place of honor in the home, *"He would pour forth His Blessings and Graces."* Margaret Mary said that this was the last act of His Love that He would grant to all men, in the *latter days*, in order to save them from Satan. When *priests* like St. Claude Colombiere, and *religious* like St. Margaret Mary, and every member of the *Body of Christ* really understand this promise, when all become completely immersed in the Sacred Heart of Jesus, the Heart from which the Church flowed, when His Sacred Image becomes a stamp upon their hearts, when every action of their ministry will flow out from a promontory inspired by a tender devotion to the Sacred Heart of Jesus, the Catholic Church will know a renewal in the fervor and passion of the most beautiful and glorious era of our Christian heritage.

St. Louis Marie de Montfort

Slave of Mary
Prophet of the Last Days

Saint Louis Marie de Montfort

A few years ago, we wanted to write a book entitled *Mary's Heroes*. There are many brothers and sisters who have had a love story with Our Lady. They are so powerful! They are so filled with the Holy Spirit! They have such a great love for Mary, a devotion, a willingness to live or die for her, we really didn't know where to begin. Which brother or sister would we write about who had such a burning love for Our Lady? All the people that you will meet in this book had a deep, special love for Mary. The Mystics did; she spoke to them and through them to the Church. The Visionaries did; she appeared to them, shared her Son with them, and their lives were changed forever. The Stigmatists did; she stood by them as she stood by her Son during His Passion. They all had a close, personal relationship with Mary. But who has brought devotion to Mary to the forefront of our Church? What form of Marian Devotion did our Pope John Paul II memorize while a youth working in a factory in Krakow, Poland? The answer rang loud and clear, *St. Louis Marie de Montfort*, Hero of Mary, prophet of these *Last Days*.

The writings of St. Louis Marie de Montfort have left such a mighty impact on those who follow, that in these, the Last Days of the Twentieth century of the Second Millennium, thousands upon thousands of the Faithful have been making a *"Total Consecration to Mary"* through his *"True Devotion to Mary."* Come with us now, as we share the life of one of Mary's heroes, one of our Powerful men in the Church.

Mary's sends a light to shine in the Darkness

We can just envision the blustery night of January 31, 1673, when the midwife scurried around the little cottage of Jeanne de la Vizeule[1] and Jean-Baptiste Grignion, making ready for the coming of the new child. It had been a tempestuous day, with gusts of harsh cold winds blowing off the Atlantic Ocean, sweeping east towards the little village of Montfort, some twenty four kilometers from the nearest big city of Rennes. Did St. Michael leave his perch atop the abbey at his most commanding shrine, Mont St. Michel, to the north off the English Channel? Did our Lady give him instructions to take a legion of Angels to this little hamlet of no account, deep in the province of Brittany, to surround the house of this future Saint, this prophet of a time that St. Paul speaks about in Romans 8:28?[2] Did Jeanne or her dear husband, or any of the people gathered around, have the slightest idea what God had predestined this child to be, and the works He would do for the Kingdom?

Do we know, do we have a tiny clue as to how important that child *we* may be bearing, is in the great scheme of God? If the people of the world had even a minute inkling of the mammoth effect their opposing the plan of the Creator would have on the history of the world, Abortion would be wiped off the face of the earth.

---

[1] In Europe, and in many Hispanic countries, the wife keeps her maiden name.

[2] *"We know that God makes all things work together for the good of those who have been called according to His decree. Those whom He foreknew He predestined to share the image of His Son, that the Son might be the first-born of many brothers. Those He predestined He likewise called; those He called He also justified; and those He justified, He in turn glorified."*

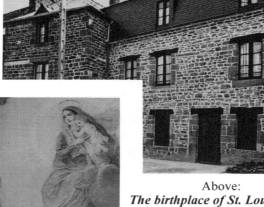

Above:
***The birthplace of St. Louis Marie
de Montfort in
Montfort, France***

Left:
***Banner used during the
Canonization ceremony of
St. Louis Marie de Montfort in
St. Peter's Basilica,
July 20, 1947***

***The living quarters of Montfort Missionaries at
St. Laurent-sur-Sèvre, France***

Left:
**Statue of Our Lady
and Baby Jesus
carved by St. Louis
Marie de Montfort**

Right:
**Crucifix carved by
St. Louis Marie de
Montfort**

Below right:
**Statue of
St. Louis Marie de
Montfort in St.
Peter's Basilica,
Rome**

Above:
**St. Louis Marie de Montfort meets with
Pope Clement XI**

Jean-Baptiste Grignion was particularly concerned about his wife Jeanne. Their first child had caused her much suffering and had died in infancy. Was this one also going to cause her great distress? Would the child or the mother survive the hard winter of Montfort and radiate the sun's bright rays in the warmth of the Spring, or would the child waste away to nothing and blow away as so much dust? Jean-Baptiste prayed, as did all in the household that evening.

We can see with the eyes of faith, the Angels standing guard as the curtain opened in Heaven, and a great light emerged. It formed a solid ray to the little cottage on the street of the Lawyers, Rue de la Saulnerie in Montfort, where the residents of the house were breathlessly waiting with their Guardian Angels for the miracle of birth to take place. Envision Our Lady descending on that beam from Heaven to earth, to a baby, the child who would be christened the following day, Louis Grignion. Is Our Lady entering the cottage and placing her precious hands on the baby inside the womb of the expectant mother? Within a moment, is the child fighting his way past all obstacles, and out of the womb of the mother into the world, screaming and yelling for all he is worth? St. Louis Marie Grignion de Montfort was born. The Angels rejoiced; all Heaven sang praises to God. An era was beginning, the era of Our Lady. [Did it happen this way, or is this just the musing of another *"slave"* of Mary (Bob Lord), another man helplessly in love with Mary? What do you think?]

The following day, the baby was wrapped securely in woolen blankets and brought to the Parish Church of St. Jean where he was formally baptized and welcomed into the Church. Then he was brought back to his home, that solid building where he would spend the next few years of his life. We visited that house in 1977. We stood among the solid beams which held up the structure, strong as the man who was brought forth from there, he who would make this town famous throughout all the world with his love for Our Lord Jesus and His Mother Mary. We could feel the presence of the Saint in that house, as much as we could in St. Laurent-sur-Sèvre, where he took his last breath in 1716.

Although he made the village of Montfort renowned by taking its name, Louis only spent two years there. His father bought a farm outside the town in a hamlet called Bois-Marquer, in the town of Iffendic. His father had good reason to buy the farmhouse. He was to sire eighteen children, although not many of them survived to adulthood. But Bois-Marquer was a place where the young Louis could spend time in the church as an *enfant du coeur*,[3] his first opportunity of being close to Our Lord Jesus in the Tabernacle and on the great and wonderful Altar of the Church.

Louis came from a very pious, very Catholic family. He acquired some of his father's traits which would be considered shortcomings in his ministry. The father had an explosive temper; which Louis had also. He inherited his father's big build. Louis was a big man, solid, strong. He never backed down from a brawl, and there are those who say he may even have started one or two when his adversaries were saying or doing something which offended God, or His beautiful Mother Mary. It is believed his piety came from his very devout mother, and thanks be to God, more piety was given to him than billowing temper. Our Lady worked with his piety; our Lord Jesus turned his anger to zeal for his Mother and the Church.

From the time he was a youth, Louis had a great devotion to Our Lady. He was fascinated by pictures and statues of her. He would spend hours on his knees in church, praying to her, his eyes fixed on images of her. All his life she was his ideal. He prayed for her intercession before every major move in his life. We have to believe that she was very instrumental in his bold move to enroll in the Jesuit College in Rennes at *11 years old!* That time was excellent training for Louis, especially for the work ahead of him. It was at this college that he was enrolled in the Sodality of the Blessed Virgin. We're sure he was not aware of the importance of it at the time, but Our Lady was. Because of

---

[3] altar boy

his membership in the Sodality, he was given access to all the services in the Sodality - such as lectures, sermons and instructions which were prepared especially for its members. We very often think these are coincidences, but they are not, unless they are *holy coincidences.* Our Lady is here; she's with us. She guides us through life and helps us when we need her. She also orchestrates our lives, if we allow her to, so that we are directed to areas where she can influence our walk towards the Kingdom.

We break here for a moment to give you two solid examples of how this has happened that we know of: Once in the life of *St. Louis Marie de Montfort,* and once in the life of our *Pope John Paul II.*

As we said above, St. Louis Marie was given exposure to Our Lady in, what would have appeared, a very innocent gesture on the part of the priest. He was enrolled in the Sodality. When he arrived in Paris, at the Seminary of the Sulpicians some eight years later, he had to work to support himself. He was given the job of *librarian,* which gave him access to all the books ever printed on Mary. So when Louis began to write his books on Our Lady, he already had all the resource background given to him by guess who? Our Lady!

Pope John Paul II has stated on numerous occasions that the reading of St. Louis de Montfort's book, *True Devotion to Mary* had a profound effect on him. He stated,

"...the reading of the treatise on True Devotion to the Blessed Virgin was a turning point in my life (at a time when he was secretly studying for the priesthood). *Whereas I had initially been afraid lest devotion to Mary might detract from that due to Jesus instead of giving Him His rightful place, I realized, when reading the treatise of Grignion de Montfort, that such was not the case. Our interior relationship with the Mother of God is a result of our association with the mystery of Christ."*[4]

---

[4]André Frossard, "Dialogue avec Jean-Paul II," p. 184-185

In the Marian Year 1987, in his Encyclical, *"Mother of the Redeemer"* Pope John Paul II recommended to the faithful, the writings of Louis Marie de Montfort.[5]

Louis Marie desires to become a martyr

Louis Marie became very close during his college years with Claude Poullart des Places, founder of the Holy Ghost Fathers, and an intimate friend of St. John Baptist de la Salle, founder of the Christian Brothers. Louis spent more time among the Jesuit priests at the college than he did with the students. He cared more for their company.

Through these priests, Louis was given the great desire to become a Missionary and a *Martyr*. Remember, these were Jesuits who taught in this college. Stories floated back from the Missions in Canada, from the Blackrobes (Jesuits) who fought and ultimately won the battle for Jesus against the false gods of the pagans in North America. While he was in college, Louis probably read in *"Relations"*[6] how conversions were coming about in the missions in Canada. Kateri Tekakwitha, who died during the time Louis was in the Jesuit college at Rennes, was one of the most inspiring of the native converts. Louis wanted to go to Canada and evangelize to the Natives. But Our Lady had other work for him to do. She would give him his heart's desire, to become a Martyr, but not in the way that he thought.

Louis was always a very bold person. He truly believed he was being guided by Divine Providence. He cared not whether he had money in his pockets, clothes on his back, or a roof over his head. He just walked the road on which he believed the Lord had sent him. An example of this happened when he was at the Jesuit College in Rennes. His family moved there, most likely to be close to him, although they all went back to Iffendic in the summers. But Louis felt the call to the priesthood. He prayed for hours in front of the statue of our Lady of Mount Carmel in the

---

[5] We know of no other writer whom Pope John Paul II has recommended in an Encyclical.

[6] the diaries or histories of the Jesuits

Carmelite church in Rennes. What discussions he and Our Lady must have had throughout his life! At any rate, when the decision was made to become a priest, a young woman from Paris, Mlle. de Montigny, who had come to meet Louis' father on business, offered to be his benefactor; she would pay his way to study at the Seminary of St. Sulpice in Paris. She told him how it was the model of all seminaries in the world, founded by the friend of many Saints, who had as a teacher St. Francis de Sales.[7] Louis was so excited, he could taste it! He advised his parents he was leaving Rennes to study theology in St. Sulpice in Paris. He had been at the Jesuit College in Rennes for eight years, and it was time to move on. He was being called.

He felt the need to be completely free of any earthly burden, as he walked his way from Rennes to Paris, 348 kilometers (or 226 miles). It was a bold stroke and took a great deal of courage for a young man of nineteen to make his way on his own. As he traveled by foot, it took him *ten days* to get there. To be sure that he was dependent only on the Lord, after he left the confines of Rennes, he gave his money and his possessions to a beggar. He even exchanged his clothes with the beggar; so that when he arrived in Paris, he looked like a beggar himself. The ten days journey had been atrocious. He looked terrible! His huge looming stature, coupled with his unkempt appearance, caused people to be frightened of him, or at least desirous to keep him at a safe distance from them. He begged for food and lodging. Whatever help he did get was given to him begrudgingly. But he didn't care. These things meant nothing to him. Only the Lord. He created a battle cry, *"God alone."*

Young Louis embraced the poor in Paris. It was not difficult because he was one of them. For the first six months, his benefactor Mlle. de Montigny paid for his board (the room was free) in a poor seminary run by a saint of a priest, who had no skills in the kitchen. But after a time her reserves diminished, and he was on his own. He lived in communities with starving seminarians, all

---

[7]who had been canonized just thirty years before

of whom were studying for the priesthood. For the first two years, he went to the University of Sorbonne, and the last six were spent under the priests at St. Sulpice.

Louis experiences many crosses in Paris

Louis was exposed to the best of Paris and the worst. St. Sulpice was located on the Rive Gauche, the Left Bank, the Bohemian section, most likely even at that time. But he concentrated his time and efforts on the courses afforded him in these halls of learning. As he progressed in his studies, using Sacred Scripture as his basis, his mission manifested itself to him. He was to be an *itinerant preacher*, going from village to village proclaiming the Good News of Jesus. He wanted in effect to do as Jesus had done before him. Where he would carry on his ministry would be up to the Lord to decide.

Louis was a challenge to the Sulpicians. They were a spiritual-enough group of religious, but they were no match for Louis. Perhaps they were more sophisticated, being from the area of Paris, or having been brought up under more genteel circumstances than he, or they might not have been given the same mandate from Our Lord Jesus and His Mother Mary, to go out and save souls. Did they see in Louis something that they had seen in themselves, a long time before? Was there a holiness in his eyes and in his demeanor that forced them to look away, because the brightness showed them the imperfections in themselves? Did they feel that by joking about his piety and reverence, accusing him of being a charlatan or a country bumpkin, they could soothe their own consciences? One Sulpician priest in speaking about Louis said, *"Monsieur Grignion's pious air was only affectation, his conversation was beneath contempt; his silence, stupidity; his meditation, illusion; his zeal, the result of his temperament; his acts of gentleness and humility but means to attract the esteem of others."* And this, of a man whose book, *True Devotion to Mary,* has been memorized by our Pope John Paul II.

Louis experienced many crosses during that time with the

Sulpicians in Paris. But had he known in advance, he would have welcomed them anyway. He had learned to embrace the Cross passionately. And to accommodate him, God sent him *heavy* crosses, because He loved Louis so much.

A very scary thing, we've found out since we began this book on the Visionaries, Mystics and Stigmatists, is that they all loved the Cross, and they were all given heavy crosses, to the point that we would think they couldn't have survived under the weight of them. When they were at their spiritual peak, the crosses became heavier and heavier. But the Saints accepted them as a sign of God's love. The more He loved them, the heavier the crosses. In our society, we have a tendency to cry out, *"Lord, what did I do? Don't You love me anymore?"* when we are given heavy crosses. The Visionaries, Mystics and Stigmatists cried out these words when they *were not given* crosses.

After eight years in Paris, under extreme conditions, Louis Marie de Montfort was ordained on June 5, 1700, in the Church of St. Sulpice on the left bank of Paris. He celebrated his first Mass at the Chapel of Our Lady which had been such a special haven for him during his time at the Seminary. She had given him inspiration, wisdom, courage. He was finally ready to go out on his mission, whatever that was. Just because he was ordained, didn't mean his crosses at the hands of the Sulpicians were over. Although they ordained him, they did not give him his faculties as Preacher and Confessor, two extremely important duties of a priest. He accepted this as another cross from the Lord. Louis believed and lived the Gospel where Jesus addresses Pilate with the words: *"You would have no authority over Me, if My heavenly Father had not given it to you."*[8]

We would have thought it was more like the evil one, doing anything and everything possible to stop Louis from beginning, for he knew that once Louis started, nothing would stop him. Souls would be saved *en masse,* and the evil one didn't want that.

---

[8]John 19:11

Louis Marie was like a race horse at the starting gate. He was so primed, so ready to get out there and do the work the Lord and his beautiful Mother Mary had planned for him. He really envisioned himself walking through the forests of Canada, looking for Hurons or Iroquois whom he could convert. He even asked his Superior, who made no bones about how he felt about Louis, if he could be sent to Canada. The Sulpicians had been there for a time and had been fairly successful in the missions. The priest, Father Leschassier, laughed contemptuously, and answered with a wave of the hand, *"You in Canada? No. No. Looking for the Indians, you'd get lost among the trees."* And so Louis waited.

An old priest came to St. Sulpice who took a liking to Louis. He asked him to come to his Community in Nantes, which was about 85 kilometers from Rennes, near Louis' hometown and a long way from Paris. The priest wanted Louis to be a missionary for his Community. Louis jumped at the chance; his Superior jumped at the chance of getting rid of Louis. So he began his walk to Nantes. When Louis arrived, much to his dismay, he found the Community was more worldly than the Sulpicians in Paris. They wore silks and gold buttons and lace. He couldn't wait to get out.

Providence came to him in the form of his sister being clothed in the habit at a convent some distance from Nantes. The convent was run by the King's former mistress, Madame de Montespan, who had converted after the king dropped her, but who wielded much power in all circles, church and otherwise. She was taken with Louis and his strange appearance, but it was his sincerity and piety which overwhelmed her. She asked him what he wanted to do. He said he wanted to work with the poor in the missions. She suggested he speak to the Bishop of Poitiers, which was quite a distance (considering that Louis always walked). But he accepted her invitation, and set out for Poitier. However, before he did so, he celebrated Mass for the nuns. After finishing Mass, Louis spied a blind beggar at the door of the chapel. He asked if the man would like to see. The response was an excited *Yes.* Louis moistened his fingers with his saliva, put them on the man's eyes, and prayed to Our Lord Jesus and Our Mother Mary. The man opened his eyes and saw! This is the first recorded miracle attributed to St. Louis Marie de Montfort. But there's a cute twist to this. Madame de Montespan, whose convent it was, and who owned the chapel, claimed the miracle was not to be attributed to Louis Marie, but to her, because *she* had invited him in to celebrate Mass at *her* chapel. Louis could not have cared less who got credit.

When he arrived in Poitiers, the bishop was out of town, so Louis Marie asked permission to spend the four days waiting for him in the hospital chapel. He went there and prayed for four hours on his knees. When the hospital personnel saw him, they took him for a beggar and took up a collection. When Father Louis came out of the chapel, he began ministering to them - first the personnel, then the patients, then the people in the streets and in the prison. By the time the bishop arrived, Louis had won the hearts of all the people in the area. The bishop didn't know what to do with him. He wanted Fr. Louis to take charge of the spiritual direction of the old hospital, but he wanted to know a little more about him first. He wrote letters to Louis' previous Superiors. Meanwhile, the bishop asked him to remain in Poitiers until he received answers from his inquiries.

The bishop had to leave town for a month or so, and so he told his vicar to let Louis do whatever he thought best to bring the souls of Poitiers to the Lord. That was possibly the greatest thing he could have said, as far as Louis was concerned, but not as far as the priests and religious of Poitiers were concerned. Louis took the bishop at his word. He went all over the town, ministering to everyone in sight. He went to the hospital, to the schools, to the prisons, to the market place. He started lay organizations; he gave alms to the poor. He virtually took over Poitiers, and the people loved him. By this time he received word from his Superior in Paris, criticizing him for not having given more time to the old priest in the mission in Nantes, where the priests had been more decadent than in Paris. But Fr. Louis was obedient, and so he walked all the way back to Nantes, about 180 kilometers (97.5 miles). The great gift he was given by making this sacrifice was that as soon as he arrived, he was given all his faculties, to hear confessions, as well as to preach.

He was sent on his first mission to a small country parish outside Nantes. It was small, and the people were poor, but he loved it. He didn't change his lifestyle at all. He remained poor, begging for everything and anything he received. He begged for alms, and then gave whatever he received to the poor. He dressed like a pauper, which he was in the eyes of the world. But in the eyes of God and of his Lady, he was their Prince; he was rich beyond compare. He taught the school children in the daytime, as well as spoke to the adults in the parish three times a day. He baptized, heard confessions, administered first Holy Communions, consoled the sick and dying.

Fr. Louis was on a roll. He went from the one town to another town, then to another and still another. By the time the Bishop of Poitiers caught up with him, he had been out in the countryside for three months. *And the people loved him!* But the people in Poitiers loved him as well. The bishop wanted him back. He was too overpowering for the priests at the mission in Nantes, so the good Superior was more than pleased to let Louis go back to Poitiers, with his blessings and a healthy stipend,[9] for all his labors in the field of evangelization. Fr. Louis naturally gave the money to the poor on the way back to Poitiers.

It was here, on the second go round at the hospital at Poitiers that he met his first spiritual daughter, *Marie Louise Trichet.* She was to become the first *sister* in his religious order, Sisters of Wisdom. She came to him in 1702 to ask for counselling on her vocation. She was from a well-known family in Poitiers; she wanted to become a nun. Louis didn't feel that she should be enclosed in the cloisters. He prayed. Maries Louise began to work in the hospital with him. She kept asking him about her vocation. He held her back. He knew there was something Our

---

[9]gift of money

Lord Jesus and our Mother Mary wanted with Louise. Finally, a few months later, Fr. Louis had to go to Paris. On his return, Marie Louise pleaded with him for a decision. He brought her to the hospital with him. In February, 1703, on the Feast of the Purification of Our Lord Jesus, Marie Louise was dressed and capped in the Order of *"Daughters of Wisdom,"* the Order for women that she was instrumental in co-founding.

There were a lot of ramifications to this action, all of them against Fr. Louis Marie. He instructed Marie Louise to walk up and down the streets of Poitiers, in her new habit, and evangelize in the districts where she used to socialize. This was, at best, *unusual* in those days. Nuns were in cloister. This one was not. She became the brunt of many snubs, insults, attacks, and general estrangement. Marie Louise's mother, who felt she had been publicly ridiculed, went after Fr. Louis Marie. She didn't stop until she had most of the people in the town against him. Complaints found their way to the bishop's office by the droves. Fr. Louis Marie was discredited, fired from his job as manager of the hospital, and asked to leave the diocese. The girl, Marie Louise Trichet went to a local convent and was guided by the sisters there. Fr. Louis Marie went back to Paris for a short time, and then found that the people of the hospital at Poitiers did indeed want him to return. He went back for a third time. Marie Louise joined him with another girl, Catherine Brunet, who was to become the second entrant into the order of Daughters of Wisdom. *[Marie Louise Trichet was Beatified on May 16, 1993 by Pope John Paul II.]* But again, things went bad for Fr. Louis Marie and he was to leave the hospital for the last time. He would never come back.

Poitiers was to be a place of valleys and high places for Fr. Louis. The Lord and our Lady blessed him in all the missions he gave. He experienced his greatest successes in towns where most would not have given him the slightest chance of reaching the people. He was able to get the most incorrigible citizens back to the Church; people who had never heard the name of Jesus now prayed the Rosary and marched in procession. He, the huge blustering oddball priest, was known as the gentle priest when it came to the confessional. The people loved him and wanted him to stay with them. The number of conversions were in great swells. They called Father Louis Marie *"The Good Priest from Montfort."*

For this reason, the devil brought out all his guns to destroy Louis and hopefully, in the wake of that, destroy the souls of all those to whom he had ministered. You would think the pounding and beating Fr. Louis Marie was subjected to, at the hands of the demons at night in his little room, would have been enough. They were the least. The slings and arrows of ungrateful men were what wounded him the most. They went after him, no matter where his mission took him in the Diocese of Poitiers, to belittle him and discredit him. They couldn't kill him; that would have created a *"Wet Martyr."*[10] Instead, they went about making him a *"Dry Martyr."*[11] They would make him look foolish, so that all he preached would appear foolish. The Bishop of Poitiers wanted him there; he could see very easily all the good that was being done through his work. But he bowed to the pressure of political powers, villainous powers, and Fr. Louis Marie de Montfort, Mary's hero, found himself exiled from the diocese *again*.

Fr. Louis Marie *walks* to Rome!

Fr. Louis Marie knew what he wanted to do - preach missions. If he was not able to do that in Poitiers, he would ask the Pope where he should preach his missions, or what he should do. Louis was completely open, completely obedient. He just needed direction. He enjoyed the slurs and slings of outrageous men, because it brought him closer to the Kingdom, but he felt he may possibly have been spinning his wheels in Poitiers, or that his work was done there, and the Lord was trying to tell him in so many words that it was time to move on.

It's very difficult to visualize anyone walking from Poitiers, France to Rome, Italy. Look on a map. You will see the great

---

[10] one who willingly dies for the Faith.

[11] Archbishop Fulton J. Sheen says these are those who do not die for the Faith, but suffer persecution, all their lives for the Church.

expanse, and somewhere, you have to cross the Alps mountains. But Louis began his journey. Now, in light of what we said above, we want you to again look at the map of Italy, and find Loreto, where the Holy House of Nazareth rests. If you can't find Loreto, look for Ancona on the Adriatic sea. Loreto is about ten miles inland from Ancona.

On St. Louis Marie de Montfort's way to Rome, he made a detour to the Holy House[12] of Loreto. He spent time there with our Lady and the Angels, communicating with them. He may have gone to the Pope for his instructions, but we believe he got most of them right there in the Holy House of Loreto. Strengthened by the love of our Lady, his bloody feet bathed in the light of her love, Louis gathered enough strength to continue his journey to Rome. As he approached within view of St. Peter's dome, he took off his shoes and walked the rest of the way barefoot.

The Lord put a priest in his path, who just happened to be the *Pope's confessor*. Well, that took care of that. An audience was arranged without any difficulty, and in June, 1706, Fr. Louis Marie de Montfort found himself in a special audience with Pope Clement XI. Louis Marie was completely taken back. He was in the presence of a descendant of Peter the Apostle. But Louis had the courage of Our Lady and the Angels behind him, and so he shared about the work he had done in the diocese of Poitiers, probably leaving out the problems he encountered there, or at least minimizing their importance. He talked about his ongoing wish to go to Canada to the missions of Ontario or Quebec and minister to the natives of North America. We believe the interview ended with a commitment to submit himself to whatever the Prince of the Apostles felt he should do.

The Pope answered immediately, without hesitation: *"Go back*

---

[12]Read about the Holy house of Loreto in Bob and Penny's book: *"Heavenly Army of Angels"* or see the video they filmed at the Shrine entitled: *The Holy House of Loreto.*

to France, and to work. It is a field big enough for your zeal. Work against Jansenism.[13] *Teach the children their catechism. Teach all Christians to renew the promises they made, by themselves or through their godparents in Baptism.* ***And always be obedient to the bishop of the diocese."***

Louis had always been obedient to his bishop, but it always created a problem. However, in the lives of the Visionaries, Mystics and Stigmatists we have shared with you in this book, the key thread which bound all of them together was *obedience*. Louis knew that and accepted it. Therefore it was no great surprise to him when he returned to the diocese of Poitiers, feet bleeding terribly, his condition badly run down from lack of food and water, and sleeping under the stars as often as not, that the bishop sent an emissary to the monastery where he was convalescing, to tell him in no uncertain terms that he was not allowed to celebrate Mass in the diocese of Poitiers. In obedience to the Bishop of Poitiers, Louis got up from his bed and walked *eighteen miles* until he was outside the boundaries of his diocese. He was provided shelter by the generosity of a friendly priest. He recuperated from his trip to Rome on the one hand, and prepared himself for the journey ahead on the other, the journey of Evangelization through the Missions.

He was not going to let anyone stop him in his mission; after all it had been given to him especially by His Holiness, Pope Clement XI. The Pope had given St. Louis Marie the title *"Apostolic Missionary,"* and Louis Marie was taking it seriously. The Pope had blessed Louis Marie's Crucifix, at which time he placed it on top of his staff to carry with him everywhere he went. He also gave Louis Marie the power to grant a Plenary Indulgence to anyone who would kiss the Blessed Crucifix on his or her deathbed. The only condition was that they repent of their sins, and call out in reverence - the names of Jesus and Mary.

---

[13] A heresy running rampant at that time, which taught that man was unable to resist temptation, and denied the doctrine that Christ died for all men. It spawned an elitist society of *"predestined saints."* During Louis Marie's time, the Jansenists expanded the heresy to state only persons with perfect contrition could receive the Sacraments of Penance and the Eucharist.

Father Louis headed in the direction of Rennes, where it had all begun for him twenty-one years before. But as in the case of his trip to Loreto, he made another out-of-the-way trip on his way back to Rennes. This time it was to the shrine of St. Michael the Archangel, Mont St. Michel, in Normandy. He arrived there for the Feast of the Archangels, September 29.

We know that St. Louis Marie had a very special relationship with Our Lady. She appeared to him many times, and you can be sure that they communicated with each other often, through apparitions and inner locutions. We also know that Our Lady's champion in Heaven is St. Michael the Archangel. Wherever you see anything about Our Lady, you will see a statue, a painting or something relating to St. Michael the Archangel. We have to believe that with all the struggle St. Louis experienced in the years of his ministry, the dangers he was subjected to, he had to implore the Prince of the Heavenly Hosts for help. And there is no question in our mind that he was aided by Michael and all his Angels. Whether the Angel actually ever appeared to Louis or our Apostolic Missionary just felt his presence is not important.

In the case of Don Bosco, his enemies actually saw and *felt* the fangs of Il Grigio (the grey one), the ugly dog that defended Don Bosco, whom he later referred to as his Guardian Angel.[14] In the case of Charles Garnier, in the missions of Canada the Indians saw a huge Angel walking beside him. In St. Louis Marie de Montfort's case, it could have been any of the above. At any rate, St. Louis spent time there, honoring the Heavenly Army of Angels on this special feast.

Returning to Rennes was an interesting experience for him. He was asked to speak at many churches and seminaries, although he still looked like a vagrant. On his way to Dinan, he had to pass through his own village, Montfort, and the place where he had spent his youth, La Bachelleraie. He begged for food and shelter, not telling anyone who he was. Everyone turned him away. The poorest man in town took him in, and that was before he recognized

---

[14]*"Memoirs of the Oratory"* by Don Bosco - Don Bosco Multimedia

him as the son of M. Grignion. Before long, everyone in the district was standing outside the beggar's home, apologizing for not taking Louis Marie in. A statement Louis Marie made to his aunt Andrée, sums up what he meant to say to all of them:

"You have committed a great fault, not against me but against Jesus. You are making it up to me now, but not to Him. You are showing me your affections, not because He is in me, but because I am in me. Jesus abides in the poor, even the least of them. The next time a poor man asks anything of you, give what you can - for you give it to Jesus as well as to him."

St. Louis continued on to Dinan where he gave retreats and missions, opened hospitals, worked with the poor and the sick, taught the children catechism because that was beneath the other priests who were giving missions. He worked wonders with the military men at the local garrison, because the local missionaries didn't want to get involved with what they thought was an impossible situation. The soldiers were only interested in the things of the flesh, and nothing the good priest from Montfort could tell them would change them. However, the Lord worked through St. Louis here as He had in so many other places. By the time he was finished with them, they were praying the Rosary, they had put up a painting of Our Lady in their barracks, and lit a perpetual candle in honor of her. When Louis left them, they promised with all they were worth, to keep it lit forever.

Father Louis Marie was recruited by a very famous priest, a Father Leuduger, to join a group of secular missionaries in a diocese in Brittany, St. Brieuc. Louis thought this was exactly what he wanted, but it was not necessarily the Lord's plan. As in every other place he went, he was well accepted by the people. But he was a very firm man when it came to Our Lord Jesus and Our Lady, and the teachings of the Church. Because of this, he always found himself an outsider with other missionaries in the group, with other priests. He was too stern, unbending, and altogether too overpowering for their tastes. So after he single-handedly gave

(Le Calvaire) The Calvary at Pontchâteau

powerful missions, the priests asked him to leave their group because he was not really of them.

No, he was not! He was an Apostolic Missionary. He was completely committed to his cause. Father Louis was not a compromiser. He didn't give in, for the sake of peace within the group. He had given up his entire life; he had ill-treated his own body, for the sake of his soul. He couldn't allow himself to settle for something other than his convictions, just because he ruffled some feathers. That was his calling card, *ruffling feathers*. But he was not popular with the other priests, and so he had to leave, and go his way on his own. *"His preaching was a source of admiration for many, of resentment and anger for others."*[15]

The Shrine of Calvary in Pontchâteau

In 1709, St. Louis went to a little town called Pontchâteau, between Nantes and Redon, to give a mission. The people were on fire. Louis had always wanted to build a Calvary, in honor of Our Lord Jesus, Mother Mary and the others members of His Passion. After giving a mission in this town, he received an inspiration from the Holy Spirit. He shared his plan with the people at the mission who became very enthused. They chose a spot, a distance from the town and began to dig. In short order, it was determined this was not the right spot. So he brought everyone into the Chapel to pray for guidance from Our Lady.

When they went back outside, they saw two white doves come

---

[15]*God Alone*, Montfort Fathers - Pg. xi

down out of the sky, and settle on the mound which had already been dug out. The doves took dirt into their mouths, and flew off. They did this quite a few times. Louis prayed all the while this was happening. Eventually he realized that the doves were trying to bring them to a place. Louis Marie and the workers followed the doves to where they landed, some distance from where they had been. There they found a *"hive-shaped"* mound, on the highest point of the area. From this vantage point, a Calvary could be built and the crosses seen from miles around. They began to work.

Little by little, old-timers from the town came to the site. They shared a story which had happened some thirty six years before, whose meaning they had never been able to figure out. The people testified that they had seen crosses coming down from the sky, during the daytime with banners flying from them. The crosses hovered over this spot and stayed there for a time. Then there were very loud noises which frightened animals for miles around. This was followed by singing, Angelic singing, as if floating down Heaven to earth. They said the date this happened was *January 31, 1673, **the day St. Louis Marie Grignion de Montfort was born.***

At first, just the people of Pontchâteau took part in the project. But soon people from all over the district came with tools, ready to build Calvary. Statues of all the participants of the Passion, Our Lord Jesus, Our Lady of Sorrows, St. John the beloved, and St. Mary Magdalene were carved at the same time the mountain was being built. The statues were placed in the grotto which had been formed by the digging. Every evening, after the workers were finished digging, they went down to the grotto and prayed to Our Lord Jesus and the other members of the Passion.

The main tree for the Calvary was cut from a neighboring village. It took twenty-four oxen to bring it to the mountain. The trees of the two thieves were placed on either side of it, one on the right and one on the left. One hundred and fifty fir trees were planted for the Hail Marys, and fifteen cypresses for the Our Fathers. It was a most beautiful tribute to our Heavenly Family.

But as had plagued Louis all his life, the powers of evil were ready to destroy what had been built in honor of God. There was a war with England going on. Word got out that all this digging was going on. Those who hated the Church and especially St. Louis Marie de Montfort complained to the authorities: *Le Calvaire* (The Calvary) was in Brittany, which was right across the English Channel from England; if the English should attack, the Calvary would make a perfect fort to use against the French. The project had taken over a year. The solemn blessing was to take place on September 14, 1710, Feast of the Triumph of the Cross. A few days before the blessing, the bishop was pressured by a small group of very vocal, special interests with an agenda, and orders were given to Fr. Louis Marie and the people of Pontchâteau to *tear down* the monument built to Our Lord Jesus.

The words of Pope Clement XI came rushing back into the mind of this heartbroken priest, "***And always be obedient to the bishop of the diocese.***" The people of Pontchâteau and the surrounding villages tore down the mountain, *Le Calvaire* (the Calvary), the shrine to the Crucifixion of Our Lord Jesus. Louis Marie was to learn again, *God Alone!* Strangely enough, however, that's not the end of the story. *Le Calvaire* was rebuilt *again* in 1747. Then the crosses had to be replaced *again* in 1774, after they had collapsed. And then *again* they were replaced in 1785. The Reign of Terror that spread throughout France tore down the crosses *once again*. But, the Church will never stay down, and after the French Revolution a *new* Calvary was built on the same site. Bronze crosses were erected in 1854, the same year that the Dogma of the Immaculate Conception was proclaimed. Pilgrimages began in 1873.

Today, it is a major shrine in Brittany. We visited it, this summer and it is a majestic tribute to Our Lord and His Passion. *Le Calvaire* cannot be wiped from this countryside, no more than His Death and Resurrection. The crosses loom high in the sky, a testimony of love and hope for the world.

Miracles and Conversions in St. Louis Marie's life

The stories of Louis Marie de Montfort's missions are classical. Here was a man who did not go out of his way to become attractive to those whom he encountered, and yet he captured their hearts. There are stories of many miracles attributed to St. Louis Marie de Montfort during his lifetime. There are reports of apparitions of Our Lady.

One time, in La Garnache Louis was in the rectory garden praying his office before dinner. A young man was sent to call him for dinner, but he returned, saying the priest *"was having a conversation with a lady who was floating in the air."*

Another time, Louis was leaving a church when a woman came up to him with her child whose head was full of scales and sores. The mother prayed for a healing. He put his hands over the child and prayed for a healing to reward the mother's faith. The scales dropped off the child's head, and she clapped her hands and laughed. She was healed. There are many, many stories about miracles attributed to St. Louis Marie de Montfort, but the greatest miracles were the conversions of hardened sinners, Jansenists and Calvinists,[16] who came to his missions to disrupt and destroy them.

In many instances, because of conversions of hardened Protestants, Calvinists and Jansenists, murderers were sent to kill de Montfort at these missions. In one instance, a man came into the room where Louis was praying and drew a sword, threatening to kill him if he didn't leave the mission immediately. Louis stayed kneeling and told the man he would die in glory if the man would change his wicked ways. The hands of the man shook so much, he had to leave the place.

There was a report that Louis threw a bunch of well-dressed Protestants out of a mission because they were trying to disrupt it. They vowed to get even with him. That evening, he was to go

---

[16]followers of John Calvin, who came after Martin Luther. He was ruthless, determined to destroy Catholicism and replace it with his own religion

to the home of a sculptor to look at his work. But as he was approaching the place, he was given a word from Heaven not to go any further, but to turn around and go back to his quarters. It was discovered later that there were seven men waiting to kill him, some of whom had been at the mission that night. They waited in different places to ambush him on subsequent nights but were never successful.

But one attempt on his life almost got him, and weakened him to the point of being the beginning of the end for St. Louis. After the Lord had successfully converted a high-ranking Protestant, an assassin sneaked into the dining room and put a strong poison into Louis' wine. He drank some of it and immediately spit out the rest. Father Louis took an antidote, which prevented him from dying, but his strength gave way. He was never the same.

Louis Marie de Montfort preaches his last mission

Fr. Louis' last mission was in St. Laurent-sur-Sèvre. It began on April 5, 1716. It was a strange mission, he commented, in that no one attacked him. There were no insults, no barbs, no bishops coming after him. There must be something wrong, he joked. But it was different for him also in the fact that his strength was leaving him rapidly. He never looked so bad. The poison had taken its toll on him. During this mission he tended to give his talk and then return to his room in the hovel where he was staying. One morning he was late for Mass. The little altar boy figured that he was probably sick and may have overslept. He went to fetch him at the boarding house. As the boy approached the house, he could see through the window the holy priest in conversation with a beautiful lady, whose shape radiated with a great light. He knew who she must be.

The altar boy waited until the heavenly conversation was ended, and then brought the priest to the church. He mentioned seeing the Lady with Fr. Louis Marie. Father just smiled, and put his arm around the boy. *"You are a happy boy. Only the pure of heart may see that Lady."*

He could feel himself slipping away. He took to his bed. He asked for the Last Rites of the Church. One of his priests from the Company of Mary, later to be called the Montfort Fathers, gave him the Last Rites. Then Fr. Louis Marie made out his will. Everybody became extremely nervous. After having been virtually invincible for years, it actually seemed like their beloved Father, Louis Marie might actually die. One priest in particular, the one who would be natural to carry on the ministry, Fr. Mulot, was a *worker*, but had none of the charismatic qualities of Fr. Louis Marie. On the day of his death, Fr. Louis Marie spoke softly and firmly to this young man. He would have to take over. The work could not die with Louis Marie. He told him, in no uncertain terms, Our Lady was giving him a mandate. He countered all the young priest's arguments with *"Don't worry. I will pray for you. Have confidence in me."*

Father Louis Marie focused his attention on his Crucifix, that great Crucifix which had been blessed by the Pope when he had been given the mandate and the title *Apostolic Missionary*, and a statue of Our Lady. These had been his weapons as he went forth to conquer evil and do good. He kept saying, *"Jesus and Mary."* He weakly began to sing the first verse of a hymn he had composed:

> *On, on, dear friends, to Paradise,*
> *God's Paradise on high!*
> *Whatever be our gain on earth,*
> *'Tis surer gain to die!*

His voice trailed off into a coma. He stayed that way for some time. Everyone assembled prayed for the soul of a man they knew to be a Saint, Louis Marie Grignion de Montfort. After some time, he woke abruptly and cried out, *"Your attacks are quite useless; Jesus and Mary are with me; I have finished my course, I shall never sin again!"*

With that, the Slave of Mary left his withered and wasted body behind, as he went off to Heaven to continue fighting battles from a different vantage point.

Louis keeps fighting the good fight

Satan would have loved if the entire movement of the good priest from Montfort would have ended on that April 28, 1716. The enemy did everything in his power to make it so. The little Community that St. Louis left behind consisted of four Daughters of Wisdom, two priests and six lay brothers in the Company of Mary. They didn't know what to do after his death. They hid out and prayed for almost two years. We believe that from Heaven the Founder was having a fit, because an almost impossible thing happened in Lent of 1718; they were sought out by the Curé of a local church to work in the Parish for that Lent.

They were not too shocked by it until they arrived at the Parish. They thought they would only have to teach Catechism, hear confessions, and say Mass. No! They were to give a full blown Parish Mission, with all the fire and spirit of their Founder, St. Louis Marie. They called themselves the Followers of Montfort. Their mission was a success. They didn't speak the way Fr. Louis Marie spoke, but they allowed the Holy Spirit and Our Lady to speak through them. Fr. Mulot, who was very soft-spoken, was able to get the message of Fr. Louis Marie across without alienating anyone. They did so well that three other missions were set up for them during that same period.

The Daughters of Wisdom and the Company of Mary bought the property at St. Laurent-Sur-Sèvre which had been the inn where their founder had died. They were able, through donations, to buy enough property for a house to be built for the Sisters and another house for the Priests and Brothers. They set forth on their missions from that headquarters. The little Community grew beautifully. But Satan would have to have his way. Through some of the Jansenists, the book *True Devotion to Mary* was blocked from being published. No matter what the Community did, they couldn't get it printed. Add to that the French Revolution at the end of the Eighteenth Century, where nine Priests and Brothers from Louis Marie de Montfort's Order were guillotined, and you can see Satan was having a field day.

With all of that, the manuscript of Fr. Louis Marie's works was misplaced, or lost, or hidden by the devil. Thank God that the Community never left St. Laurent-sur-Sèvre. The Revolution ended; Napoleon had his way and perished, and the little country began to mend itself from its ignoble ventures. On September 7, 1838, one hundred and twenty two years after the death of Fr. Louis, Pope Gregory XVI declared him *Venerable*, the first step towards canonization. The little Community was elated.

Then, possibly the greatest gift, Our Lord could give to the Church and to St. Louis took place in April 22, 1842, when a Priest of the Community was rummaging through old manuscripts which he found in a beat-up trunk. As he began reading one of them, his hands shook, his heart beat excitedly. This had to be the writings of their father in faith, Venerable Louis Marie de Montfort. The Lord had allowed the writings of St. Louis Marie to lay dormant for almost one hundred thirty years. Did He do that so we would never take this powerful Saint or his writings for granted?

This is an amazing Saint! He is possibly more popular now than he has ever been, even when he was alive. His collection of letters and books are not only brilliant, but so Scripture-solid that any Catholic can firmly stand on the teachings. Especially in our world today, the writings of St. Louis Marie de Montfort are having a greater influence on Catholics, not only on the role and importance of Mary in our Church, but on our obligation to Our Lord Jesus and His Vicar on earth, our Pope.

In this short biography, it's not possible to give you even a sampling of the powerful writing of St. Louis Marie de Montfort. He has written extensively. His writing is not difficult to understand. You owe it to yourself to give yourself the gift of Louis Marie de Montfort. Read and practice *True Devotion to the Blessed Virgin*. Read *The Secret of the Rosary* and *The Secret of Mary*. These are powerful writings that are as needed today, as they were three hundred and fifty years ago, maybe more so.

Okay, those are his writings. But there's more. There is his life! Unfortunately, more people know about the writings of this great Saint than about his life. He is a model of so many things, we don't know what to focus on. The very first would have to be his battle cry, his motto, *"God alone!"* In his quest for his Lady, he brought people closer to Jesus. He never for a minute focused on Mary, at the cost of Jesus. It doesn't happen that way with the Saints. When they bring you Mary, you know they're bringing you Jesus.

Another example or virtue which we can imitate from this great Saint is *Obedience.* We know there had to be others in the history of our Church who practiced obedience as much as St. Louis Marie de Montfort, but no one ever practiced it more. His greatest struggles came in practicing obedience. His greatest crosses were given to him in the name of obedience. He embraced these crosses and carried them with joy.

Humility - While he was never given great plaudits in his life, Saint Louis Marie knew that the Lord was working powerfully through him. He personified an old proverb, *"Fools rush in where Angels fear to tread."* He could not help but know when conversions were coming about in areas where everyone had given up, or would not even venture. Louis Marie had courage, knowing that God was always with him, and so he had the freedom to be a fool for Christ. However, he never took credit for any of the successes of his missions. He never even gave himself credit for the strength he had to forge on against tremendous odds. He gave all credit to Our Lord Jesus and His Mother Mary.

We told you at the beginning of this chapter that *Louis Marie de Montfort was a prophet of the Last Days.* The reason we call St. Louis Marie de Montfort a prophet of the last days, even though he lived between the last half of the Seventeenth Century and the first part of the Eighteenth century is because of what we read in his prophecies which deal with these last days:

"....towards the end of the world, ...Almighty God and His holy Mother are to raise up saints who will surpass in holiness most other saints as much as the cedars of Lebanon tower above little shrubs."[17]

*"These great souls filled with grace and zeal will be chosen to oppose the enemies of God who are raging on all sides. They will be exceptionally devoted to the Blessed Virgin. Illumined by her light, strengthened by her spirit, supported by her arms, sheltered under her protection, they will fight with one hand and build with the other. With one hand they will give battle, **overthrowing and crushing heretics and their heresies, schismatics and their schisms, idolaters and their idolatries, sinners and their wickedness.** With the other hand they will build the temple of the true Solomon and the mystical city of God, namely, the Blessed Virgin... "[18]*

"They will be like thunderclouds flying through the air at the slightest breath of the Holy Spirit. Attached to nothing, surprised at nothing, they will shower down the rain of God's word and of eternal life. They will thunder against sin; they will storm against the world; they will strike down the devil and his followers and for life and for death, they will pierce through and through with the two-edged sword of God's word all those against whom they are sent by Almighty God. "[19]

"They will be true apostles of the latter times to whom the Lord of Hosts will give eloquence and strength to work wonders and carry off glorious spoils from His enemies. They will sleep without gold or silver and, more important still, without concern in the midst of other priests, ecclesiastics and clerics. Yet they will have the silver wings of the dove enabling them to go wherever the Holy Spirit calls them, filled as they are, with the resolve to seek the glory of God and the salvation of souls. Wherever they preach, they will leave behind them nothing but the gold

[17]True Devotion to Mary #47
[18]True Devotion to Mary #48
[19]True Devotion to Mary #57

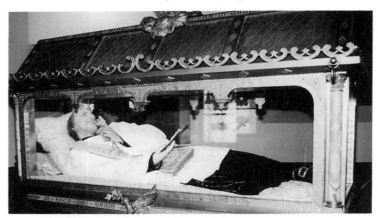

Wax image of St. Louis de Montfort in St. Laurent-sur-Sèvre

of love, which is the fulfillment of the whole law. "[20]

"They will have the two-edged sword of the Word of God in their mouths and the bloodstained standard of the Cross on their shoulders. They will carry the Crucifix in their right hand and the rosary in their left, and the holy names of Jesus and Mary on their heart.[21]

"Mary scarcely appeared in the first coming of Christ... But in the second coming of Jesus Christ, Mary must be known and openly revealed by the Holy Spirit so that Jesus may be known, loved and served through her."[22]

Thank you Jesus and Mary for St. Louis Marie de Montfort.

---

[20]True Devotion to Mary #58
[21]True Devotion to Mary #59
[22]True Devotion to Mary #49

Saint Veronica Giuliani

Visionary, Mystic and Stigmatist, Mystically married to Jesus

Saint Veronica Giuliani

Pope Pius IX said, after reading Veronica Giuliani's Diary that she was not merely a Saint, but a *great* Saint! A bishop, in 1927, two hundred years after her life, wrote that Saint Veronica Giuliani was a Saint for all time: a **Penitent** like St. Rose of Lima[1] who suffered for the redemption of sinners, a **Mystic** like St. Margaret Mary Alacoque[2] to whom God revealed His Love and Passion, a **Visionary** like St. Teresa of Avila[3] passing on the infused knowledge she received from the Lord in her Diary,[4] a **Stigmatist** who like St. Francis,[5] (her father in faith), bore the Wounds of Christ's Passion on her body; she was **Mystically married** to Jesus as was St. Catherine of Siena,[6] a Saint who stands shoulder to shoulder with all the greats before and after her who have

---

[1]Read chapter on St. Rose of Lima in this book.

[2]Read chapter on St. Margaret Mary in this book.

[3]Read chapter on St. Teresa of Avila in Bob and Penny Lord's book: *"Saints and Other Powerful Women in the Church."*

[4]which we pray will someday make her a Doctor of the Church. It contains over 20, 000 pages in 23 volumes.

[5]Read chapter on St. Francis in Bob and Penny Lord's book: *"Saints and Other Powerful Men in the Church."*

[6]Read chapter on St. Catherine of Siena in Bob and Penny Lord's book: *"Saints and Other Powerful Women in the Church."*

molded this Glorious Church which Jesus founded.

Ursula Giuliani (who will later become Sister Veronica) was born on December 27, 1660, in Mercatello, a small village in the Province of the Marches in Italy. Her father was a well-respected member of society. Her mother was a deeply religious woman. She would die before she reached her 40th birthday, leaving Ursula and her four surviving siblings (two having died) to their father's care. *But before she died,* her mother would consecrate each of her five children to the precious Five Wounds of Our Lord Jesus. To the Wound in Our Lord's Side, she entrusted Ursula, who was all of seven years old. Without her understanding the full implication of her mother's bequest, nevertheless this was the beginning of Ursula's betrothal to Jesus' Heart, the very Heart Which bled on the Cross.

Ursula walks with Jesus from the very beginning of her life

From the time of her infancy, little Ursula sought only paintings and statues of Jesus, His Mother and the Saints, pointing to them from as young as a few months old. Barely able to walk, she cried until someone would carry her to a picture of Mother Mary holding the Baby Jesus, so that she could kiss them.[7] She would talk to them saying, *"I am Yours, and You are all mine, dear Jesus!"* The Child Jesus at that time would reply *"I am yours, and you are Mine!"*

Ursula had her first vision of Jesus, seeing Him as a Baby holding out His Hand toward her. She would dream of Jesus. He would play with her in her dreams; her family said they could hear her gleefully talking and laughing.

One day, when she was still a little girl, picking flowers in her garden, Ursula beheld the Infant Jesus. He said, *"I am the real flower."* Then He disappeared! She thought He had run into the house. She ran after Him with such speed, she later wrote it

---

[7]It reminds us of our grandson when he was a little baby pointing to a picture of Jesus, saying *"God!"* and then *"Man!"* and then *"God-Man!"* He was barely able to talk but he knew that Jesus was the *God-Man*; a truth that many with supposed higher intellect deny, today.

Above left: *The entrance to the garden, chapel and the pear tree*
Above right: *The pear tree is now saved as a relic inside the courtyard of the Monastery*

Above: *The cell of St. Veronica Giuliani where she received the Stigmata*

Above:
St. Veronica Giuliani receives the Stigmata

Above: *The original diary of St. Veronica Giuliani*

seemed[8] as if her feet were not touching the ground. Jesus would later call her "**His** *little flower*."

Ursula knew Jesus and loved Jesus in the Blessed Sacrament, from as early as two years old. When the priest raised the consecrated Host, her mother had all to do to keep her from running up to her Lord Present in the Eucharist. She would stand next to her mother and sisters and watch them receive Holy Communion, drinking in the *outer* sign on their faces of the real change taking place *inside*, her mouth opened in joyful anticipation that maybe *this time* she would receive her Lord.

When she first heard her mother read to her about the Martyrs, Ursula was all of three years old. She was so filled with love of Jesus she too wanted to suffer just like them, to be burned for the love of her Lord. As it was winter, she went over to the stove and placed her hand on the fire. Imagine her family's grief, when they saw what she had done. But, Ursula later writes, she did not remember shedding a tear.

She began doing penances from an early age in silence, striking her body with rope, all in a desire to imitate the Saints before her. She began walking on her knees, her little arms outstretched in the form of Jesus Crucified. Like St. Rose of Lima, Ursula desired to carry the Cross as her Jesus had done. She fashioned a Cross, putting two pieces of wood together. She later wrote that it was so heavy, she could not carry it; she found herself falling with every step she took. Our Lord, too, fell under the weight of the Cross made heavy by our sins and the sins of the world.

Ursula had a deep love for the poor, never sending a beggar away empty-handed. Now, she had a new pair of shoes that she had carefully placed by her bed. Oh, how she treasured those shoes. She would have worn them to bed, if she had thought she would not spoil them. One day a beggar came to the door; she knew she had to give him one of her new shoes, and she did.

[8]The Saint uses *"seem"* often, out of humility, never presuming that all or any part of what was revealed to her was of the Lord and His Mother, obediently waiting upon the decision of the Church.

Then, the beggar returned and asked for the other shoe. She gave it to him. A book could be written around that one sentence. Many years passed when Jesus appeared to Ursula, holding out golden shoes in His Hands. He said, *"These are the shoes you gave to Me when you were a little child. I was that beggar."* And He disappeared! Ursula not only invited beggars into her home to share her meal, she led them to pictures of Jesus and Mary, feeding their souls as well as their bodies. And all this began when she was just a little child.

Ursula had an earthly mother who read to her about the Saints, prayed with her and guided her toward Sainthood. Death would bring that to an end, when Ursula was barely seven. She watched her mother die, moment by moment. Ursula was devastated. She was with her mother when she received her last Communion, her Viaticum. Desiring to share this last Gift her mother would receive, she begged the priest for a piece of the Host. He was sad, as he refused her. The child bent close to her mother, to be near her Lord in the Host; she smelled the heavenly fragrance of roses and said to her mother, *"Oh what a beautiful thing; oh what a sweet perfume."* When they returned from the grave, Ursula refused to go to bed, as her mother was no longer there. The only thing that quieted her was when her family placed the statue of the Blessed Mother holding Jesus in her arms. *She* would be her Mother from now on.

On February 2, 1670, at the age of ten Ursula was to finally receive her heart's desire, her Lord Jesus in First Holy Communion. When she received her Lord this first time, she said she felt a fire blazing inside her, *"her heart burning."* From that time on, she would consecrate herself to the Lord *alone.* She wrote:

"In First Communion, I think the Lord was teaching me that I had to be His bride. I experienced something special. I don't know quite what; I was beside myself, but I couldn't understand a thing. I thought it was always like this at Communion."

After receiving Communion, young Ursula had a burning desire to become a nun, to belong to Jesus completely. She would have to wait for the mystical marriage that would take place between her as the beloved and the Lord as her Spouse.

She asked the Blessed Mother to teach her how to suffer. And the Baby Jesus, speaking from His Mother's precious arms said, *"I have suffered so much."* To which Ursula replied, *"I want to do everything You did."* Jesus then said, *"The Cross awaits you."* But little Ursula was so filled with her Lord, so overflowing and abounding was His love, she wanted to offer herself completely to Him. So, at only ten years old, she offered the Lord her total abandonment, in the quiet of night pleading:

"My God, don't delay, any more. My Lord, I do not want to separate from You, until You give me the grace to be Crucified with You. Crucify me with You! Give me Your thorns, Your nails, Your Cross, and all of You; here I am, hands, feet and heart. Wound me, O my Lord!"

Jesus calls Ursula to be His own, and the Courtship begins

Ursula, now a young woman of seventeen, told her father of her desire to be the spouse of her Lord Jesus. He answered by bringing eligible suitors to the house. But seeing the holy stubbornness of his *fiery daughter,* as she had been called since early childhood, he finally gave in and granted her permission to enter the Monastery.

Writers write one liners which cover a lifetime of struggles and temptations. *The road to the Monastery was not to be a smooth one.* Ursula always had a very charismatic personality. Her laughter and joy were infectious. She was beautiful, her blonde hair and blue eyes, a decided attraction to young would-be suitors. She later wrote how she was tempted by a relative who always managed to walk with her in the garden, saying all sorts of worldly, upsetting things to her, bringing her messages from eligible young men asking her hand in marriage. She fought him off, saying,

"If you don't keep quiet, I'll go away. Don't keep bringing me messages. I don't know anybody and I want nobody.

My Spouse is Jesus. He is the One I want. He is mine."

This pursuit by the devil, to tempt her from her Spouse in Heaven lasted two painful years. After much struggling with family, the day finally arrived when Ursula knelt before the bishop and asked for his approval to enter the Monastery in Città di Castello. He was so impressed with her, he suggested to the *Capuchinesses*[9] they admit her, *immediately.* He told them, *"Take care of this new Sister as precious treasure, because she will be a great Saint."* The day she had anxiously been looking forward to finally came about. As she excitedly anticipated her appearance before the Superior of the Monastery, *Ursula went into ecstasy,* and when the nuns came to escort her before their Abbess, they had to wait until she returned to this world!

Ursula begins the Way of the Cross as Sister Veronica

On the day she received her heavy coarse maroon-colored habit, Ursula was given the name of the Saint who had the courage to wipe Our Lord's Face on His Way to the Cross - no longer Ursula but now *Veronica of Jesus and Mary.* This was to be the sign of her life with the Lord, that of His Passion. When did it begin? Was it at age seven when she saw Our Lord covered in wounds? At that time He told her to be devoted to His Passion and then disappeared. When He again appeared, He looked so wounded, His Wounds forged a stamp onto her heart, carving themselves so deeply into its cavity, she was unable to think of anything or anyone else.

Jesus called out to her *"To War! To War!"* when she was still a young girl. As with her Seraphic father Francis, she misunderstood and began to study the art of fencing. Our Lord then appeared to her and said, *"This is not the war I want from you."* Jesus was preparing her for the battles she would have to wage in His Name.

When she was vested in her habit, *Sister Veronica* asked three things of the Lord: *One,* that she would have the strength to live up to the life she had pledged to follow; *Two,* that she never

---

[9]Capuchin nuns

wander far from His Will; And *Three* that He keep her on the Cross with Him. [That last one makes me tremble! I know the Cross He could have me share and I am not inviting my Lord to do that.] He promised Veronica she would do all she desired, but cautioned her that the price would be much suffering. She would drink from the cup of bitterness, as she shared the Lord's Way of the Cross.

The Lord was calling her to *"make up in her flesh what was lacking in the sufferings of Christ"*[10] **for the good of the whole Church**. The Lord has always turned to His Mystics and Saints calling for *sacrifice* for His beloved Church, the Church which flowed from His Heart on the Cross. Saint Catherine of Siena, another powerful Visionary, Mystic and Stigmatist, *"had a Vision in the early part of 1380, in which the ship of the Church crushed her to the earth. At that moment she offered herself as a willing sacrifice. She was to be ill from that time (until) on April 29th of that year she went to her reward."*[11]

In the first year of her religious life, her novitiate, Veronica was to suffer the slings and arrows of the devil through her sister novices. They constantly strived to show her in a very bad light in front of her Novice Mistress who took up the persecution of Veronica with gusto, causing the little novice to struggle against the temptation to fight back! She later wrote, *"What a struggle went on inside of me, to overcome myself!"*

The enemy never lets up. He barely allows you to catch your breath, when he strikes again, more furiously than before. The attacks would be ongoing throughout Veronica's life as a religious. They were so brutal, they could only have been waged by the number one archenemy of God, Lucifer himself. He took on the identity of some of her fellow sisters accusing her of vile misconduct. When that was not enough to destroy her, they began

---

[10]St. Paul

[11]from chapter on Saint Catherine of Siena in Bob and Penny Lord's book: *"Saints and other Powerful Women in the Church."* Read more about Saint Catherine and other powerful Saints who were also Visionaries, Mystics and Stigmatists.

to abuse her physically, inflicting wounds, bruising her body mercilessly. And then, as with her Seraphic father Francis before her, the enemy thought to do her in by having his fallen angels appear as monsters performing disgusting obscene acts. But wherever the enemy of God is, the Shepherd is not far away. The Lord gave her the strength to not only withstand the assaults, but to infuriate the devil as she laughed at his stupid antics.

Where are You, Lord?

It has been called the **Dark Night of the Soul** by the Mystics, like Saint Teresa of Avila and Saint John of the Cross, and rightly so. [We can still remember when we lost our son, the pain of not having the consolation of the Lord and His Mother. Only with us, it was not He Who withheld Himself from us but we who turned our backs on Him. And till today, when we are ever slightly tempted to go with the crowd and run from Jesus and his persecuted Church on the Cross, we remember life without Jesus and fight the good fight. Nothing can compare with that Dark Night of the Soul when you no longer feel the Lord inside you. Not even the devastating loss of a loved one can compare with the loss of *the Loved One*.] Saint Veronica was to write:

> *"One occasion, when I was dry and desolate and longing for the Lord but unable to find Him, I would come out of myself and run from one place to another. I called for Him out loud, using all kinds of magnificent names, repeating them several times. At times, I seemed to hear Him, but in a way I cannot explain....I felt as though I were on fire, especially around the heart."*

Sister Veronica would apply cloths soaked in cold water to allay the pain, but upon contact, the heat that was emanating from her body quickly dried them, leaving her in excruciating pain.

Pain was the road she would travel to complete union with Jesus. Most of us can stand almost any kind of pain - physical, spiritual or mental, if we have a loved one at our side. Veronica was all alone, without earthly or *Divine* consolation! Through this pain, she would know the Spouse Whom she had chosen and

Who had chosen her. Her walk was to be to the Cross, to *literally* hang there with her Spouse Jesus *alone*, deserted, mocked and rejected. She would cry out, as He had before her: *"My God! My God, why have You forsaken me?"* in her Dark Night of the Soul.

When we went to make our documentary on Saint Veronica, we stood in front of the Cross upon which she would hang almost every evening (and during the forty days of Lent *every* evening), after her work was done, for anywhere from an hour to an hour and a half. She would tell the nun who helped her climb onto the cross, to return and help her off the cross when her time was up. One evening, the nun overslept and did not come for Veronica until the following morning (around three hours later, possibly more). When they found Veronica, she was close to death. Her confessor forbid her to hang on the cross from that time on, and she obeyed.

Veronica began suffering from aridity. She was longing for the Lord, trying to find Him, to have Him talk to her; He seemed to be nowhere to be found. Where did she go for help? To the Sacraments! She went to confession sometimes four or five times a day! She desired a complete union with her Spouse; He was not responding. Well, she would not give up; she would wait for Him! She lived as though He would come at any moment. While she was waiting for Him, she would go about making her house (soul) spotless for Him to enter. Even as He withheld Himself from her, she had an unexplainable urgency to prepare herself for that moment when He and she would be one. It reminds us of what someone once said, *"When a woman loves you, you can't drive her away; she will never leave you."* And so, it was with Saint Veronica and Jesus, only more so.

Veronica is shown Hell

Veronica asked Our Lord for His sufferings, and He said *Yes!* An eye-witness attested to the following:

"One day, I saw her suspended in midair, shedding tears of blood which stained her veil. Later, she told me that

God was greatly offended by sinners and that she, in a trance, had seen the wickedness of sin, and of sinners' ingratitude."

Having been shown hell, Veronica devoted her life to keeping souls from ending up there. She wrote:

"At that moment I was once again shown hell opened, and it seems that many souls descended there, and they were so ugly and black that they struck terror in me. They all dropped down in a rush, one after the other, and once they entered those chasms, there was nothing to be seen but fire and flames."

Upon seeing this, Sister Veronica offered herself as a victim to hold back the Hand of the *God of Justice.* [Today, when we are being told God is Love (and He most certainly is) and God is merciful (and He most certainly is), we are not being taught He is also the God Who is Just, the God of Justice. Prophets and Visionaries tell us that in the final days, when the time of the God of Mercy is over, we must stand before the God of Justice.] Veronica pleaded, she be allowed to block the entrance to hell, so that no one would be able to enter, and lose the Lord for all eternity. She outstretched her arms, as if on a cross and said to the Lord,

"As long as I stand in the doorway, no one shall enter. O souls go back! My God, I ask nothing of You but the salvation of sinners. Send me more torments, more crosses!"

On the Cross Our Lord said *"I thirst!"* He thirsted for souls! As Veronica shared His thirst for souls, He allowed her to experience the pains of Purgatory and Hell. Our Lady who had prepared her told her that *"Many do not believe that Hell exists, and I tell you that you yourself, who have been there, have understood nothing of what hell is."*

The Mystical Marriage of Veronica and Jesus

On Easter Sunday, 1694, Jesus appeared to Veronica, seated on a golden throne adorned with sparkling jewels. Before Him, on a throne of alabaster, sat His Mother the Blessed Virgin praying to Him, in readiness to offer Veronica to Him as His bride. Saints Rose of Lima and Catherine of Siena, acting as her ladies in waiting were there encouraging Veronica. Jesus took the wedding ring, embossed with His Name, from His Sacred Heart. Our Lady held out her hand to Veronica and guided her to the Royal throne of her Divine Spouse. She handed Veronica's right hand to the Lord and He placed the mystical wedding ring on her finger. Veronica wrote in her Diary:

> *"I felt the pressing of the ring, on my finger; and so it is every time I receive Communion, I feel I am again at the wedding."*

Jesus asks Veronica to make her confession

Before Jesus would share His Wounds with His beloved Veronica, He would require she make a general confession before the entire Heavenly Court. On Good Friday, in the year 1697, she had a vision of the Risen Lord, the Virgin Mary most holy, all the Angels and the Saints. The Lord asked her to begin her confession. She began, *"I have offended You and confess to You my God,"* when suddenly she could not go any further because there before her, were all the times she had offended her Lord, and the sorrow she felt was indescribable. The Lord turned to her Guardian Angel and commanded him to speak for her.

Then Our Lady came before her Son. She stood at His Feet, just as she had done at the foot of the Cross. She began to pray for Veronica, interceding for her. The Lord revealed to Veronica the unconditional love that He has for all souls, particularly ungrateful souls like hers that have been singularly gifted. As the Lord revealed His Hurts and Wounds, suffered by Him because of the unfaithfulness of His children, she was filled with such overpowering sorrow for the times *she* had caused Him pain by *her* sins, she asked the Lord for His suffering, especially His Wounds, His Pain to become her pain. The Lord looked at her and said, *"I forgive you, but I want faithfulness in the future."*

How would Veronica remain faithful to the Lord? She walked the *Way of the Sacraments*, those Graces of Light in our path to the Father! She was ordered by her Spiritual Director to write down all she was experiencing, in a diary. She wrote that when she went to confession:

"I feel an inner tenderness and would like the confessor to penetrate every thought of mine, not only as it exists in me but as it exists before God. I feel such great sorrow that I don't know how I shall manage to speak a word. When I come before the one who stands in the place of God on earth, I have such sentiments that I cannot put them into words."

She wrote that an unexplainable peace filled her after she received absolution for her sins, as if *"a mountain of lead"* was lifted from her back. She could feel the Lord embracing her soul, and through this Love from the Lord, love began to flow from her to others.

[They say that when we stand before Jesus, it is not He Who condemns us, but we condemn ourselves as our life unfolds before us, revealing to us how many times we have put human respect before Divine love, how many times we have run away from Him and the Cross, how many times we have worshiped the subtle false gods of this world over Him, our One True God. Yes, and at that time we will beg to be purified in Purgatory; at that time, even those who have not believed there is a Purgatory will be grateful for its existence.]

"Many are going to hell because there are so few who pray and sacrifice." This message, given to the three children at Fatima by our Blessed Mother, has been true from the time of Adam and Eve. Veronica's vocation would be, singularly, to fulfill that need. The Lord not only chose her to be a victim for sinners, a sacrificial lamb as He had been before her, but He also *trusted* her to fulfill this act of love, day in and day out. She accepted the role of intermediary, acting as a go-between, between God and the people of God living in a state of sin. She knew that, as with her Jesus before her, the only road to forgiveness of the sins that still stain the world that God created, was through atonement! And she

said *Yes*! It reminds us of Blessed Edith Stein[12] who went to the Cross in atonement not only of her Jewish brothers and sisters but for the Nazis who killed them and her, saying if she did not, who would?

Veronica receives the Stigmata

One day, while praying in her cell, Sister Veronica had a vision of Jesus. He was carrying His Cross on His Shoulder. He asked her, *"What do you wish?"* She replied, *"That Cross and I wish it for You, for Your Love."* He took the Cross from His Shoulder and placed it on her shoulder. It was too heavy! She fell under the weight of it, and her Lord lifted her.

Still another time, Our Lord appeared to Veronica, covered with open sores, a Crown of Thorns on His Head. Blood spilled from His precious Body, as He said, *"See what sinners have done to Me."* Veronica wrote in her Diary:

"Seeing the great agony that my Lord was in, I begged Him to give Me His Crown. He placed it on my head; I suffered so much, I thought I was dying."

Another time, Jesus came and showed Veronica a Chalice full of liquid. She wrote that it seemed as if the liquid was on fire. The Lord told her, *"If you want to be Mine, you must taste this liquid for My Love."* She later wrote that when He placed just a few drops of the liquid on her tongue, she was filled with such indescribable bitterness and sadness, she thought she would die. Her tongue became dry and from that day on, she could not taste anything.

On Christmas Day, the Infant Jesus appeared to Veronica. He sent an arrow deep into her heart. When she awakened, she found her heart bleeding. The burning flame roaring inside her heart was so painful, she could not rest day or night. He told her He wanted her heart to bear the marks of His Wound; He said, her heart had to feel the lance and her feet and hands, the nails He felt on the Cross.

---

[12]Read more about her and other Martyrs in Bob and Penny Lord's book: *"Martyrs, They died for Christ."*

Our Lord chose to make Veronica as much Himself as is possible, and what better way than to share His Passion with her. He had asked her many times what she wished, and she had replied, His Cross. Well on April 5, 1697, Veronica had a vision of Jesus Crucified, accompanied by His Mother *Our Lady of Sorrows* as she appeared at the foot of the Cross on Golgotha. Veronica's heart, as with her Savior before her, was pierced. She experienced the crowning of thorns, the scourging, the crucifixion, *her* own death and that of Our Lord Jesus Christ.

Mother Abbess Mary Catherine told us that the other nuns could see the impressions of the crown of thorns on her head through her veil, the blood at times dripping from her eyes because of the deep wounds inflicted by the long sharp thorns. Sealed with this stigmata, Veronica's body became an indelible sign of the Lord's total communion with her, one of everlasting unity and love. She wrote:

"In an instant, I saw five shining rays shooting out from His Wounds, coming towards me. I watched as they turned into little flames. Four of them (the flames) contained the nails, and the fifth one contained the lance, golden and all aflame, and it pierced my heart. The nails pierced my hands and feet."

Veronica took the crucifix off the wall in her cell and embraced it saying:

"My Lord, pains with pains, thorns with thorns, sores with sores, here I am all Yours, crucified with You, crowned with thorns with You, wounded with You."

Veronica takes up the Cross

Veronica received the stigmata. Now it was time for her to take up the Cross! She could not help Jesus carry His Cross, that dark and infamous day He walked to Calvary. He had told her, she would be the bride of the Crucified Savior. Now to be completely *one* with Him as His bride, in imitation of her Spouse, she would carry *her* cross each evening. At those times she would wear a robe, lined with sharp long thorns which pierced her body, especially doing damage to the shoulder upon which she carried the cross.[13]

Laden down by the weight of the cross, she staggered as she tried to maintain her balance. She would walk through the monastery's orchard or within the monastery itself until she was to the point of collapse. When she completed her Way of the Cross, she would then climb up many steps to a painting, in the convent, of St. Francis receiving the stigmata, where she would flagellate herself. At other times, she would levitate up into the tree in the cloister gardens, the other nuns saying she looked like a little bird in flight.

At times Veronica would take a very heavy log and carry it across her shoulders as a cross beam to reenact more authentically Our Lord carrying the cross to Calvary. There are crosses there till today, which the nuns carry on Good Friday.

Our dear Lord asked Veronica to fast for three years. Upon receiving permission from her Superior, she fasted for the next three years on bread and water alone.

Veronica experiences internal suffering

Archbishop Fulton J. Sheen said that the *Wet Martyrs*, those who died for the Church, suffered and died, all pain ending with physical death. But the *Dry Martyrs* suffered and died an ongoing pain and death, day in and day out, for the Faith. As the physical pain ended for Veronica, a new form of suffering would begin.

She described in her Diary the pain she had in her heart resulting from her Lord's great *Love,* and the *purification* she underwent through those within her own convent. Sister Veronica's internal suffering was so intense, that after she died they found the traces of her life as a victim. Her heart had Divine incisions on it of the instruments of Our Lord's Passion: the *Cross* He had carried, the *Lance* which pierced Our Lord's Heart, the *Pliers* used to rip the nails from our Lord's Hands and Feet so He could be taken down from the Cross, the *Nails* that mercilessly ripped away at

---

[13]Our Lord shared with St. Bridget of Sweden that He suffered the greatest pain on the shoulder upon which *He* had carried *His* Cross.

the Flesh on His Hands and Feet as His Body collapsed, completely exhausted, after trying to summon enough breath to speak, begging forgiveness for us all.

As you can not separate the Son from the Mother, Veronica's heart also bore the seven swords that pierced the heart of Mother Mary. It was further engraved with letters representing the vows she had taken, a sign of her faithfulness to her vocation: **P** for Passion, **O** for Obedience, **V** for *Volunta*,[14] **F** for Faith and **C** for Caritas.[15] She described each sign to Blessed Florida (one of her nuns), as it was being imprinted on her heart by the Lord, and Blessed Florida would sketch the heart with the sign. And then, as a new one was added, Blessed Florida would sketch the new sign, including the signs that she had previously received, until finally, she sketched the heart containing all the signs the Lord had inscribed. When Veronica died, the bishop, doctors, and nuns, including Blessed Florida, were present at the autopsy. They saw the signs Veronica had spoken of, clearly imprinted on her heart when it was dissected in half.

Attacks from within the Monastery, from within the Church

There is no pain like that from *within*, whether it is within your family, your church, your ministry, your village, your friends. Veronica was Novice Mistress several times but not without terrible conflict within her own Community. As if that persecution and pain was not enough, when there was peace with her fellow nuns, she had attacks from priests, confessors and bishops, her Superior and then even the Holy See adding to the severe tests she had to undergo.

After she received the stigmata, Veronica was ordered by her confessor to remain locked away in a room in the infirmary for 50 days, to leave only to go to Mass, and then accompanied by two other nuns. The devil kept attacking her, throwing her against the walls and door in an attempt to scare her into disobeying her confessor. Veronica obeyed her confessor! At

---

[14]the Will of God
[15]Charity, love, compassion

other times, the *Holy Office* ordered she be placed under round-the-clock scrutiny for days on end. She never refused or complained, as they examined and probed her mind and her body. She submitted without complaint.

Finally satisfied, the Holy Office lifted the ban which they had imposed on her being elected Abbess, and so in the month of April, 1716, Veronica was elected Mother Abbess of the Monastery. Although she reluctantly agreed to being Abbess, the Lord blessed the Monastery with many vocations under her very able headship. She had a wing built, to accommodate all the new sisters. [It reminds us of a modern day Abbess, Mother Angelica, who has to keep expanding the monastery because, in this time of shrinking vocations, she has a struggle keeping up with the number of young women who desire to live the cloistered life of the *Poor Clare Nuns of Perpetual Adoration*, and now the young men who desire to be part of the Order of Missionaries of the Eternal Word that she founded.]

Veronica became so spiritually attuned to Christ's suffering and passion she asked to not die, but to be allowed to remain on earth so that she could suffer *more!* She, like the Saints and Mystics before and after her, knew the value of Redemptive suffering. Someone once said, *"Catholics know the saving merits of the Cross."*

The Diary written by a reluctant author lives till today

When they were investigating the cause of Saint Veronica's beatification, as with so many Mystics and Saints who have written so extensively, the process had to have been slowed down considerably; the Church, always prudent in making a proclamation, so as to not face possible scandal some day. Under obedience to her Abbess and confessor, Veronica had written 20,000 pages. [We had the privilege of holding one of her manuscripts and filming its handwritten pages for our documentary.]

Veronica never allowed her daily tasks to suffer, in order to write her diary. She, like St. Teresa of Avila, found Jesus among the pots and pans, cooking and baking for the nuns, a loving task she really enjoyed, especially for Feast Days. She devotedly cared for the sick nuns in the Infirmary, seeing Jesus in each and every one of them. At times, when Veronica was going about performing her duties among them, she would pass by the Crucifix in the Infirmary, and Jesus would take His arm off the cross and scoop her up to Him, holding her close to Him. When He lifted her onto the Cross and embraced her, it is the same as when we receive Him in Holy Communion; He embraces us.

She spent very little time sleeping. She walked the Way of the Cross, prayed and wrote down all the Blessed Mother and Jesus dictated to her in the *evening hours*, after her chores were completed.

At night, when she retired to her cell and would begin writing her diary, the devil would throw huge cobble stones against her door to frighten her and disrupt her thoughts. The last fifteen years of her life, she was so very ill and under such ferocious attack from the devil, she could barely remember what to write. *Our Lady of Sorrows*, the Blessed Mother in the painting in her cell, came to life and dictated the last chapters of Veronica's diary.

Through the Diary, we are able to glimpse not only into the life of Saint Veronica but of the Church and world at that time. We, in the Catholic Church have such a wealth of role models, beacons of light to guide us. Saints are like lights placed strategically along a pathway leading to our home that go on when it gets dark. When it seems the light has gone out of our life and there is darkness, and we are approaching despair in our families, in our Church, in our world, the Lord places these lights, these Saints in our path to lead us to our final and eternal Home.

Veronica, daughter of Mary Most Holy

Veronica drank mystically from the *Chalice of the Blood of Christ* and that of the *Tears of Mary*; she shared in what really happened at the foot of the Cross. Do you not believe that Jesus' Chalice of Blood was not mingled with Mary's Chalice of Tears? Were not the Blood and Water from His Side, that of Mother

Mary, as well? Was His Blood not her blood and His Water not her water? Had she not given all to her Son, right up till the very end?

Mother Mary assigned a *second* Guardian Angel to Veronica, to help and console her through her difficult journey to the Kingdom. She was further strengthened one time, by the Angel transporting her in a vision to the Holy House of Loreto. Again, as with Saint Joseph of Cupertino, a Saint is brought to the House of the Holy Family in Loreto.

Veronica solemnly consecrated herself to Mary on November 21, 1708, as her *"slave."*[16] In addition to being *Veronica of Jesus and Mary,*[17] she became *"Veronica of the Divine Will, daughter and devotee of Mary Most Holy,"* her heart melting into those of Jesus and Mary, the three hearts *becoming one.*

There was a statue of *Our Lady of Sorrows* in the infirmary, before which Veronica spent hours praying after caring for the infirmed. One night Veronica pleaded she was not worthy to be Abbess; Our Lady came to life in the statue and spoke to her, *"I'll be the Abbess and you will be my Vicar."* When Veronica received the keys to the convent, she handed them to Mother Mary; whereupon the Blessed Mother assured Veronica that it was *she* who was the true Superior of the Monastery:

"Daughter, be calm. I am the Superior and I will provide all the necessary sustenance for you and your sisters. That is my task. You don't have to see to anything."

Mother Mary even took over the instruction of the sisters in Chapter. One time Veronica journeyed into ecstasy, and did not awaken until the Chapter lesson was over. Mother Mary had taught the entire lesson. *"She it was who did and said everything."*

Mother Mary never left her daughter alone, always walking beside her, supporting Veronica as she walked closer and closer to perfection in her Son Jesus. Veronica became more and more

---

[16]Louis Marie de Montfort gave himself to Mother Mary as her *slave*, during this same time and advocated everyone do likewise.

[17]her religious name

Jesus, and more and more His Mother Mary.

Mother Mary is our true Mother. Sometimes, thinking of her as Our Queen, which she most certainly is, we lose sight of the fact that she is a Mother, our Mother. And what do mothers do? They help their daughters in everyday tasks. One day, as Veronica was washing clothes in the laundry room, the Blessed Mother appeared to her and said, *"Do you want to wash all the clothes, yourself? Move over and leave some for me."* As Mother Mary began to wash the clothes, the ice cold water turned into hot water. We saw the primitive laundry room inside the cloister of the convent, (which we filmed for our Documentary).

Veronica, Mother Mary and the Holy Trinity

She wrote in her Diary that Mother Mary guided and groomed her, as she walked toward becoming *"daughter of the Father, spouse of the Word and disciple of the Holy Spirit."*

Mary called her *"heart of my heart"* and then brought her before the Holy Trinity. Veronica wrote, powerfully:

"I became recollected with the vision of the Blessed Virgin Mary. I behaved as usual, and she had me perform an act of adoration of the Holy Trinity. Then, three rays, with three arrows, came into this heart of mine. It seemed to me, the three Divine Persons were confirming, by a sign of love, what they had graciously shown me on many occasions. Mary explained to me: `The Father confirms that you are His daughter, the Eternal Word confirms you as His spouse, the Holy Spirit, that you are His disciple.' Meanwhile, the three arrows that were in my heart went straight to the heart of Mary, and one arrow came from Mary's heart to mine, each heart drawing the other to itself. Then the three arrows became like flashes of lightning, and went back and forth from my heart to that of Our Lady."

Through that experience, Veronica said that it *seemed* her heart and soul became one with the heart and soul of Mother Mary. That night, the convent began to shake with the force of a huge earthquake. The nuns ran out of their cells, frightened half to death. Veronica told them to go back to sleep; she was having a vision of the Holy Trinity.

The Lord reveals the graces He bestowed upon Veronica

It was as if the Lord was unfolding before her a video of her spiritual life with Him. He told her He had renewed the sorrow in her heart 500 times to bring her closer to Him. When we are under attack, do we consider, the Lord may be trusting us to share in His Passion on the Cross? Jesus gave her the grace to have true repentance for her sins, as He revealed to her who she was and who she was called to be. He made her aware of her faults that she might use the gifts He had given her to perfect herself. Then He helped her to understand all the *virtues* His generous Heart had instilled in her that they might help and guide her, and through her others on their journey towards sanctity.

He told her, He had renewed His marriage to her *sixty times*, and He would allow her to experience His Passion *thirty-three times*, for every year He had spent on the earth that she might know the price, He had paid for His children on earth. He said, He revealed this only to His specially chosen ones.

[It reminds us of St. Clare of Montefalco, when the Lord told her He had been waiting so very long for someone He could trust with His Cross, as He plunged His Cross into her heart.][18]

The Lord showed Himself to Veronica wounded and bleeding, His precious Blood spilling from His open Heart and other Wounds. He once again asked that she do His Holy Will. It's so simple, isn't it? All we need to do is listen for His Will and do His Will. It's simple but it's not always easy to *discern* His Holy Will. One thing is certain, Our Lord is in charge and nothing is going to happen unless He allows it. As Jesus said to Pilate, *"You would have no authority over Me, if My Heavenly Father had not given it to you."*[19]

---

[18]from chapter on Saint Clare of Montefalco in Bob and Penny Lord's book: *"Saints and other Powerful Women in the Church."* Read more about Saint Clare and other powerful Saints who were also Visionaries, Mystics and Stigmatists.

[19] John 19:11

How loving Our Lord is to those who carry the Cross with Him. Veronica wrote in her Diary that on *three* different occasions, Jesus pulled His Arm away from the Cross, and lifting her, brought her close to Him and held her beside Him on the Cross. *Five* times Our Lord allowed her to drink the Blood and Water from His Side. *Fifteen* times He washed her heart in His precious Blood which shot forth from His Side like a ray and struck her heart. *Twelve* times He searched her heart, purifying it, emptying it of all imperfections and remnants of past sins.

Was this to strengthen her so that she could, with her sacrifices make retribution for the Church that flowed from that Holy Side? She wrote, *"He gave my soul delightful embraces in a special way, not counting the others which He gave constantly."* He pierced her heart with *one hundred* loving Wounds, to be known to the world only after her death when all would see the signs Our Lord had imprinted on her heart.

This and so much more He gave to her, always after she would receive Holy Communion. What gifts of Grace, Our Lord has ready to give us in the Eucharist! If only the faithful knew Our Lord's generous Heart to those who receive Him worthily.[20]

Veronica had such a love for the Lord and an awareness of His Real Presence! The night before the convent chaplain was to bring Holy Communion to the bedridden in the infirmary, Veronica would climb four flights of stone stairs on her knees, making the Sign of the Cross with her tongue on each step.[21] It was as if she were laying out a red carpet for her King, the Eucharist, upon which He would ascend to the infirmed, in the hands of his ambassador-priest. When she got to the top, her tongue, now bleeding profusely, would leave a visible bloody Sign of the Cross on the last steps.

---

[20]to worthily receive, one must not be in a state of sin, nor separated from the Church Community of believers.

[21]approximately 60 steps

Veronica goes *Home*

Veronica's last years were spent in total communion with God, enjoying the special Graces of being one with God, a new perfected creation, as are all the Saints in Heaven. When it was revealed to her that she had received the gift of sanctifying Grace, she exclaimed, over and over again, *"Forever and forever...Love has conquered and love itself has been overcome."* The more that we accept God's Love in our hearts, the more we become aware how small our love is, in comparison to His unconditional never-ending Love for us.

The time for her to enter the Kingdom was at hand. We believe, it must be like the state we are in when we are about to go on a journey, especially (for us) a pilgrimage. You are physically with your loved ones, but your heart and mind is already on the way and you can think of nothing but the place where you are going. What a peaceful death, this Faith gives us.

Our Lady appeared to Veronica. On March 25, 1727, the Feast of the Annunciation of Our Lord, His Mother, who had been dictating the *Diary* to Veronica for fifteen years, gave her the final message: *"Call a halt!"* She was telling Veronica it was time to stop writing the Diary.

Veronica suffered a stroke on June the 6th, right after having received Holy Communion. Now paralyzed, the nuns carried her to a bed in the infirmary, she had so faithfully served. But, the Lord would not take her Home to Him, until she suffered *thirty-three* days of Purgatory on earth. She, and others who have had visions of Purgatory, will tell you, it is God's Mercy that we be able to suffer our Purgatory here and not after we die. For those *thirty-three* days, she was attacked mercilessly: *physically*, as she knew the most excruciating pain; *spiritually*, as she had all the temptations of such Saints as St. Thérèse, the Little Flower, the devil taunting her with her sinfulness and unworthiness to enter Heaven, how she had been a poor nun and led many to sin; on and on, *diabolically* torturing her, pulling out all stops, in a last ditch effort to have her for himself.

But you see, Veronica knew the devil's game, having prophesied she would suffer his slings of poisonous arrows. She suffered all the pains and sufferings of Our Lord, the complete Passion of Christ, a day for each of His *thirty-three* years on earth. As you meditate on the last days of Jesus' life, you get a glimpse of what pain, rejection, abandonment, complete vulnerability Veronica shared with Him.

At dawn, July 9th, Veronica asked permission from her confessor to go to her Spouse in Heaven. Having received it, she closed her eyes! Then she uttered final words to her sisters at her bedside: *"Love has let Himself be found!"* No more pain, no more Passion on earth, job well done, her soul soared up to Heaven where she would experience the Beatific Vision[22] for all eternity.

Mother Church declared Veronica **Blessed** in 1804. Then in 1839 she entered the Company of Saints and became known to the world as **Saint Veronica Giuliani**. There is a movement within the Church to declare Saint Veronica a *Doctor of the Church* because of her invaluable teachings, through her writings: *her Diary, her Reports* and *her Letters*. Please continue to read about Saint Veronica Giuliani. Her road to perfection is a loving, spirit-filled journey to the Lord for all those reaching for eternal life with the Father.

Saint Veronica Giuliani speaks to us, today!
on the Sacraments of the Eucharist and Reconciliation
"In some way, the Three Divine Persons, present in the most Holy Sacrament revealed Themselves to my soul, and my soul received a deep and penetrating understanding of this Divine mystery.

"There is no way I can find to explain how this was seen. I can only say it was presented to me as a precious joy. Every time we receive Communion, our soul and heart

---

[22] *"The blessed see God as He sees Himself"... "the fulfillment of happiness, seeing all in the light of supreme Truth"* John writes: "...*we are God's children now; what we shall later be has not come to light. We know that when it comes to light we shall be like Him, for we shall see Him as He is."* (Jn 3:2) The Catholic Encyclopedia - Broderick

become a temple of the Most Holy Trinity and, with God
coming to us, all Paradise comes. In this joy, I saw how
God exists, enclosed in the most Holy Host, and this Grace
was for me superior to all the other Graces, I have ever
received during my whole life.

"I sensed Divine Love intimately in my soul which united
itself to Him and it gave me strength and momentum, light
and clarity about my faults, the like of which I have not
experienced. Also in that moment, I had a very vivid
understanding of the special Grace of the Sacrament of
Penance. These two Sacraments are such great Graces
for our souls. We do not comprehend; we do not really
esteem them as we should."

Whenever we have given a Retreat or Mission on the
Miracles of the Eucharist, as the faithful became more and more
aware of the Miracle that comes about on the Altar at the moment
of Consecration and of that Lord Who dwells in the Tabernacle,
we would see them line up outside of the confessional to receive
the Sacrament of Penance. The more we know Jesus in the
Eucharist, the more aware we become of our unworthiness and
sinfulness; and we want to be washed clean. Normally the
Sacrament of Reconciliation brings us to the Sacrament of the
Eucharist. In this instance, the Eucharist brought us to
Reconciliation.

Saint Veronica speaks of the Sacrament of Reconciliation or
Penance as a *"Tribunal of Mercy...the confessor takes the place
of God: he speaks in the very Person of God (*in Persona Cristi)."

"When I go to this Tribunal, I am terrified from head to
foot. I do not seem to have a tongue to confess my failings...I
wish that the confessor would be able to penetrate every
thought I have, not only as it is in me but also as it is in the
Eyes of God. I feel such sorrow, I do not know how I can
utter a word.

"In the act of receiving absolution from the confessor I
seem to feel myself renewed and so lighthearted that really,

it seems like I have had a mountain of lead lifted off my shoulders. I experience the loving embrace God gives my soul.

"I sense that Divine Love makes it clear to me what He has and is doing, so that I may say everything to him who stands in His place. Thus with entire frankness I reveal everything just as if I were at the feet of God, and while I am speaking I feel myself changing into someone else, so much so that I remain astonished. He has made me to understand that the obedience of revealing things (about my visions) is my cooperation as is the Penance of writing about them."

Veronica speaks on God's Grace

"Revelation teaches that God dwells in us through Grace, that the soul becomes a temple of the Holy Spirit and in addition, a dwelling place of the entire Trinity."

St. Veronica lived in the *reality* of the Presence of God. She was not a theologian but a Mystic, a vessel through which the Lord and His Mother could speak to the children of God. As God spoke through the prophets at the time of the Israelites, now Veronica, under the guidance of the Holy Spirit, simply recounted and reported all that had been passed on to her by the Savior and His Mother.

Whether we realize it or not, we seek the Divine from the day we are conceived. It is as if God keeps a small piece of our hearts with Him, and we long to be united with that part of ourselves. Some of the problems facing the faithful today is, with the de-emphasizing of the Divine by some theologians, we find people fulfilling their need for the Supernatural in the wrong places, running from one *alleged* Mystic to another, or substituting age-old heresies that deify man.

Saint Veronica said, *"God is in me and I am in God."* She also cried out, *"Lord, I want to love You and to be completely one with You."* All of God's children yearn for God. Alleged mystics who give no credit to Divine Revelation and the Supernatural, bringing the faithful to focus on *them* and not God and his Divine Power to do all things, will invariably end up in Pantheism[23] or the Pantheism of today, *New Age*! We have two problems: *one*, those who fall into the danger of *Pantheism*; and *two*, those who, fearing Pantheism or *New Age*, fall into the equally dangerous heresy of *Naturalism*.[24] Mystics, accepted by the Church, who have passed the test of time, have had a Supernatural oneness with God within themselves - as St. Paul said to the Galatians: *"Yet I live, no longer I, but Christ lives in me; insofar as I now live in the flesh, I live by faith in the Son of God Who has loved me and given Himself up for me."* [25]

So, unlike those practicing Pantheism, true Mystics experience God within, and are raised to the Divine through that indwelling of *God* within them, God taking over the soul, not the soul becoming God. Veronica said:

"O Love, O Love, what are You doing with this soul? I am no one, dust, ashes, and nothing. I sense this fullness which is God, without limit, united, made One very substance with my soul, and my soul made one and the very same thing with God." (Diary)

Although the soul continues to live, it now experiences itself living in God. Do we not say: Empty me, Lord, of all that is not of You and quickly fill me with Yourself? Our soul continues to live with the Free Will which God has given to it; but completely abandoning itself to God and His Will, we no longer live but God lives within us. And then, God lights that flame that cannot be extinguished.

---

[23]*Pantheism* denies a personal God; it advocates that God is in everyone and everything, that we are all God and there is no One God. For more on Heresies, read Bob and Penny Lord's book: *"Scandal of the Cross and Its Triumph."*

[24]*Naturalism is a rationalistic system of philosophy and theology, which denies the Supernatural and centers on nature alone.* The Catholic Encyclopedia by Broderick

[25]Gal 2:20

**The Incorrupt body of St. Veronica Giuliani
Monastery in Cittá di Castello, Italy**

St. Veronica says that when God takes possession of the human will, what results is *one single will* and from this *one will, one Love* alone flows. As a result, everything the soul does from this moment on is not the soul acting, but Love Who is present inside.

This day, turn your will over to the Lord, to do with as He Wills. Invite Jesus into your heart, mind and soul. Ask that your thoughts be His Thoughts, your eyes His Eyes to see, your ears His Ears to hear, your words His Words to speak, your arms His Arms to embrace, your legs His Legs to bring you closer to Him, your heart lost in His Heart that you might love as He does. Adore Him, as did Mother Mary, the Saints, the Angels and the Mystics before you.

Blessed Anna Maria Taigi

*Loyal Wife,
Loving Mother,
Faithful Daughter of
the Church
Mystic and Stigmatist
Advisor to the Popes*

*Blessed Anna Maria Taigi
and the sun*

In our book *"Martyrs, They Died for Christ"* we tracked the walk of two people born into a time of infamy, that of a Blessed Edith Stein[1] and Adolf Hitler. One went to her death in reparation for the sins of the other who had caused such death and devastation. One will be remembered for her generous heart and the other will be accursed for generations to come.

This story is about another who suffered, only as a *Dry Martyr*[2] for her Lord, a willing victim of sacrifice for her Church. Just as Blessed Anna Maria Taigi was being born in Italy, another child was coming into the world, Napoleon Bonaparte. When Anna Maria opened her eyes and let out her first cry, it was to a

---

[1]chapter in *"Martyrs, They died for Christ"* by Bob and Penny Lord

[2]"Dry Martyr - one who doesn't die for the Faith (Wet Martyr), but dies each day in defense of the Faith." Archbishop Fulton J. Sheen

world groaning in pain, a world inundated by sin and perversion, very like our own. The throne of France was heading madly toward its own destruction and demise, taking Christianity down with it. Because of the decadence of that court, with its greed and disregard for its own people, anger was fueled by a few with an agenda; and the furor spread throughout France, with the Church becoming a target of the holocaust, innocent priests and religious falling alongside the nobility, victims of the guillotine in that insidious French Revolution.

It looked like the end of all that was decent and traditional. Whole nations, known for their faithfulness to the Church, were swept away by the deadly current, their leaders drowning in sin. Masonry entered holy Poland through the betrayal of its own king, he whom his subjects so loved and trusted. Helpless lambs of Catholic countries like Spain and Italy were sacrificed as their royalty flocked to the Masonic Temple erected in Warsaw, seeking the prestige and power that this diabolical society could offer them. But its head is the father of lies and he always betrays. As he was making promises to the unscrupulous nobility, he was placing his fallen angels among equally decadent peasants who would fan the flames of discontent and cause the demise of not only the Royal Houses of Europe but the destruction of the Church as well.

A Blessed is born

In Siena, on May 29, 1769, a baby girl was born to Mary Santa Masi[3] and Luigi Giannetti. Our little future *Blessed* came from a very well respected family. Two and a half months after *her* birth, Napoleon Bonaparte I was born, he who would destroy and plunder all that was good and holy. Like Anna Maria, Napoleon was born of Italian and Tuscan lineage. His background was again like hers, in that he came from a middle class family who had fallen on hard times. It would be thirty years before we see the Lord's plan, this powerful Blessed He raised up, defending

---

[3]In Italy, as well as in other foreign countries, the woman maintains her maiden name until death.

Right:
***The Basilica of Saint
Crisogono, in Rome***

Below:
***Bl. Anna Maria Taigi
with her family at her home***

Above:
***The Triumph into Heaven of
Bl. Anna Maria Taigi***

Left:
***The remains of Bl. Anna
Maria Taigi in the
Church of Saint
Crisogono***

the Chair of Peter that this other child would strive to overthrow. As Napoleon would seek to conquer the world with its empty promises, Anna Maria would live only to serve her Lord with the World *above* in her sights.

The fourteenth century had had another *Sienesse*, Saint Catherine, who was born to save the Papacy and die for the Church, *"crushed by the Ship of the Church."*[4] Now in the eighteenth century, the Papacy was again in danger; the Lord once more went to Siena and raised up a powerful woman who would wage battle on all those who would destroy the Prince of the Church, our sweet *"Christ on earth."*[5]

Anna Maria was baptized the day after her birth in the church of St. John the Baptist. We cannot be sure what happened to cause the demise of her father Luigi's business in Siena; however, at age six the family moved to Lucca, but not until Anna Maria's father had sold all his worldly goods to pay off his debts. Still proud people, they left the town under the cover of the night so that their neighbors would not see the sad state of their affairs.

The family leaves for Rome

Pope Pius had declared 1775 the year of their exodus, *a Holy Year!* We can just see the little impoverished family walking beside the pilgrims heading towards Rome. Unlike them, our little family did not know what awaited them. They settled in the *"dei Monte"* area of Rome, a quarter teeming with families jammed together in small hot dwellings. As they lived on the street *dei Vergini*,[6] close to where the holy Saint Benedict Labre lived, it was very possible they knew him. God puts holy people in the paths of other holy people to bring about His Will, the Holy Clusters we write about in our books. Eight years passed quickly and Saint Benedict Labre died at the age of thirty-five. Anna Maria's mother Santa, known for her acts of charity, washed his body and wrapped him in a

---

[4]Catherine of Siena's last words. Read more about St. Catherine in Bob and Penny Lord's book: *"Saints and Other Powerful Women in the Church."*
[5]what Catherine of Siena called the Pope.
[6]of the Virgins

shroud. Her mother and then Anna Maria after her always carried a picture of the Saint, turning to him for his intercession.

God is putting the chess pieces into place. Pope Pius VI was elected after a long and arduous conclave. Luigi, Anna Maria's father found a job as a domestic. Anna Maria went to the *"free school,"* carrying her dinner in a little basket. There she was to receive a good education. She would learn how to care for the home, how to sew and cook; she would receive a deeper understanding of religion, and become proficient in worldly subjects like arithmetic, reading and writing. But *"the best laid plans of mice and men often go astray."*[7] Small Pox struck; Anna Maria took ill, and her schooling was cut short. Although there were no physical scars, she never returned to school. Her family needed her to remain at home and help her mother with the household chores. This girl, who was never taught to write, her schooling having stopped shortly after she learned how to read, would someday dictate volumes of messages that she had mystically received from the Lord. And through these revelations, change would come about, not only molding circumstances of her time, but giving *our* generation much needed instruction and wisdom for *our time*.

There are volumes of very powerful teachings this simple servant of the Lord left to the whole world. Although she was unable to write, Anna Maria had highly respected priest-secretaries with impeccable reputations, faithfully taking down all she dictated. One of these was Cardinal Pedicini, a former Marquis from a noble family, who, upon becoming a priest agreed to be her personal secretary.

Anna Maria made her first confession at age seven and was confirmed at eleven in St. John Lateran, the Cathedral of Rome. At thirteen, she received her First Holy Communion. Her family, very pious, brought her to Mass early in the morning each day. On Sunday, Anna Maria would attend Catechism classes at the parish church.

---

[7]From John Steinbeck's book: *"Of Mice and Men"*

Times were hard, and Anna Maria's father took his sad plight out on the little Blessed. As he piled abuse upon abuse, Anna Maria just bowed her head. The Lord was preparing her for the way of the Cross she would walk, sharing in His pain and persecution. The parents would never be able to fully know this special gift from Heaven.

Anna Maria battles the temptations of the world

Anna Maria was thirteen years old, when the world was about to explode. France helped the colonies in America to fight for its independence from England. Little did the world know that France would start a revolution of her own, based on America's success. Unlike America, what France lacked was the most important Ingredient - God, in their revolution! And without God, man will sin and sin will kill, and finally turn on the sinners themselves. Civilization was at a new low. *Sound familiar?* To mock all that is traditional became the vogue. King Louis XVI of France himself joined the crowds at the theater, as they applauded shows which jeered at nobility and royalty, religion and morality, ridiculing them, cruelly mimicking them, grouping them all together. Again, we repeat: *Sound familiar?* Anna Maria went to work sewing fine dresses at a shop owned by some very kind older ladies. Then she returned home each night, cooked, cleaned, washed clothes and tried to bring some cheer into the very gloomy world her parents had settled in.

When Anna Maria turned sixteen, she was breathtakingly beautiful! She soon began to notice eyes constantly upon her. She enjoyed going to dances. She found herself not only enjoying the attention and complimentary glances, she began to cater to the accolades, fussing over her appearance, until one day, she realized her new found vanity could lead her to sin. All who testified at her Beatification affirmed that she did not fall victim to even venial sin, as a result of this temporary temptation. A priest who testified, said that even at this time, Anna Maria never ceased praying, receiving Holy Communion every Sunday, as well as attending *Daily* Mass.

Anna Maria offers herself as victim to God for the Papacy

It was March, 1782. Their parish priest asked all parishioners to pray for Pope Pius VI who was leaving Rome for Vienna, to try to dissuade Emperor Franz Joseph and his minister, who were under the deadly influence of the philosophers, from turning the Church into a heretical *State Church*.[8] It was at this time, that Anna Maria had what might be called an *inner locution*. *She had a thought*: She must offer herself as a victim to God for the triumph of the Papacy over enemy forces who desired to destroy the Church.

Anna Maria was among the Faithful who saw the worried face of the Pope as he addressed the Church. Franz Joseph had broken promises as quickly as he had made them. The aristocracy of Vienna was as intoxicated as the Parisian society before them, by the success of *"The Marriage of Figaro"* with its philosophy: *"Behold what alone distinguishes us from other beasts is, to drink for the sake of drinking and to make love all the year round."*

But as we are seeing today, philosophies of this type of lunacy, expounded in prose, do not end up only in the written word but in bloodshed as well.

In Anna Maria's family change for the better was coming about, and God was weaving His plan. Her father Luigi obtained a position in the Maccarani palace. When he discovered that the mistress of the palace, Madame Serra had need of a maid, he recommended his daughter Anna Maria. Madame Serra was so pleased with the genteel, gracious Anna Maria, she offered a post to her mother. And so the whole Giannetti family moved into the palace with their few possessions.

Now, that's not the end of the story. It seems that Madame Serra was separated from her husband. Therefore, the gossip-mongers of the area, with nothing better to do, spread conjecture

---

[8]In Bob and Penny Lord's book: *"Martyrs, They died for Christ"*, in the chapter on the Mexican Martyrs, you read how *all* but two priests became fugitives rather than swear allegiance to the Masonic State Church that the Mexican Revolutionaries wanted to set up as the official church of Mexico.

as to Madame Serra's character. As she received food from the Chigi palace, the busybodies used this to question her friendship with the prince who extended this gesture of charity. But if Anna Maria was aware of any weakness of character, instead of joining those committing a serious sin by their spread of malicious innuendos, she probably brought about, through her prayers and holiness, the conversion of her mistress who died at an advanced age with an honorable and irreproachable reputation of piety, chastity and humility.

God sends a husband into Anna Maria's life

Now, Anna Maria had been working in the service of Madame Serra for three years when the Lord sent Domenico Taigi into her life. The life at the palace was far from austere, and because of her sweet personality, Madame Serra loved to shower fine gifts of clothes, jewelry and perfumes on Anna Maria, and she being a young girl found herself once again loving these things of the world too much. When she confessed this, her confessor advised marriage.

Domenico's family was almost as prominent as the Chigi family in whose palace he now served. Before misfortune fell on them, they had been honored by kings and dukes in the fifteenth century. This was a wound which impregnated Domenico's personality to the point of ruining his life. But, the good Lord sent him Anna Maria. The young Domenico who delivered food to the Maccarani Palace was good looking, and he knew it! But in spite of his blustering temperament, he was known for his strong spirituality. He would learn, through Anna Maria's prayers, that God sent him to her that she might soften his rough edges.

Now, although Domenico was a humble servant in the Chigi palace, the Prince trusted him with the *sensitive* business of bringing food to his friend, Madame Serra. He held him in such high regard, he not only charged him with this mission, he also commissioned Domenico to accompany him to three Papal Conclaves where he, the Prince, presided in his capacity as Marshall of the Holy Roman Catholic Church and Perpetual

Guardian of the Conclave (an honor bestowed on his family by Pope Clement XI). As we follow the steps in Anna Maria's life, we can see God orchestrating the libretto which will bring her in contact with *four* Popes.

Each evening, after he arrived at the servant's entrance, with food meant for their mistress, Luigi and Santa would invite Domenico to sit with them and have a glass of wine. Upon seeing the beautiful Anna Maria, he was convinced he would marry her. As he was very handsome and could be quite charming, the twenty-year old Anna Maria found him equally appealing. After *Domenico* made inquiries about Anna Maria, and *her family* about him, they were all convinced this was a suitable marriage; and he made all the arrangements for their wedding within one month's time. The wedding Mass was celebrated in the parish church of St. Marcel in the Corso on January 7, 1790, the morning after Epiphany. There was a joyful dinner that followed. But all too soon, we discover that courtships and honeymoons can turn into nightmares. It was the marriage of a lamb and a wolf. But instead of the wolf eating the lamb, the lamb tamed the wolf. And this is the strong part of the story of this Blessed who so powerfully influenced the Church of her time and we pray, the Mystical Body of Christ[9] in our time.

Prince Chigi kept Domenico in his service and the couple moved into two rooms on the ground floor of the Chigi palace. Domenico, unaware of his mother-in-law's difficult ways, offered her one of the rooms. Sadly, this was something he would soon regret. His father-in law refused the invitation and remained in the service of Madam Serra in her palace. Anna Maria soon decorated the otherwise drab little apartment into a cheerful home for Domenico and ultimately seven children who would be born

---

[9]Members of the Mystical Body of Christ, according to Pope Pius XII are: *"Only those...to be included as members of the Church who have been baptized and profess the true Faith and who have not unhappily withdrawn from body-unity or for grave faults been excluded by legitimate authority."* This expression has been used in the Church since the ninth century, but its scriptural basis is secure in St. Paul's letter to the Colossians (1:18) when he refers to the *"head of the body."*

there.

Now, Domenico loved to show off his wife. She was his showcase. He loved to see and hear the admiration all his friends had for her beauty. She, a young girl of twenty, was filled with the typical Italian fervor and excitement of living. She enjoyed dressing up and her one weakness, her biographers say, was at this time that of vanity.

God is ready to lower the boom on sinful man

But, God had a job that had to be done, and He would not wait too long for Anna Maria to grow up. We are in the terrifying period of 1790-1791. [We hear the wailing of people complaining, today: *"How can a loving God allow all these disasters that are happening?"* God is a patient God, but when His children refuse to listen and change their lives, He gets their attention the only way He can, with a two by four!] As Anna Maria and Domenico were spending their first years of marriage in their own world of newly wedded bliss, the rest of the world was about to explode. The Revolution in France was gaining violent momentum. In Paris, the Constituent Assembly, formed by a band of renegades and misfits, ignored the rights of God as it proclaimed the *"Rights of Man."* These hoodlums took over Church property. They closed down Abbeys, Convents and Religious Chapters; religious were thrown out, churches desecrated in the vilest ways. The fifty thousand priests who refused to take the oath of allegiance to this *illegal, civil* constitution were hunted, incarcerated and, after unbelievable torture, martyred.

Pope Pius VI condemned the renegade Assembly and its heartless massacre of the King and thousands upon thousands of lay people as well as priests and nuns. The Assembly retaliated by decreeing the end of the Papacy and the Church in France. Although news of these happenings had reached Rome, Anna Maria and her young husband were too busy being married to pay too much attention. But Anna Maria could feel the pull of the Lord.

One day, as Anna and Domenico were strolling outside St.

Peter's Basilica, she was jostled by someone in the crowd and was thrown against a Servite Priest. Father Angelo had never seen Anna Maria before, but an inner voice told him: *"Notice that woman, for I will confide her to your care, and you will work for her transformation. She shall sanctify herself, for I have chosen her to become a Saint."* She could not understand why she suddenly felt an overpowering wave of remorse come over her for the times she had not put the Lord first. When she confessed this her confessor told her that as long as she obeyed her husband and was faithful to him, she need not be concerned. As much as she wanted to be reassured by his words, Anna kept hearing a voice inside saying: *"This is not enough."*

Anna was twenty-one years old, and she was struggling between her desire to please her husband and the pull of the Lord to perfect herself in His Image. She went to confession. As the priest did not recognize her as one of his parishioners, he refused to hear her confession. After wrestling with this wounding rejection, she tried again. She went to the church where she and Domenico had been married, and with more than a little apprehension, she entered the confessional and began to confess. She was before the priest she had bunked into at St. Peter's Basilica! He said: *"So you have come, at last, my daughter. Our Lord loves you and wants you to be wholly His."* Father Angelo told her all the Lord had told him in front of St. Peter's. She praised God for this affirmation. Her heart began to soar, as her new life was about to begin.

Father Angelo had been given the gift of spiritually directing a Mystic. He knew he had his work cut out for him. He could not turn to the life of Saint Teresa for help, to guide this obviously chosen vessel of the Lord. After all, she was not a religious nor was she a widow; she was the young wife of Domenico and would give birth to seven children within a twelve year period. Anna Maria's prayers and penances, her ecstasies, *everything* would have to play a secondary role to her vocation as wife and mother. [As Mother Angelica said: *"The Lord does not raise up copies of*

other Saints, but Saints unique in their own walk with the Lord."]
Father would have to direct this future Beata, according to *her*
calling in life.

Anna Maria knew it was time to ask Domenico to allow her
to do without the luxuries he so loved to give her. No more
promenading on the Corso in the latest fashions; no more theaters
and puppet shows that he was so fond of; no more pride in
parading her before all his friends; no more admiration in
everyone's eyes for her beauty; no more delight in hearing the
complimentary remarks of his friends. *He said Yes!*

Anna and her walk with confessors

Anna Maria told her confessor she desired to go to confession
before receiving Holy Communion at Daily Mass. He told her to
receive each day and go to confession *once a week*. She did not
look kindly upon those who brag of going from one *famous*
confessor to another, and said that once you have the right confessor
you should stay with him. But like St. Teresa of Avila, Anna had
to change confessors frequently. But as with the other Saint, it
was not through her design.

Her *first* confessor *Father Angelo* soon discovered he was in
above his head, and sent her to *Msgr. Strambi* who remained with
her, counselling and being counselled by her, until he became
Bishop of Macerata and his duties made it impossible. He
recommended her to a Passionist, *Father Philip Salvatori,* who
expounded on her gifts to so many people he drew huge crowds to
her home. *Another confessor was sought.* At this time Anna
Maria went to Father Angelo and told him that she was to atone
for the sins of the world. He recommended she become a Tertiary
of the Order of the Trinity, as she had such a great devotion to the
Holy Trinity. Father Ferdinand of the Trinitarians would be her
new confessor. Anna Maria asked Domenico's permission to
become a Tertiary, and again he gave his consent.

Upon receiving the Habit of a Tertiary, Anna Maria was so
overcome, she had one of her now almost ongoing ecstasies and
began sobbing loudly. Fearing she would disrupt the proceedings,

Father Ferdinand ordered her to awaken. And she obeyed! Everything went well until Father then told her she was to live with Domenico as brother and sister. Domenico flatly refused, arguing that if that was what she wanted, she should have become a religious, not a wife. But wife she was, and Domenico expected her to be faithful to that commitment. Father Ferdinand then ordered her to wear her Habit out in the street. Domenico rebelled, insisting it was not fitting for a married woman to be dressed as a religious, especially when carrying his child! Anna and the Lord agreed, and she changed confessors. The Lord told her that He would make up for what was lacking in her confessors; *He* would guide her in the way of perfection. And He did for fifty years, until the day of her death.

Anna Maria dictates to her priest-secretaries

As she could not write, Anna Maria dictated all that the Lord said[10] to her priest-secretaries, especially one who would later become Cardinal Pedicini. This highly respected prelate faithfully recorded it all for thirty years, filling in anything the other secretaries might have missed. This was crucial when the Cause for her Beatification opened.

Anna Maria always worried whether it was *the Holy Spirit or the evil spirit who was speaking to her.* The Lord told her, the way that she would know that it was *He* Who was speaking to her would be by: feelings of *compassion, serenity, regret for her sins,* and above all *humility.* He said:

"Man has within himself a dust that settles around his heart; it is called self-love. Man is full of pride and I have nothing to do with the proud."... "He who wishes to taste My delights must despise the world, and expect to be despised by it in return."... "I make my abode in humble souls that are full of simplicity. The more lowly and uncultured they are, the more I take pleasure in them. As

---

[10]St. Catherine of Siena, who never learned to write, also dictated all that the Lord said, to secretaries, and because of her works, was made a Doctor of the Church.

*to these wise and learned professors whose heads are full
of the fumes of pride, I put them down from their seats, and
you yourself shall soon learn where I send them."*

Anna Maria sees the future in the sun of light

Anna Maria's husband and mother were quarreling. There
was barely enough bread to eat. Envious housewives were
spreading scandals about Anna Maria and her priest-secretaries.
A devastating sadness came over her.

When she approached the door of her home, Anna Maria saw
what appeared to be a blinding sun encircled by a crown of thorns,
with two thorns wrapped around it as if in an embrace. A young
woman was seated in the center and appeared to be meditating.
Anna Maria was made to understand she represented *Eternal
Wisdom.*[11] A hazy film covered the sun, dimming the brightness of
its rays. An inner voice said this would clear, and the light would
become brighter as she reached a higher degree of purification.
Sounds poetic, doesn't it? But gold is purified by *fire*! Anna Maria
would suffer greatly to bring about the sanctification necessary to
burn away the veil of fog that blocked her vision from seeing all the
Lord had prepared for her, how she could grow in God's perfection,
how she would be able to aid the Church Militant and pray for the
Church Suffering.[12]

Right up to her death, whenever she looked into the sun, Anna
Maria was able to prophesy the *future* and discern the *present*; she
could read the secret recesses of men's hearts and reveal the most
hidden dreams and thoughts of the rich and the poor, the famous
and the infamous alike.

For *forty-seven years*, day and night, at home, in church or in
the street, as the light became increasingly brighter, Anna Maria
was able to see things on earth, both physical and spiritual. She
penetrated the depths of hell and soared to the heights of Heaven.

---

[11]Our Lady has, as one of her titles: *"Seat of Wisdom"*. On his TV program
on the Catechism on **EWTN,** Bishop David Foley explained this title in the
following way: Jesus as all-knowing God is Infinite Wisdom. Mary, as His
Mother, provides the perfect lap (perfect seat) for her young Son.

[12]The Church Suffering are those in Purgatory

She saw shipwrecks in far-off seas and heard the anguished cries of those drowning. She entered prisons in China and Arabia and heard the agonized cries of prisoners whose only crime was they were priests. She suffered with them, as she witnessed the inhumane torture endured by religious, slaves and prisoners alike. Cardinal Pedicini said that although she withheld nothing from him out of obedience, she took equally strong measures to keep herself hidden from those who had benefited from her revelations from the sun. She wanted no reward, no recognition, no recompense of any kind.

She was a seer at twenty-one years old and would live for close to fifty years, till her death, in almost continuous, never-ending ecstasy. She derived no pleasure from it and feared it was of diabolical origin, until her spiritual advisor assured her it was the work of the Divine. Jesus told Anna Maria she was to convert sinners, console people of all walks of life, priests, bishops, religious and even *"His Vicar."* He spoke of the Graces, those who listen to her words, would receive. But he also warned, she would meet false and treacherous people, she would be scorned and ridiculed and scandal would be spread about her, but she would live through it, out of love for Him. She protested, she was too weak for this great task. Our Lord replied, *"It is I Who will guide you by the hand, as a lamb is led by the shepherd, to the Altar of Sacrifice."*

God had chosen from the humble and poor, a wife, a mother, a servant to save His Church, to save the world. She was called by Him to obtain the remission of the world's sins. We were again at a time when the people of God were living in a world where God was ridiculed if at all acknowledged, the clergy massacred, Pope after Pope was dragged from prison to prison, churches desecrated, Christianity drowning in a bottomless pool of blood. Our Lord said to Anna Maria that He had chosen her to be a martyr! The Church has always been sanctified by the blood of those who not only loved her but freely gave all, shedding their last ounce of blood for her.

Word got out, in spite of all her attempts at anonymity. Bishops, Kings, Queens, Popes and Saints came to learn the mystery of Heaven from this humble young woman.

Anna Maria, first and foremost, wife, mother and daughter
As wife: Her husband testified, at the Cause for Beatification, she never failed in her duties toward him, and asked little for herself. He said she would stop speaking to royalty, bishops, even Popes, to wait on him when he came home from work. When she finished serving him, she would resume her duties as prescribed by the Lord. She found it painful to go out socially, especially to the puppet show, but she quietly submitted until her husband, seeing how distasteful it was to her, stopped pressuring her to go.

Domenico testified that he recognized more and more his wife's virtue and holiness. His blustering rages and frequent outbursts caused great stress and anguish in Anna Maria's life, as she tried to sooth his unpredictable mood swings. He said that between him and his mother-in-law, they did a good job at insuring the purification of Anna Maria, as she went about trying to bring the message of peace and reconciliation from one to the other, receiving nothing but abuse in the process.

As daughter: Although her mother grew more and more argumentative, Anna Maria never lost patience with her. When she would ask her mother to accompany her to Mass, she was told, in no uncertain terms, to mind her own business. But Anna Maria never stopped praying for her. When she cried because her mother was suffering so, the Lord reassured her that it was better her mother suffer more pain here and less in Purgatory. Through Anna Maria, her mother died in a state of grace.

Madame Serra, Luigi's employer, died, and Anna Maria's father went about Italy squandering his pension and causing terrible scenes. He carried on shamefully. That did not stop Anna Maria from going to him. When he was irrational and violent, she responded with love and she was able to calm him. She cleaned him, fed him and then prayed for him. At the end he landed in a hostel, consumed by leprosy. His daughter went each day to visit him; she washed him like a baby, tended to his open lesions and cared for his body and soul. As her last act of love, Anna Maria arranged for him to receive the Sacraments before he died.

As mother: Her children testified at her Beatification that their mother always put them, and their needs, before all her other acts of charity. Her daughter Sophie said that her mother brought up her children to know and love their Faith. She had them confirmed at the age of six or seven, and earlier, if they were sick, or if there was a chance they would not be confirmed. When the French invaded, and there was fear the bishops would have to flee, she had little Maria confirmed at *five*. After carefully preparing them, Anna Maria had her children receive First Holy Communion at age twelve which was the customary age at that time. Upon rising early in the morning, the family started their day with prayer. After supper, before bed, they prayed the Rosary together, she read them a story of a Saint and very often ended the evening with the family singing hymns. They went to Mass *as a family* every Sunday. She brought her girls to the hospital so that they would learn how to care for others. She was prudent and never allowed her girls to go out without a chaperone. She showered much love and affection upon them, but when they had need of punishment, rather than use a stick, she had them go to bed without eating dinner or with just a piece of dry bread.

Domenico testified, his wife had a small Altar in her room where she always had a votive lamp burning in front of a painting of the Virgin Mary and a Crucifix. The oil from this lamp was an instrument the Lord used many times to bring about miraculous cures. Anna Maria kept the water font in her home filled, as she blessed her children before they left the house and before they went to sleep.

As good and holy neighbor: As Anna Maria was generous to her husband, mother and children, she was also charitable to her neighbors, even those who mocked and accused her of witchcraft. Now Domenico could not figure out if it was that they were envious, because so many dignitaries were seen coming and going from

her house, or if it was the work of the devil. All he knew was that
when he wanted to quiet their venom, Anna Maria begged him to
leave them alone. Imagine how frustrated this wild man was,
when she insisted on giving more of their little rations to *them*,
than even to those who appreciated it.

Monsignor Rafaele Natali comes into Anna Maria's life

Monsignor Rafaele Natali comes up over and over again in
the Beatification Process. Born at Macerata, in 1781, this priest
who was twelve years Anna Maria's junior would become her
priest-confidant and secretary. Although he was warned to be
careful of possible gossip, he was soon won over by her holiness.
But that does not mean she accepted *him*. In the beginning she
judged *"he was like a young bird that flew from tree to tree and
needed to be placed in a cage."* But since she never learned how
to write, she had to dictate all the revelations that she was receiving,
to him. As a result, he found himself learning, and she saw him
growing in sanctity. He lived in a tiny room in their small flat and
shared the voluntary poverty of Anna Maria and Domenico until
he too went to the *Father* at age ninety.

Anna Maria foresees the ransacking of Rome

It was time to turn to the Lord, and Anna Maria did! She
looked in the sun and foresaw Napoleon Bonaparte confiscating
all Papal holdings. Napoleon sent one of his generals to occupy
Rome; the sacking and desecration of churches began. This was
a death blow, and Pope Pius VI died shortly after. Anna foretold
the day and hour of the election of his Successor to the Chair of
Peter.

God took care of Domenico, Anna Maria, and the whole
family. They, and others who attended Mass, were spared during
the systematic slaughter of the citizens of Rome. On March 14,
1800, the new Pope was elected, and on July 3rd of that same year
a heartbroken Pope Pius VII entered the bloody remains of what
had been a glorious Holy City.

Healings take place through Anna Maria

The gift of healing was granted to Anna Maria by Jesus, shortly after her conversion. She was dying. Jesus appeared to her, wearing a grand blue cloak. He clasped her left hand in His and told her she was to be His spouse. He also said with that hand she would heal, and from that day, she did. Then he told her to rise from bed for she was cured.

Anna, who was an instrument of healing for others, was to bury four of her children before her death. She loved her children passionately! When the time came, she would not have anyone else touch her children. She had cared for them in life, and she would care for them now in death. This strong and brave holy woman prepared her children's bodies and placed them in their shrouds. But she never gave up on God! She trusted Him, implicitly.

When Anna Maria's grandchild tore the pupil of her eye while playing, and the doctor told the family that the sight of that one eye was gone forever, and there was every likelihood the child would lose the sight of the other, Anna Maria made the Sign of the Cross with some oil from the lamp that burned before a statue of St. Philomena, and the child was able to return to school the following day, her sight completely regained!

A time came when Domenico suffered a seizure and passed out in the street. He awakened to find Anna Maria kneeling beside him, praying to the Virgin Mary. He was instantly cured without any aftereffects. Some time passed and Domenico began suffering from unbearable headaches. He began to roam the streets, half-mad, acting insane. Anna Maria was not afraid to go to her husband; she made the Sign of the Cross on his head, and he was not only immediately cured, he was never afflicted in this way again.

When her daughter Sophie lapsed into a coma, Anna Maria made the Sign of the Cross on her daughter with a relic (she always carried) and Sophie awakened immediately. One day soon after she had recovered, Sophie began to writhe in pain from horrendous stomach pains; she couldn't walk and was having difficulty breathing. It is believed she had cancer. Anna Maria placed her hands on her daughter's stomach and the pain disappeared and Sophie began to walk. The testimonies are so numerous it would take miles of pages to list all the miraculous healings attributed to her intercession, during her lifetime and after she went to the Father.

One of the healings which was particularly well-known was that of Marie-Louise of Bourbon. The deposed queen[13] was locked away in a convent with a small contingency from her former royal court. She grieved inconsolably, almost losing her mind and contracted epilepsy. Hearing of the miraculous healing of a princess, the queen called for Anna Maria. She asked her to intercede with God for a cure for *her*. Anna Maria blessed her with a statue of the Blessed Mother, saying, *"Turn to the Mother of God."* The Queen rose from bed, completely healed and spread what had happened to all Rome. Anna Maria preferred praying for the poor, as no one paid attention to them when they were made well

Man trades in the Creator for the created, and God groans

Man, who is always prey to any fancy that tickles the ear, was at it again. God was being substituted for philosophers, the likes of Voltaire, and Christianity looked as if it was taking its last labored breath. Shallow gurus with fancy titles were spouting the philosophy that man was a machine, or a plant, or at most an ape. Sound familiar? This lunacy began with the *intelligentsia*, and then trickled down to the man on the street. It was nothing to hear the highly-respected spouting this blasphemy. *God* was out and *brotherly love* was in.

But God does not leave us to the wolves. He raises a powerful woman who fights for lambs and shepherds alike; he gives this

---

[13]She was the widow of Louis de Parma and daughter of King Charles IV of Spain, and forced to abdicate when Tuscany (Italy) was absorbed into the French Empire

troubled world and society Anna Maria[14] who boldly says, *"the world is an open book consisting of one word - God!"* She first humbled and then influenced the most educated theologians by *her love of the Cross.* They called her living example a *"homily in itself."* They marveled at her astounding knowledge of theology; But first and foremost, they admired her desire to be *anonymous.* Insisting they were gifts from God, she refused to take credit for the revelations she received from the sun.

Anna Maria, instrument of conversion

Msgr. Natali's elder brother Joseph's road was diametrically opposite from his. Although they had the same pious upbringing, Joseph as a youth took up with, and finally left home with, disreputable friends. He returned home wounded and dejected. His brother nursed him back to health. But Joseph had not had enough. The French occupied the Papal states; Joseph quickly gained the enemy's trust and became a messenger for them. He went from bad to worse. Deep in a society where there is no sin, he was to stoop closer to hell. He moved in with a woman of nobility who was separated from her husband.

But God continued to send Joseph warnings. When crossing a river on horseback, he got caught in a current and almost drowned. Next, he was seated at a window smoking, when lightning struck him. He barely escaped death but was left lame. As if that wasn't enough, he was crossing a plain when bandits attacked him and his party; his cohorts were all killed, and he escaped unharmed. Did he understand? No! Then Napoleon was banished to St. Helena; all lands were returned to the Papacy, and Joseph was left broken, penniless, and ill. And if that was not enough, Joseph was confined to his bed; his mistress came to take him home and was struck dead before a priest could give her absolution. On hearing this, were it not for his brother, the Monsignor, the young man would have taken his life. All seemed hopeless; Msgr. Natali

---

[14]As we read about the life of Blessed Anna Maria Taigi, although she was not a religious and Mother Angelica is, we can see God's action in the parallel road each travels to save Mother Church.

brought his brother to Anna Maria. It looked like she had gotten to him, when the demon prompted him to shatter *her* faith. After a furious battle that lasted three days, Anna Maria's belief in God was intact and the young man left. He left untouched, and later returned, still without remorse. Joseph's friends avoided him. He was in a state of despair. But Anna Maria's prayers saved him in the end. He asked for a priest, confessed his sins, received the final Sacraments of the Church, lapsed into a coma and died.

Then there was the priest who had betrayed his Sacrament of Holy Orders and left the Church to become a Protestant. He agreed to go to see Anna Maria. What he saw, as he entered her very austere dwelling, was a woman wearing the cone shaped headdress of a poor working woman. She also was wearing a bandage on her head to cover the wounds inflicted by the devil. She asked him to sit. She then told him all the sins he had committed. At first he was amazed at what she had revealed, but soon pride took over and he was his arrogant self once again. Anna Maria sent him a message that his days were short. He soon fell gravely ill. Then she followed with the message: *"You will never get up again."* He repented his sins, confessed and died in peace through the Sacrament of the Anointing of the Sick.

For the conversion of souls, Anna would walk barefoot to St. Paul-outside-the-Walls and pray before the miraculous Crucifix,[15] or on other days she walked the Way of the Cross around the Coliseum.[16] She was particularly interested in the Jewish people and prophesied there would be great conversions among them which would bring the chosen people to the fullness of the Word of God. Alphonse Marie Ratisbonne[17] converted three years after her death and his brother Theodore ten years before her death. She foretold through the sun, the founding of the *Daughters of*

---

[15]This is the Crucifix that came to life and Jesus shared with St. Bridget of Sweden what had transpired during His Passion.

[16]Our Pope John Paul II walks the Way of the Cross every Good Friday around the Coliseum.

[17]Read more about his conversion from Judaism to Catholicism and on to the Priesthood, in the chapter on the Miraculous Medal in Bob and Penny Lord's book: *"The Many Faces of Mary, a love story."*

Zion by the Ratisbonne brothers, the first congregation dedicated to the conversion of the Jewish people and understanding between Christians and Jews. Her daughter Sophie testified that one day when she accompanied her mother to the Church of the Holy Apostles to witness the baptism of a Jewish convert to the Faith, she saw Anna Maria hide herself, afraid she would be noticed and attention be directed at her. After the baptism, she went into ecstasy. As she came out of it, she was heard exclaiming, *"This convert is a great soul. She will go to Heaven without passing through Purgatory."*

You alone, Lord

Anna Maria counted on no one but God. She refused the gifts of those whom she had helped, in any way, saying, *"I do not serve God for personal reward. Thank the Blessed Mother, not me."* When her children were hungry and many urged her to accept gifts for their sake, she flatly refused, saying, *"Would you dare say that I and my family could not trust in Our Lord and His infinite generosity?"* And *"Do not insult God by suggesting that He would abandon us."* Through God's providence they were always cared for.

Anna Maria was real! She was human. At her Process of Beatification, people came forth and testified witnessing the time she went to St. Paul-outside-the-Walls and asked our Lord for help, pleading her family had no more bread. He told her to go home and she would find some. When she arrived home, she did not find bread but instead, a letter containing a draft for just enough money to buy bread. Another time when there was no bread, she again turned to the Lord: *"Lord,"* she pleaded like Abraham and Moses before her, *"Your unworthy servant expects her daily bread from Your Hands."* No sooner had she stopped praying when there was a knock in the door; she opened to a stranger she had never seen before. He handed her a letter which he said came from a far-off place. It contained alms and a message: *"I hear you are in need; allow me to help you."*

Msgr. Natali testified that he had the joy of studying the

"servant of God" for thirty years during which time she faithfully practiced complete self-abandonment, turning completely to the Lord, shunning the gifts of *this* world for the Gifts of the *next* World. Princes, Kings, Queens, Cardinals all tried to use some kind of subterfuge to help her without her knowing it, but Anna Maria found out (through the sun) and refused! Her Lord wanted her to be completely dependent on Him, and He gave her the strength to walk that walk.

Anna Maria and twenty years of the Dark Night of the Soul

The Lord told Anna Maria she was to be His instrument to bring about the conversions of many. He warned she would have to fight many battles and withstand brutal attacks by those who would like to destroy her because she was doing His Will. With little earthly understanding and support at times, God was to plunge her from the glorious days of His consolation to the bleakness of the Dark Night of the Soul - for twenty years! Sometimes after receiving Holy Communion, Anna Maria would see a slim ray of light, but then the Lord would withhold Himself and it was all the darker. When the Master spoke to her it was to invite her to Calvary. Suddenly she was to understand the meaning of the crown of thorns around the sun. She spent sleepless nights, weakened by illness and tortured by demons. Although she was like one lost in a desert, parched and weary, she never gave up on her Lord. Loving Him the more, she never asked for the end of her martyrdom.

It was not enough that Heaven had closed its doors to her; earth became a roaring hell! She was attacked by local women spreading scandal about her and her daughters. Desolation of the spirit was compounded by diseases of the flesh mounting one upon another, robbing her of what little strength she had left, completely debilitating her. Her pounding headaches increased on Fridays to such an intense pitch, it was difficult for her to stand, no less work. At these times she could do little more than go to bed. Her head was like that of Jesus when He was crowned with the Crown of Thorns, the pain piercing her eyes as well as her entire head. She went about her chores bravely trying to hide the agony she was enduring for this Lord she so adored, Who appeared to having deserted her. As a result of her continuing to work on her close-up needlepoint at this time, the pain in her eyes became so severe and the damage she suffered so critical, it resulted in the complete loss of sight in the one eye and the little that was left in the other, by the time Anna died. The pain in her ears was so excruciating, she had to wrap a band tightly around her head which nearly stifled her in the hot humid weather. Her senses were affected with an ongoing bitter taste of vinegar in her mouth. Her sense of smell was violated by the horrible stench of sin she perceived in the world, which became more pungent when a sinner approached her. As in Psalm 22, she, like Jesus *"could count every bone in her body,"* racked with pain.

Anna Maria and Jesus in the Eucharist

One time, a priest who thought she was a fake, gave her an unconsecrated host. In that way he would expose her, or so he thought. Anna Maria *knew* this was not her Lord, but *instead* an unconsecrated host that had been substituted for her Lord, and she refused it. The Lord told her she had to tell her confessor of the priest's deception. She did; the confessor approached the priest and he admitted his deception and attempt to trick Anna Maria.

Another time, during the Mass, when the priest turned around[18] and said, *"Behold the Lamb of God Who takes away the sins of the world,"* the consecrated Host left his hands and glided through the air; it suspended in midair for a moment and then *soared* toward Anna Maria where It came to rest on her lips. After the Mass the priest went into the sacristy, fuming that this was an abuse of the Eucharist and Anna Maria was a witch. He threatened to report her to the Holy See, when he was dissuaded by two Trinitarians who spoke up, telling him that *"God was the Lord of the Liturgy."*

Anna Maria never saw Jesus as a piece of consecrated Bread, but instead Our Jesus alive in the Host, at times as a Child, and at

---

[18]prior to Vatican Council II, the priest celebrated the Liturgy of the Eucharist with his back to the faithful.

other times as a King dressed in majestic purple robes. He mournfully shared with her:

"In this crowd of people that you see in the church, there are scarcely two souls who are truly sincere in their love. The others are equally ready to come to Mass or to go to the theater."

When Anna Maria received Our Lord in the Eucharist, she would become so lost in ecstasy she often fell to the ground, as if struck by lightning; she remained motionless until ordered by the priest to get up. The priest would silently motion her to leave the area of the Altar, so as to not create a scene with her loud sighs which invariably accompanied her ecstasies.

There was a priest who refused to give her Holy Communion. If she came by herself, he declined to open the Tabernacle. Anna Maria kept this to herself, but witnesses reported it to her confessor Msgr. Natali, who acquainted the priest of his duty. The priest refused to remedy the situation. The good Monsignor threatened to denounce him in front of the whole church. Suddenly the priest changed his mind. Although she had been devastated when she could not receive the Eucharist, Anna Maria was more upset with her confessor for chastising the other priest.

Anna Maria and the Sacred Heart of Jesus

She consecrated all her Fridays to the Sacred Heart of Jesus. But rather than with devotions, practiced by the Church for centuries, she contemplated the Sacred Heart in Jesus' life beginning in Nazareth and ending in Calvary. She saw His Sacred Heart beating inside His Mother's womb after Incarnation, in Bethlehem as He first opened His Eyes to the world, in the Baby Who had to flee with Joseph and Mary to Egypt, in the young God-Man Who had been lost for three days in the Temple, to the Savior Whose Sacred Heart was pierced out of love for us on Calvary.

For as long as she could *physically*, Anna Maria walked, *barefoot*, to the Mamertime prison, where she would adore the Crucifix. One day, as she was praying before the Crucifix in the church of *St. Andrew della Valle*, Jesus came to life on the Cross and asked her, *"What do you wish? To follow Jesus poor and naked and stripped of all, or to follow Him in triumph and glory? Which do you choose?"*

She answered: *"I choose the Cross of my Jesus. I will carry it, like Him, in pain and infamy."*[19]

Anna Maria and the poor souls in Purgatory

She continued to pray for the poor souls who never ceased pleading to her, at great cost to herself, physically as well as spiritually. One day during Mass, she experienced excruciating pain and sorrow. Then during the following Mass, Anna Maria saw the poor soul, she had been praying for, released from Purgatory, rising up to Heaven. She would ask those souls to pray for the Pope and the Church.

One other time she saw a priest who had been held in great esteem while on earth, for his preaching and his charismatic gifts, suffering brutal, torturous agony in Purgatory because instead of giving glory to God he centered on himself, drawing the Faithful to himself and not the Savior.

Another instance of suffering for Anna Maria was when she saw one of her friends writhing in pain in Purgatory because, while on earth, she had advertised the supernatural gifts she had received from the Lord, rather than keeping them to herself.

Anna Maria saw a lay person, whose goodness had been above approach while on earth, suffering dire anguish in Purgatory because she had ingratiated herself to those in power, flattering them to receive their favor.

But she also knew great joy as she saw lay brothers of the Capuchins and the Friar Minors, as well as a young Jesuit novice and two priests from the missions, rising out of Purgatory.

She saw in her sun, the martyred souls of the Superior General of the Trinitarians and his companion who had been tortured and then murdered by French soldiers, soaring straight to Heaven.

---

[19]disgrace

Anna Maria and false prophets

A religious, known for his sanctity, believed that he had had a vision of two Angels who assured him his ambitious project was of Divine origin and would bear much fruit. When he told this to Anna Maria, she smiled sadly and gently informed him it would fail miserably. It did!

Then there was a Poor Clare who spread stories of having visions and receiving many mystical gifts. Because of this, she was able to establish a Reformed Franciscan Third Order. One of her sisters led many astray by alluding she had the gifts of St. Teresa of Avila. Bishops, priests, religious and laity alike were deluded by this nun who wrote and spoke cleverly, convincing everyone that she had *the infused knowledge* from God that Teresa once had. Anna Maria went to the two nuns and let them know that she was on to them and their deception. They brazenly denied it, insisting the Poor Clare did indeed possess all the Divine gifts of Teresa of Avila.

Although at times it seems the innocent will never know the truth, Our Lord Jesus will ultimately bring all things to light, not allowing his children to fall, if only they will use their eyes to see and their ears to hear. The nun's Spiritual Director, Most Reverend Father General of the Friars Minor of the Observance, brought her to Bishop Natali's attention (Anna Maria's confessor). The bishop asked Anna Maria what she saw in the sun about this alleged visionary. Although she would not speak unkindly of the Sister, she told him not to waste his time visiting her. He understood all too clearly what she meant. It was not long after that, the Poor Clare nun was exposed, and she, the Most Reverend Father General and her nuns were brought before the Holy See and censured.

One time, a Cardinal came to Bishop Natali and asked for prayers, as an alleged Mystic had told him he would die shortly in Naples. Bishop Natali asked Anna Maria to look into the sun; she sent word to the Cardinal to have peace; he would have a peaceful trip to Naples and would return to Rome. But while there, he was to go to a certain convent where he would find two nuns: one with a reputation of being very pious and one who is believed to be a fool. He was to ignore the sanctimonious one, as she would lead him astray. He was to listen to the other one, as she would give him the proper guidance. When the Cardinal returned to Rome, he tried to reward Anna Maria. She refused the monthly allowance he offered, to help feed her impoverished family, insisting he give it to a family she was not able to help because of her limited resources. When the Cardinal later became ill, Anna sent word that although the doctors said there was nothing seriously wrong with him, he should prepare to meet the Lord soon. The Cardinal put his house in order and died a peaceful death, a few days after Anna Maria had so prophesied.

Anna Maria - Saint of Charity to Humans and Animals

She not only had a tender heart for the sick, caring for them, answering ingratitude and harshness with love and compassion, she never turned away anyone in need. One day, seeing how little food was left in the cupboard, Anna Maria's mother sent a beggar away, empty-handed. When Anna Maria heard of this, she searched for him, brought him home and cared for him. She not only cleaned him and fed him, she affirmed him, endearingly telling him how precious he was to the Lord.

She was walking to church one day when she spotted a woman lying in the street. People were passing by, looking away from her, trying to avoid the sight of the poor soul who so obviously had epilepsy. The woman was foaming at the mouth. Anna Maria wiped her mouth, picked her up and brought her to a little shop where she fed the starving soul. Others seeing this act of charity, joined in and took up a collection for her. Later, in church, Anna Maria immediately went into ecstasy and heard the Lord say, *"Thank you, dear one, for caring for Me."*

Another time, hearing the daughter of one her most vindictive persecutors was dangerously ill, Anna went to the house, tended the girl and comforted the mother. She brought her some cookies each day. Her last visit, Anna blessed the girl with the Sign of the Cross and she was immediately cured.

Anna Maria did not only have love and compassion for God's *human* creatures, but for His four legged ones as well. She would pick up stray animals, care for them and then find them homes, saying, since their only time was on earth, we have the obligation to give these sweet, helpless, loving creatures who live only to love us, the best life we possibly can. [We highly agree with her.]

Martyrdom for the salvation of the Church

Anna Maria suffered, for almost fifty years, the most excruciating pain for Jesus and Mother Church. She saw in her sun a world filled with evil, dominated by Christ-hating Masons. She saw Europe destroyed and destitute as despots took over, thousands of the Faithful dying in battle without the Sacraments because of no priests. She saw Spain burning as brother killed brother. She saw illegal councils called in Paris which would rob Catholics of their Church. She saw the evolution of a schism by which many bishops, priests, and religious would lose their lives for refusing to reject the supreme authority of the Papacy over the Church. She saw the Emperor Napoleon running the Church as if she was part of his army, claiming since the Pope and the prelates were weak, it was his God-given duty as supreme emperor of the world to rule over the Church.

Two boats sail - One for Christ and one for Self

Two children came into the world in Italy in the Eighteenth Century. One desired the crown which Jesus wore on earth so that she would one day wear the golden crown of sanctity and eternal life in Paradise; and she bore all the pains, the rejection, and the wounds He bore for the redemption of the world, to share with Him, His Cross. The other, coming from very similar circumstances, sought and wore the temporary crown of gold on earth which tarnished, robbing him of all the world had promised.

Anna Maria Taigi, through her sun, followed the footsteps of the other child, Napoleon, from his early days as a lieutenant to his bloody grasp at ruling the world and the Church to his lonely miserable death on the Island of Elba. She witnessed the seventeen years of bloodshed covering the four corners of the earth, the ruthless annihilation of those who opposed him or who threatened his ascendancy to the throne as Emperor of the world, the brutality toward Princes of the world and the Church, the imprisonment and torture of her Vicars, her priests and religious. And she saw his humiliating end on a lonely island. She described, to her confessor Bishop Natali, Napoleon's death more than two weeks before his *mother* heard of his death. Anna Maria saw his grave, his funeral and his destiny in time and eternity. His destiny? His uncle, Cardinal Fesch said of him, *"God did not break him; God humbled him and in humiliation lies salvation."* As Napoleon did to others, so was done unto him. His last days were with rats, lice and bugs as companions, and a heartless jailer who took delight in reducing him to a pitiful state. As the Lord so many times said to Anna Maria Taigi, when she begged Him to alleviate a sinner's terrible suffering on earth, *"Better he should suffer on earth than in Purgatory."* Did the jailer spare Napoleon time in that dark abyss? Anna Maria Taigi not only prayed for the soul of his proud mother who pushed her son into temporary glory, but for Napoleon!

Our Lord promised Anna Maria He would take care of her children, with these words, *"I am yours, as I am to all who take up their cross bravely. The children of the Beloved are My well-beloved."* Anna Maria foretold her own death. She told Bishop Natali, as she stood before the Crucifix in St. Paul Outside the Walls, *"It is the last time."* She had just received Holy Communion and she felt such a wave of peace. Our Lord spoke to her, *"Live in peace my daughter, and do not trouble yourself over what people say about you. You will soon be with Me in My Kingdom."* These words would ring through her heart and mind during her final pain-filled last seven months of her life.

On the 26th of October in the year 1836, Anna Maria took to her bed, never to leave it. Was there pain for this obedient, humble child of God? You bet! But the difference was, she had the peaceful assurance that God was with her and would be with her family, always providing for them. Confined to bed, Anna Maria continued her sewing and directing the servants caring for the family.

Her faithful confessor Bishop Natali said Mass for her every day in her home and gave her the Lord in Holy Communion. On Sunday the 2nd of June in 1837, she was burning up with a raging fever. After Communion, she went into such a deep and long ecstasy, everyone thought she had passed on. But during that ecstasy, Our Lord told her she would die on the following Friday, the day of His Passion, the day they had shared over the years. When she awakened from her ecstasy, she told Bishop Natali the Good News the Lord had revealed to her. She was radiant!

She first called Domenico in and thanked him for all the loving care, he had given her through all the years of their married life. Then one by one she called in her children, blessing them, imploring them to be faithful in saying their prayers, reciting the Rosary daily, and attending Mass. And then, knowing how, when a mother dies, the family splits apart, Anna Maria begged them not to fight among themselves, to remain a strong united family. She cried, not because she was going to be with her Lord and his Mother, but because she would not see her children until that time when they would meet once more in Heaven.

At half past four, Friday morning, June 9th, 1837, our future Beata closed her eyes and was silent. No more would she look into her sun on earth. But she would be a sign and an inspiration to those of us who have not entered religious life, but who want to serve Our Lord. As she had counselled Popes on earth, now her Vicars would bring honor to her, recognizing and proclaiming the holiness and virtue of this great wife, loving mother, and faithful daughter of the Church. Pope Pius IX introduced the Cause of Beatification in 1863 and on May 30th, 1920, Pope Benedict XV raised Anna Maria Taigi to the royal roll call of Blesseds. She was soon after proclaimed by this same Pope - *Special Protectress of Mothers of Families* and *Patroness of the Women's Catholic Union.*

When Pope Pius heard that Anna Maria had desired to be entombed in the Church of the Trinitarians, he had her body brought to the Basilica of San Chrysogono (where she is till today).

> *"Three years later the coffin was again opened, and though the clothes had decayed, her body was still intact.*[20] *The sisters of St. Joseph took off the poor clothing and replaced it with new. For eight days, the body was exposed for the veneration of the Faithful; the whole neighborhood of Trastevere*[21] *seemed on the move and troops were needed to ensure order. The body, enclosed in a double coffin of lead and cypress, was near the Chapel of the Blessed Sacrament in a memorial tomb, and later on, in the chapel to the left, under the Altar within a large glass shrine which allowed her to be seen in the habit of a Trinitarian Tertiary. The hands were joined in front of the breast. The face, giving an impression of infinite serenity, was covered in a light wax mask beneath the white coif."*[22]

When someone like Anna Maria died, they would make a death mask, so that the faithful down through the ages could see how she really looked. We were blessed to be able to see all the relics, left behind, including her death mask. We can never describe the feeling we had, as we knelt before her tomb and prayed for the intercession of Blessed Anna Maria Taigi. God raised up a Blessed from people like you and me, ordinary simple people who said yes, the same people to which Jesus, Mary and Joseph belonged. Anna Maria is that sign to the laity, that in communion with our Pope, his faithful prelates, priests and religious, we can usher the Church into a new glorious age. The world must know of this great but humble woman; know and have hope that we can make a difference; believe that there will be victory in the twenty-first century for Jesus and his Church.

Blessed Anna Maria Taigi, may we seek to do God's Will as faithfully as you did. Pray for us.

---

[20]incorrupt
[21]in Rome
[22] *"Wife, Mother and Mystic"* by Albert Bessieres, S.J., Tan Publications

Saint Gemma Galgani

Saint Gemma Galgani

Mystic who bore the precious Wounds of Our Savior

The curtain is falling on the 19th Century. The Heresy of *Modernism* would soon show its venomous fangs and the Church, through her holy Pope Saint Pius X, would fight it, dispelling it for all time, or so he hoped. *We, know now at the tail end of the 20th Century that this did not come to pass. We are, once again, suffering the same Heresy combined with centuries of other condemned heresies, all in one deadly poisonous attack disguised under the name of enlightenment.*

The Lord was wounded by His sons, those He had commissioned to be guardians of the Faith. He needed a *victim-soul*. His priests and bishops, who were supposed to be *victim-priests* with Him, had once again betrayed Him, and He needed a soul who would be faithful and obedient until death, one who would share His Wounds and Passion. And so, a *Gemma*[1] was born!

---

[1] Italian for gem

The Lord sends down a Gem from Heaven to bless the world

In Camigliano, a small village not too far from the historic city of Lucca, the Lord blessed Aurelia Landi[2] and Enrico Galgani on March 12, 1878, with a tiny, precious little baby girl (as the priest who baptized her, exclaimed upon seeing her), *una Gemma del Paradiso!*

Gemma's mother had hesitated naming her new-born child Gemma, as it was not a Saint's name, but did so, taking the priest's words as prophecy that the Lord had blessed them with a gem from Heaven.

Once again, we find *"Holy Clusters"*[3] as we discover, Gemma's father descended from the *same family* as a Saint, St. John Leonardi. Gemma would bless the *same city*, Lucca, that another Saint, *St. Zita*[4] blessed in the 13th Century. As her father had relocated his family to Lucca, soon after Gemma was born, she spent most of her twenty five years of life there, and now after death, rests there for the faithful to come and venerate till today.

Although she was one of seven children, she and her brother Gino were their father's favorites. He liked to take Gemma and her brother for walks. But when he showed special favors to them, they both rebelled, not wanting to be treated better than the other children. Nevertheless, we can be sure, the rest of the family probably resented the two and did not look upon them, kindly.

Gemma showed signs of sainthood from a very young age. One day, her grandmother noticed her precious, chubby, little

---

[2]In Europe and Mexico as well as other nations around the world, the wife maintains her maiden name until death, when she is buried under that name.

[3]In their books, Bob and Penny show how Miracles of the Eucharist, Apparitions of Mary and the Angels, and the births of Saints will often come from a certain area. We call those areas, so blessed over and over again by the Lord, *Holy Clusters*.

[4]St. Zita spent her life serving the Lord, as a lay person and servant. She was blessed by many Miracles happening through her lifetime and after, her virtuous life and Miracles raising her to the company of Saints. Her body never decomposed.

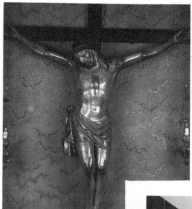

Left: *Crucifix in dining room of the Giannini home*

Above: *St. Gemma's diary with the hoof prints of the devil*

Above: *The habit of St. Gemma Galgani*

Above: *St. Gemma Galgani receives the Stigmata*

Left: *Dream of Saint Gemma Galgani where Venerable Gabriel gives her a heart*

granddaughter, all of four years old, kneeling before a picture of the Immaculate Heart of Mary. When her grandmother called an uncle over, they asked the child what she was doing. She replied, she was praying the Rosary and to please leave her alone, so that she could continue. Needless to say, this little feisty future saint had her way; they left her with her Blessed Mother. Even from this young age, it was obvious, Gemma would belong to no one but the Lord and His Mother.

Gemma was her mother's life! They would pray together, the little girl joyfully keeping up with her mother. Each day, she excitedly looked forward to the time when her mother told her stories about Jesus and *His* Mother. But that was tragically to come to an end when Gemma was only five years old. Her mother became ill. The next few pain-filled years, her mother would hold her little girl close to her, cradle her in her arms and ask the Lord why He had sent this precious girl to her so late. She would tell Gemma, she wished she could take her up to Heaven with her.

Gemma, in later years, gave full credit to her mother for the great love, she had for God through the Cross. Her mother taught her the Faith, through the Lord Crucified, speaking of that loving God the Father Who sacrificed His only begotten Son for her, and of Jesus the Son Who willingly suffered and died for her. Knowing suffering first hand, her mother taught Gemma the value of the Cross. As death approached, her mother, completely bedridden, continued telling her stories about Jesus. But when she was nearing the end, she told her little Gemma that soon, she would learn from Jesus Himself Who would speak to her from the very depths of her heart.

As she could feel the debilitating ravages of consumption draining her of life, her mother, Aurelia, requested Gemma be allowed to receive the Sacrament of Confirmation, before she died. Although she was only seven years old, her mother's instructions had fared her well and the Pastor agreed. The day of her Confirmation came and she was confirmed. After that Mass was over, she and her family stayed to give thanksgiving at the *next* Mass. As she was deep in prayer, praising the Lord for the gift of this Divine Sacrament that He had given her, Gemma heard a voice interiorly ask her: *"Will you give me your mother?"* She replied she would, but asked the Lord to take her, along with her mother. The Lord asked her to give her mother to Him, *unconditionally.* This was to be the first of many sacrifices that He would ask of her throughout her life, as she would join Him on the Cross.

Gemma carries her first cross, as her mother dies

It was September 17, 1886, and it was time for the young Aurelia (age 39) to go Home to the Lord, she had so faithfully brought to her daughter, the future Saint. Now that her mother was with the God she had so often spoken of, Gemma knew, there would no longer be anyone to tell her stories about her Jesus. Believing with all her heart that her mother would now help her from Heaven, did not heal the emptiness she felt, losing her beloved mother and holy story teller.

She was to remain on earth with her father and her brothers and sisters. Her first Christmas, after her mother's death, was a very quiet one. She looked like a little girl who had lost all her toys, as she tried to find the joy she had shared with her mother, when, in former Christmases, they had welcomed the Baby Jesus into their hearts. She sat at the window, looking off to the *Place* from where, she knew her mother was watching over her and tears began to flow. She cried, remembering how she had breathlessly helped her mother roll the dough to make ready all the baked goods, in anticipation of the precious Baby's birth.

Jesus in the Eucharist comes to dwell in Gemma

At age nine (although she was frail, and barely looked six), she was sent off to a fine school run by the Sisters of St. Zita. The wise and holy Sisters soon discovered she was a special soul, untouched by the world, who would, one day, be singularly blessed by the Lord.

When she pleaded to be allowed to receive her Lord in Holy Communion: *"Give Him to me; I long for Him, and I cannot live without Him,"* her confessor had no choice but to say Yes! It was then, she said, that she received her first embrace from Jesus *Crucified.* From then on, she would desire only to walk with Him, sharing in His Passion. She later wrote,

> *"Do grant, oh my God, that when my lips approach Yours to kiss You, I may taste the gall that was given You; when my shoulders lean against Yours, make me feel Your scourging; when my flesh is united with Yours, in the Holy Eucharist, make me feel Your Passion; when my head comes near Yours, make me feel Your thorns; when my heart is close to Yours, make me feel Your spear..."*

When we approach Our Lord in Holy Communion, are we aware of the price, Our *Crucified* Lord paid that we might receive Him in His Body, Blood, Soul and Divinity? As we receive the Risen Lord, do we ever contemplate the action of the Mass, the ongoing *Sacrifice* of the Cross[5] which brings the *Risen* Lord to us? Should you ever begin to walk beside Him on the Way of the Cross and join Him during the Sacrifice of the Mass, you will begin, as Saint Gemma before you, to know the Savior Who suffered and died for you.

On June 17, Feast of the Sacred Heart, Gemma received First Holy Communion. As she was preparing for *"His Kiss,"* she meditated on no longer being herself but becoming the Jesus Who would live in, and love through her. She said that when she consumed the Host, for the first time, she had a glimpse of what life in union with Christ would be like when she shed the shell of her body and was with Him in Paradise. During her remaining sixteen years, whenever she remembered, or better *relived* that day, she again tasted that special morsel of Heaven, she knew the first time she received Holy Communion.

---

[5]Read in Bob and Penny Lord's book: *"This is My Body, This is My Blood, Miracles of the Eucharist- Book II"*, chapters on the Mass, the ongoing Sacrifice of the Cross.

She was an outstanding student in school, excelling in all her studies, secular as well as religious. She was liked and loved by students and teachers alike. As one of the few things she feared most intensely, was that she might offend God, she would answer simply *No* when she meant *No* and *Yes* when she meant *Yes*. For Gemma there were no gray areas (so popular today, where we no longer know what is right or wrong); it was either black or white. One of the Sisters who spoke of her child-like frankness remembered the day, the girls at the school were practicing for a play, when the Mother Superior came to the Sister in charge and asked her to have the girls pray for a dying man who refused the Holy Sacraments. The girls knelt with the Sister and prayed for the poor soul. After they finished praying, little Gemma came over to the Sister and whispered: "*The grace has been granted.*" They received word that evening that the dying man had converted and died after having received the Holy Sacraments of the Church; Penance, Holy Communion and Extreme Unction.[6]

Gemma always strived to keep her senses under control; sometimes using quite severe (by today's standards) means of mortification. Her principle fear was being in any way, guilty of the sin of pride. When she was once *accused* of pride by one of her classmates, she said she did not know what to answer because she did not know what pride was and did not want to offend God by answering incorrectly. But, with years, comes knowledge, and with knowledge comes the loss of such child-like innocence. As she grew older, Gemma became aware of the dangerous subtleties of pride and how they devour souls, once allowed to enter the smallest corner of the soul. Because of this concern, she would plead with her teachers and fellow students to forgive her if she had been guilty of pride in any form.

No matter what was going on around her, Gemma's heart always longed for her Lord in the Tabernacle. Although she obeyed the Sisters when instructed to play with the other girls, she still looked toward the often locked door of the Chapel, saying that

---

[6]now called the Sacrament of the Anointing of the Sick

love breaks down all barriers. One day the Sister asked the class, "Who wants to be a Saint?" Without waiting for the Sister to add *"in the play,"* Gemma shot up and answered *"I will become a Saint."*

Gemma goes through The Dark Night of the Soul

Honeymoons end, and then the reality of living a life together comes into play. Jesus had wooed little Gemma; she was ecstatic, sharing the sweetness of being loved by Him. But all good things come to an end. Gemma was to now know the Lord in His Passion, the Lord Who suffered in Gethsemane. She would share the abandonment that He felt as she went through the *"Dark night of the Soul,"* experiencing *nothing* after receiving Holy Communion. Feeling spiritually alone, afflicted in body and soul, finding no consolation in prayers, nothing to affirm her faith, Gemma, like her Jesus before her, still *knew* and *continued to believe* she was not abandoned by God and tried even harder to please Him.

Things improved at home. Whereas she had formerly been chastised for wanting to go to church to be with her Lord, after her two aunts came to live with her family, she was able to go and had the joy of receiving her sweet Lord once more in Holy Communion every day at Mass.

On a retreat in 1891, at the Convent of St. Zita, Jesus gave Gemma deep insights into herself and how she could please Him *more* with her *heart* than her lips. As she listened to His Voice beckoning her to be like Himself in His humility, obedience, and sweet unconditional love, she resolved: to visit Jesus in the Blessed Sacrament, each day, speak to Him with her heart and not her lips; and when she prayed, to speak of Heavenly things, not earthly concerns.

Gemma has to say good by to her brother Gino

It was 1894 and Gemma was sixteen years old. Once again, she had to say good-by to a loved one who would precede her to Heaven. Her brother Gino had always shared her love for Jesus.

When he heard Jesus' call to become a victim-priest with Him, he did not know that it was to be in Heaven. He had studied industriously and had just graduated from Minor Seminary with highest honors when he contracted the same disease that claimed his mother's life. He was only eighteen years old. And so little Gemma's heart knew heartbreak once more, as her brother left her to join their mother and beloved Lord Jesus in Paradise.

Devastated by the death of her dear brother, Gemma became so ill, she was unable to rise from bed for over three months. Her father, seeing his precious child near death, pleaded with Jesus to take him and not her. The Lord answered his prayers and two years later, his spirit spent from the crosses he had borne, Gemma's father went *Home* to his wife and son.

[It reminds me of the time my father was seriously ill with Cancer. I had not been feeling well either. After the results were in from my x-rays, the doctor told me, by the size of the mass and how quickly it had grown, it most likely was malignant and I had to have an operation, immediately! I did not want to upset my parents so I said it was just a little minor surgery, nothing serious, and I would not be in the hospital long. My father went into the bedroom and prayed to the Lord (like Gemma's father) to take him and not me. My father died a few months later. I never had an operation. Such great love! Does the world know that kind of love anymore? If not, we are truly poor!]

Gemma has an encounter with her Guardian Angel

As her illness had taken a toll on her strength, Gemma was not able to return to school. She remained at home and taught her sisters and brothers. At her beatification, one of her brothers said, *"Gemma always brought the olive branch."*[7] She lovingly cared for the needs, both spiritual and physical of her family, often at the neglect of herself. She had no use for fancy clothes, and adorned herself in simple, extremely austere black dresses. One day to please a relative, not wanting to offend him by refusing

---

[7]the symbol of peace

his gift, Gemma wore a gold watch and a gold cross and chain when she went outdoors. When she returned home, who should come to her but her Guardian Angel. He scolded her: *"Remember, the spouse of the Crucified King should wear no ornaments but thorns and crosses."* She immediately pledged never to wear nor speak of things of the world. She went back to the severity of the clothes she had been wearing, and when she ventured out, she donned a simple black cloak to cover a shapeless black dress and a straw hat. This did not detract from her fine patrician looks, but instead enhanced them.

Her Guardian Angel stressed obedience! He would repeat over and over again: *"Obedience! You must obey! You must be like a dead body; whatever is asked of you, you must obey quickly and joyfully!"* He was not above reproaching her, scolding her: *"If you do not obey, I will not show myself to you, again."* He taught her that to disobey would always lead to sin. He told her there was no shorter road to Heaven than through obedience!

The new year brings more crosses

At the end of a very difficult 1895, burdened down by heavy crosses, Gemma placed herself at the Lord's Feet on the Cross. The new year did not promise to be any better:

"I do not know what will happen to me this year. I abandon myself to You, my God; all my hopes and affections shall be for You. I am weak, oh Jesus, but I trust in Your help and I resolve to live differently, namely, closer to You."

When we pray as Gemma prayed, do we not expect Jesus to turn everything around and grant us peace on earth? The new year came and with it, crosses. The Saints wanted to be like Jesus; that always means the Cross!

Her first cross was when, her leg became so infected, the doctor was going to amputate. Instead, he performed an extremely painful operation. Gemma, refusing all anesthetic, her eyes on Jesus on the Cross, cried out only once, for which she later begged forgiveness from the Lord.

That battle over, a worse attack was to ensue. Her father, a chemist, had given much credit to the poor and to those in financial straits *temporarily*; except *temporarily* became *forever*, and they never paid! His wife's and son's illnesses and then deaths had drained whatever resources he had; the authorities sold his farm and its machinery and his entire pharmacy. When Gemma's father was struck down by cancer of the throat and died November, 1897, his worries and pain were over; but those of Gemma and her brothers and sisters were only beginning.

Although they were left penniless, Gemma grieved more for the loss of her father than of all they had lost *materially*. The hurts were there though, and till her dying days, she recalled the creditors coming in, her father still laid out at home, taking what little they had left. But with all of this hitting her at one time, bitterness would have been an acceptable reaction. However, instead of vindictiveness, she prayed to that God Whom she never gave up on, the One Who never gave up on her. Gemma faced this at all of nineteen and a half years old!

She had been living with her brother and his wife. An aunt offered to have Gemma live with her. The family agreed to this sacrifice as it would be one less mouth to feed and a little less pressure on the brother and sister-in-law. And so she went to live with her aunt. The distractions of her aunt's family and friends who were good people, but definitely of the world, were more painful for her than the deprivations she faced back home. When two different suitors came and asked for Gemma's hand in marriage, she knew it was time to leave. Although this life, her aunt offered her appeared to be one of comfort and plenty, to one promised to the Lord it was poverty of the soul, a kind more threatening than any she could suffer back in Lucca. She complained of back pains, and her aunt agreed to let her go. Although it was difficult to say good by to such loving family and friends, she longed to return to the suffering, she faced at home in Lucca; for there, she knew her Spouse was waiting for her to take up her cross.

She returned home, and the pain in her back travelled down

her spine, crippling her so badly she was bent over. This was further magnified when she suffered attacks of meningitis. As if that was not bad enough, Gemma lost her hearing, her hair fell out, and her legs became paralyzed. Every means of relief her family and doctors attempted, failed. Then a woman left her a book on the life of *Venerable Gabriel of the Sorrows*.

At first Gemma was not interested in reading about Gabriel. It was not until she was attacked by the devil one evening. She had been undergoing great suffering, not only in body but in spirit. Just when she was about to despair, thinking she could not stand anymore pain and suffering, who should appear? *The devil* who loves to move in at times like this. He told her, he would take away her pain, he would cure her, he would make her happy! There he was, the father of lies, telling half truths which grow into full blown lies.

Just as she was about to give in, she felt impelled to call on Venerable Gabriel for help. No sooner did she have the thought when a wave of peace came over her. When Gemma was tempted a second time, she called on him again. She was now filled with such serenity, she was *eager* to learn about this great intercessor who had rescued her from the enemy, *twice*. She read his biography over and over again. Gemma grew so close to Gabriel, when the woman came for her book, Gemma wept. That evening, Gabriel appeared to her in a dream and told her to be good and he would come back to see her.

Gemma feels called to the religious life

Life was one failed operation upon another failed operation, pain upon more pain. Then one day, Gemma had a thought: she would like to enter the *religious* life. It was the Feast Day of the Immaculate Conception in 1898. When she received permission from her confessor to become a religious, she had another dream of Venerable Gabriel. He told her to simply make her vow to be a religious and say no more. Then, he gave her a cloth emblem in the shape of a heart (worn by the Passionists) to kiss. He then placed the heart on her heart and called her *"Sister."* The next day, Gemma made her vow and received Holy Communion. A calm came over her like the quiet after a storm. She neither understood Gabriel's words nor why he covered her heart with another heart, yet Gemma was destined to be a Sister of the Passionists, if not officially, then assuredly as the Bride who shared in the Passion of her Spouse, Christ the Crucified.

Jesus asks Gemma if she wants to be healed

Although Gemma's soul was at peace, her body was still racked with pain. Her health declined drastically until, on February 2, 1899, a priest was called and she received what was to be her Viaticum, her final Holy Communion. But it was not time for the little suffering servant to go to her Spouse. One of the Sisters of St. Zita brought her a novena to *St. Margaret Mary Alacoque.* Having started and stopped several times, she finally began a novena to the Saint of the Sacred Heart on February 23rd. That evening around midnight, she heard the gentle tinkling of rosary beads gently rubbing against each other, and a hushed voice intoning the Our Fathers, Hail Marys and Glory Be's. The voice asked her if she wanted to get well. He then told her to pray with faith to the Sacred Heart of Jesus and he would return each evening and they would pray together. It was the same one who had placed the heart on her heart; it was *Venerable Gabriel*!

On the last day of the novena, Gemma went to confession and received Holy Communion. Afterward, Jesus asked if she wished to be cured. She was so overwhelmed, she could not speak. She recovered immediately! The Lord took her into His Arms and said: *"I give all to you; will you give all to Me?"* It was time for plain talk, for trust! Gemma complained that He had taken her mother and her father, leaving her abandoned, alone. Jesus looked deep into her soul and said, *"I will be your Father and My Mother will be your mother."* Seeing a bright light coming from Gemma's room, a servant entered and saw persons surrounding Gemma, saying *"We want to cure you."* Gemma asked the servant to say nothing until she was dead.

Gemma has a vision of Jesus on the Cross

On Holy Thursday, 1899, Jesus came to Gemma for the first time in a vision and told her to sacrifice herself in atonement for the sins of the world. When she had been ill, the Sisters of St. Zita, in addition to giving her the Novena to St. Margaret Mary Alacoque and the Sacred Heart, suggested she make a *holy hour* in remembrance of the Passion. Gemma had promised she would, as soon as she was physically able. *Now she was well!* She thought she had better cleanse herself by going to confession. As she prepared for this mercy-filled Sacrament, she started to meditate on her sins. When she reflected on how deeply she had wounded Jesus by her sins, she began to cry as if her heart would break.

As she was grieving, Jesus appeared to her, Blood spilling from His Wounds, and said, *"Look at My Wounds and learn how to love. Look at this Cross, these Wounds, these nails, these bruises and lacerations, and this Blood. See to what extent I have loved you, Do you want to love Me? First, learn to suffer; suffering teaches how to love."*

Gemma receives the Stigmata

Because she had been healed through the intercession of St. Margaret Mary Alacoque, Gemma felt this was a sign she was called to be a Nun in the Convent of the Visitation. The days before her entrance were filled with God speaking to His little Spouse and she answering, offering Him her total abandonment to His Will.

When the sun came up on May 21, 1899, Gemma thought she would never forget that day. As she walked up the steps of the convent, she was filled with such joy and anticipation of becoming a nun in the Visitation Order. But it was to be short-lived, as she was judged too fragile for convent life as a result of her illness. No amount of tears and begging would dissuade the Mother Superior or the Archbishop who had given the order she not be accepted. Therefore, the day which had begun with hope and happiness, ended with devastating grief as Gemma shared her Lord's rejection.

After St. Francis' heart was broken (resulting from his friars changing his Rule), he received the Stigmata; so it would be with Gemma. Several days after she had been rejected, Jesus spoke to Gemma: *"I am waiting for you on Calvary."* On June 8th, two weeks after her rejection, she had an *inner thought*. She was about to receive some very special grace! She went to her confessor to shed herself of any sins she might have so that the Lord would have a spotless soul, ready to receive whatever blessing, He willed to give her.

When Thursday came, Gemma began to think of all the sufferings, Jesus had endured for her. She became filled with such overwhelming remorse, she became rapt in *ecstasy*! The Blessed Mother appeared, accompanied by Gemma's Guardian Angel, and told her that Jesus had forgiven her sins. Then Mother Mary opened her mantle and placed it over her. Jesus appeared and showed her His Wounds which were no longer bleeding. Instead flames of fire leapt forth from them and pierced Gemma's hands, feet and heart. She was in such excruciating pain, she thought she would collapse and die, were it not for Mother Mary supporting her and covering her with her mantle. After she remained like this for hours, Mother Mary kissed her forehead and the vision vanished. *Gemma had received the Stigmata, and now bore the five Wounds of Jesus*! She was in such agony, she needed the aid of her Guardian Angel to help her into bed. The next day, she carefully bound and hid her bleeding hands and went to Mass.

From that time on, Gemma would receive the Stigmata, the five Wounds of Jesus, each week on Thursday evening, beginning at 8 P.M. They would continue bleeding until 3 P.M. Friday, then completely disappear that evening or early Saturday; by Sunday, freshly healed flesh would cover the wounds; the Stigmata was gone. The only visible signs left, were white spots where the five open Wounds had been. The following Thursday the bleeding would begin again.

The last three years of her life, the ecstasies stopped. Her

Spiritual Director forbid her to have them because of her weakened condition. Always working through the Saints' obedience to their Superiors, the Lord no longer shared His Five Wounds with Gemma.

Gemma becomes a child of Jesus' Passion

That same June, 1899, when she first received the Stigmata, Gemma went to a mission given by the Passionist Fathers. It was then, she recognized that the habit worn by Venerable Gabriel in her vision was the habit of the Passionists, and the heart he had placed on *her* heart was the symbol the Passionists wore on their habits, over *their* hearts. A sign! Aren't you glad that the Saints, too, sought *signs* to know God's Will? And that they too, were sometimes wrong? Over and over again, we will come to realize that whereas we *interpret* with the mind of the world, God works *through* the Mind of the Divine.

Gemma levitates to embrace Jesus on the Cross

The Gianninis, a wealthy, very pious family in Lucca, having heard of Gemma's holiness, begged her brother and his wife to allow them to adopt Gemma. And so Gemma was adopted as a daughter of their family in September, 1900. There was an atmosphere of sanctity in this otherwise affluent home. Here Gemma had an opportunity to meet and listen to Passionist Fathers.

After attending Holy Mass each day, Gemma would return home to get the children dressed and ready for school. She would also help the servants around the house. Setting the table in the dining room was one of her favorite tasks, as a huge Crucifix hung on the wall. Although venerated by the whole family, it was most especially adored by Gemma who would pause in front of it during the day and keep her Lord company with consoling words of love. Many times, she so desired to kiss the Wound on His Side, she would find herself rising into mid-air up to Christ on the Cross, embracing Him and kissing the Wound on His precious Side.

One day, as she was placing the tablecloth on the dining room table, her heart beating wildly, she cried out to the Lord, *"Let me get to You. I am thirsting for Your Blood."* As happened to Saint Francis of Assisi and Saint Paul of the Cross, the Image of Christ on the Cross came to life; Jesus held out one of His Arms from the Cross and beckoned Gemma to come to Him. She levitated up to Him; Jesus held her in His Arms and Gemma drank from the *Holy Spring* in His Side, staying aloft as if resting on a cloud. All this became known to the Church through a member of the Giannini household, Aunt Cecilia, her adopted mother. Gemma was under obedience to tell all her experiences to her; if not for that, all that came to pass would have remained a buried treasure inside Gemma's heart.

Gemma's Stigmata and Ecstasies come under investigation

After examining her, the Archbishop of Camerino declared there was no evidence that the events in Gemma's life were of Supernatural origin. He ordered her to cease having *manifestations* (supernatural experiences) at once, and to return to an ordinary way of life. As hard as she tried to obey, the ecstasies continued and the Stigmata reappeared each week at the same time. Monsignor Volpe, her pastor, decided to bring in *Science!* Jesus had revealed to Gemma beforehand, what was going to come to pass. He gave her a message to give to the good Monsignor: The sign would only be given to *him*; and as this was not an illness, a man of Science would not be able to detect it. Nevertheless, a doctor came; he examined her, and declared the wounds and ecstasies were due to hysteria, nothing else.

When our Gemma came out of the ecstasy, she could see that everyone's attitudes had changed. When the tide turns and threatens the ship, everyone deserts the ship and its captain. As with Jesus, so it was with Gemma. All who had been attracted to her because of the miraculous occurrences in her life now turned away from her, filled with doubt, suspicion and contempt, almost glad to see her fall. [Isn't that sad about human nature, how we delight in one another's adversities, almost having a love/hate affair with one another?] So, once again Gemma shares in Jesus' suffering as she drinks from the bitter chalice of rejection and condemnation from which Our Savior drank on the Cross.

As Gemma walked away, accompanied by Aunt Cecilia, the wounds began to appear and bleed! Nothing would convince her confessor Monsignor Volpe, she was authentic. He told her, he would never believe her or in her alleged manifestations. Gemma was beside herself; she turned to Jesus. As she was praying, she became engulfed in ecstasy and found herself before Jesus and someone else, a Passionist Father whom Jesus told her would be her Spiritual Director, the one who would recognize in her the mission that He had given her. At that time, Jesus revealed the Passionist's name. In January, 1900, Gemma wrote to her future Spiritual Director, Father Germano, revealing as Jesus had directed, all that had transpired and the prophecy that a convent of Passionist Nuns would open in Lucca, describing it to the minutest detail, just as she had seen it when Jesus sketched it in a vision.

Father Germano spoke with Monsignor Volpe who was more than willing to hand over the responsibility of what he judged a hot potato. That evening, Father Germano came to supper at the Giannini home. Although *he* did not know who Gemma was, and *she* did not know how *he* looked, upon seeing one another, they both got down on their knees, and weeping, began to pray before the Crucifix in the dining room. It was Thursday. When supper was over, Gemma cleared away the dishes and retired to her room. She had not been in her room long when Aunt Cecilia went to check up on her. She returned quickly to ask Father to accompany her. What they saw was Gemma in ecstasy pleading with Jesus, the God of Justice, for mercy on a sinner for whom she had been praying.

It was another Abraham pleading and arguing with God, as Gemma bargained and debated brilliantly with the Lord. When it appeared that Jesus would not budge, she cried out, *"I do not seek Your justice but Your mercy."* Jesus replied, He would not yield to her petitions, no matter how much pressure she exerted, because the sinner had sinned beyond mercy. When all seemed lost, Gemma pulled out all stops and brought in His Mother:

"It is Your Mother herself who is praying for him. Will You say no to her? And now, answer me, Jesus, and tell me You have saved my sinner."

She was so excited, she blurted out, *"He is saved! He is saved! Jesus, You won!"* and she came out of her ecstasy.

Father Germano left the room. Then one of the Giannini household told him there was a man who wanted to speak to him. *"Father, I want to make my confession."* It was the sinner!

Jesus reveals God's imminent punishment on mankind

Father Germano saw in Gemma a holy soul who, like a child without guile, simply loved God and saw Him in all the circumstances surrounding her life, recognizing Him most in her suffering. Discerning her to be holy and pure, Father Germano believed her ecstasies were authentic and accepted her wounds as *the Stigmata*, a gift from the Lord of *His* five Wounds. Father spent the rest of his life being her Spiritual Director. But that did not mean Gemma's life would be without strife and dissension, the devil doing all he could do to cause problems. At times, Gemma even doubted Father Germano and all those who had been the first to believe in her.

Gemma's life was one of: *rejection* - God's gifts to her were often doubted and she, mistrusted; *hurts* - ill-will, spite and jealousy in the hearts of those around her; *abandonment* - feeling most sharply the absence of a family, she grieved because she judged she was a burden on those around her.

Gemma could see the sins within the souls of others

Not only could Gemma see the sins within the souls of others but those within herself as well. This caused her so much anguish, she asked to suffer even more. She desired with her whole heart to suffer that *her* pain might alleviate the pain *God* suffered because of sin. *One day the Lord appeared to her and gave her a new mission.* Jesus said that God the Father was highly offended by the sins of the world, and that there was a dire need for more victim-souls to appease His anger.

Jesus speaks of the new convent that is to be formed

Jesus told Gemma that God's mighty wrath would be held back by and through the foundation of a Convent of Passionist Nuns in Lucca, and that she was to tell her spiritual director, Father Germano that this was to be done.

Gemma was so happy! She knew this was the Community she was to enter! Since Venerable Gabriel had been wearing a Passionist's habit when he had appeared to her, surely she was called to be a cloistered Passionist Nun in that Convent. Now it is often difficult to discern. Is it God's Will she be a Passionist Nun or not? Believing, it was His Will, Gemma sought entry in the Community of Passionist Nuns. Someone had spoken maliciously about Gemma to the Mother Superior, and so she was rejected. Not only was she turned down, she was also chastised contemptuously for sins she had not committed. She neither defended herself nor sought pity. As her Spouse Jesus before her, she forgave those who persecuted her.

Was it the devil who was blocking Gemma or God? After all, God is in charge! All we can count on is that God is in charge, and whatever comes to pass, God will use it for His Glory and the sanctification of the world. All we have to do is cooperate with His Grace, give Him all of ourselves to use as He wills. Jesus never wastes any experiences in our lives, especially the carrying of our crosses. Gemma told a tender soul who was undergoing grave trials:

"...an interior voice seems to tell me we must remain at the foot of the Cross. If Jesus is nailed upon the Cross, we must not complain if we have to stay at its feet."

Gemma told this poor soul, we must all walk with Jesus on the way to Calvary, to the Cross and His death; or was she speaking with the *Heart of Jesus* asking *that* soul and us, *do we run away from Our Lord at the Pillar, not wanting to be wounded by and for the sins of others? Are we silent when we are mocked and humiliated, as Our Lord was when they put a Crown of Thorns on His precious Head? Do we deny Him when the going gets rough, like Peter? Do we choose the world's answers to our problems, as they did when Pilate asked "Which one do you want me to release to you, Barabbas or Jesus Who is called Messiah?"*[8] *Are we willing to stand beside His Mother and die, as she did, with Him for His beloved Church, this Church which flowed from His pierced Heart on the Cross?* Be not afraid! Be not intimidated by your weakness. Gemma confessed to this soul that she was speaking out of her weakness, not her strength. Whenever we are afraid that we cannot do all that is required of us, we remember the Lord's words to us before the Blessed Sacrament one day, *"In your weakness, I will be strong!"* Although it is hard to live, it keeps coming back to us when the going gets rough.

In a vision, Venerable Gabriel revealed to Gemma, she was to advise Father Germano that it was *he* who was to start the Convent of Passionist Nuns and then proceeded to give her the name of the *woman* who would bring the mission to fruition. When Gemma said she did not know her, he even gave her the city where she lived. Gemma had a problem accepting all that Venerable Gabriel was saying. This did not phase him, as he prophesied that in two years, on a Friday, the work would begin.

Although it did not seem feasible to her, Gemma said *Yes!* She made herself a beggar, pleading wholeheartedly for funds to begin the Convent. Accompanied by Aunt Cecilia, she sought a house for the Monastery. She passed on Jesus' words that it was *His* wish this be done to all she encountered. It became exciting as she saw the Lord moving the hearts of the miserly to generosity.

But her joy was to be replaced by sadness when Jesus appeared to her and told her that the convent life was not for her, that there was a better life for her. She was confused and hurt! After all, had not Gabriel told her in a vision, that she would be his sister? But Our Lord does not leave us alone for long. During Midnight Mass, at the time of the Offertory, as the priest was

---

[8]Matt 27:17

offering the gifts to the Father, Jesus appeared and offered *Gemma* as a victim to the Eternal Father. The Lord was radiant as He embraced Gemma and then presented her to her *Mama*, His Mother Mary, as *"the fruit of His Passion."*

Mother Mary tells Gemma that she is taking her to Heaven

It was around the end of May, 1902. Gemma became seriously ill. Our Blessed Mother appeared to her at this time, and gave her a message for Father Germano: *"Tell your father that if he does not listen to you, very soon I will take you with me to Heaven."* With that, the Virgin Mary kissed her little daughter Gemma, and left. Gemma said that after being with Mother Mary, the world and its empty treasures were paltry and pathetic.

Gemma went to her Spiritual Director and shared all that Mother Mary had said to her. She told him that she had asked the Blessed Mother for a sign, to let him and Gemma know that it was really *she* speaking to Gemma and not her imagination or a deception from the evil one. Mother Mary said the sign would be that Gemma would be healed! Gemma warned him, Mother Mary had stressed that he listen to her message and do as she requested, or she would *take back the sign* and carry Gemma off to be with her Son in Heaven. It was not for her, she pleaded. Although Gemma had hoped to live long enough to see the convent opened in Lucca, she assured Fr. Germano that she was at peace, and looking forward to the *better Convent* Jesus had prepared for her.

For some reason, the priest delayed. Gemma pleaded that if he did not act soon, it would be too late; Jesus was tired of waiting for her; He had told her He would take her to Him in six months if the Convent was not begun. Father and the others did not listen. Jesus appeared to Gemma and informed her she would not live to see the foundation of the convent. Now she shared Our Lord's agony in the Garden of Gethsemane as she grieved that she would not see her dream come true. But she was content to salute it from afar in Paradise with her Spouse.

The long painful journey *Home*

She was coming to the end of her journey to the Cross. Gemma's physical suffering was extremely painful. But the *physical* could not compare with the *spiritual* attacks to which this sweet soul was subjected, at the hands of the devil. He did not let up, right up to the very end. He gave her no rest day or night. The devil tried to force her to despair; he brought fear, anxiety, doubt, sadness, and then tried her soul by bringing bitterness into her heart. He taunted her with: *She had led a useless life; all her suffering was for nothing; God had abandoned her because she had fooled people into thinking her pious; her gifts of the Stigmata and ecstasies were not of God and the devil used her to deceive everyone into believing they were divinely inspired; God was angry because she was a hypocrite, her humility and purity were false, and she was in truth a big sinner.*

The devil had her so convinced of her sinfulness that she wrote the story of her life, accusing herself of being sinful and deceitful. Seeking absolution for the dreadful sins the devil had deluded her into believing she had committed, she gave her story to her confessor. The holy priest read her story and assured her of her piety, charity and holiness. The devil filled her head with unclean thoughts which she fought to the point of exhaustion. She could not eat, as the devil made it appear as if her food was covered with crawling insects. She would become so repulsed, she would vomit. She asked to be exorcised, and when the authorities refused, she tried to exorcise herself. When she wrote, the devil smeared the pages with black hoof-prints, of black ink and carbon from the fires of hell. These marks can still be seen on the pages of her writings.

Gemma communicates with her Guardian Angel

In a vision, her Guardian Angel had previously appeared to Gemma and showed her two crowns, one of lilies and one of thorns. When the Angel offered them to her, inviting her to take *one* of them, Gemma responded, she wanted the crown that belonged to her Lord Jesus. The Angel handed her the crown of thorns!

Gemma embraced the crown and kissed it. Then pressing it to her heart, she said, *"Be always praised my God! Long live Jesus! Long live Jesus' gifts! Long live Jesus' Cross!"*

Well, here it was, the end of Gemma's life, and she was wearing the crown of thorns she had chosen and would wear to the Cross. As with other Mystics who had had the Stigmata, she had desired to share Jesus' Passion. Jesus allowed her to carry His Cross, bear His humiliation, loneliness, anguish, abandonment, yes, and even the taunts and temptations from the devil. Now, she would know the full meaning of her *Yes* to the Lord. Her final hours strongly paralleled those of her Savior. Gemma was walking the way of the Passion that her Lord before her had tread.

We never know what is going on while we're on earth! And when we are before Our Savior, we probably will not care. We wonder, though! Was this an attack on Gemma because she had dared offer to Jesus the *obedience* and *love* that the devil had refused to accord Him? Or were all these horrendous blows dealt to Gemma, an attack on *God*, the devil now using Gemma, as he did Job, to try to hurt Him: "Wait till I throw everything at her, at the last moments of her life, making her doubt in You, making her question You even exist! Then we'll see if she loves You."

When the pain and the bombardment got heavy, the Lord came to her, accompanied by her Guardian Angel.[9] He tried to reassure her and encourage her to persevere in fighting the temptations of the devil. But as soon as He left, the battles began to rage again; the enemy was back again, more vicious than ever. As her Lord Jesus had cried out to the Father on the Cross, ***"Why have You forsaken Me?"*** now Gemma cried out, *"Jesus where are You? You know my heart; where are You?"*

Gemma goes to the Convent Jesus had prepared for her

Gemma ceased speaking of becoming a nun. She was now on the *last leg of her journey*. She had worked diligently trying to

---

[9]For more experiences of Gemma and her Guardian Angel, read Bob and Penny Lord's book: *"Heavenly Army of Angels."*

fulfill Jesus' Will to open a convent in Lucca, and although it was not completed, it was time for her to go to Him. Oh how she would have loved to have seen it open, with her a Passionist Nun, if even for one hour. But now it was time for Gemma to let go, to turn over the foundation to the Blessed Mother. Gemma was divorcing herself of all worldly desires, looking ahead to the final stop. Aunt Cecilia could not understand her wanting, no, *longing* to go to Heaven. She asked Gemma, "Why are you so anxious to go to Paradise? Do you not see Jesus here?" Gemma replied, *"But it is not the same as He is in Paradise. One time when I saw Him a little better, He was so brilliant, so radiant, my eyes burned."* When Gemma said that, Aunt Cecilia suddenly remembered the time, she had scolded Gemma about her health because her eyes were so red.

Gemma could be heard crying out in ecstasy, *"Make haste, Jesus. Cut off the chain that binds me to earth, separating me from Heaven. Let me come to You."*

Gemma had asked Jesus to allow her to die on a Solemn Feast Day. Gemma had suffered the 40 days of Lent, and now it was Holy Week. Gemma would be given the final gift from Jesus: she would share fully in His Passion, agonizing with the suffering *Spotless Lamb.* On Holy (Spy) Wednesday, Gemma received Holy Viaticum with joy and thanksgiving. Prior to that, because of her constant vomiting, even the Lord in His Eucharist had been withheld from her. Since March 23rd, she felt as if she was alone in a desert, her lips and heart parched as she thirsted for the *Living* God. She had suffered the loss of her most precious consolation on earth, Holy Communion, and she was inconsolable.

When at last she received her Lord, Gemma fell into a deep ecstasy, and when she came out of it, she told the nurse, *"Oh, if only you could see the smallest part of that which Jesus has revealed to me, you would die of ecstasy."*

On *Holy Thursday*, she again requested Holy Communion. Soon after receiving her Lord, she fell deeply into ecstasy and was overheard saying, she saw a crown of thorns, and she had more to suffer.

On *Good Friday*, the last one she would share with Jesus on earth, Gemma turned to her Aunt Cecilia and asked her not to leave her until she was nailed to the Cross. She said: *"I must be crucified with Jesus. Jesus told me, His children must be crucified with Him."* Everyone wept at Gemma's bedside as they witnessed that final dying on the Cross.

The morning of *Holy Saturday* the priest came to anoint her. Gemma, like her Savior before her, summoned her last ounce of breath, just enough to pray with the priest. She had asked to die without any comfort as her Savior before her, and the Lord complied. When the devil launched his last attack, taunting her that she had been abandoned by the Lord she so loved, she replied, *"A Crucifix and a priest are all I need."*

At half past one, Holy Saturday, April 11, 1903, Gemma died, her Crucifix in her hand, exclaiming, *"Jesus, if it is Your Will, take me."* And then turning her eyes to a picture of Mother Mary on the wall, she cried out, *"My Mamma, I commend my soul to you. Tell Jesus to be merciful to me."* She kissed the Crucifix, placed it on her breast and closed her eyes.

Gemma died as Venerable Gabriel's sister, the title he had given her the first time he appeared to her. She had *lived* the life of a Passionist, suffering each week the Passion with her Lord; and now with the imprint of Jesus' Passion, His five Wounds indelibly on her flesh, she was *dying* a Passionist. When they laid her out, they placed a heart, the symbol of the Passionist Fathers and Nuns, on her heart, the same symbol that Gabriel had placed there years before.

Easter Sunday the church bells peeled; the Lord had risen, Alleluia! At sunset, the body of the precious little spouse of Jesus was carried through the streets toward the cemetery. The bells were sounding once more as they had at sunrise that morning. Gemma Galgani had died with Jesus and now she was living eternally with Him, feasting on what she had always desired, His Beatific Vision in Paradise.

On her tombstone was inscribed: *"The faithful virgin of Lucca, consumed with love rather than disease, has flown to the loving embrace of her Spouse."*

The First Convent of Passionist Nuns is founded in Lucca

His little charge gone to the Lord she'd so passionately loved, Father Germano recalled how, one year before her death, Gemma had told him to go to Rome and speak to the Pope. Now it was as if she were speaking to him even more insistently, and he felt compelled to go and speak to Pope Saint Pius X. The Pope responded just as Gemma had foretold; he granted the new Community of Passionist Nuns the needed sanction to open the Monastery in Lucca. In his own handwriting, he declared that the Passionists of the new Monastery were to offer themselves as *victims of the atonement* for Mother Church. And somehow, we can see Jesus smiling, saying to Gemma, *"Job well done, little one. See what I can do with each little Yes!"* On a *Friday* in July of 1908, the first Community of Passionist Nuns was canonically founded in Lucca.

But this was not the only prophecy of Gemma that came to pass. She had said that although the Passionists would not accept her in life, they would accept her in death. And so another prophecy was to come true. The coffin, containing the precious remains of Gemma's body, was removed from her *first* resting place and carried in solemn procession to their final home. On September 4, 1923, they were interred in the Chapel of the Monastery in Lucca, the one she had so desired to enter in life. Here she remains till today. When you come to visit her, as we have, her loving testimony greets you, and you hear the Lord's message: *"Safety and peace is found only in the Cross."*

Gemma's crown of thorns turn into a halo of light

Father Germano published her biography four short years after her death, and Gemma soon became known over the four corners of the earth, as far east as China and Japan.

In 1917, the Church began to scrupulously investigate her

The Tomb of St. Gemma in Lucca, Italy

life. After long and thorough study of all she had written and careful examination of the sworn testimonies of those who had known her, on May 14, 1933, Gemma Galgani was Beatified. Bishops, priests, religious and thousands of the laity crowded into St. Peter's Basilica to do honor to *the little poor one*, Blessed Gemma Galgani.

Miracles were submitted and painstakingly studied. Science agreed with Mother Church that the healings were truly miraculous. And then, on March 26, 1939, on Passion Sunday, they were approved and proclaimed Miracles, supernaturally obtained through the intercession of Gemma.

On the triumphant anniversary of Christ's Ascension into Heaven, May 2, 1940, Gemma Galgani was hailed for the first time: *"Saint Gemma."* In the midst of war and hatred, of death and cruelty, of man's inhumanity to man, a light shone in the darkness and love was crowned.

Blessed Dina Bélanger

Victim of Love
Apostle of Love
Martyr of Love

Blessed Dina Bélanger

We praise You, dear Lord Jesus. We bless your Holy Name. You give us everything we need just when we need it. In a time when virtues like *Obedience, Commitment, Chastity, Modesty, Accountability* are all but lost to our modern society, you give us a Dina Bélanger, a precious child of Jesus, who embraced all these qualities. She was a nun who died at 32 years old in 1929, and was *beatified* by His Holiness Pope John Paul II on March 20, 1993.[1] What blessings the Lord has given us through this woman of the Twentieth Century, whose most important attribute was her total, unconditional love of Jesus. We are allowed to delve into the life of this most special friend and child of God. Researching the life of a beautiful servant of Jesus and Mary has been a treasure for us, from which we can learn and prosper in our relationship with our Heavenly Family. Blessed Dina was aided man times in her lifetime by our Lady, and by the Saints and the Angels who were assigned to her, to protect her on her pilgrimage of life, her Journey of Faith.

---

[1]An exciting aside, the foundress of Dina's Order, Sr. Claudine Thévenet, was *canonized* on March 21, 1993, the day after Dina was beatified.

The life of Dina Bélanger is so peaceful, so like who she was. Even her times of struggle, her Dark Night of the Soul, were unique in that she was constantly trying, in everything she ever said or did, to please and give honor to Our Lord, her Lover.

Whenever we write a book on a Saint or Blessed, we make a television and video series. We visited Sillery, in the province of Québec, Canada, which is in itself a charming, peaceful reflection of the Saint who lived most of her life in that spiritual atmosphere. We went to the convent of the *Religious of Jesus and Mary* on St. Louis Road in Sainte Foy, and the school where she taught, St. Michel de Bellechasse.

The convent in which Dina spent her nine years as a religious burned to the ground in 1983. Therefore there was no room where she had lived, no infirmary where she died, nothing physical, that you could touch in the new convent and school which was built after her death. But she was there, in every room we visited, every corner we turned, in the chapel where she is buried, and most importantly, in the eyes and spirit of every Sister in the Community. They all reflected the spirit of their Sister in Christ, the precious little Saint of Québec. There were mementoes of her life, pictures of her (She is a *Twentieth Century Blessed*, a product of our own century), needlepoint which she made, a musical score which she composed, and Sisters whom she knew. She died sixty-six years ago and we were able to talk with people whom she touched and, while they have become senior citizens, their memories of Blessed Dina are crystal clear. Everyone had something special to share about her, a word, a smile, something which touched their lives. She remained with them, and they would never be the same.

We walked with some of the Sisters out to the little graveyard to the left of the convent, in between the primary school and the gym. All the members of the Québec Community who have passed on are buried there, including a close friend, Bernadette Létourneau. She had been a roommate of Dina's in New York when they both went there to study music, and followed Dina into

Above:
***Dina Bélanger as a young girl with her
friends ready for a concert***

Below: ***Dina Bélanger's piano***

Above:
***Baptismal font of Dina
Bélanger located in
Saint Roch's Church,
Sillery, Quebec***

Bl. Dina Bélanger - Original Convent that burned

the Community of the *Religious of Jesus and Mary.*

Dina's body has been removed from the rows of other Sisters who have gone on to their eternal reward, where she had originally been put to rest. At the head of the cemetery, there is a large stone with her name on it, in memory of the Blessed from their Community. But her body is in the chapel of the convent, forever to be remembered by her Sisters, and everyone who comes here to be touched by her. As we were looking at the various tombstones, one of the nuns pointed to the grave of Mother St. Elizabeth,[2] Blessed Dina's Novice Mistress, and who was with her at her deathbed. The Sisters told us that Mother St. Elizabeth had always prayed that one of her nuns would become a Saint. Did she have the feeling, when she met Dina Bélanger that she was in the presence of a Saint?

The Life of a Saint in our time

Dina Bélanger was born in Sillery, Québec, Canada on April 30, 1897. There are those who believe that there was a connection between the little Saint and the Little Flower of Lisieux, St. Thérèse, because Dina was born exactly five months before St. Thérèse died. Also, during Dina's time in the convent, she was given the Little Flower as a protectress by Our Lord Jesus. There are also many other similarities between the two Saints, which we will see as we go on with the life of Dina.

The church where she was baptized was not the church where the well-to-do people of the town worshiped. To the contrary, St. Roch's was in the working man's section. She was born at ten before nine in the morning and baptized in the afternoon of the same day. She was named Marie (after our Lady), Dina (after her father's mother), Marguerite (after St. Margaret Mary Alacoque). Dina wrote of that time in her life, as she was given to see it in her heart:

"It seems to me that, in the earliest moments of my life,

---

[2] All the nuns of this order took the names of Saints, placing St. in front of their names

God wrapped the protective cloak of the Blessed Virgin around me; my eyes first saw light on the eve of the month of Mary, a Friday, and that very evening the grace of Holy Baptism drove the devil out of my soul to let the Divine Spirit reign as its master."

Her father, Octave Bélanger, and mother, Séraphia Matte, were very spiritual people. They gave this child of God the solid Christian formation that she needed to open herself to the working of God in her life. Everything centered around their Faith, their morals, and their Christian behavior. Dina's mother Séraphia talked about her dreams for her child even before she was born:

"I asked God that this child, soon to come into this world, accomplish something good in its life, and not by halves, that this child become a religious man or woman, if such was His Will. Every time I went to Mass, I renewed this request."

The Lord surrounded Dina with Saints and Angels to protect her from her very earliest age, even to where she lived and the names of the streets. She lived up from Our Lady of the Angels Street on the street of St. Joseph.

From Dina's childhood, she recalled her mother signing her with the Sign of the Cross while she was still in the cradle. Dina remembered hearing Bible stories and accounts of the famous Angels and Saints in our Church. She would sit on her mother's knee while she read to her. She learned how to kneel very early, about twelve months old, and prayed the Hail Mary before she was two years old. She prayed the Angelus with her family, as did all French Canadians in the little town of Sillery, located on the outskirts of Québec, off the St. Lawrence River. This was God's country; these were God's people; they enjoyed the peace of the Lord.

Dina predicted her Sainthood at the very beginning of the writing of her autobiography.[3] She did not believe it would happen

---

[3]This was written under obedience to her Superior, who was inspired by the Holy Spirit to have it done.

because of any great attribute of hers, but in repayment to her parents, whom she once called her visible Guardian Angels on earth. She truly believed she had to pay them back for the suffering they endured, in allowing their daughter to follow the path, she felt the Lord had planned for her. She said in her Autobiography:

> *"Admirable parents indeed! Only in Heaven shall I fully understand the vigilance, devotedness and love of my mother and father...I thank Thee for having spared, until this day, these two beings who ever preferred Thy good pleasure to their own gratification and did not hesitate to sacrifice what was dearer to them than life itself...To prove my gratitude, I am in duty bound to become a Saint. I have contracted a sacred debt which I must discharge at all costs...Yes I will become a Saint. I will become holy to the degree God has marked out for me. Thus may I repay them for the pains they have taken for my education and console them in their grief over our separation."*

For Dina, growing up was a time of learning obedience, self-control, controlling, or at least, hiding emotions. She became a contradiction of sorts. One the one hand, she was very shy, sensitive, and disciplined. On the other hand, she had a volatile temper which could very easily manifest itself into tantrums. There is a story of how her father nipped her rages in the bud. She was still very young, not yet four years old. She was in a mood. She argued over everything her mother said. Whenever young Dina was told to do something, she refused. When her mother finally had it up to her eyeballs with her little precocious child, she *insisted* she obey. This threw Dina into a full-blown tantrum. She began yelling and screaming, jumping up and down, stamping her feet, actually dancing. To an outsider it looked extremely funny, but to those involved in the situation, it was anything but that.

Her father, however, saved both the day, and suppressed a bad precedent, all in one act. He took her in his arms and began dancing with her. He said, "Come, I'll help you dance and scream so we can get this over with sooner." The little child came out of her tantrum in shock. She could not understand what was happening. She listened to her father imitating her. She didn't like what she heard. She immediately stopped crying. She looked at him strangely. He was dancing peculiarly. She didn't want to dance anymore, but he continued. She was embarrassed. Her pride was crushed. Obviously, she could see how she looked in his eyes and those of her mother, and she didn't like it. It was a hard lesson which she learned immediately. She never did that again.

An instance of learning *obedience* the hard way occurred before the temper tantrum incident, but the same result took place. It happened when Dina's mother first began bringing her to church. She was a little over three years old. She was excited about all the wonders of the Church and the Mass, but tended to lose her attention span during the homily. She took out of her pocket, a little doll she always carried with her. The doll was called Valéda. Dina began playing with the doll. Her mother was scandalized when she saw her daughter behaving this way in front of the priest who was giving the homily. She whispered in a shout, *"Put that away!"* Dina obeyed, but she wasn't happy about it.

A few minutes later, the homily was still going on at full steam. She put her hand in her pocket and took the doll out again. This time her mother grabbed the doll, and put it in her purse. When they got home, Seraphia (Dina's mother) hid the doll. This would be the end of the matter. However, she didn't count on Dina's resourcefulness. The child searched the entire house until she found the doll. She put it back in her pocket and brought it to church with her, the next day. During the homily, Dina took it out again, in full disobedience to her mother. No sooner had her mother caught sight of the doll than it was confiscated; this time in such a way as to telegraph a strong message to Dina. It was clear, her mother meant business by the stern manner with which she took it away. Dina never brought that doll to church again.

Dina had dreams as a child, which showed her great love for

Jesus and His Church, and her great disdain for, even fear of, the evil one, the devil, to whom she referred as *"the capudile."* One time, after having accompanied her mother to a novena to St. Francis Xavier at church, Dina had nightmares about terrifying devils, a result of the priest's overly descriptive homily: *"They were as red as fire, rushing about, in and out of a long railroad train. They were constantly in motion and very agitated."* Needless to say, that was the end of the novena for poor Dina's mother. But the dream had a positive effect on Dina. She said, *"Having such a dreadful fear of the devil inspired an equal hatred for sin."*

By the same token, little Dina had *wonderful* dreams, dreams of Jesus as a Child, and dreams of being in Paradise. She had such a longing for Paradise.

She shared with her family, *"Last night I dreamt I was in Paradise; but it was a dream, such a beautiful....dream. Could it be one of the causes of this nostalgia for Heaven which has pursued me all my life?"*

Another time she shared, *"I could feel the Lord drawing me to Himself. On the third day, I loved my little Jesus so much, I desired so much to be with Him, that I begged Him earnestly and with all the fervor I could muster, to take me to His beautiful Paradise. I was surprised to wake up during the night and find myself still on earth, and the following morning I was very disappointed that my prayer had not been heard."*

Dina's Burning Desire for Jesus in the Eucharist

Possibly the greatest goal Dina had given herself, other than being in Paradise immediately, was to receive the Body and Blood of her Savior, our Lord Jesus Christ, in Communion. She waited and waited, counting the years. When she was nine years old, she thought she was old enough to receive Communion. To give her credit, Dina was far beyond any of the other children her age, spiritually. She was well-educated in the Faith, and she was bigger than most of the children her age. She kept pestering the nuns at her school to let her receive at nine years old. They suggested she have her mother bring her to Monseigneur Roy, the parish priest, and ask his permission. While he agreed that she was an exceptional student and knew the Faith better than she need know at her age, he did not feel it proper to break the rule. There was no urgency, no fear of death overtaking her before she reached the age of ten.

When they left the priest's office, Dina was crushed. While she normally hid her feelings, she very visibly showed her disappointment at having to wait another year. But she was obedient! Her mother said, *"The parish priest has spoken. You must accept his decision."*

Dina's disposition would have been to brood and sulk for the next year and let everyone know just how unhappy she was about this determination which she judged to be unfair. However, that's what makes the difference between a Saint and a sinner. She accepted the decision, and went on. Actually, she used this time to prepare herself interiorly, so that when the time came, she would be completely ready to invite the Lord into her life through the Sacrament of the Eucharist.

On May 2, 1907, Dina was to receive our Lord Jesus in her body for the first time. Before receiving Holy Communion, however, she had to receive her first Penance. She worked her way up to this event *meticulously.* She made a list of every possible sin she could ever have committed. When she went into the confessional, she had more sins to confess than someone who had not been to confession for many years. Needless to say, this was less the product of an overscrupulous mind and more a heart full of love for the Lord.

When she went up to the Altar to receive Our Lord in the Eucharist, Dina concentrated on what was about to happen. She rejected all other thoughts. The devil tried to distract her with thoughts of various things, in particular a silver watch which was given to her for her First Holy Communion. She threw out that thought. She wanted to go up to the Altar with a pure heart and a pure mind. She writes of that first encounter with Jesus in the Eucharist:

> *"Great was my happiness! Jesus was mine and I was His. This first intimate union left in my soul, together with other graces, a hunger for the Sacrament of Love, a hunger which increased with each ensuing visit."*

Dina was invested that day in the Society of the Scapular, as well as receiving Confirmation. She felt truly like a Soldier of Christ, ready to do battle and give up her life for her Savior.

The Making of a Saint

Dina had always been a girl devoted to the Lord. But her first Holy Communion and Confirmation, which she received when she was only ten years old, sealed the bond with the Lord. It was at that time that she began to discipline her body, her mind and her soul to be as perfect an offering to the Lord as is humanly possible. She consciously avoided anything which could be considered even worldly or distracting. She walked in a way which would not show any unnecessary movement or tend to highlight her femininity. She focused on any and every part of her daily life, disciplining and correcting herself scrupulously. In prayer she became more recollected, to the extent of avoiding the slightest movement, even the raising of her eyes when reading her prayer book.

She became aware that she had developed a habit of looking at herself in the mirror, when she would pass it on the way to her room. She gives credit to the devil for having persuaded her to do this.

> *"The devil attempted to set a new snare for me, the habit of looking in the mirror. The wily deceiver had many a victory to register, alas, victory upon victory. Jesus, then, took pity on my weakness and folly and gave me strength to overcome this habit. He armed my will to conquer."*

The key phrase here is, *"He armed my will to conquer."* For the rest of her life, Dina used this weapon the Lord had given her to conquer herself, all her temptations, and all her inclinations. She fought any attempt to give in to the slightest enticement which was sent her way. Naturally, this type of ramrod determination has to give way to scrupulosity.[4] She admits to having fallen prey to this affliction.

"Little things appeared to me worthy of the minutest fidelity. At this period of my life, a new trial was awaiting me, that of scruples. God happily sent me an enlightened and holy director, who took charge of my soul and was my guide during thirteen years. Words cannot express what I owe this priest."

The beginning of her Inner Locutions

On the Feast of the Annunciation in 1908, the year after she made her first Holy Communion, the Lord spoke to her soul, very clearly, unquestioningly.

"The following 25th of March, Feast of the Annunciation, and also Holy Thursday, during my thanksgiving after Communion, Our Lord communicated with my soul in a hitherto unknown manner. It was the first time, I understood His voice so well, inwardly, of course, a sweet, melodious voice that filled my soul with bliss."

Dina gave herself slogans, strong sayings which brought her through difficult times in her life. One of her first powerful ones was, ***"Death rather than defilement,"*** which she adopted at age 13, and which stayed with her until she entered the novitiate. She also consecrated herself to the Blessed Mother and became a child of Mary.

She embraced the teachings of St. Louis Marie de Montfort, another of the special people about whom we have written in this book.

"About this time, I surrendered myself wholly to the

---

[4]Scrupulosity - Because of confusion over the morality of actions, scruples arise when a troubled conscience, prompted by imaginary reasons, causes one to constantly dread sin where no sin exists, or to hold a venially sinful action mortally sinful. - Catholic Encyclopedia

Blessed Virgin, by means of the perfect devotion of Blessed Grignon de Montfort. This entire relinquishing of self and possessions to the Queen of Heaven brought me great consolation and peace."

Dina was always a very focused girl. She knew exactly what she wanted and worked her entire life to achieve her goal. There were many obstacles thrown in her path, and often she had to go a far distance around them, but her eyes never left her goal, never lost their direction. In an endeavor to break her bonds with everything of this world to which she clung, she aimed at her most vulnerable spot, her relationship with her parents. She adored them completely. She would do anything for either of them and do nothing that would hurt them in any way. But we can just hear the perfect Lover asking her the question, *"Dina, how much do you love me? Enough to give up your parents?"*

She could feel the call to the religious life pulling at her very forcefully. She asked her parents to allow her to go to boarding school. This was to be a giant step in embracing her Heavenly Family and shedding her dearest family on earth. She knew this would hurt them. As they loved her so much, they would suffer greatly without having her with them. However, she asked permission, and they gave it.

This time in boarding school changed Dina completely. She did not have the luxury of her own way as she had had at home. She was under the scrutiny of her instructors more than when she was a day student living at home. But an entry in her autobiography, describing her state of mind those first few weeks, opens a window to Dina Bélanger and the formation of this future Saint:

"The first Sunday after my entry, which had taken place the previous Wednesday, I cried all day. During Mass I sobbed and choked, and I did the same in the parlor that afternoon. My parents were greatly distressed and Papa offered to take me home. `No, thank you,' I replied, `I shall get used to it.' I wept on fourteen consecutive nights, and then for a few weeks every two or three nights. Finally

my will was strengthened and I wept no more."

That, to our way of thinking, is the most powerful statement of who this girl/woman was and was becoming, and how her entire life would be governed. It was a systematic, ongoing breaking of her will, her spirit, to be open to being filled by the Lord. If there were only one phrase we could use to describe Dina Bélanger fully, to tell you who she was totally, it would be the paragraph above. She spent her entire life dying to self, so that she could more fully embrace the Lord.

One of the greatest hurdles she had to overcome in the boarding school was interaction with her fellow students. She was a shy girl; she had always been introverted and removed. At home, she was able to afford herself this luxury. Her parents allowed her to be reserved. In primary school, her teachers talked to her about her relationship with her fellow students, but she had been able to be her own boss in this area. Now, she was not only going to school with them, she was *living* with them! She made a statement to her mother during this test, *"Mama, it is no easy matter to live with other people."*

But when she finally realized, and when her teachers and counselors made her aware what part she was playing in this estrangement, she threw herself headlong into developing relationships with her fellow students.

"These years spent outside my home and family were a great help in the formation of my character. From the common life, I derived more energy and forgetfulness of self. On many occasions, I was forced to come out of myself. I had a fault that one of my teachers had the goodness to point out to me, in the first months of my life as a boarder, namely that I did not communicate with others, that I never revealed my impressions, desires or feelings, but kept them all to myself; whereas, if I had expressed them, others might sometimes have benefited from them. In short, I had an opportunity to fight egoism and try to do good...When I returned to my parents, my soul was stronger and more

loving. "

During her time in the boarding school, Dina was exposed to many religious communities, including the Congregation of Jesus and Mary, the order which she finally joined. But at the time of her first exposure to the Community, she never thought she would be a part of them.

"While we were going around the house, we met a group of postulants. I observed them and was edified by their recollected demeanor. I retained a very happy memory of the visit. " But that was the extent of her interest.

After her two years in boarding school, she came out a fine young lady. One of her teachers described her as follows: "She was a girl of fifteen years, tall, intelligent, gracious, pleasant, and so perfect! There was nothing affected or studied in her manner...Just imagine a girl of fifteen years who, during a whole year in boarding school, never showed any sign of impatience or of being out of humor...This complete self-possession, this perfect control of her feelings possessed by the dear child intrigued me. Once or twice I found an opportunity to test her by little contradictions, but her virtue remained unchanged."

At sixteen, Dina left boarding school. She went back to live with her family, but she was determined, at all costs, not to lose what she had gained by such hard work and discipline in two years. She set up a rule of life:

† Morning prayers and evening prayers
† Daily Mass and Communion
† Daily Rosary
† At least ten minutes of meditation every day
† Weekly Confession
† Nightly examination of Conscience

While Dina committed to these practices, and would like to have added others - such as the *Little Office of the Blessed Virgin* once a week, and a day's *retreat* once a month, she did not want anyone to become aware of her activities. As important as these works were in her life, she did not want to let anyone know the secret workings of grace in her soul and her exclusive attraction for the spiritual life. In order to find enough time for meditation and extend her prayer time she gave up sleep time, so that no one would suspect what she was doing, not even her parents.

The burning desire, Dina had always experienced, to enter religious life, compounded and multiplied itself after she left boarding school. She wanted to tell her parents, but she did not want to shock them or cause them distress. She was able to keep her aspiration for the religious life a secret from her parents for seven months. After that, she couldn't hold it in, any longer. She asked their permission to enter a religious Community.

You can imagine their devastation! Her parents had just gone through two years without her, at her request, so that she could have boarding school experience. They knew she was a very spiritual girl, but she didn't share very much with them. She kept everything to herself. Now this! But being the parents of a future Saint, they thought of themselves last. As much as they wanted her with them, Octave and Seraphia were willing to abide by the decision of the parish priest on the matter. Msgr. Cloutier, their parish priest, advised Dina to wait; she was too young; she should see some of the world. He earnestly believed that she owed it to her parents to remain longer with them. He recommended she wait until she were at least twenty-three or twenty-four, before entertaining this vocation.

Dina was obedient. She had conditioned herself mentally and spiritually to obey her superiors, and she considered this to be the Will of God. But she didn't change any of the rules of life which she had drawn up when she left boarding school. To the contrary, she embraced her spiritual life more so, now that she would have to wait for seven or eight years. Actually, the regimen which she gave herself, disciplining herself, was a good training for this new burden that was being imposed on her.

Dina did all the things her parents wished - going to social gatherings, wearing jewelry, silks and fine materials. She spent time with her relatives and her parents' friends. She made a good impression on everyone she encountered. If they had any complaint about Dina, it was that she did not spend enough time with *them*.

But Dina was an active girl. She couldn't just sit around for seven years. She had to do something. She had been extremely gifted as a pianist during her teenage years. She threw herself into her piano, spending hours each day, practicing. She very quickly obtained a Superior Diploma, Laureate, and a Teacher's certificate. She also played the piano in concert tours. This was very difficult for her. She was given rave reviews. She accepted them with much humility.

"I wished to recognize my God-given talents, but I aimed at so sublime, so unattainable an ideal that I knew very well, I did not deserve so much praise...My deep-seated conviction increased my keenness to improve and I slaved at my study...No one could suspect what martyrdom (I do not fear to use this word) I endured in the midst of applause and flowers."

She was so proficient at the piano that her parish priest, Msgr. Cloutier, recommended she go to the Conservatory of Music in Manhattan, New York. There was a residence there called "Our Lady of Peace" which was kept by the *Religious of Jesus and Mary*. Plus, he said, there were two other girls going from Québec, and so she wouldn't be alone in the big city. Although this would mean additional separation from her parents, they bowed to her desire, coupled with the priest's recommendation, and gave their permission.

Just before Dina was to leave for New York, her mother was in an automobile accident and was left seriously injured. Dina immediately assumed the role of being mistress of the house. She took care of her mother, as well as a little two and a half year old girl whom Madame Bélanger had taken in while the little girl's mother was ill. Dina loved children and happily accepted the responsibility of taking care of the child. However, it seemed as if the Lord was telling her that her trip to New York was not to be. She had really been looking forward to this adventure.

*"At the moment of carrying out serious, important plans
on which my future sometimes depended, Jesus used to ask
me to sacrifice my desires. How I suffered at these times!
I needed a powerful grace to be able to give up joyfully this
or that hope in order to respond to His Will. And when I
had made my act of renunciation, circumstances would
change, obstacles would vanish, and my desires were always
granted."*

And so the Lord, generous to all who say *"Yes"* to Him,
healed Madame Bélanger. In addition, the little girl went back to
her mother and the way was cleared for Dina to depart for New
York.

The Dark Night of the Soul

The enemy used this time when Dina was away from her
parents, and for all intents and purposes, anyone who could help
her spiritually, to attack her with an interior struggle which was
to last for six years. We call it *the Dark Night of the Soul*. All the
greatest Saints have endured this time and fought this battle. It
began about four months after Dina had arrived in New York. It
was a ferocious battle between Jesus, her great Lover, and Lucifer,
with her as the victim and the prize. She could not believe what
was happening to her. In her own words,

*"It was the rage of Satan who was bent on assailing me
by multiplied assaults, wiles and stratagems. Jesus
showered upon me thousands of graces to keep me entirely
His during these terrific struggles. The devil was
determined to conquer and what means he did not invent
to attain his ends!...I felt unutterable agonies and passed
through moments of profound darkness, of excruciating
trial."*

She threw herself into her studies and into her prayer life.
The pressure of the new environment, the work load, and the
spiritual plight she was experiencing, all contributed to a
breakdown of her health, although not serious, and not for any
length of time. But her companions suggested that perhaps she

should take time off from Daily Mass, until she was feeling better. This shocked her. Dina couldn't possibly think of doing anything like that. She consulted a priest who advised her to continue with Daily Mass and Holy Communion.

During her time in New York, Dina was able to overcome one of her long standing weaknesses, that of communication or relationship with others. She was thrown into an association with two Canadian girls who came with her to New York from Québec. The first girl, Bernadette Létourneau, was virtually thrust upon her. When they arrived at Our Lady of Peace, both girls were supposed to be given single rooms. But as it turned out, there was only two rooms available at that time, one single and one double. Their other companion, Aline, was given the single room. Dina and Bernadette had to room together but were told it would only be for a short time.

This was very difficult for Dina, as she was used to privacy and the ability to study and pray as she desired. However, she would not let Bernadette, or anyone else for that matter, see her distress. She became friendly with Bernadette. Their friendship went far beyond the two years they spent together in New York. As a matter of fact, when they were told a month later that the single rooms were available, they chose to remain together.

This was extremely good for Dina. She was able to be free with her two friends. She opened up to a degree. Although she retained her selflessness and her charity towards others, she became very lively, and as she got to know her two friends more, she began to tease them.

She even took to boisterous and uncontrollable laughter. One evening, Bernadette heard the sounds of laughter coming from Aline's room. She ran to the room to find the two girls, Dina and Aline, in wild fits of merriment. Dina had turned the lights out in the room, sat on Aline's bed, and opened an umbrella. When Aline entered the room, after the initial shock of fright wore off, both girls broke into joyful exhilaration.

The time in New York was good for Dina. She became highly

accomplished in her music. This would prove to be important for her during her years with the *Religious of Jesus and Mary*. But at the time, she wasn't sure why the Lord wanted her to wait before entering religious life. She was just saying yes, knowing that He would make whatever He was doing in her life, work. She was a willing victim, ready to do whatever her Lord asked of her.

Dina's novitiate with Jesus - a time of Visions and Locutions

In June 1918, Dina's time in New York came to an end. She returned to her home in Sillery and her parents. She was happy to be home but missed the life in New York. Her parents were extremely happy to have her with them. She still had three years before she could enter religious life, according to the timetable established by Msgr. Cloutier with her parents. She didn't know it when she first returned home but this was to be a time of learning, a time of close relationship with the Lord, a time of *Mysticism* and *Inner Locution*. At times, Dina heard the voice of Jesus speaking to her, and she saw a very bright light and images which were unfamiliar to her.

"When entering upon this period of my life, I see myself submerged in an ocean of graces. Here, first of all, let me extol the intimate, divine work achieved in my soul which I have always been most averse to mention. This is a secret between Jesus and myself which I kept and pondered in my heart." She was being taught by the Master!

But while she was being filled with unexplainable joy and wisdom, Dina was being attacked bitterly by her old enemy, Satan. [You have to know that whenever the Lord is working powerfully in your life, Satan is right behind Him, trying to destroy all that the Lord has given you. This was the predicament the Saints experienced all their lives; this is what we can expect when the Lord embraces us with His blessings.] In the case of Dina, the bright light was always followed by the darkness of the deepest night. She continued suffering the trial which began in New York in March, 1917. She was bombarded by assaults from the enemy, but now in addition, she found herself in a continuous state of aridity and spiritual dryness.

She countered these attacks with rigorous and relentless prayer, spiritual reading, and attendance at Mass. The Mass was where she encountered the greatest onslaughts. The enemy was constantly trying to block her spiritual ascent to Jesus at Mass by distractions and vile thoughts.

The times when Jesus came to Dina were worth any anguish she had to endure. He would only come to her in moments of calm and tranquility. If her soul was not at peace, He would first quiet its agitation and attract her to the sentiments of humility and sorrow for her faults.

"I asked Him one day, not to let me be deceived by the devil. He explained how I could always recognize the difference between His Divine Voice and that of the tempter who so loves to play the role of imitator and deceiver. The Savior makes Himself heard only in hours of deep recollection, peace and silence. His Voice is soft, so soft that in the soul all must be hushed; it is a melodious voice, while that of the devil is noisy, abrupt and discordant, and his words are uttered in the midst of agitation and tumult."

Dina's spiritual journey and enlightenment of the soul were extremely important to Jesus. He knew what a cherished emissary this child would be, how she would project His love and His instruction to His people. To that end, He gave her particular attention. He and our Mother Mary personally took charge of her development.

*"Jesus gave me for guide and luminary the **Host** and the **Star**. The Host was Himself, the Star, none other than His incomparable Mother. He showed me a path bordered with thorns wherein he wished me to tread, after He had first walked on it. At the outset, the trials were not numerous, but as I advanced they increased in number; in order to be faithful, I was not to allow myself to be dismayed by any suffering. The path was narrow and grew narrower as it became more infested with thorns. The latter were to*

become so thick and tall as to nearly choke up the route. I had to push them aside as I advanced...And I saw ever before me the Host and the Star representing Jesus and Mary in the path I was obliged to follow. At the end of the route which sloped upward I could see, as on the summit of a mountain, a blessed door, that of my eternal Home. There the Savior and His beloved Mother would open for me in a few years that tightly closed door, and what waves of joy would then inundate my whole being. I seemed already to see the door ajar, to behold the reflection of the pure rays of dazzling light that radiated from it and to hear the echoes of Angelic melodies."

In her heart, these scenes were very clear. Dina was able to distinguish them more clearly than if she had seen them with her eyes. She was able to go beyond that curtain which separates our world from the world of God. Dina was approaching that level of unity with Jesus of which all souls only dream. And with the joy and ecstasy came the assaults by the enemy. He instilled in her heart a desire for humiliation and contempt.

"Every morning I repeat the same request, `My God, grant me the grace of being scorned and humiliated as much as Thou desirest me to be...If thou desirest that I should taste no more joys on earth, I am willing to forego them all.'"

By means of Heavenly images, Jesus acquainted her more and more with the idea of suffering. One image reminds us that of another Saint and Mystic, St. Clare of Montefalco - Jesus thrust His Cross into her heart, telling her *"At last I have someone I could trust with My Cross."* With Dina, He held a Cross in His Hand. The first time, He pierced her heart with the foot of the Cross. Later, He plunged it in more deeply, and finally, He thrust the entire length of the Cross in her heart, letting it tear and lacerate her body as it went. She said, *"This last action meant that the Savior and His Cross reigned in me. Then He surrounded my heart with a crown of thorns, symbol of His own."*

During all of this, the Lord mentioned at various times that

He was preparing her for a mission. She accepted and embraced the idea, although she had no idea what it could be. She continued practicing the piano, but she could not see how this would have any importance in whatever mission the Lord might be planning for her. Jesus said to her:

"Your musical studies will protect your vocation, but you will do good particularly by your writings. Yes, in the convent you will devote yourself to literary work."

Dina knew she was predestined to be a religious. Her whole life had been pointing in that direction. Also, since she began to have conversations with Jesus, her vocation was never in question. She understood, when Jesus told her she would use her musical education in the convent, but she had never thought about writing. She was not really versed in literature. How would she devote herself to literary work? She wondered; she might have even questioned the Lord; but she never doubted. She knew that if the Master and Lover said it, it would happen.

The end of the beginning; the beginning of the end

The year was 1920. Dina was twenty-three years old. She had waited for seven years for this time to come. She had worked and studied, given her heart and soul to her Savior, especially in the two years since she returned home. She groomed herself as well as possible, for this time. Now the question was, *Where should she go?* Her only real exposure was the Congregation of Notre Dame. But she didn't feel drawn to them anymore. In addition, the Lord had spent a lot of time teaching her music. This, it would seem, indicated that He expected her to use it in a teaching Community. But where? There were three possibilities: the Ursulines, the Ladies of the Sacred Heart, and the Congregation of Jesus and Mary. She was completely open but not excited about any of the three. Then one day the Lord made the decision for her.

"I want you in the Congregation of Jesus and Mary." He said to her. She replied,

"Wherever you wish, my Good Master. You know I have

no taste for teaching, but I want to answer your call and to go anywhere according to your good pleasure."

To which He replied, ***"You will not teach long."***

The die was cast; the decision was made. Dina applied to the Congregation of Jesus and Mary and was accepted immediately. Her parents put no block in her way. They were convinced it was God's Will that she enter the Community. But they loved her so much. The last year she was home, her parents showered her with love and attention. They couldn't think of enough things to do for her, and she accepted all willingly and joyfully because she felt she was giving this last gift to her parents. As the day of her entry, August 11, 1921, came nearer and nearer, Dina came to terms that this might be the last time she would have to spend with her parents. She was sure she was leaving her home for the last time, although it was not that far from the convent of the Congregation of Jesus and Mary. The strong, driving force, which gave all of them the fortitude to go through with this separation was that they all agreed she was doing God's Will.

Dina had worked for twenty-four years to perfect herself. She had disciplined her body and soul, her emotions, every area of her life. We would think that the young lady who entered the convent would be firm and secure in her commitment. And yet she experienced the same problems she had when she went to the boarding school at age fourteen, and again when she went to New York at age seventeen. She was still shy, inhibited, didn't communicate very well, and worst of all, she was extremely homesick for the first few weeks.

It was worse, however, possibly because Dina was so close to home. There were times when she wanted to leave in the middle of the day, as she was walking on the grounds of the convent without taking anything, not even coat and hat, just leave and go home, never to return. Other times she planned to leave the next day, in which case she would bring some of her things with her. She had fought so hard for so long to distance herself from any of the ties that kept her earthbound. But it was still the same. Dina missed home, terribly.

However, that made the gift she gave Jesus even more precious. She had to fight everything in her to give up all her habits. She threw herself into her new life. She felt free to practice all the forms of mortification, abstinence and humility she had practiced in the secular world. But now Dina had a Superior, to whom she could confide. This was a great gift, being able to unburden herself of all her questions, especially about her inner locutions and visions of Jesus. She developed a bond with this Superior, an affection which she began to fear was too human. She appealed to the Lord Who gave her the grace to understand the purity, sweetness and strength of the bond. She was helped greatly in her spiritual life by this Superior.

The Lord threw in a special bonus for Dina when she entered Community. Her dear friend from her years in New York, Bernadette Létourneau, entered the convent of Jesus and Mary on the same day as Dina. This was a good thing for Dina, because now she had a familiar face and a good friend to help her through those first six months. But she felt it could be a problem because she might tend to lean too heavily on her friend or become too much of a shoulder for her friend to lean on. Her Mistress of Novices allayed her fears in that area.

After six months of preparation, Dina was ready to be clothed on February 15, 1922. She took the name, Marie St. Cécile du Rome, after St. Cecilia, a Virgin, Martyr and Disciple of the early Church. It was those three virtues of St. Cecilia which attracted Dina so much. She had been given St. Cecilia by the Lord as a protectress, some time before. Now she could make it official.

At the beginning of her novitiate, Dina embraced poverty, chastity and obedience with a passion. She asked to take the vows *privately*, prior to her public profession which would take place a year and a half later. She was given permission. She took her vows on March 25, 1922. She felt that by this ceremony, she had given herself completely to Jesus.

"I dare not speak of my happiness. It was not surpassed

*by that of my public profession nearly a year and a half
later...At this last ceremony my gift of myself was not more
complete than at my private profession at which I
surrendered myself without any reserve and with the
determination never to take back any part of my offering."*

Dina changed her motto. During her postulancy, she had taken
the motto *"To suffer joyfully."* Now she was more mature. She
changed it to *"To suffer with love."* She also changed her
childhood motto, *"Death rather than defilement"* for *"Jesus and
Mary the rule of my love, and my love the rule of my life."*

Her life as a novice brought her closer and closer into
relationship with Jesus. She took part in all the duties and
activities of the other nuns. All during this time she was
communicating with Our Lord Jesus. After Dina's death, her
Mistress of Novices shared much of what Dina was experiencing.
She testified that at one time, while the Community was enjoying
a picnic, Dina, laughing and playing with the others, was receiving
instruction from the Lord. No one could tell she was having an
inner locution at that very moment.

A short time in the infirmary encouraged Dina to begin
writing. She didn't know what the Lord wanted, but she was
told by Him, *"You will do good by your writings,"* and so she
began to write. She wrote poetry, verse, plays and musical
compositions. The Lord blessed all of Dina's endeavors.

In 1923, the Congregation was given the inspiration to ask
Monsignor Cloutier to request permission for the Blessed
Sacrament to be reserved in their chapel when he went to Rome.
The request was granted; the entire Community was in a state of
anxious expectation. What would they name the chapel? Mother
Elizabeth, the Mistress of Novices, was given a strong word by
the Lord to call it the Eucharistic Heart. Thus it was named, and
on June 7, the first Mass was celebrated in the *Oratory of the
Eucharistic Heart*.

It was also at this time that Jesus told Dina that her mission
would be focused in love of, and adoration to the Blessed

Sacrament. He told her of the promises and desires of His Eucharistic Heart:

> *"Our Lord asked me to console His Heart, outraged in the Blessed Eucharist. One first Friday of the month, during my private adoration before the Blessed Sacrament exposed, I seemed to see a multitude of souls rushing to their eternal damnation. Some were on the brink of the abyss and on the point of falling. Jesus told me that I could save these souls by praying fervently for them and offering Him little sacrifices through love. I did so immediately, and I saw these souls, conquered by Divine Grace, leaving the camp of Satan."*

At these times Dina had the spiritual direction and guidance not only of St. Cecilia, her namesake, but the Little Flower, St. Thérèse, whom she had been given as another helper.

On August 15th, 1923, she made her profession. Jesus asked her to *"climb into His Boat."* By this, He meant that she was to leave Sillery and go to the school at St. Michel de Bellechasse,[5] which was operated by the Congregation of Jesus and Mary. She was to teach music to the children. Dina spent five weeks there. The students adored her. She treated them well. But she was only there for a week when she contracted Scarlet Fever from nursing a student who had contracted it. She became very ill, and was sent back to Sillery, to the infirmary. This illness was the beginning of many illnesses which would lead to Tuberculosis and eventually her death.

Back at Sillery, Dina felt completely useless in the infirmary. What could she do there? However, the greatest sacrifices she had to make was to abstain from receiving the Eucharist for ten days. She had to be isolated and quarantined from everyone, because her condition was so contagious. It grieved her each

---

[5]Since her beatification, the name of the school has been changed to Collège Dina-Bélanger. We visited and taped St. Michel de Bellechasse for our television program.

morning to hear the little bells ring when the priest was coming to give Communion to the patients in the infirmary, and she could not receive. But the Lord makes the most of everything. He did not cause her to get Scarlet Fever, but He was able to use that time of seclusion in the infirmary to teach her. Jesus said to her,

"From now on, I am giving you the grace of feeling My Presence within you, that is, of enjoying the felt Presence of God in you."

Dina added *"Immediately, the life of the Blessed Trinity manifested itself in me, with unutterable sweetness, peace and love. I remained motionless in respect and gratitude."*

Dina had always reached for the goal of complete abandonment to God, a death to self. She worked at this from the time she was a child, all through her secular life, and now into her religious life. In effect, she wanted Jesus to take charge, to do with her as He pleased. On November 3, she began a ten-day retreat. Jesus told her that at the end of that retreat, He would allow her to undergo a transformation which would put her in a state of annihilation and death to self. Dina explains what happened in a dramatic, and very aesthetic manner:

"He showed me an Altar, rather elevated, above which rose brilliant flames of fire; this was the Altar of His love. In His Hand, I saw my heart, my very own heart which He had taken from me during the postulate retreat. He made me look at it, so as to provide me with the opportunity of giving myself to Him again, more completely and freely. Then He placed it on the Altar, the fire surrounded it, and I saw it being consumed to its last fiber; there remained nothing of it, absolutely nothing.

"Then, Jesus invited me to go up the Altar myself. There were five steps to climb in honor of the five Sacred Wounds. What went on within me is beyond description. I felt, as it were, my nature overtaken by repulsion, in revolt against this; in my soul there was peace and happiness. I placed my foot on the first step, the second, and kept on in a spirit

of abandonment. I soon reached the center of the Altar. The flames moved apart on each side of me and did not touch me. The Good Master, His eyes always upon me, made me open out my arms as on a cross; immediately, the flames rushed upon me with violent intensity, but they were, nonetheless, moving slowly as they consumed my entire being. As this divine fire consumed me, it seemed to me that my being shuddered, moaned and finally, to me, it appeared to be dead at the moment of its complete destruction. When there was no longer anything to burn, the fire subsided and went out. In the center, there remained some ashes; Jesus drew near, breathed on them and destroyed them totally. I no longer existed!"

From that time on, for the rest of her life, Jesus alone would live in her. Dina's role was to live in complete trust, abandonment and love, to let Jesus do as He wished with her. [There is such an important lesson for us here. Jesus stands at the door, asking us to open it so that He can enter, and become part of us. For those who are chosen, He asks us to give ourselves completely over to Him. But why does He have to ask? Why can't He just take over in our lives? He is God, after all. We don't exist without His permission. But that's the whole key, to give of ourselves, totally and freely. If we truly love Him with our entire being, we want to give ourselves to Him.] Dina had reached that level of unity with the Lord. She had climbed the mountain so high, yet there was so much more climbing to do.

Dina's Autobiography

Dina was not the only person at the convent at Sillery who was receiving messages from the Holy Spirit. Sister St. Romauld, her Superior, had had a inner locution directing her to have Dina write her autobiography. She presented it in council to *her* Superiors, asking permission. At first, she was turned down. They thought it might not be good for humility, and it was contrary to the policy of the Congregation. Sr. Romauld was obedient, but went back again in February, 1924 with the same request.

She just felt it was important, not only for the Community, but for Dina as well. Finally they gave their permission, and from the beginning of March, 1924, until June 30th, she wrote, under obedience, her life story to that point in time. She gave it to her Superior. Then she continued writing, as time went on, until her death.

It was difficult at first, for Dina to go back into those years before the convent. She had lived her whole life, to bring her to where she was at this time. She did not want to go back. And in analyzing those years, she had to become aware of the pain she experienced growing up, as well as the pain inflicted on her mother and father whom she loved so dearly. But as she continued writing the story of her life, Dina was able to put into words all the feelings she had stored up, the love story she had shared with Jesus, and how everything she had experienced could be put down on paper, with such beautiful words which the Lord had given her. Through her writings, she was able to leave behind a living witness of what her life had been.

What the Lord gave Dina was definitely for her, but not only her. It was for the thousands, and possibly millions who would read her testimony and feel the warm embrace of the great Master. As with her predecessor and mentor, the Little Flower of the Child Jesus, St. Thérèse of Lisieux, Dina would live on in her autobiography. And because she said *yes* to Jesus, we have this treasury of spirituality, this gift, this glimpse of how much Jesus wants to give us, how He wants to embrace us, and consume us, and make us His.

The Lord did not cause Dina's illness which incapacitated her for most of the rest of her life. But He was able to use her illness to get her attention, to be able to work with her, to bring her closer to Him and the Kingdom. For all her years in the convent, she taught school whenever possible; she composed beautiful, peaceful music, and she wrote her autobiography. But the Lord worked powerfully in her as well.

During the next two years, she felt herself being drawn as

victim-soul, closer and closer to the Trinity. She came up with another motto, ***"To satisfy fully all the attributes of the eternal and adorable Trinity."*** She had to have had a very close relationship with the Trinity to be able to use the word *adorable*. But God works that way with those whom He loves. Most likely, the Trinity looked upon Dina as being *adorable*. She was going to the Trinity through, guess who, Our Lady, the Blessed Virgin. She didn't realize it, as often we do not, but she was using all the tools, the weapons of the Church, what we need to bring us through this Journey of Faith, from here to the Kingdom.

Dina was just completely open to anything and everything the Lord would have of her. She spoke about immolation, love. She learned that she must live her life, going through the Twin Hearts, the Sacred Heart of Jesus and the Immaculate Heart of Mary. This was given to her on June 20, the month of the Sacred Heart. She may not have known the terminology we use today, but her own words were *"...to radiate the Heart of Jesus on all souls, through the Blessed Virgin."* To do this, she had to love and let Jesus and Mary have their way; she had to sacrifice herself through love.

The Lord also gave her another gift, a Weapon to fight off the attacks of "le capudile." That was, and naturally is, the Eucharist, the Real Presence of Jesus, there for all of us in the Tabernacle. She would feel herself *physically drawn* to the Blessed Sacrament, like a magnet.

"When I pass by the chapel I feel an irresistible impulse to go in. Before the Tabernacle I feel an indefinable joy. When the Blessed Sacrament is exposed, I am enraptured and as it were, paralyzed by the Eucharistic Heart. When I leave the chapel, I have to tear myself away from the Divine Prisoner..."

Dina shared in the Passion of Our Lord Jesus

Dina had a practice of setting aside Thursday to honor the Eucharistic Heart of Jesus. On September 2, at noon, while she was meditating on the Heart of Jesus, He spoke to her soul: ***"Do***

you desire to drink of the chalice of My Passion?"
She was honored. She answered *"Oh yes. How good Thou art."*

He repeated with vigor, ***"Do you wish it?"***
The force of the words were like a dart of love, piercing her heart. *"My Jesus, Thou knowest that not only do I desire it, but that it is the only object of my desire."*

At that moment, an excruciating interior suffering took possession of her, a suffering that she could not put into words.

Dina wrote, *"During the night between Thursday and Friday, I was overwhelmed by a deep sentiment of compassion for my Savior. The physical pain was nothing compared to what my soul endured; my suffering had its origin in the heart and from there it spread out over my whole being, seeming to bruise every part. I was oppressed by a crushing sense of loneliness, and yet drank deep draughts of joy."*

The following Friday, September 10th, Jesus asked her again: ***"Do you wish to drink of My Chalice?"***
She replied, *"Oh! yes indeed, my Jesus."*

From that time on, Dina was given the gift of sharing in the Passion of Jesus every Thursday and Friday. Dina was ecstatic to be able to console Our Lord Jesus, as if they were in the Garden of Gethsemane. She felt so close to Him, sharing in the cup of His Passion. This was enough to bring her to the edge of ecstasy. It could never get better than this. And then the Lord gave her His most special Gift.

Dina Received the Stigmata

On January 22, 1927, Dina was given the gift of the Stigmata of Jesus, the Five Wounds in her hands, feet, and side. She described it in breathtaking description:

"On the 22nd of January, a Saturday and the Feast of Our Lady of Fourvière, we had the closing ceremony of the Forty Hours Adoration. During my mediation before the Blessed Sacrament exposed, I suddenly felt myself enveloped in profound peace. I was already conscious of

the presence of my Divine Master, but this was something more than the ordinary union of Thursdays and Fridays. In fact, Our Lord was granting me a great favor: the Stigmata of His Sacred Wounds. From His Divine Heart flames radiated on the feet, hands and heart of my annihilated being. The Blessed Virgin applied these flames to my hands and feet, and Jesus imprinted on them the Stigmata of love of His Sacred Wounds. He was granting one of my most cherished desires, but He astonished me by granting it at this moment when I was not expecting it and in this manner which I could never have imagined."

As with most genuine Stigmatists, Dina begged Our Lord Jesus not to let her Stigmata show. She didn't want anyone to know that she had been given this special gift. And the Lord answered her prayer. Padre Pio begged for his Stigmata to remain invisible, and for a time, the Lord gave him this gift. But when the Lord felt it necessary for the Stigmata to be visible for all the world to see, Padre Pio said yes to all that it entailed.

[Let us say something at this point, which is really important. We've been given a great gift here, in having the autobiography of a Mystic and Stigmatist. We get to know what is going on inside of her, what she's thinking, what she's feeling, what her focus is throughout her life. She wanted to be *a nothing*, hidden in a corner, just adoring her Lord. She wanted no attention, no publicity. Hopefully by now, you've read about Sts. Martin de Porres and Rose of Lima. They didn't want to be in the public eye. It was thrust upon them. They wanted to be contemplatives. Dina was the same. To have had the visible Stigmata, would have been asking for a cross which would have been very heavy for her to carry. The publicity and notoriety that comes with a gift like the Stigmata would have been completely contrary to how she wanted to adore her Lord.]

Throughout her life, Jesus told Dina that she was going to die at a given date, and she did not die. When questioned by her Superiors, rather than make an excuse, she would say, *"I made a mistake.*" That wasn't so. Jesus would never lie to her. He can't lie and still be God. She did not understand what He meant. He was telling her she would be dying to herself, things she was hanging onto. When He would say *"Next August 15, you will be with me in Heaven,"* she would go into ecstasy on that particular date. She may have even had an out-of-body experience. Her autobiography doesn't specify.

But a time was to come when the Lord told her He was taking her *Home*, and He did. In the Spring of 1926, she began to show signs of pulmonary Tuberculosis, which was a very life-threatening and debilitating disease. She suffered greatly until it became full-blown. It would lead to an early death for our little Saint. She managed to hang on until she made her final vows on August 15, 1928. But after that, she was preparing for the road Home. She had always desired Heaven. She was promised Heaven by her Lover, Our Lord Jesus. Now it was time to go Home. On April 30, 1929, her birthday, she was moved into the isolation ward for Tuberculosis patients. While it was a more pleasant and a brighter atmosphere, it was the place from which few ever come back. She was on her way.

Actually, from what we can gather from her autobiography, she was more in Heaven than on earth towards the end of her life. She was just shackled to her body, but her soul had already been lifted to the summit. She had soared to the High Places, and it would not be fair to bring her back to earth. She had sacrificed herself for the Divine Wishes of her Master, and He was now going to reward her. But "le capudile", the devil, was not about to let her go peacefully. He kept pulling her back to earth with doubts, trying to break her faith and her relationship with Jesus. Dina fought valiantly, but could only succeed through the saving efforts of her God Who was by her side to the very end.

In the early days of September, 1929, she had been given the last Sacraments of the Church. She called the Mother Superior over to her, reporting to the end all that had been told to her. Dina

Below:
Dina Bélanger's tomb

Above:
*Dina Bélanger on her
deathbed. This photo
was taken just moments
before she died.*

said to her, *"Mother, I heard voices saying to me and repeating
fifteen times, `Blessed, Blessed.'"* On September 4, 1929, at three
in the afternoon, she took her last breath. She looked at the two
Superiors on either side of her bed. She smiled such an angelic
smile to them that it was imprinted on their hearts for the rest of
their lives. When she died, she looked very much like the Little
Flower of Jesus, St. Thérèse of Lisieux, sitting up with her head
back on the pillow.

We want to share with you an excerpt from Dina's diary,
regarding the Eucharist.

*"If souls but understood the Treasure they possess in the
Divine Eucharist, it would be necessary to encircle the
Tabernacles with the strongest of ramparts for, in the
delirium of a devouring and holy hunger, they would press
forward themselves to feed on the Bread of Angels; the
churches would overflow with adorers consumed with love
for the Divine Prisoner, no less by night than by day."*

Most Catholics don't know much about this little Saint. The Lord put her in our path recently, and we were so enthralled with her that we followed her up to Québec, Canada, to learn as much as we could, to get to know her through the people she touched, to see the places where she lived. We can't recommend too highly that you read more about little Blessed Dina, beatified on March 20, 1993, whose greatest gift to the Lord was to surrender herself to His Love. ***Praise Jesus!***

Blessed Brother André

*Miracle Worker of
Montreal
Healer, Religious,
Doorkeeper, Dreamer
of Dreams*

Blessed Brother André

As with many Saints that we have written about, when Blessed André died on January 6, 1937, the Faithful had already proclaimed him a Saint. In the case of Blessed André of Mont Royal, or Montreal, Canada, not only the citizens of that city, but indeed all of French Canada considered him a Saint during his lifetime. There was an expression which circulated French Canada during the early 1900's when something could not be done, *"Hey, I'm not Brother André. I can't get it done."* One of the resource books we're using for this life of Blessed André is *"Brother André, Miracle Worker of Mont Royal."* This title just about expresses what Brother André was and did. The Lord worked powerfully through him and all was done through the intercession of, and to give honor to St. Joseph. The monument to St. Joseph, high on a hill overlooking all of Montreal, is a tribute from Brother André to St. Joseph; but we believe it's also a tribute from St. Joseph and our Heavenly family as well as the people of Montreal to their own Brother André.

No one wanted the humble doorkeeper forgotten, nor did they wish his memory to be romanticized or altered in any way. Therefore, for the eight years following his death, forty-nine of the most reliable witnesses were individually questioned regarding events surrounding Blessed André's life. Everything was carefully taken down in short-hand, so that the investigators could later read their answers and make sure their testimony had been accurately recorded. Having agreed that it had, they then signed documents, swearing under oath that all they had testified was true.

Over *three thousand* pages of eye-witness testimony was accumulated, only to have Rome, twenty-five years later in 1962, appoint other Church officials in Montreal to conduct an inquiry delving *more specifically* into Blessed André's life. This would result in *nine hundred* more pages by another twenty-two witnesses. You would be hard-pressed to find anyone in the Church or in the world more documented or better known than the humble Doorkeeper who founded Saint Joseph's Oratory.

Blessed André, the child

Alfred Bessette (later known as Brother André) came from very humble beginnings, much like those of Jesus. He was born on August 9, 1845. The baby was so frail and sickly, his parents were afraid he would not live; and so Alfred was baptized the moment he was born. He was conditionally baptized (when there is doubt concerning a previous Baptism) the following day in the church. With the loving care and prayers of a very pious mother, our future Blessed lived to an old age! But, like other great Saints before and after him, Brother André would have serious bouts with debilitating illnesses to the day he died.

His parents, Isaac Bessette and Clothilde Foisy were young when they married. The little family had virtually no money; Isaac was, like St. Joseph before him, a carpenter. We believe that Brother André's first exposure to St. Joseph, and the great devotion he had for the foster father of Jesus, came from his own saintly father. Isaac married Clothilde when she was only seventeen years old. As she was from the Parish of Saint Joseph in Chambly, she taught her son Alfred about Jesus' earthly father, at an early age. When questioned later on in life, Brother André

Above:
Bl. Brother André's cell

Above:
Bl. Brother André, the doorkeeper

Above: **Bob & Penny, Luz Elena
and Brother Joseph praying at St.
Joseph's Oratory in Montreal**

Above: **Altar in the orginal
chapel at St. Joseph's Oratory,
Montreal**

Left:
**St. Joseph's Oratory,
Montreal, Quebec**

would tell everyone about the great devotion and love he had for
St. Joseph came from his mother who taught him from the cradle
to know and love this great Saint, and his own father who
represented St. Joseph on earth for young Alfred.

Alfred loved to pray from the time he was a little boy. He
later spoke of those special moments when the family gathered
to pray together, how he would sit close to his mother and finger
the beads on her Rosary as they recited the mysteries. The two
people who meant so much to little Alfred were taken away from
him at an early age. First, his father died in an accident, and then
six years later, he lost his mother to a dreaded, debilitating illness,
tuberculosis. Family life as he knew it, would never be the
same. Alfred had no mother and father; he had his heavenly
Mother and father, Our Lady, and St. Joseph.

The family had to be dispersed. His siblings each went to a
different home. Alfred, frail, delicate, and a very sensitive boy
of twelve was required by his adoptive uncle to be a man! Right
after the funeral, he told the grieving boy to stop crying; there
was work to do. There was no time for mourning; that was for
weaklings and girls. Alfred was twelve; he had to be a man and
carry his weight. Poor Alfred had no weight; he was such a
small, fragile child. But he did what he was told. This cross he
carried would give him a love for the Cross of Jesus and a heart
and compassion for the suffering people of this world who would
later come to him. He prayed and practiced means of penance
from an early age; but when the means of mortification, which
could be a hairshirt, or a wire belt, were discovered by his aunt,
he would obey and remove them, only to put on different ones.

Alfred was protected and looked after all his life. One night
he went to a party. He was disturbed by the language and behavior
among the young people there, and so he left by himself. As he
was crossing a bridge on the way home, he heard a murmuring
coming from below. He looked, but there was no one there. He
heard the sounds again. Realizing they were not coming from
the brook, suddenly thoughts of his mother came to him. He

called out: *"Dear Mother, if this sound is you warning me not to return to that place, let me hear it again."* Again he heard the sound, only now more clearly. Alfred knew both his earthly mother as well as his heavenly mother were looking out for him.

When Alfred was twenty years old, we find him following the pattern of other young men, venturing out to new worlds and more rewarding horizons. This was most likely encouraged and possibly mandated by his uncle who felt that André was a means to earn some money. And André obeyed. He went to the United States where he first worked on a farm and then in a factory. This was what other young men his age were doing; it seemed like the right thing to do. However, that was his agenda, or his uncle's. He did not know that the path God had chosen for him was not *in* the world but *for* the world.

Alfred has a *dream* that points to his vocation

Brother André never spoke of ecstasies, visions or inner locutions; he called them *dreams.* Although he would later call this time in a foreign country, away from all he knew and loved, his time *in exile,* he was not alone; his Saint Joseph was with him. *Alfred had a dream* that he was working in a field. In his dream he leaned tiredly on a rake, and asked Saint Joseph: *"Where shall I die?"* Before him he saw a huge stone building unlike anything he had ever seen. He never forgot this dream; years later, when he entered Notre Dame College in Montreal, he recognized it as the building in his dream. Although he did not die there, he would spend forty years of his life in this college as an instrument of God.

When he was twenty-three years old, Alfred returned to his beloved Canada and settled down with his family. Or so he thought. Here, we see the Lord intervening powerfully in the life of Alfred Bessette, our future Brother André. The Lord put another Saint-maker in his path, his parish priest, Father Provençal, whom everyone called a Saint. From the time he was a little boy, Alfred loved to assist at Mass. It was obvious the boy had a great devotion to the Eucharist and to the Mass. He would stay in the church long after Mass was over to pray. He wanted to remain in the presence of God Whom he could feel in the church, especially after having received Communion.

Now, years later, Alfred had returned and Father Provençal saw in the young man the little boy who had served him so zealously, so faithfully; he asked him if he had ever thought of a vocation as a religious! [Do we ever ask that question? We wonder how many young people have a vocation in their heart, and only need someone to light that flame with a spark of a suggestion like: *"Have you ever thought of becoming a religious?"* How many young people need that affirmation of what might have been burning in their hearts from childhood? How many potential vocations are lost because no one ever asked the question?] When Alfred protested that he had nothing to offer to religious life, as he could not read or write, Father spoke of him becoming a *brother of the Holy Cross*, a Congregation that had come to his parish. He told him that this Order had brothers who served the Community in ways not requiring any kind of formal education. Alfred prayed and realized his searching, his longing had been for the Lord and His Will, not for the world's empty rewards.

After praying for two years, Alfred applied to the *Brothers of Holy Cross*. Now they were reluctant to accept him, not so much due to his lack of education, but because he was so frail and sickly, they were afraid he would be a burden on their Community. But the Novice Director, who had interviewed the young Alfred, was touched by the Lord. He saw in André what Our Lord Jesus could use, humility and a great love of Jesus and the Church. The Novice Director stepped in; he said, if Alfred were to become so incapacitated that he was unable to work, he would always be able to pray! He believed Alfred would be a powerful prayer warrior. *He was accepted!*

Father Provençal wrote to the Community of the Brothers of the Holy Cross: *"I am sending you a Saint."* It was 1870, the year that Pope Pius IX proclaimed Saint Joseph Patron of the

Roman Catholic Church. Little did Alfred or the brother who admitted him realize that he would be an instrument to bring millions to a deeper devotion to Saint Joseph. *Alfred* donned the habit of a Religious of the Holy Cross, but it was *Brother André*[1] who entered the novitiate that day. He immediately plunged into caring for the sick in the infirmary, sweeping and scrubbing the hallways, washing linens, always available to the needs of the other brothers day or night. All this he did joyfully. André was part of something, part of a great work for the Lord. Little did he know at the beginning just how great his work was to be. He prayed a great deal and always asked others to pray with him.

Father Hupier, a priest known for his holiness, was assigned to him as Spiritual Director. One evening *Brother André had another dream!* He dreamt that Father Hupier had appeared to him. Brother André asked him which prayer pleased God most. Father recited the Lord's prayer three times, and then told the young novice he was to repeat over and over again, *"Thy Will be done."* Had his Spiritual Director come to him in a dream to prepare him for the road he would have to travel, one of heavy crosses and great trials? Soon after his dream, a cross would be handed him.

Several months passed, and his vocation as a religious seemed doomed. Judging his poor health would cause him to become a tremendous financial and physical burden on the Community in the future, his Superiors made the decision to dismiss him. Brother André was destroyed.

But the Lord is in charge; He is always in charge. He sent the local bishop to the monastery. The Lord had done the hard part; now it was André's part. He summoned all his courage, (remember, he was very shy) and prostrated himself before the bishop. When he told the prelate of the Community's decision to let him go because of frail health, the bishop looked into his eyes and said, *"Do not fear, my dear son, you will be allowed to*

---

[1]Alfred took the religious name of Brother André in honor of his mentor, Father André Provençal.

make your profession." Now it *just happened* that this bishop had had a desire for most of his priestly life to bring recognition to the Saint second only to Mother Mary in the Heart of Jesus, *St. Joseph.* He wrote:

> *"We must have a church specially dedicated to his cult in which he may receive daily the public homage worthy of his eminent virtues....We wish to consecrate all our strength and the rest of our life to making him honored in such a church, establishing there a place of pilgrimage where the people will come to him."*

He was seventy-two years old, and his dream had not as yet been realized. This bishop was known for his holiness. Did the Holy Spirit speak to his heart and tell him that this humble brother was to be the instrument God would use to fulfill his prophecy? Was he passing on the gauntlet to Brother André? Perhaps he was saying in effect, "I was not able to see the dream accomplished. Like the biblical characters in Hebrews 11, I see it from afar and salute it. You will be the one, the Lord will use to make it happen." And is it possible in André's soul he accepted the challenge? The results of his life would have to agree with this.

Brother André, Prayer Warrior and Healer

The Novice Master whispered in Brother André's ear: *"Do not worry; I shall see to it that you make your vows."*

At the end of his novitiate, Brother André was assigned to be Doorkeeper of Notre Dame College, the college-seminary of the Order. As he entered the grounds of the college for the first time and looked at the building he realized, *it was the stone building, he had seen in his dream!* He stayed in this position as doorkeeper for forty years.

André had many tasks which he took very seriously, and he did them all faithfully, snatching precious moments during the day to pray. Although he was a man of prayer, he never neglected his assigned responsibilities. As a matter of fact, all of the activities for which he became famous, were done for the most part in his off-duty time as doorkeeper. As doorkeeper he answered the doorbell and welcomed visitors. Part of this position involved looking for religious or students for whom the visitors had come. This gave him an opportunity to talk to them about Jesus, Mary and Joseph, as he was leading them to the parlor. Besides being the porter of the door, another duty was to keep the parlor and the three corridors of the college neat and clean. In between all these loving tasks, he was the school barber. André loved this job particularly because, as he was cutting the brothers' hair, he had a captive audience. It was one on one; he could lead them to a deeper understanding and consequently a more profound devotion to Saint Joseph. He remembered always the words of the bishop about making the homage to St. Joseph well-known.[2]

He also had chores outside the college. He was given the responsibility to go to town on different errands. One of these was picking up the mail. Another was driving to the students' homes on Saturday and doing their laundry. He considered all of these tasks very important, offering everything he did to the cause of St. Joseph. He prayed as he performed these tasks. As André went about his varied duties, the townspeople got to know him. They started to tell him about people who were suffering with illnesses. He went to their homes, visited with them, prayed with them, and then rubbed the ailing person with some oil from the lamp which burned in front of Saint Joseph's statue in the college chapel. Somehow this angel of mercy was able to do all this and not neglect his appointed duties. As Mother Angelica says, *"Unless we are willing to do the ridiculous, God cannot do the miraculous."*

As the ill began to heal miraculously, the word spread. More and more people stopped him and asked him to go to a loved one who was ailing. They lovingly called him: *"good Brother André."* He healed the sick. They told everyone *he* was a saint, to his deep dismay. Brother André constantly corrected them,

---

[2]see on page 389

insisting always that it was through Saint Joseph's intercession that the healings took place.

This frail brother, whom his Superiors thought would be a burden, did the much needed work of *ten* religious. He was kept so busy, he would sit off in a corner of the dining room, barely taking time to eat. It is miraculous in itself when you think how this man, who could just about eat a mouthful of food because he suffered terribly with pains in his stomach,[3] could have had all the energy he had, never complaining as he humbly and diligently went about doing his work.

Pupils and parents alike soon discovered in this unaffected, humble doorkeeper, a man of deep faith, someone they could turn to. In a world where no one cared whether most people lived or died, Brother André sat with them, listened to them, held their hands and cried with them. With his openness and friendly, loving disposition, he touched many, and they opened up to him, sharing illnesses of mind, body and spirit. He always consoled them by saying, *"I'll pray for you."* Which he did, and miracles started to happen!

One day, while working in the infirmary, Brother André visited a boy who was burning up with an extremely high fever. He ordered him to get up! He said *"You are in perfect health. Get up and go out and play."* Although the boy was reluctant at first, he jumped up and went to join his classmates in the playground. College authorities were livid! They scolded, "You had no right to interfere; the boy is ill!" André gently implored them to have a doctor examine the boy; *he* would tell them, the boy was completely healed. He insisted: *"St. Joseph cured him!"* The Superior became very upset with André and his claims of St. Joseph healing all the time, but when the doctor came and examined the student, he dismissed him with a clean bill of health.

Cases of Smallpox attacked students and religious alike in a neighboring school, Holy Cross College of St. Laurent. Many

---

[3]These excruciating pains never left Brother André.

were dying! Brother André asked to minister to the sick. When he stepped into the infirmary at Holy Cross, his heart went out to the sick and dying jammed into the room. He knelt down at the entrance and prayed for all he was worth to Saint Joseph to relieve the sick. There was not one death recorded after that time.

Brother Alderic, the treasurer of Notre Dame was known for his fine education and sound judgment; he was highly respected in the college and in the Community. He had been suffering intense pain from a severe leg wound which refused to heal, despite the doctors trying everything they knew for two months to no avail. Brother Alderic rubbed some oil from Saint Joseph's lamp on his leg, and the next morning he awakened without any pain! He later told a newspaper that within two days the wound was completely healed. Not satisfied with the recounting of this miracle, he enthusiastically shared about three of the many miraculous cures that had come to pass through the healing hands of Brother André.

Jesus said, *"I tell you, if they keep silent, the stones will cry out."*[4] Word got out and spread! It was alright, as long as it was limited to the confines of the school, the students and their parents, but that was not to last. Although Brother André always insisted vehemently that full credit went to Jesus through the intercession of St. Joseph,[5] people started to flock to the school entrance of Notre Dame College where he was doorkeeper. Soon crowds of the poor and helpless came, without money but with hope. The lame came; they had heard of how the crippled were cured, and they wanted to walk. The sick came; they knew of the infirmed miraculously healed, and they wanted to be cured. The disabled came; they wanted to be whole again, to function as their brothers and sisters. He welcomed them into the small cell he occupied next to the parlor. As he had little use for his cot, because he spent most of the night on his knees praying, Brother André would

---

[4]Luke 19:40
[5]This is much like the Curé of Ars, St. Jean Vianney, who gave credit for all his miraculous occurrences to the intercession of St. Philomena.

sometimes have an ill person rest in his room. He spoke to them all; he told them to pray; he then anointed them with some oil from a lamp which burned in front of a statue of St. Joseph.

This caused unbelievable problems! The parents of the university students complained. Because the sick came in the same door as the students, the mothers and fathers were afraid their children would catch contagious diseases from them. Furthermore, they did not want their children distracted by the noise and commotion of the great numbers (at the beginning, in the hundreds) who crowded the entrance, pleading for Brother André to heal them. His Superior disapproved; his brothers mocked him. The school doctor insisted, *"He was practicing medicine!"* He accused Brother André of being a *"quack"* and demanded, he be stopped from caring for the sick. The students' director added fuel to the fire; he accused Brother André of using superstition: "He was placing oil on the patients; that was not prayer!"

The Superior ordered Brother André to stop the sick from coming into the college. Brother André obeyed, as always. There was only one problem, *the sick!* They kept coming, and since he was the doorkeeper, what could he do? He let them in. Isn't that what a doorkeeper does? And so, they came in greater and greater numbers. When, out of obedience, Brother André refused them entry, they congregated on the grounds outside the door in faithful anticipation. You see, they believed in miracles! And if miracles healed others, then miracles could come about for them; they would see Brother André and they would be healed. Faith! It was not very complicated; people just made it that way. What everyone at the college did not realize was that it was not oil, but faith that brought about the healings. Brother André tried to tell that to everyone, but no one really wanted to hear his explanations; neither those within the college who were opposed, nor those who were being healed.

The Superior's directives were ineffectual. The suffering poor came and would not leave. It got so critical, he allowed

Brother André to open the parlor to them *after hours*. That did not help, so the college asked for and received permission for the crowds to wait for Brother André across the street in the trolley station. But, that did not solve the traffic situation of the sick coming to the college, as many had not heard about waiting at the station, and some did not care. So many people waited at the trolley station that a traffic jam was created there as well. They had an urgency, and they had a singular focus: They wanted to receive the prayers and blessing with the *miraculous* oil and be healed.

The Brothers of Holy Cross had a legitimate concern; they did not doubt their Brother André's intentions; however, because of his lack of education, they were afraid he might try to give spiritual direction which could lead many astray and bring scandal upon the Community. The local Archbishop had similar worries. He turned to the Superior of the Community: "Would Brother stop seeing the sick if you should tell him so?" When the Superior responded: "He would obey blindly," that was a powerful sign to the Archbishop. Obedience, especially blind obedience, is a true sign of a pious soul. He told the superiors to leave Brother André alone, for if his work was from God it would live; if not, it would crumble.

Satan was so angry with the powerful results the Lord was having on the souls being touched by Brother André, he kept poisoning the hearts of many people. Those who were opposed to Brother André's ministering to the sick for one reason or another, continued their campaign and would not rest until they stopped him. They were relentless in their attacks on this simple servant of Christ. They went to his Superior. The parents threatened to have their children removed from school. They went to the Archbishop and filed a complaint. Not having received the satisfaction they had expected, they spread all sorts of scandal about Brother André, attacking his reputation. He touched the sick as he was healing them; his enemies accused him of immodest behavior. This wound was even dealt by a visitor whom he had helped. Brother André always tried to make his explanation as simple as possible. He said, *"My hands produce the same effect as Saint Joseph's oil."* Now this is an obvious oversimplification of the facts, but the truth might have been difficult to accept. Jesus was giving the people miracles at the hands of His servant Brother André. But this only infuriated his foes.

Suffering from false accusations, smeared by dreadful scandals, suspected by those within and violently maligned by those outside his Community, harassed to a point of collapse, Brother André trusted a layman who appeared sympathetic. He shared his hurts and attacks; he even allowed this man to see him crying. He needed someone he could trust; he felt so alone, without any earthly consolation. This man, in whom he had confided, joined Brother André's enemies and began to circulate all that he had told him, warping and twisting it to discredit him. As God *reveals*, this layman's treachery came to light and he was exposed for the liar he was. However, Brother André felt the hurts from this betrayal for years to come.

Nevertheless the miracles did not stop. The devil was completely unsuccessful in this. One day there were so many people in the waiting room of the college, and they looked so helpless, Brother André decided drastic situations required drastic measures. He asked each of the sick people to take a medal of St. Joseph which he gave them. He told them all to rub themselves where they had the affliction with the medal of St. Joseph and make a novena to him. They just stared at him. So he walked into the crowd of them.

He looked at a cripple, took his crutches away from him, and ordered him to walk. The cripple walked perfectly. The man was in shock at what had happened. When the reality of his healing finally hit him, the man ran out of the building, yelping and screaming, praising God. He went across to the trolley stop, got on a trolley and left the area. The other people looked in awe at Brother André.

He then went to the next person. *"And what can I do for you, sir?"* The man shared that his arm was paralyzed. Brother André told him, *"Go to confession and then start a novena* (to St. Joseph)."

The man looked at him incredulously. "But I haven't been to confession for twenty-five years."

The man's daughter, who had brought him to Brother André, cautioned her father, "Be careful, father, people will hear what you say." To which the father replied, "If I have been bad enough to spend twenty-five years without going to confession, I should be brave enough to admit it."

Brother André did not have time for this. He interrupted the two, *"Take your hat with your right hand and put it on."* The man obeyed instinctively, and lifted his paralyzed arm with ease. He looked at Brother André with shock. Our Saint said to him, *"Come tonight to sleep in the room under the chapel roof. Tomorrow you will receive Holy Communion."* The man and his daughter left ecstatically. A bystander asked Brother André, "You have let him go. Do you think he will come back?" Brother André smiled and said, *"Yes, I am sure of it."* [P.S. - The man did come back, went to confession, and received Holy Communion.]

Brother André also prepared people for death and laid them out after death. But this had to be done after hours. Nothing was allowed to interfere with his duties as doorkeeper of the college. Now, the Lord doesn't always take his people to Heaven based on Brother André's off-hours schedule. A situation arose where a young man came to Brother André on a Sunday morning. His grandfather had died, and he needed Brother André to come and prepare him for burial. He told the young man his grandfather would have to wait until he had finished his chores at the college. The young man went back to his parents to report what Brother André had said. They sent him right back, insisting he come at once as rigor mortis would set in, and the body would be too stiff to clothe. Brother André told him, *"I will go about seven o'clock.*

I cannot go now, because I am not allowed to leave the college on visiting days."

That evening, Brother André went to the young man's house; the grandfather's body was still soft and supple. He prepared it for burial. The moment Brother André was finished putting the last of his clothing on the dead man, he had difficulty moving the head into the position he wanted, because his body became stiff as a board.

It was at these times in particular, that he was attacked by the devil. On this particular evening, when he returned to the college, he said his evening prayers and retired to his little cell. He heard the most god-awful sounds coming from the dining room. It was like an earthquake had hit, and all the dishes and stemware had plummeted to the ground. Brother André ran into the room and turned on the light. Nothing had been touched.

This happened many times after preparing dead people to go to the Kingdom. He came to realize that it had to do with the work he was doing. He said, *"Every time I go to lay out a corpse, I hear that noise."* He would also see black cats, or strange animals in the dining room. He reasoned that *"the devil, enraged on account of my errands of mercy, is trying to frighten me."*

We could go on and on about the miraculous events credited to Brother André and still not be able to account for all of them. One author suggested a book be written, similar to *the Fioretti (Little Flowers) of St. Francis* and *the Fioretti (Little Flowers) of St. Clare of Assisi,* in which all the special instances of Divine intercession worked through the hands of this special Saint could be recorded. Blessed André's life is so remarkable. But we have to go back to the problem at hand; what to do with all the sick people at the college door, and how Jesus and St. Joseph get what they really wanted in the first place, a monument and shrine to the foster-father of Jesus, the husband of Mary.

Jesus wants a chapel in honor of His foster father Joseph

Everything looked so black. The situation kept getting worse; something had to be done! If we look closely, we can see

God working through all this. We learned an expression in our beloved Louisiana: *When you're up to your ears in alligators, it's hard to remember that your original aim was to drain the swamp.*
They desperately needed an alternative! The Community could not keep the people from coming. If the sick continued coming to the doors to Brother André, the college would lose all its students. A solution, that's what was needed. *Purchase the land across the street on the hillside!* Brother André and some students buried religious medals of Saint Joseph on the hillside.[6] A student had watched Brother climb the mountain every evening after Brother was finished working. When the boy asked him what he did there each night, Brother André told him he prayed and invited him to go with him. From that time on, you could see man and boy going up the mountain and praying. Brother André prophesied, *"We will obtain this piece of land. Saint Joseph needs it."*

When the boy returned to the college as a young man, he was unable to walk without assistance. He asked Brother André if he did not recognize him; whereupon Brother replied: *"You are my little companion who used to come and pray with me on the mountain. How are you?"* The young man told brother that because of an injury he had sustained at work, the doctors were saying he had to have his leg amputated; and that he knew that brother had the power to heal him, if he would. As always, Brother André insisted: *"No, not I, but Saint Joseph, if you have faith. Send your carriage and stay with me."* He placed him in a room adjacent to his, away from the curious and the critical. At night, he brought the young man to *his* room. He massaged the injured leg for a few minutes. The gangrene that had set in, disappeared; the leg, swollen and black and blue, was now normal, so much so, he walked home *alone* on the slippery snow-covered road. Miracles continued happening.

[6]This might be why some people may have gotten the practice of burying a statue of Saint Joseph on their property in order to sell a house. We don't recommend it to anyone. We're not sure if St. Joseph really likes it.

We have to say here that Brother André was not the only one who wanted the Community to buy the property across from the college. We have to give credit to the brothers as well. They had wanted to buy the property for years, in fear that someone would build something objectionable, or completely contrary to the spiritual climate which had been created for this area. Finally, the owners agreed to sell the land to the Order.

The Heavenly plot thickens. Brother André had been trying to have a chapel built in honor of St. Joseph for some time. He had pleaded with his Superiors, with no success. While it's true they wanted to buy the property, they didn't know what they wanted to do with it. They were sure that if there was any cost involved, they wanted nothing to do with it. Brother André had hit a stone wall; so he turned to Saint Joseph.

Years before Brother André had placed a statue of St. Joseph on the top of the hillside and carefully covered it with a small wood shelter. Now he placed a statue of the Saint in his window facing Mount Royal, the mountain across from the college. When visitors questioned him on why the statue was with his back to him, Brother André would say it was facing the mountain where someday there would be a special Shrine to Saint Joseph.

Well, God is in charge and He will get their attention one way or the other. He placed Brother André in the infirmary. Whereas, it was not unusual for Brother André to be there, to be sick and be placed in the same room with his Superior was too much to be mere coincidence. He had a captive audience. We kind of smile thinking of that persistent servant of God very possibly going on and on until his idea became the Superior's. Brother André got permission to build, but no money to do it. His Superior would not budget anything toward the project; it was up to the little Brother.

He was told *he* had to get the money if the chapel was to be built. He had been cutting the students' hair for years and saved the few nickels they gave him. His Superior also granted him permission to keep the small offerings, he received from those who had been healed. And so, finally, he had two hundred dollars; enough to begin. But, he would not need to do it alone. One of the students' fathers donated the wood. The school carpenter, a fellow religious, did the work, and André went about raising the money. His Superior's words to him had been: "Go and tell St. Joseph that there will be a chapel *only* if you can find the money."

When God wants something done...it gets done! The laity got involved, giving him their backing financially, physically and more importantly, affirmatively; encouraging him every step of the way. Things were going slowly. Brother needed more help. Saint Joseph came to his little one's aid. One day a stone mason suffering from a malignant tumor in his stomach, came to Brother André. He told him he was unable to eat; he was wasting away, more and more with each passing day. Would brother pray for him? Brother, like Abraham and the other prophets, bargained with him: *"If Saint Joseph heals you, will you come and work with me on the mountain?"* The mason agreed, not taking too much stock in brother's proposal. He would have rather had an anointing with the holy oil, but he felt he had nothing to lose. The next morning the mason arrived at André's room and marveled at the fact that he could eat a hearty breakfast. He was cured! He began working on the mountain that very day; it was the first full day he had put in for months. He told everyone he met about his miraculous healing through the intercession of St. Joseph; and more came to help, because of his testimony.

Do not, for one minute, think it was an easy undertaking. Land had to be cleared and leveled, a gazebo torn down, ground excavated, huge stones carried away and trees cut down. Finally, with sweat and tears, a road was open to where the chapel would be. There were those times when, at the end of the week, André had to say to his employees: *"I have no more money, and I do not have permission to go into debt. I am afraid we will have to stop."* But, the Lord heard, and He would provide for this chapel, being built in honor of His earthly father. [Sometimes, we marvel at how different Jesus looks, as He comes to our ministry's aid, at the last moment!] And so, our eleventh hour God, through some benevolent benefactors, provided additional financial backing, and the men were there Monday morning, bright and early, working away.

The chapel was ready by the middle of October. It was so small, it had barely enough room for an Altar, a priest and two altar boys. To accommodate the Faithful who wanted to attend Mass at the little chapel, they placed two rows of benches on the grass; and then opened the double doors, so that they could face the Altar.

The sick continue to come to the college

The ill continued to come to the door of the college. They were told that Brother André could not see them there; they would have to go to the trolley station across the street. They went obediently. But, then because of the crowds of sick people who were now congregating at the trolley station, the passengers began to protest. They filed a complaint with the Montreal Board of Public Health. A doctor came to assess the situation. After speaking to Brother André, the doctor submitted a favorable report, and the Board granted Brother André permission to continue using the station.

The chapel was too small, and it could not accommodate the many who wanted to attend Mass there, especially in the cold Canadian winter. It didn't begin to accomplish what everyone was hoping it would. The people ignored the chapel and came back to the door for Brother André. His backers determined that an extension to the chapel needed to be built. On June 5, 1908, they had a meeting to which they invited the Superior of the Brothers of Holy Cross. The men told him they would finance the entire project; and he agreed to the extension. One month later, it was completed. What the laity can do, when they get started! Six hundred people attended the opening of the new extension, and all found shelter from the hot summer sun.

Winter came; the cold winds cut through the new shelter, chilling the pilgrims who came there to pray. The committee of lay people had another meeting. They then handed a petition to the Superior, signed by two thousand people, proposing the chapel be enlarged and heated in the winter. The people assured him they would be responsible for the financing. The Superior agreed and work began the very next week. *It was completed in two months!* They now had a proper oratory, not the great oratory which would one day grace the hill across the street from the college. But they had a good chapel. Brother André was happy. He felt that St. Joseph was being honored, and the sick people had a place to come for healing, which would take the pressure off the door of the college, and subsequently, take the pressure off him.

More and more pilgrims came to the oratory to such a degree, they needed to have someone take Brother André's place as doorkeeper several times a week. The number continued to grow to such proportions, they had to eventually replace Brother as doorkeeper of Notre Dame College altogether. He was by this time sixty years old. He had served faithfully as doorkeeper and Saint Joseph now had another job for him. His Superior assigned him the full time position of *"Guardian of the Oratory"* and Brother moved his cell to the Chapel area.

Brother André had mixed emotions about leaving his position after forty years. Who would wash and polish the floors? Who would take care of the brothers the way he did? Who would cut their hair? The door of the college was such a part of his life, it was difficult for him to envision not being there anymore. But he was given an order; he had to be obedient. He could not covet his position as doorkeeper, no matter how he loved it, or felt it had been given to him by God. The Lord gives; the Lord takes away. Brother André moved all his possessions, very little in the eyes of the world, but to Brother André they were his very life. He moved across the street and up the hill to his new home. It was as if he were moving to another country. But St. Joseph had to be respected and venerated in the new oratory, and Brother André had been chosen to do the job.

Within one year the oratory grew to include a religious book and gift shop, a restaurant, an office for Brother André, a waiting room for the sick and a long wood staircase which connected the Shrine with the street.

At last, *after thirty-five years*, the Superiors of Notre Dame College could rest easy; the sick followed their Saint to the mountain. Whereas the oratory was originally constructed to alleviate the overcrowding from the many sick who came to the door of the college seeking help, now it had a life and a purpose of its own. The Superiors thought that they had consented to have the oratory built as a remedy to a problem; the laity were convinced it was for the poor and the sick, so that they could come from all parts of Canada and upper United States for healing. But the Lord had His own plan, and it surpassed anything that could be imagined by man. The number of needy would grow and come from all parts of the *world*, especially North America, petitioning St. Joseph; he would answer their prayers through the Miracle Worker of Montreal. As Saint Teresa of Avila said, *"Saint Joseph will never let you down."*

Brother André, man of prayer

The throngs of pilgrims came, and Brother André devoted every waking moment to serving them. He led the pilgrims along the Way of the Cross. They went to confession to the many priests who came and made themselves available to the oratory. Having received the wonderful Sacrament of Reconciliation, they then attended Mass.

Brother André was a man of prayer. He prayed long hours, several times a day, sometimes alone, at other times in the chapel, while traveling, with the sick and in a packed church. [It reminds us of Mother Angelica; she and her Nuns pray and God does the miraculous!] Brother André prayed and miracles happened! Sometimes people would only have to mention the name of St. Joseph and healings would take place. On other occasions Brother André would just *be* in a room where there were sick people, and they would be healed. He might hand out medals of St. Joseph, or St. Joseph's oil taken from the lamp at the chapel of St. Joseph and have people pray together. Healings took place. In 1916, there were 435 cures; this did not include those never reported. He quickly and adamantly corrected anyone who asked *him* to heal them, or who credited *him* with having brought about miracles, always pointing to Jesus, Mary and Joseph. He would scoff, *"As if human power can heal!"*

It was important to André that the crutches and other evidence of healings be displayed for all the visitors to see and upon seeing, have faith. When the Provincial of his Order saw the many crutches, he ordered him to take them down. Brother obeyed!

As God would have it, the Provincial became ill and was in the same infirmary as Brother André. Now, he would have an opportunity to talk to *him!* He began, *"You have always taught us that Miracles are signs given by God."* He went on, saying *"crutches are signs by God that miracles have taken place, through the healings that have come about at the Oratory."* He continued, telling the Provincial that God has given these *signs* to His children to show that He cares so much, He will bring about miracles to heal them. Just as miracles are signs given by God, so are the crutches. And if God has granted these signs, who would dare take it upon himself to hide them? Besides, they were the outer signs of His foster-father's love and concern for us. *"Jesus spoke, using signs that the people could relate to,"* André insisted. These are the signs that the faithful of today understand. Needless to say, the crutches were replaced, lining the walls, with new ones added each year.

Saint Joseph sends a priest

The sick came; they were cured. There was need of the Sacraments so that no one would take his or her eyes off the One and Only True Healer. Yes, Brother André *did pray*, and Saint Joseph *did intercede* and does till today; but the Healer was, and always will be, the One Who walked the earth and healed, Our Lord Jesus Christ. The people needed a priest!

It was 1910; a professor, Father Adolphe Clement came to the oratory. The young priest was sent by his Superior to help Brother André. Brother was overjoyed to be working with him. He was so excited! He explained how people came with more involved ills than he could handle; their needs were more often *Spiritual* than physical; they needed forgiveness. Remember, Jesus first said: *"Your sins are forgiven you,"* before He healed them physically. Suddenly Brother André's face changed from happiness to consternation. The priest explained that he was happy for the privilege of helping Brother André, but it was only fair to tell him it would be for a short time, as he was going blind. He went on to say, he had to cease teaching because of this crippling ailment. Father Clemente insisted he had not come for a cure, but only to serve as long as he could. Brother André must have looked at him in the same way that Jesus had looked upon the rich young man, with so much love. He turned to him and said, *"Leave it up to Saint Joseph. He is the one who sent you here, and you can be certain he will not desert you. He will help you to help others."*

Had the priest expected Brother André to say, as he had so many times, *"Open your eyes and see! You are no longer going blind?"* Is that why he looked so downcast? Brother André gently said, *"Wait till morning."* If the priest heard him, he did not believe that was enough. Was he like the man in the Old Testament who refused to go into the Jordan River, not accepting that God could heal in any way He saw fit, from the grandest Miracle to using something as simple as a body of water? Did he, too, not understand? He staggered out, his head mournfully bent.

The next morning, the priest whom Brother encountered, was filled with the joy of the beggar (only one of the ten who had been healed) who had returned to thank Jesus. *He could see clearly!* It was obvious to him, as he had read his Breviary for the first time in months, that he had been healed. Brother said, *"I told you Saint Joseph was the one who called you here. It was he who gave you your sight back, because you are so sorely needed here."* The Heart of the Church, the Eucharist, came into the oratory through this priest, and many others would follow to come and feed the hungry, the lost, and the hurting with the Sacraments of forgiveness through the Sacrament of Penance, the Bread of Life-the Sacrament of the Eucharist, and healing through the Sacrament of the Sick. *The Oratory was complete!*

The Power of the Intercession of St. Joseph

Healings became like the mustard seed of Holy Scripture. What started with a few healings, grew to monumental proportions, and with it, curiosity. A priest who lived with Brother for nine years, asked him one day, "How do you know that someone is going to be healed? You do not say the same thing to everyone, and yet they are healed. You will say to one, 'Make a novena to Saint Joseph;' to another 'Rub yourself with this oil from the lamp which burns in front of the statue of Saint Joseph, and pray believing that Jesus will heal you.' Then to some, 'Get up and walk!' and they walk. How do you know they will walk?"

To all this, Brother André humbly said, *"It's obvious."* And yet, if we just pause a moment and listen with our hearts, we will hear behind those simple words, the makings of a Saint, humility. It would have been so easy to say what really appeared obvious, that *he was receiving this wisdom and knowledge from the Lord.* But, fearing that the enemy of *Pride* would find an open door and sneak in, the Saints only spoke of the Lord's gifts to them, under the vow of obedience. What he did not explain or try to humanize was the way he knew those who would be healed. Thousands of witnesses spoke of how miracles happened in front of their eyes through the intercession of Brother André. But if he were alive, he would argue with them that it was strictly through the intercession of Saint Joseph, and he had nothing to do with it. Whether he chose to acknowledge it or not, he was a powerful instrument whom the Lord gave the gift of knowledge and that of healing.

Only in man's tiny brain do we categorize everything in small, medium and large. In God's Vision there are no small miracles; for what miracle is not grand! There are so many miracles that occurred through Brother André. But some that seem to stand out are the following:

One is the healing of an Irishman from Quebec. His name was Murtin Hammon. One day, as he was unloading heavy marble blocks, Murtin looked away for a brief moment when one of them fell on top of his legs, crushing them, shattering them into pieces. That happened in October, 1908. He suffered through one unsuccessful surgery after the other, and after failed treatments and lost hopes, Mr. Hammon was no better. He could not walk without crutches, and that was with the most horrendous pain and difficulty. Then he heard of Brother André and the Oratory. This miracle has been carefully documented by an early biographer of Brother André.

On January 10th of 1910, Murtin Hammon left his village, taking the train to the oratory, accompanied by a friend who helped him to go up to Brother André's office. He did not have to wait long. Brother touched his legs; they were made whole and were completely healed. He left his crutches at the oratory to show that God was still bringing about miracles, and it was happening on this holy mountain. The account of the miracle appeared in all the newspapers. The patient testified. All his doctors as well as the Chief Surgeon at the Hotel Dieu, the hospital in Quebec where he was operated on, signed a document attesting to the irreversible damage done to Hammon's legs. They all agreed on the condition of his legs prior to his visiting the oratory as well as his family and his fellow workers on the railroad where he worked, all swearing, under oath, how badly crippled he was before visiting Mount Royal. You can imagine the crowds braving the fierce Canadian winter of February to come and receive some of the bountiful miracles that the Lord was bringing about through Jesus' foster-father, Saint Joseph, and a little brother with a great gift. That year, the Oratory welcomed between four and five hundred pilgrims a day. Again the chapel became too small.

As with the other Saints and Mystics, Brother André offered freely to everyone, friend and foe, what so freely had been given to him. Recognizing them strictly as gifts from God, they were not his to possess or withhold. There was a certain doctor in Montreal, Charette by name, who was quite outspoken in his public criticism of Brother André, alluding to him as being a quack and a faith-healer. The doctor went so far as to accuse Brother André of misconduct, breaking his vow of chastity when he touched the women. Now, it just came to pass that Dr. Joseph Charette's wife became quite ill. Her nose began to hemorrhage, and there was nothing her husband or any of the other doctors could do to stop the bleeding. *"Bring Brother André,"* she pleaded. The doctor protested, *"I love you very much but what you ask of me is just too much."* But, like the persistent woman in the Gospel, she insisted: *"Get me Brother André. You say that you love me. Do you want your wife whom you say you love, to bleed to death?"*

We can just see the doctor going off to call Brother André, hoping against hope that no one would see him bring that *"fake"* to his home. His love was more for his wife than for himself, and God can always work through that kind of reluctant future saint. When you think about it, it took quite a great deal of love for this doctor to go for help to someone he had maligned so brutally, doing everything in his power to discredit him. When Brother André saw the doctor approaching the Shrine, he went to him, smiling: *"Go home, doctor, your wife is healed; her nosebleed has stopped."*

The jury is still out on whether the doctor was happiest because his wife was healed or because he did not lose face in front of his neighbors and patients, by letting the word out that he had appealed to Brother André for help. Oftentimes, to our shame, human respect takes precedence over Divine respect, and we get drowned in what people think of us. Our God Who is faithful then takes second place to his unfaithful creatures.

The dream to build a Shrine befitting Saint Joseph

They came; they prayed; they left changed. But Brother André knew his work was not over. And so, although now past sixty, he forged ahead with his dream to build a towering, magnificent Shrine, paying homage and loving respect to the man who cared for Jesus most of His life on earth.

For almost thirty years of his final days on earth, Brother André worked, begged and prayed toward the fulfillment of that dream. He never used words like visions and apparitions or inner locutions. But as you read about his life, and between the lines, you can still see the Hand of God and that of His Mother Mary and foster father Saint Joseph, infusing him with this dream, and giving him the many gifts which would attract the Faithful to help to bring about this dream. For, as a holy priest once said, *"It has always been the laity who have fostered devotions."*

The work on the gigantic, magnificent Shrine went at a snail's pace, the Superiors of the Community insisting it be a pay-as-you-go project, no debts! But André never lost hope! He just kept walking toward that goal, although he knew he would never see it. His eyes and heart already set on saluting it from afar, he would often say, *"I will not see the completion of the Oratory, but the work will be done. It is not my project, anyway. It's Saint Joseph's."* And at that moment, if you looked in his eyes, they would appear to be *twinkling*, almost playfully. But looking closer, you could not fail to see that peace, that calm assurance, shining with anticipation of things to come, that only doing the Will of God can produce. He prayed that row upon row of stones would mount until they reached the top, and the glorious tribute to St. Joseph would be completed.

He never became discouraged. Neither did the Faithful who continued to come from the nearest and the farthest regions of Canada and the United States. As man was destroying the fine monuments to the Glory of God, God's houses, our churches, in Canada a man of faith walked toward *a dream*, not looking behind him or to what was before him. He, like Jesus, lived the moment. The walls finally rose thirty feet above Mount Royal, towering over the countryside, visible from thirty miles around, a message of hope to a world gone mad. However, the roof was still not completed.

In 1931, man was too busy getting over wholesale decadence of the flapper days of the twenties, and heading toward the worldwide depression of the thirties, as well as the prospects of total annihilation at the hands of the Nazis in Europe to complete a Shrine to Saint Joseph. They were counting on human resources for their answers, and as always they would be betrayed, and God would bring them back to Himself. The Shrine, without a roof, stood like a giant open crater, not a fitting home for the Lord or for His foster-father Joseph. Although now in his eighties, and suffering from the same ulcerated pains in his stomach he had known all his life, Brother André went begging for money. Because of the Great Depression, there was little money other than for survival. But that did not stop Brother André from traveling to the United States and to every hamlet of Canada.

But, sadly, there was just no money; years later, in 1936, the Provincial called a meeting to decide whether to keep on going or to abandon the project, as hopeless. Incredulous that they should, for one moment consider stopping the project, this man of faith once again, insisted; *"It's not my work; it's Saint Joseph's!"*

Place a statue in the middle of the Oratory

A very tired Brother André spoke to the Council: *"Put a statue of Saint Joseph in the middle of the building. If he wants a roof over his head, he'll get it."* That very afternoon his brothers, wanting to see their beloved brother's dream fulfilled, solemnly processed the Statue of Saint Joseph up the mountain. Brother André tried to follow, but his age was catching up to

---

[7]artistic renditions of incidents where there have been prayers answered miraculously (usually through the heavenly intercession of some Saint or Blessed after they are dead).

him, and he was too exhausted to make this last act of faith. But his Saint Joseph heard him and observed the Community scaling the mountain, believing a miracle would come to pass. And he honored that faith! The brothers, seeing the magnitude that the dream had reached, voted to take out a loan to complete the project.

Brother André, now ninety years old, persisted till his Superior gave him permission to make one last fund-raising trip to the United States. All the signs of many years of suffering and illness seemed to fade, and it was the old enthusiastic vibrant André who greeted the Community after he returned from a successful trip. After all the brothers had retired to their cells, Brother André climbed to the mountain and entered the crypt. He placed, as ex-votos,[7] the crutches and other instruments formerly used by the invalids whom he had healed during his *last* trip.

Brother André predicts his own death

Brother André started to slow down. Oh, he kept up his arduous schedule tending the sick, the suffering, all the poor souls that came to him seeking a miracle. But his health was slipping quickly, as if someone was draining the vehicle that was his body of all fuel. But, the brothers were still hopeful that he would see his dream completed before he went to the Father.

André prophesied his death. As he was reluctantly posing[8] for the bust his Superior had ordered made of him, Brother André told the sculptor, *"I will not see the completion of the Oratory. I am going Home; my work is done here."* A few days before Christmas one of the brothers told him, *"The people were right. You will be alive to see the Oratory finished."* To which Brother André replied, *"I said I would never see it realized."*

He knelt all during Midnight Mass in his stall behind the Altar, his head in his hands, lost in adoration. He was so tired,

---

[8]under obedience to his Superior

he had to leave the crypt before the third Mass was over. He was smiling as he was helped to his cell. Was he dreaming of the Christmases that would follow? He told the priest accompanying him, *"I have done all that I had to do; the work has no need of me, now."* He told everyone that this Christmas was his last; and when they insisted he had so much more to do, he replied: *"If one does good on earth, how much more can he do in Heaven!"*

On the evening of the day after Christmas, André began to suffer excruciating gastric pains. On New Year's eve he was rushed to the hospital in Saint Laurent. As the orderlies placed him on a stretcher, and wrapped him snugly in a blanket, Brother joked with them: *"I look like a man going to the North Pole."*

He told his nurse: *"The Great Almighty is coming."* She asked, "Why do you not ask Saint Joseph to heal you?" And he, whom the Lord had used to heal so many, simply replied, *"I can do nothing for myself."* To the very end he was his cheerful, loving self, playfully begging the nurses' forgiveness when he had to summon them. *"It is your old nuisance ringing again."* he told them. For three days he suffered on a bed of thorns, every inch of him wracked in pain like his Savior before him.

His thoughts were on the completion of the Oratory to the very end. It was January 4, 1937, eleven o'clock at night. He was dying; he was approaching the final corridor, and he would be Home soon with that Heavenly Family he had spent his life on earth, knowing and sharing. He kept on speaking of St. Joseph and all the miracles that had come about through his intercession.

As he entered the last stages of his life, Brother André cried out, *"O Mary, my sweet Mother, Mother of my sweet Savior, be merciful to me and assist me."* Then he called out, almost inaudibly, to his lifetime friend and partner, St. Joseph. Were they there? Had he seen them waiting to bring him Home? For three hours before he lapsed into a coma, he kept repeating with complete resignation: *"My God, how greatly I am suffering."*

We're not sure if Brother André or St. Joseph or the entire Heavenly Family decided that he would wait until fifty minutes

Bob and Penny Lord praying at the Tomb of Bl. Brother André

into the 6th of January, 1937, to go to the Father, so that André could pass on to *eternal life* on the Feast of the Epiphany, one in which his good friend, St. Joseph was involved. There was much weeping at the bedside of the little doorkeeper.

However, the picture must have looked quite different on the other side of the curtain, in Heaven. We can just see St. Joseph ushering the little brother up to the gates of Heaven to meet another doorkeeper, St. Peter. How did Brother André feel when St. Joseph brought him to meet in person, his wife Mary, and his Foster Son, Jesus, the Son of God? It had to be a glorious day in Heaven.

The Church most likely agreed with the people of Montreal that Brother André was a Saint during his lifetime. But the process for the Beatification of Brother André took its time, and on May 23, 1982, Pope John Paul II entered his name into the company of the Blessed who had gone before him. We believe the little doorkeeper of St. Joseph's Oratory in Montreal, Canada, was certainly watching over the procedures, smiling, his arm around his best friend, St. Joseph. Take an example from Blessed André. Make friends with St. Joseph.

Blessed Sister Faustina

God's Messenger of Divine Mercy

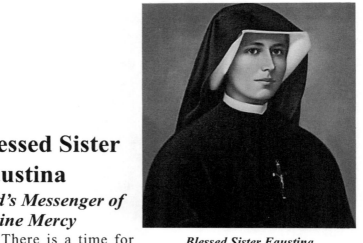

Blessed Sister Faustina

There is a time for Mercy and a time for Justice. Expelling Adam and Eve from the Garden of Eden was an act of God's Justice. But even then, as the Angel was blocking the way to the Tree of Life in the Garden of Eden,[1] and ushering our first parents out into the cold world, God was showing His Mercy to us through His promise of the Messiah, the Redeemer. God has always lived up to His Word. Throughout Salvation history, we have been beneficiaries of God's Mercy. And very few times has He let loose His Justice. Sodom and Gomorrah was God's Justice. Noah and the Ark was God's Justice, but also mingled with God's Mercy. The miracle of Moses and the Jews crossing the Red Sea was God's Mercy, coupled with God's Justice on the Pharaoh's charioteers. When finally we are in the last days, with possibly the end of the world at hand, and we are about to face the Last Judgment, at that time the God of Mercy will give way to the God of Justice.

God has continued to give us the benefit of His Mercy down

---

[1]Genesis 3:24 - "And when He expelled the man, He settled him east of the Garden of Eden; and He stationed the Cherubim and the fiery revolving sword, to guard the way to the Tree of Life."

through the centuries. A powerful messenger of God's Mercy, which parallels Blessed Sr. Faustina and devotion to Divine Mercy, is St. Margaret Mary Alacoque and the promises of the Sacred Heart Devotion.[2] Through her, God manifested and made known His Mercy through His Sacred Heart in the seventeenth century. We come to the Twentieth Century, the Dawn of the last century of the Second Millennium, and we find that God has sent us Prophets and Visionaries once more, to warn His children. There have been many prophecies, including one by St. Don Bosco, that lend credibility to the strong belief that the Second Coming will occur at the end of this last decade of the Twentieth Century. The world is behaving with the same insane euphoria as it did at the time of the fall of Greece and Rome. Decadence, promiscuity, concupiscence, and apostasy are rampant. If we were ever in need of God's Mercy, it is now. And so, Our Lord answers our prayers, before we even know we need His aid.

Early in the twentieth century, the Lord gave us a simple servant, Helen Kowalska, born in the small village of Glogowiec, Poland, on August 25, 1905, the day before the National Feast of Our Lady of Czestochowa. Poland is much like Mexico, 95% Catholic, but *98% Czestochowan.* They have always had a great devotion to Our Lady under that title. She has saved them from utter destruction, many times in the history of this troubled country.

Poland has been dominated throughout the centuries to a great extent by her next door neighbors, Germany and Russia. From time to time, each would take turns invading and pillaging Poland. The period of time when Helen Kowalska grew up in the little village of what is today central Poland, was a turbulent time in the stormy history of the country. Just prior to Helen's birth, Poland had been chopped up by its neighbors. In 1918, when Helen was only 13, a new Republic was created which gave the country just a fraction of its former land, small enough to

---

[2]Read more about Saint Margaret Mary and the Sacred Heart devotion in the chapter on her in this book.

Above: *The birthplace of Blessed Sister Faustina in Glogowiec, Poland*

Above: *Bob & Penny at the Baptismal font of Bl. Sister Faustina in Glogowiec*

Above: *Statue of Divine Mercy Image at the Convent in Plock*

Above:
The Convent in Vilnius, Lithuania

Left:
Eucharistic Adoration in the Chapel inside the Convent at Plock

guarantee, it would never be a threat to either Russia or Germany. But even that only lasted twenty one years, when Nazi Germany invaded Poland, and Russia (then part of the Soviet Union) then followed by occupying her until 1989.

We believe this period, this thirty three years in the life of Helen Kowalska, later to be known by the whole world as Sr. Faustina and now *Blessed* Sr. Faustina, was to give us strength, courage and trust in God's Mercy which we would need desperately in this last century of the Second Millennium. But on an immediate scale, it was to prepare the people of Poland for the hell this dear country would have to endure for the next fifty one years following the death of Sr. Faustina. Our Lord knew what strength the people would need, and He began giving it to them through His apparitions and messages to Sr. Faustina.

Sr. Faustina's early days

As with many families of that time, Helen's father was a stern man, a disciplinarian, who maintained a strong grip on his family. He was also, however, a very spiritual man who prayed diligently. In her diary, Sister Faustina writes how impressed she was with the way her father prayed. But for the most part, the children received their religious training from their mother. Marianne Kowalska was a very loving, pious woman, who insisted she give her children a strong foundation of the Faith so that they, too, would be able to pass this on to *their* children. Daily prayer, the Rosary, observance of Lenten and Advent fasts and abstinence were all part of Helen's upbringing. Although they never had money, the parents gave high priority to trying whenever possible to save a little to buy books on the Saints. Helen loved to hear stories of the monks and hermits. She used to share these stories with the children with whom she played.

Helen felt the strong presence of the Lord Jesus in her heart, from an early age. She tells us in her diary that when she was seven years old, she felt a call to the Religious life.

"From the age of seven, I experienced the definite call of God, the grace of a vocation to the religious life. It was in

Visionaries, Mystics and Stigmatists

*the seventh year of my life that, for the first time, I heard
God's voice in my soul; that is, an invitation to a more
perfect life."*

Helen's strongest fusion with Jesus came during
Communion, or in front of the Blessed Sacrament. Receiving
Jesus in the Eucharist was a high point of her life.

*"When I was present at Vespers and the Lord Jesus was
exposed in the Monstrance, it was then that for the first
time God's love was imparted to me and filled my little
heart."*

At another point, she wrote in her diary,

*"The most solemn moment of my life is the moment when
I receive Holy Communion. And for every Holy
Communion, I give thanks to the Most Holy Trinity.*

*"If the Angels were capable of envy, they would envy us
for two things: one is the receiving of Holy Communion,
and the other is for suffering."*

And yet as a child, Helen was willing to sacrifice this most
special gift - going to Mass, so that her Sisters could use the one
Sunday outfit available to go to Mass. At these times, she received
Spiritual Communion. She would hide in a corner, and just pray.
She closed herself off from the whole world and spiritually joined
them at Mass. Even her dear mother, who might call her to perform
one task or another, would have to wait until the Mass in the church
was over, because Helen became so lost, communicating with the
Lord.

Helen's formal education was very short. This created some
problem in the translation and use of her diary as a source of
information about her life and the Mission of Divine Mercy. *It
was written by a person with less than two years education.*
Sentences were not properly structured; grammar was incorrect;
meanings were not clear. There would come a time when the
enemy would cause this lack of education to be a major stumbling
block, the major grounds for having the devotions to the Divine
Mercy of God suspended by the Vatican for twenty years.

Does this not reminds us of the story of Gideon in the Old Testament? The Lord made Gideon send home most of his soldiers because He wanted all the world, especially Gideon and his people, to know that *He* was delivering them from the hands of their enemies, and not the power of Gideon or the soldiers.[3] The same occurred with Faustina. The Lord was probably saying to us, *Don't get the idea that anyone but Me gave this devotion to Faustina, and that anyone but Me will have it accepted in the Church.*

Helen's whole life was centered around visions and inner locutions. She talks about them in her diary extensively. She believed that every one of her visions had a special meaning for her. When she went to Lodz, it was to help her family. She became a domestic and housekeeper at the home of a woman who owned a bakery. She was only fourteen. The family needed her income to help support them. One day, Helen had a vision in broad daylight. Actually what she experienced was a brightness more radiant than the sun. She knew it was the Lord speaking to her heart. She returned home and asked her mother and father to allow her to enter a convent.

Now, we know that her parents were indeed pious people. They believed in vocations but would not even *consider* allowing Helen to enter a convent. It was an open and shut case. Years later her mother Marianne confessed they were reluctant to give up their most beloved child. However, they did feel a certain guilt about suppressing Helen in her desire to follow a vocation. Being an obedient daughter, she went back to Lodz and continued to work as a domestic. As part of her job, she worked for a group of women who were Third Order Franciscans. She regained the courage to ask her parents again; and again, she was refused.

Helen decided to go with the program. If she were not to be a religious, she might as well adapt to the secular world. She went to a dance with her friends at a park in Lodz. By this time, she was eighteen years old.

---

[3] Read Judges 7

"While everybody was having a good time, my soul was experiencing deep torments. As I began to dance, I suddenly saw Jesus at my side, Jesus racked with pain, stripped of His clothing, all covered with wounds, who spoke these words to me: `**How long shall I put up with you and how long will you keep putting me off?**"*

Helen, completely shaken by this, left the party in tears. She immediately ran to the Cathedral of St. Stanislaus and prostrated herself on the floor near the main altar. She prayed for what seemed like forever. She heard in the depths of her heart, **"Go to Warsaw; you will enter a convent there.***"* The die was cast. Helen could not ignore what the Lord was saying to her. She had put Him off long enough. She couldn't do it any more. It was time. She left the same day for Warsaw.

This reminds us of St. Joseph who was sleeping in the cave in Bethlehem when, after the Baby Jesus was born, the Angel Gabriel came to him and said, *"Rise, take the Child and His Mother; flee to Egypt."* Talk about obedience. But this situation was even more ominous. Helen had never been to a big city. Lodz was the biggest city she'd ever been to. It was big, but not like Warsaw. We've been to both cities. It had to be a frightening experience. At least in Lodz she had Sisters, an aunt and uncle. She didn't know anyone in Warsaw. It had to be at least 130 kilometers from Lodz. But she said yes to the Lord, and she went. Helen only brought one dress with her and whatever little things she owned, which was not much.

When she got off the train in Warsaw, her reaction was natural. She panicked! Everyone was heading in different directions. They knew where they were going. She had no direction to take. She was quite alone, except for her Holy Family. She prayed to Our Lady, *Lead me in a direction, please.* She was given the message to go to a nearby village where she would find safe lodging for the night. It was as if Our Lady was saying to her, *You made the big hurdle today. We'll take care of the little one tomorrow.* She did as Our Lady had instructed her, and behold, everything was as it should be.

"Immediately, I heard these words within me telling me to leave the town (Warsaw) and go to a certain nearby village where I would find a safe lodging for the night. I did so and found in fact that everything was just as the Mother of God told me."

The next morning Helen headed into Warsaw again. She had a little more confidence, knowing she was under the mantle of Mary. She was given a thought when she got off the train: *Go to the nearest church* (which was St. James Church). She stayed in the church during many Masses, until she felt she was being told to speak to a particular priest, the pastor of the church. She went into the sacristy and spoke to him, explaining all that had happened. He sent her to a woman parishioner who invited her to stay with her while Helen searched for the convent which was right for her.

That turned out to be more of an undertaking than she thought it would be. No matter where she turned, the doors were closed. Lack of dowry was a major factor. In addition, her limited education was a stumbling block as well. She knew the Lord had sent her in this direction. She couldn't understand why she was having such a difficult time. She begged Jesus, *"Help me; don't leave me alone."* She may have been discouraged, but she had a lot of spunk. She just kept going from convent to convent. The Lord had told her to do this, and she knew He would not let her down. But there were times when she found herself becoming discouraged in her quest.

The Lord answered her prayer in *His* timetable. That's really something we all have to learn. Prayers are always answered. They are not necessarily answered according to our schedule, but they are answered. The response is not always what we want to hear, but the powerful teaching is that the Lord is always with us, always listening, always watching out for us. And when the time is right, and the request is right, He answers.

Helen walked to the door of the Mother House of the Congregation of the Sisters of Our Lady of Mercy on Zytnia Street in Warsaw. She was interviewed by Mother Michaela, the Mother General of the Community. We believe, it was the Lord who touched the heart of the Mother General. Helen had not said anything differently to her than she had to any of the other Communities. But at the end of a relatively brief interview, Mother asked her to speak to the *Master of the House*, and ask *Him* if this was the Community for her. Helen knew this was it. She was told to speak to the Lord. Well, He was the one who sent her on this quest in the first place. She went into the chapel, and heard in her heart, **"I do accept; you are in My heart."** Helen returned to the Mother general and told her what she had heard. Mother told her, "If the Lord has accepted, so do I accept." Helen was home.

[We went to the Mother House of the *Congregation of Sisters of Our Lady of Mercy* for the first time in May 1993, to videotape the life of Sr. Faustina. While the building looks the way it did when Helen Kowalska entered in July, 1924, it is not the original. The entire building, indeed 85% of Warsaw was burned to the ground at the end of World War II, as part of Hitler's *"scorched earth"* policy. Most of the city was rebuilt according to old photos or paintings, or architectural plans. The Congregation of the Sisters of Our Lady of Mercy was rebuilt. But there is a step there, at the very entrance of the General House, which was there when Blessed Sr. Faustina set foot on it. It's the only thing in that building which is left from the time of Sr. Faustina.]

While Helen was accepted, she still had to go back to the world for one year. She had to save money for a dowry, at least enough to cover her clothing expenses. The Congregation was and still is a poor Community. There is always more going out than coming in, and so it was in 1924. But there was more to it than just that. Mother Michaela, a wise Superior, wanted Helen to reach harder for the goal, to work for it, and also to be sure of her vocation, as sure as any of us can be when we are on the threshold of entering a Religious Community. Sometimes we paint our own pictures or write our own scripts of how we believe it's going to be. We fantasize, according to our own desires and agenda. Helen was no different.

When her year of waiting was over, on August 1, 1925, she eagerly entered the Congregation. The dream that she had been so desirous of seeing fulfilled had finally come about, after myriads of rejections, and would you believe it, within a few weeks she wanted to leave! She was walking through the halls, actually looking for Mother Michaela to tell her that she was going to leave. However she couldn't find her; so she went into the chapel hoping to receive a message from Jesus, but nothing was forthcoming. Helen stayed there for a long time, long after all the others had gone to bed.

She quietly went into her cell and threw herself on the floor in prayer. She wanted desperately to know God's Will. Suddenly the room became so bright, it was like daylight. She saw the sorrowful Face of Jesus on the curtain[4] of her cell.

"There were open wounds on His Face, and large tears were falling on my bedspread. Not knowing what all this meant, I asked Jesus, 'Jesus, who has hurt you so?'"

Our Lord spoke to Helen: **"'It is you who will cause Me this pain if you leave this convent. It is to this place that I called you and nowhere else; and I have prepared many graces for you.'"**

She took this as a definite sign that the Lord wanted her to be in this place. While there was no way for her to know all that Jesus had in store for her, in hindsight we can see the whole perspective of what was to come through this servant. But the Lord insisted on her cooperation, her *Yes!* The following morning, she confessed all to her confessor who affirmed the Lord wanted her to remain with this Congregation.

Shortly after this, Helen was sent to a vacation house of the Community in a suburb of Warsaw called Skolimow. She was worn out. Apparently the rigor of religious life, while it could not

---

[4]They didn't have private rooms, or walls or partitions between cells. The living quarters of each nun was separated by curtains.

have been as physically strenuous as her life as a domestic, did take its toll on her. She was not very strong during her years with the *Sisters of Our Lady of Mercy.* At any rate, it was in this house that Helen was given a vision of Purgatory. She shared it in her diary:

> *"It was at this time that I asked the Lord who else I should pray for. Jesus said that on the following night He would let me know for whom I should pray.*
>
> *"(The next night) I saw my Guardian Angel, who ordered me to follow him. In a moment I was in a misty place full of fire in which there was a great crowd of suffering souls. They were praying fervently for themselves, but to no avail; only we can come to their aid. The flames which were burning them did not touch me at all. My Guardian Angel did not leave me for an instant. I asked these souls what their greatest suffering was. They answered me that their greatest torment was longing for God. I saw Our Lady visiting the souls in Purgatory. The souls call her `The Star of the Sea.' She brings them refreshment. I wanted to talk with them some more, but my Guardian Angel beckoned me to leave. We went out of that prison of suffering. I heard an interior voice which said, `My Mercy does not want this, but Justice demands it.'"*

We don't know if the nineteen-year-old Helen understood at that moment what the Lord was saying to her, or if she realized He was preparing her for her great mission, bringing the Message of Divine Mercy to the world. But she was beginning her journey and the Lord would do the rest.

At the beginning of 1926, Helen was sent to the novitiate in Krakow to finish her postulancy. It was a good place for her. She recalled with fond memories her time there. In April, she was given her habit and her religious name, which was to become famous the world over, Sr. Mary Faustina. From here on in, she will be called Sr. Faustina. After two years, she made her first profession of vows of Chastity, Poverty and Obedience. These were to be renewed every five years. In 1933, she would make her final profession, and would come back to Krakow to make that profession.

We mentioned that Sr. Faustina was not an overly educated girl. She had few skills, mostly in domestic and kitchen work. But these were put to good use in her vocation as a nun. She worked her whole life taking care of the door, gardening, cleaning and working in the kitchen. She never let on her mystical experiences, or her visions of Jesus. She was very quiet, and unassuming. She did not make herself well-known in the Community, but stayed very much to herself, immersed in her relationship with Jesus. But she was being molded all the time. Actually, the Lord had such a mammoth plan for Sr. Faustina that she could not have handled a really important job in the convent. She would not have had time for it. She was graced throughout her life with *visions, revelations, the hidden stigmata, mystical engagement and marriage to Jesus.*

The next few years were ones of training by the Lord. Looking back, we can see what His plan was. But it definitely not likely, Sr. Faustina had a clue what He was trying to accomplish through her. She only said *Yes!* One thing she may have been able to realize was, what He wanted was **obedience.** As you go through this book, you will find that this is one underlying trait which the Lord asked of all the Visionaries, Mystics and Stigmatists, and for that matter - all the Saints. Sister Faustina could accept that, but she probably did not know why the Lord was developing her in this way. She really didn't care, though. She had a strong, personal relationship with the Lord, and she could put up with anything, as long as that was not jeopardized.

The Dark Night of the Soul

Sr. Faustina suffered throughout most of her novitiate period. She had constant interior struggles. She was completely dry. She couldn't meditate. She could not feel the presence of God within her. She endured great torments and temptations even in the chapel. She writes,

"More than once, all through Holy Mass, I had to struggle against blasphemous thoughts which were forcing themselves to my lips.

"It seemed to me that by approaching the Holy Sacraments, I was offending God even more...God was working very strangely in my soul. I did not understand anything at all of what my confessor was telling me. The simple truths of the Faith became incomprehensible to me. My soul was in anguish, unable to find comfort anywhere."

While Sr. Faustina felt very alone, she had a great support system from her new Novice Mistress, Sr. Joseph Brzoza. She was able to see in Faustina, great gifts from the Lord. At one point, Faustina felt completely rejected by God. Sr. Joseph said to her, "Know, dear Sister, that God has chosen you for great sanctity. This is a sign that God wants to have you very close to Himself in Heaven. Have great trust in the Lord Jesus." The Mother Directress had a great sensitivity where Faustina was concerned.

Her confessor was also very supportive, but Faustina had difficulty expressing herself to him. He, too, saw very special qualities in her. He realized her trials were tests from the Lord. He told her, "This is a sign that God loves you very much and that He has great confidence in you, since He is sending you such trials." But then he also confused her in the same period when he told her to pray the Te Deum or Magnificat, and then to run fast around the garden in the evening, or to laugh out loud ten times a day. Sr. Faustina thought either he didn't understand her, or that he didn't take her completely seriously.

Well, think about it. This is not a normal situation between a novice and her confessor. This young woman has a special relationship with Jesus, and even with that, she is going through some of the greatest spiritual suffering a soul could endure. It would take a very special person to direct her spiritually. The ability to do this would have to come from the Lord. No man would have the right spirit, the right words, on his own. The

Blessed Sister Faustina
with the Image
of Divine Mercy

problem of a Spiritual Director was no different for Blessed Sr. Faustina than it was for St. Teresa of Avila, or thousands of other people specially chosen by the Lord and Our Lady to be the recipients of visions or locutions from them.

The Vision of Divine Mercy

The Lord had an urgency to give Sr. Faustina the message of Divine Mercy with or without a Spiritual Director; and so the day was to come, on February 22, 1931, in Vilnius, when the Lord's Mission would begin to be revealed to her. She was in her cell; she saw the Lord Jesus clothed in a white garment. As she explains it,

"One hand was raised in the gesture of blessing, the other was touching His garment at the breast. From beneath the garment slightly drawn aside at the breast, there was emanating two large rays, one red, the other pale. In silence, I kept my gaze fixed on the Lord; my soul was struck with awe, but also with great joy. After a while, Jesus said to me, 'Paint an image according to the pattern you see, with the signature, Jesus, I trust in You. I desire that this image be venerated, first in your chapel, and then throughout the world.'

"'I promise that the soul that will venerate this image will not perish. I also promise victory over its enemies already here on earth, especially at the hour of death. I Myself will defend it as My own glory.'"

Now, Faustina didn't know what to do with this. She herself didn't know how to paint. She was assuming that the Lord wanted her to do it. He said, **"Paint an image according to the pattern you see..."** He didn't tell her to instruct someone else to paint the image, or go out and have it made. Secondly, and perhaps even more difficult to her way of thinking was, **"I desire that this image be venerated, first in your chapel, and then throughout the whole world."** How would she go about accomplishing that? Her logical mind dictated that she speak to her confessor. The confessor got the wrong message, or perhaps the Lord did not want to make it too easy for Faustina to execute His wishes. The confessor told her the Lord was referring to her soul. "Paint God's image in your soul." As she left the confessional, she heard the words,

> **"My image is already in your soul. I desire that there be a Feast of Mercy. I want this image, which you will paint with a brush, to be solemnly blessed on the first Sunday after Easter; that Sunday is to be the Feast of Mercy."**

So much for the *Image in your soul* theory.

Faustina went to her Mother Superior, explained what Jesus wanted, and asked what should she do. The Mother Superior answered that Jesus should give some sign so that they could recognize that it was Him speaking to Sr. Faustina. Jesus told her, **"I will make this all clear to the Superior by means of the graces which I will grant through this image."** So much for the *special sign.*

This became a major cause of frustration and after a time, Sr. Faustina wanted to distance herself from the visions and the responsibility of having the image painted. After all, no one believed her, or at least no one cooperated with her. She had no Spiritual Director; she had no regular confessor. She really had no one she could turn to. Part of the reason for that was the fact that she moved around so much in her *thirteen* years of religious life. Sister Faustina was in *fourteen* different religious houses in thirteen years. The reason given was that there was such a growth in the building of houses in Poland and Lithuania, and such a need for the type of help Faustina provided in the kitchen, as well as doorkeeper and as gardener. But it played havoc with her spirituality, as each time she changed location, she also had to change confessor and Spiritual Director. None of them were able to get to know her. She was a very unique and difficult person to direct; but for priests who did not know her, or would only be with her a short time, it created a *major* problem.

She felt a great deal of pressure from the Lord to have the painting made and distributed all over the world. She could sense the importance of His directive to her, and judged she was not qualified to do the job. Because of the pressure, her behavior in front of the other Sisters was being called erratic and hysterical. Somehow, the rumor that she was having visions spread. This also caused some jealousy, as well as disbelief.

The satan of jealousy and disbelief caused some Sisters to go out of their way to hurt Sr. Faustina. One Sister in particular tortured her regarding her probations; she needed *three* probations before she could take her final vows. Being held up on these probations meant Sr. Faustina would have to wait longer than usual, before she could make her final profession. In 1932, she was preparing for her third and last probation. One of the Sisters said to her, "Sister, you will not be going for the third probation. I will see to it that you will not be permitted to make your vows." This cut Sr. Faustina to the quick. This was her most important time as a religious.

Later in the chapel, her Savior, spoke gently to her:

"At this very moment the Superiors are deciding which Sisters will be permitted to take perpetual vows. Not all of them will be granted this grace, but this is their own fault. He who does not take advantage of small graces will not receive great ones. But to you, my child, this grace is being given."

This was in contradiction to what the angry Sister had said, but naturally, you know Whose word Faustina was going to take. As the Lord had said, she was accepted to go forward to the last step prior to final vows. But again, she had to move, this time to Warsaw, for her third probation. When she arrived there, the Sister who had vowed to block her, was surprised to see her there. But Faustina just went into the chapel to speak to the Lord.

You've got to understand what was going on in her mind and heart; Sr. Faustina had to have doubts! Even though she was given so many graces, this was a very unusual situation, constantly being in the presence of God. Nobody can just take this for granted. Most of her spiritual direction, from priests who really didn't know her, and from her Superiors who were limited as to how much they could advise her, didn't really help to allay her fears and suspicions. Before the retreat which preceded her vows, the Lord spoke to Faustina. He tried to convince her that it was He who spoke to her:

"...And as a proof that it is I who am speaking to you, you will go to confession on the second day of the retreat to the priest who is preaching the retreat; you will go to him as soon as he has finished his conference and will present to him all your doubts concerning Me. I will answer you through his lips, and then your fears will end."

That's when the committee meeting with herself, as Mother Angelica calls it, began in her mind. *Should I, shouldn't I?* Old Satan got his licks in good, putting great doubts in her mind. Her committee meeting went like this.

Didn't Mother tell you that the Lord Jesus doesn't commune with souls as miserable as yours? This confessor is going to tell you the same thing. Why speak to him about all this? These are not sins, and Mother...told you that all this communing with the Lord Jesus was daydreaming and pure hysteria. So why tell it to this confessor?

This poor child went through the worst agony trying to discern if it was really the Lord speaking to her. But just as Jesus had predicted, the confessor affirmed her visions. He was filled with the Holy Spirit, and given understanding of the entire situation. He said to her:

"Sister, you distrust the Lord Jesus because He treats you so kindly. Well, Sister, be completely at peace. Jesus is your Master, and your communing with Him is neither daydreaming nor hysteria nor illusion. Know that you are on the right path. Please try to be faithful to these graces; you are not free to shun them. You should carry out what He (Jesus) asks of you, even if this costs you greatly. On the other hand, you must tell your confessor everything. There is absolutely no other course for you to take, Sister. Pray that you will find a Spiritual Director, or else you will waste these great gifts of God."

And so, like our other Visionaries, Mystics and Stigmatists in this book, Sr. Faustina carried out what Jesus asked of her, even though it cost her greatly. But the Lord blessed her mightily. He told her,

"I desire that you know more profoundly the love that burns in My heart for souls, and you will understand this when you meditate upon My Passion. Call upon My mercy on behalf of sinners; I desire their salvation. When you say this prayer, with a contrite heart and with faith on behalf of some sinner, I will give him the grace of conversion. This is the prayer:

O Blood and Water, which gushed forth from the Heart of Jesus as a fount of Mercy for us, I trust in you."

During Lent of 1933, Sr. Faustina was given the gift of sharing in the Passion of Christ, as she received the invisible Stigmata. This did not happen once, but many times during that Lent. On Easter Sunday, she was given the gift of an ecstasy. Our Lord said to her,

"You have taken a great part in My Passion; therefore I now give you a great share in My joy and glory."

She didn't share any of this with her Superiors, only her confessor. But she was to be brought back down again by doubts, because of things that different confessors said to her. On one occasion she was told, "I cannot discern what power is at work in you, Sister; perhaps it is God and perhaps it is the evil spirit." That put her right down into the pits. Then, we're not sure if it was the same confessor, but another time she was told, "It would be better if you did not come to me for confession."

But the Lord saved her again. She went before the Blessed Sacrament and pleaded, *"Jesus, save me; you see how weak I am."* The Lord spoke very softly to her, words of consolation: **"I will give you help during the retreat before the vows."**

She couldn't wait for the retreat to begin, which would culminate in her Perpetual vows ten days later. Jesus kept reassuring her that she should be in peace because He was going to take care of everything through Fr. Andrasz. He said to her, **"Be like a child towards him."**

Sr. Faustina went to confession to Fr. Andrasz, not her normal confessor; she asked for a release from these interior inspirations, and from the obligation to have the painting made. Fr. Andrasz railed into her, "I will dispense you from nothing, Sister. It is not right for you to turn away from these interior inspirations, but you must absolutely - and I say absolutely - speak about them to your confessor; otherwise you will go astray despite the great graces you are receiving from God." *"But I don't have a confessor, Fr. Andrasz. You are the only confessor I have,"* Sr. Faustina wanted to shout but she didn't.

The priest insisted she get a regular confessor who could double as Spiritual Director, at least for the time being. She needed to be able to lay out her entire spiritual life and let him get to know her, so that he could intelligently answer her questions. Father told her to pray for a good confessor.

The Lord had already given her the priest who was to be her Spiritual Director during a vision in Warsaw, Fr. Michael Sopocko. She prayed and saw him again in a second vision during this retreat prior to Perpetual Vows, standing between the confessional and the altar. She knew the Lord had given this priest to her for Spiritual Direction and to be her confessor. But she did not meet Fr. Sopocko until the following month, May 1933, in Vilnius.

The flavor of the Spiritual Direction, she received from Fr. Sopocko is as follows: He wanted her to experience *humility*. He used Ignatian spirituality. Ignatius teaches, *One is advised not only not to defend themselves against attacks when reproached, but rejoice in the humiliation.* Fr. Sopocko told her:

"If the things you are telling me really come from God, prepare your soul for great suffering. You will encounter disapproval and persecution. They will look upon you as an hysteric and an eccentric, but the Lord will lavish His graces upon you. True works of God always meet opposition and are marked by suffering. If God wants to accomplish something, sooner or later He will do so in spite of difficulties. Your part, in the meantime, is to arm yourself with great patience."

Fr. Sopocko was very sensitive to Sr. Faustina. He had heard of her before and was impressed with what she had shared with him. However, he did not want to presume that he was given this gift by the Lord. He checked with various Superiors about Sr. Faustina. He did a lot of praying. Sr. Faustina shared with him Jesus' demand for the painting, and also the Feast of Mercy to be celebrated on the first Sunday after Easter. Fr. Sopocko decided to begin at the beginning. He chose an artist Eugene Kazimierowski from the village of Vilnius, to paint the Image as directed by Sr. Faustina.

She found it difficult to communicate to the priest and the artist what needed to be done. She asked Jesus and He explained the meaning of the Image as such:

"The two rays denote Blood and Water. The pale ray stands for the Water which makes souls righteous. The red ray stands for the Blood which is the life of souls...

"These two rays issued forth from the very depths of My tender Mercy when My agonized Heart was opened by a lance on the Cross.

"These rays shield souls from the wrath of My Father. Happy is the one who will dwell in their shelter, for the just hand of God shall not lay hold of him. I desire that the first Sunday after Easter be the feast of Mercy.

"Ask of my faithful servant (Father Zopocko) that,

on this day, he tell the whole world of My great mercy;
that whoever approaches the Fount of Life on this day
will be granted complete remission of sins and
punishment."

Although a Feast Day had not been instituted yet, on the
first Sunday after Easter in 1934, Our Lord asked Sr. Faustina to
celebrate the Feast of Mercy. In honor of this Feast, she wore a
discipline wire belt for three hours while praying for sinners and
for mercy on the whole world. *Remember, she had not gotten the
words of the prayer of Divine Mercy, yet.* Jesus said to her,

"My eyes rest with pleasure upon this house today."

Sr. Faustina followed this with these prophetic words,
*"I feel certain that my mission will not come to an end
upon my death, but will begin."*

Spring came, and amid great anticipation, the painting of
the Image progressed. When Sr. Faustina saw it, however, she
was disappointed, because it was not anywhere near what Jesus
looked like. But this is the case with all Visionaries.[5] [Many who
have had apparitions of Our Lady say that the images made by
various artists could not compare with the beauty of the Lady.] Sr.
Faustina wanted it perfect. She wanted the whole world to be
able to see the beauty of the Jesus who came to her. She actually
broke out into tears in the chapel. She said to Him, *"Who will
paint You as beautiful as You are?"* To which Jesus replied,

**"Not in the beauty of the color nor of the brush lies
the greatness of this image, but in My grace."**

Sister Faustina is attacked by demons.

Our Lord sent Our Lady to tell Sr. Faustina that she would
suffer an illness. Mary said, *"You will also suffer much because
of the Image, but do not be afraid of anything."* At that moment,
Sister became ill, with what was diagnosed by the doctors as a
cold, but was not. In later years, it would be determined that it
was the beginning of Tuberculosis, which was running rampant

[5]those whom we have researched who have passed the test of time.

throughout the world and would finally take the life of our Saint.

Sr. Faustina had a late hour of adoration before the Blessed Sacrament. She didn't mind, however, because it was peaceful being with the Lord at that time. He shared his happiness with her:

"The prayer of a humble and loving soul disarms the anger of My Father and draws down an ocean of blessings."

She felt good about this, but as she left the chapel, she found herself surrounded by a pack of huge, ugly black dogs, all snarling and snapping at her habit. She realized they were devils. One spoke in a fearful voice filled with the fire of hell. "Because you have snatched so many souls away from us this night, we will tear you to pieces."

Sr. Faustina answered with complete abandonment to the Lord. *"If that is the will of the most merciful God, tear me to pieces, for I have justly deserved it, because I am the most miserable of all sinners, and God is ever holy, just and infinitely merciful."*

All the demons yelled out "Let us flee, for she is not alone; the Almighty is with her." They vanished, and Sr. Faustina was able to walk back to her cell.

But this was only one of many instances where Sr. Faustina was attacked by Satan or his followers. A few days later, she became so deathly ill, the priest had to administer the Last Rites of the Church. Suddenly her cell was filled with black figures who raged in anger and hatred against her. One of them said, "Be damned, you and He Who is within you, for you are beginning to torment us even in hell." Sr. Faustina countered with, *"And the Word was made Flesh and dwelt among us,"* at which point the demons vanished.

The Feast of Mercy

On Good Friday, April 19, 1935, at three o'clock, Sr. Faustina entered the chapel and heard the words, **"I desire that the Image be publicly honored."** At that, she saw Jesus hanging from the

Cross, only the rays of Divine Mercy were issuing from His Heart. Sr. Faustina went to Fr. Sopocko immediately and told him he had to place the Image of Divine Mercy on the *Ostra Brama,* the eastern Gate to the city of Vilnius. A three-day celebration was being held on April 26-28 for the close of the Jubilee Year of the Redemption of the world. This would also be the first Sunday after Easter, which is when the Lord wanted the Feast of Divine Mercy.

First of all, Fr. Michael didn't know anything about the Feast and questioned the feasibility of including this unknown Image as part of the celebration. You have to understand something about Ostra Brama. It is a gate to the city of Vilnius, but it is also a chapel and shrine to Our Lady of Vilnius. It is called Our Lady of the Dawn gate. Its history goes back to 1620, and it has been instrumental in bringing about many miracles. People from Vilnius and all over Lithuania go to the Gate of Dawn or Ostra Brama to venerate and petition our Lady there. So Father Sopocko's contention that there was not much chance of putting the image of Divine Mercy up there, was right on target.

"It would never be permitted." he said. But before he could completely talk himself out of asking, *he was asked* by one of the priests in charge of the ceremony if he would preach at the festivity. He was shocked and pleased and thoroughly convinced that this was the work of the Lord. He asked for the painting of Divine Mercy to be put in the window of the church near the icon of our Lady. At first, as he had predicted, permission was denied. But suddenly, the Archbishop acquiesced, and the first Feast of Mercy happened. Fr. Sopocko spoke for three days about the Lord's Divine Mercy. Sr. Faustina beamed that what the Lord had asked for had finally come to pass. She heard Him say,

"You are a witness to My Mercy. You shall stand before My throne forever as a living witness to My Mercy."

Then Jesus said to her:

"I desire that this Feast be a refuge and a shelter for

all souls, but especially for poor sinners...

"Souls are being lost in spite of My bitter Passion. I am giving them the last hope of salvation, that is, recourse to My Mercy. If they will not glorify My Mercy, they will be eternally lost...

"No soul will be justified until it turns with trust to My Mercy, and this is why the first Sunday after Easter is to be the Feast of Mercy. On that day, priests are to tell everyone about my great and unfathomable Mercy."

The Chaplet of Divine Mercy

On Friday, September 13, 1935, the world was given the most beautiful gift possible, the gift of His Divine Mercy, through the Chaplet of Divine Mercy. Sister Faustina's description of it is extraordinary:

"In the evening, when I was in my cell, I saw an Angel, the executor of Divine wrath. He was clothed in a dazzling robe, his face gloriously bright, a cloud beneath his feet. From the cloud, bolts of thunder and flashes of lighting were springing into his hands; and from his hand they were going forth, and only then were they striking the earth. When I saw this sign of Divine wrath which was about to strike the earth, and in particular a certain place, which for good reasons I cannot name, I began to implore the Angel to hold off for a few moments; the world would do penance. But my plea was a mere nothing in the face of the Divine anger. Just then I saw the Most Holy Trinity. The greatness of Its majesty pierced me deeply, and I did not dare to repeat my entreaties. At that very moment, I felt in my soul the power of Jesus' grace, which dwells in my soul. When I became conscious of this grace, I was instantly snatched up before the Throne of God. Oh, how great is our Lord and God and how incomprehensible His holiness! I will make no attempt to describe this greatness, because before long we shall all see Him as He is. I found myself pleading with God for the world, with words I heard

interiorly.

"As I was praying in this manner, I saw the Angel's helplessness; he could not carry out the just punishment which was rightly due for sins. Never before had I prayed with such inner power as I did then....

"The next morning when I entered the chapel, I heard these words interiorly: **'Every time you enter the chapel, immediately recite the prayer which I taught you yesterday.'**

"When I had said the prayer, in my soul I heard these words: **'This prayer will serve to appease My wrath. You will recite it for nine days, on the beads of the Rosary, in the following manner. First of all, you will say one OUR FATHER and HAIL MARY and I BELIEVE IN GOD.**

"'Then, on the OUR FATHER beads you will say the following words: *'Eternal Father, I offer You the Body and Blood, Soul and Divinity of Your dearly Beloved Son, Our Lord Jesus Christ, in atonement for our sins and those of the whole world.'*

"'On the HAIL MARY beads, you will say the following words: *For the sake of His sorrowful Passion, have mercy on us and on the whole world.'*

"'In conclusion, three times you will recite these words: *Holy God, Holy Mighty One, Holy Immortal One, have mercy on us and on the whole world.'"*[6]

So on this momentous day, one of the most powerful devotions, the Church has ever known was given to us. Almost immediately, from the time the first prayer cards were printed, people began praying the devotional prayer. Before Faustina's death, and before the world even knew about her, the devotion to the Divine Mercy

---

[6]In 1936, Fr. Sopocko had the Cebulski Publishing House in Krakow print that prayer on the reverse side of a prayer card, with a copy of the Image of Divine Mercy painted by Eugene Kazimierowski painted on the front. Thus began the devotion to Divine Mercy.

of Jesus had begun. Actually, that's what both Jesus and Sr. Faustina wanted, to get the word out to the people about the merciful Heart of Jesus and the power of that Mercy.

Remember, this was Poland. In the early 1920's they had been victimized by Josef Stalin in his bid to destroy the country. In 1921, twenty thousand of the military of Poland were taken by Soviet soldiers to a place called Katyn Forest, deep within Russia, and executed. The Polish military were dumped in a mass grave. Now it was 1935. Within four years the people of Poland would again be taken over by a ruthless dictator, and this one - Adolf Hitler was every bit as treacherous as Josef Stalin. Between the two, they were the most violent tyrants, our century has known. The people of Poland needed help.

The month before Sr. Faustina was given the Chaplet of Mercy, on the Feast of the Assumption, Our Lady came to her in the Chapel. She came over to Sr. Faustina and covered her with her mantle. She said to her, *"Offer these vows for Poland. Pray for her."* Poland would need a sign from the Lord that He was with them, watching over them, guarding them, protecting them. And while the Polish people suffered devastating losses at the hands of the Nazis *(5 million civilian casualties and 600,000 military)*, they still had their God to hold onto.

When we interviewed Sr. Elizabeth and Sr. Gracia at the shrine of Blessed Sister Faustina in Krakow in May 1993, the month after the Beatification of Sr. Faustina, they told us that devotion to Divine Mercy began, even before World War II; during the War, soldiers and prisoners of war carried the little prayer card given to Sr. Faustina by Our Lord Jesus on September 13, 1935. They always held onto their faith and hope in the Divine Mercy of Jesus.

Jesus had told Sr. Faustina that the Chaplet of Divine Mercy should be prayed over sick people who were dying. On Friday, December 11, 1936, she was taken to the Sanatorium for Tuberculosis. After Sister received Communion, she could feel God's Presence. She was experiencing His Passion. During the night, she was awakened. She knew she had to pray for a sick or dying person. The next day, Saturday, December 12,[7] 1936, she entered the ward and saw a dying person. She inquired when the agony had begun and was told it had begun during the night. All of a sudden, Sister heard the Lord tell her, **"Say the chaplet which I taught you."** Taking her Rosary, she knelt down beside the dying woman and prayed the Chaplet of Divine Mercy. The woman died in the aura of grace.

After staying by the woman's side for a time, Sr. Faustina walked back to her own room. God the Father spoke to her:

"At the hour of their death, I defend as My own glory every soul that will say this chaplet; or when others say it for a dying person, the indulgence is the same. When this chaplet is being said by the bedside of a dying person, God's anger is placated, and unfathomable Mercy envelops the soul, and the very depths of My tender Mercy will be moved for the sake of the sorrowful Passion of My Son."

The Hour of Great Mercy

On October 10, 1937, Sr. Faustina was given knowledge from Jesus on another great aspect of Divine Mercy, the *Hour of Great Mercy.* He instructed her:

"At three o'clock, implore My Mercy, especially for sinners; and if only for a brief moment, immerse yourself in My Passion, particularly in My abandonment at the moment of agony. This is the hour of great Mercy for the whole world. I will allow you to enter into My mortal sorrow. In this hour I will refuse nothing to the soul that makes a request of Me in virtue of My Passion."

Devotion to Divine Mercy

One of the most frustrating things about the mission given Sr. Faustina by the Lord was how to get the word out to the people, how to foster devotion to Divine Mercy. He told her many times

---

[7]Feast of Our Lady of Guadalupe

how important it was to spread the message of Divine Mercy. Sr. Faustina had no way to do this other than through her Spiritual Director Fr. Sopocko, and she had to settle for his timetable. What she did not know, but suspected every time she heard from him or saw him at the convent, was that he was having great difficulties getting permission to spread the message.

As we said before, in 1936 he was able to get prayer cards printed with the image of Divine Mercy on one side and the prayers on the other. Sr. Faustina had pressured him into having the Image of Divine Mercy present at the Gate of Dawn in Vilnius for the special three-day Feast in April, 1935. But the devotion went very slowly. She was constantly agitated about it, upset that she was not doing the Lord's will, because He kept mentioning it to her.

Her story is very much like that of the Little Flower of Lisieux, St. Thérèse. St. Thérèse was really little known in her lifetime by her own Community. But due to her *Autobiography of a Soul,* written under obedience, the whole world came to know of her spirituality. Sr. Faustina was only known in her lifetime as the doorkeeper or gardener. It wasn't until after her death that Mother Michaela began telling the Sisters at the various houses that it was Faustina to whom Our Lord Jesus had given the message of Divine Mercy. The Mission, the Devotion to Divine Mercy, really exploded after her death.

Sr. Faustina goes to her Lover

Sr. Faustina suffered terribly with Tuberculosis. It is a debilitating disease which completely destroys the body. She went through a period of suffering beginning in 1934, when the first symptoms of this dreaded disease came upon her. Her condition deteriorated steadily, until she had to be admitted to a Sanatorium in December, 1936. From that time until her death on October 5, 1938, her condition went up and down like a roller coaster. She wound up spending more time in the Sanatorium than out, from that time until her final days.

Sr. Faustina lived under the shadow of doubt and suspicion

all her life. Her Superiors had a difficult time believing all that she told them was happening with her and Jesus. She lived under the scornful eye of many of the Sisters of her Community. But the Lord always told her to accept these crosses, for the sake of His Sorrowful Passion. She even made a scorecard of how many victories and how many defeats she experienced in her endeavor to give this gift to the Lord. Even on the day she died, some of the Sisters who were antagonistic towards her would not come to make the Sign of the Cross on her forehead or pray over her. In later years, they grieved over their judgment of Sr. Faustina and prayed for her forgiveness and intercession.

Once Sr. Faustina was dead and buried in the convent cemetery, and word spread that she was the instrument the Lord had used to bring the Devotion of Divine Mercy to the faithful, many people began coming to the convent cemetery to pray for the intercession of this simple little Nun. Then, when Fr. Sopocko's booklet was released, which included parts of the Message of Divine Mercy, the devotion took off like wildfire. But for the most part, it was known only in connection with Sr. Faustina.

Sr. Faustina once prophesied;

"I feel certain that my mission will not come to an end upon my death, but will begin. O doubting souls, I will draw aside for you the veils of Heaven to convince you of God's goodness, so that you will no longer continue to wound with your distrust the sweetest Heart of Jesus. God is Love and Mercy."

The brutal invasion of Poland on September 1, 1939, a little less than a year after the death of Sr. Faustina, became an instrument to spread Divine Mercy all over the world. Wherever Poles were sent, they brought with them the Message of the Lord's Divine Mercy, and the story of the simple, uneducated little Nun in Poland, to whom the Lord gave the message - God was making His Divine Love known to this world steeped in ruthlessness and fear and so in need of His Mercy.

The work of Divine Mercy has undergone many struggles in the almost sixty years since the death of Sr. Faustina. But the

Lord has raised up powerful
men in the Church, especially
Karol Cardinal Wojtyla, who
defended the Devotion of
Divine Mercy. The devotion
had been banned from being
practiced from 1959 to 1978
because of inaccuracies in the
translations. However, during
the pontificate of John Paul II,
errors were rectified, the
devotion was reinstated, and on
April 18, 1993, the first Sunday
after Easter, the day designated
as the Feast of Divine Mercy,
Sr. Faustina Kowalska was
Beatified at St. Peter's Basilica in Rome.

*Young man praying before the
Image of Divine Mercy in the
Church of St. James in Warsaw*

In Sr. Faustina's Diary, she wrote that Our Lord Jesus said to
her, *"I bear a special love for Poland, and if she will be obedient
to My will, I will exalt her in might and holiness. From her will
come forth the spark that will prepare the world for My final
coming."*

And that spark was Pope John Paul II! Praise Jesus!

Epilogue

We pray that the Lord has given you, in reading this book, the gift we received in researching and writing it. If there was one underlying theme throughout the lives of these brothers and sisters, we would have to say they give us *hope* for our Church of the next century, and a great *love* and *respect* for who we are as a people of God.

In writing the lives of each of the Visionaries, Mystics and Stigmatists, we see a whole world laid out before us, the good and the bad, the lifelong battles being waged between God and the devil through the Saints and their adversaries. The amazing thing is that nothing changes; everything is the same today as it was a thousand years ago, and even two thousand years ago. We find that the struggles which we believe, so unique to our generation, are the same ones that were fought before; the enemies are the same, throughout Salvation history. We always win! We worry about the outcome, and it's always in the favor of the Lord.

God calls us to restrain our natural instinct to defend ourselves against our oppressors. As He told Gideon, we are to leave the victory to Him. In fighting fire with fire, losing who we are in the process, we give victory to the *enemy. Obedience* and *Humility* stand out as strong attributes found in the great Saints in this book, after whom we can pattern our lives Through their example, we can live Our Lord's words: *"....offer no resistance to one who is evil. When someone strikes you on (your) right cheek, turn the other one to him, as well."*(Matt 5:39)   We can suppress our desire for justice, and give it to God for His glory.

These are role models for the the next millennium, whose lives we can strive to make our own. This is how our Church will triumph against her enemies. We can follow in the footsteps of Jesus; we can follow these brothers and sisters and claim victory for the Lord and his Mother. Two things remain constant:

God is in charge, and we are heirs to the Kingdom.

Jesus is with us; stand firm!

Bibliography

Alphonsus, Sr. Mary O.SS.R - *St. Rose of Lima*
Tan Publications, Rockford, IL 1982
Bélanger, Dina - *Autobiography*
Religious of Jesus and Mary, Quebec, Canada 1990
Boucher, Ghislaine, RJM - *In Dina's Footsteps*
Religious of Jesus and Mary, Quebec, Canada 1984
Béchard, Henri S.J. - *Kaia'tanó:ron Kateri Tekahkwitha*
Kateri Center, Kahnawake, Quebec, Canada 1994
Bessières, Albert S.J. - Wife, Mother and Mystic
Tan Publications, Rockford, IL 1970
Bunson, Margaret - *Kateri Tekakwitha*
Our Sunday Visitor, Huntington, IN 1992
Butler, Thurston Atwater - *Lives of the Saints*
Christian Classics, Westminster, MD 1980
Cavallini, Giuliana, *Martin de Porres*
Tan Publishers, Rockford, IL 1979
Cristiani, Msgr. Leon, *St. Margaret Mary Alacoque*
St. Paul Editions 1975
Doherty, Eddie - *Wisdom's Fool*
Montfort Publications, Bayshore, NY 1975
Giugni, Guido - *St. Catherine of Bologna*
Corpus Domini Sanctuary, Bologna, Italy 1975
God alone - Montfort Publications, Bayshore NY 1987
Kowalska, Sr. M. Faustina - *Divine Mercy in my Soul*
Marian Helpers Press Stockbridge, MA 1987
Léger, Sr. Irène RJM *Courage to Love, Dina Bélanger*
Congregation of Jesus and Mary, Rome, Italy, 1986

Leonardi, Fr. John OFM Cap - *St. Veronica Giuliani*
Monastery of St. Veronica - Pesaro, Italy, 1986
Lord, Bob & Penny - *This Is My Body, This Is My Blood*
Miracles of the Eucharist, 1986
Many Faces of Mary, a love Story 1987
Saints and Other Powerful Women in the Church, 1989
Saints and Other Powerful Men in the Church, 1990
Heavenly Army of Angels, 1991
Scandal of the Cross and its Triumph, 1992
Rosary, the Life of Jesus and Mary, 1993
Martyrs, They Died for Christ, 1993
Journeys of Faith, Fair Oaks, CA
Marabotto, Cattaneo - *Spiritual Doctrine of St. Catherine of
Genoa* - Tan Publications, Rockford, IL 1989
Michalenko, Sr. Sophia - *Mercy My Mission*
Marian Helpers Press, Stockbridge, MA 1987
Nemo - *A Lover of the Cross, St. Gemma Galgani*
Santuario di Sta. Gemma Galgani, Lucca, Italy 1940
Pastrovicchi, Fr. Angelo OMC, *St. Joseph of Cupertino*
Tan Publishers, Rockford, IL, 1980
Parisciani, Fr. Gustavo OFM, *The Flying Saint*
Pax et Bonum Publishers, Osimo, Italy 1964
Rigualt, George - *Saint Louis de Montfort*
Montfort Fathers, Port Jefferson, NY 1947
Siepak, Sr. M. Elzbieta - *Blessed Sister Faustina*
Congregation O. L. of Mercy, Warsaw-Cracow 1993
Weiser, F.X. S.J. - *Kateri Tekakwitha*
Kateri Center - Kahnawake, Quebec, Canada 1972
Windeatt, Mary Fabyan - *St. Louis de Montfort*
Tan Publications - Rockford, IL 1991

Index